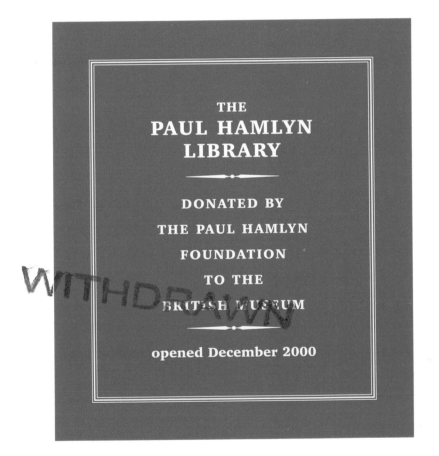

Information Seeking
in the Online Age:
Principles and Practice

Andrew Large, Lucy A. Tedd
and R.J. Hartley

K·G·Saur München 2001

Die Deutsche Bibliothek – CIP-Einheitsaufnahme

Large, Andrew:
Information seeking in the online age : principles and practice
/ Andrew Large, Lucy A. Tedd and R.J. Hartley. - München : Saur, 2001
ISBN 3-598-11505-9

Printed on acid-free paper
© 2001 K. G. Saur Verlag GmbH, München

Cover design by Juan Hayward

Typesetting by Florence Production Ltd., Stoodleigh, Devon

Printed and Bound in Great Britain by Antony Rowe Ltd., Chippenham, Wiltshire
ISBN 3-598-11505-9

About the Authors

The authors are all active in the area of information work and between them have a wealth of experience in this field. They collaborated (with Michael Keen) in the writing of *Online Searching: principles and practice* which was published by Bowker-Saur in 1990. At that time they all lived and worked in Aberystwyth.

Richard J. Hartley is currently Head of the Information and Communications Department at Manchester Metropolitan University. Previously he has held lecturing posts at the University of Northumbria at Newcastle upon Tyne and the University of Wales Aberystwyth. Prior to teaching, he worked for more than 12 years in academic, public and national libraries. He has published widely in the area of online searching and information retrieval.

J. Andrew Large is Canadian National-Phebe Pratt Professor of Information Studies in the Graduate School of Library and Information Studies at McGill University in Montreal, and from 1989 until 1998 was its Director. He was previously Senior and then Principal Lecturer at the University of Wales Aberystwyth. He has been a joint editor for the quarterly journal *Education for Information* since 1983 and has written many articles and conference papers on online themes.

Lucy A. Tedd is currently a Lecturer at the Department of Information and Library Studies, University of Wales Aberystwyth and is involved with the International Graduate Summer School there each year. Previously she worked as a freelance consultant and her work included several projects for the British Library. Since 1984 she has been editor of Aslib's journal *Program: electronic library and information systems*. She has also written many articles, research reports and conference papers related to online information seeking.

About the Authors

Preface

Information seeking in electronic data environments is no longer solely the purview of the information professional; alongside the burgeoning information available in such environments and the expansion in the variety of delivery platforms has been the tremendous extension of access to electronic information. Where a decade ago most online information seeking still took place in libraries and information centres and was concerned primarily with scholarly and technical bibliographic databases, now it is much more prevalent in the workplace and the home, and literally anyone might be seated at the computer. Such end-user information seeking has been driven by a number of factors: the eclectic range of information now available electronically, especially multimedia sources; relatively inexpensive hardware and software; easily acquired or accessed storage media such as CD-ROMs; the rapid acceptance of the Internet as a publishing and information dissemination medium; much friendlier interfaces; more powerful browsing and searching tools; and not least a general fascination with information and an appreciation of its significance in economic, political, social and leisure activities.

Despite such broadening of access to electronic information, the goal of providing straightforward, intuitive access to 'the right information at the right time at the right cost and to the right people' has remained elusive. Finding information in electronic environments may appear easy, but the seeming simplicity with which a desktop computer can be logged onto a data source in the same room or the other side of the world is misleading. Information can be found, often in mind-boggling quantities, but is this information the best available for the question in hand? Too many users maintain a rose-tinted impression of their information-seeking skills, if only because they remain blissfully unaware of what they have never been able to find!

This is not to argue that information seeking requires knowledge and skills only painfully won after years of concentrated study. But as with many tasks, a little advice backed up with well-chosen examples can save a lot of time and trouble. This book is here to offer that advice and to give those examples. It is not a comprehensive textbook on information retrieval or database construction. Nor is it an exhaustive directory of electronic information resources or the best Web sites. *Information Seeking in the Online Age: Principles and Practice* is a book with a straightforward aim: to help you, the reader, to browse and search online databases, online library catalogues, CD-ROMs of all kinds and the World Wide Web in order effectively and efficiently to find that which you are seeking. Above all it is a book about searching and browsing strategies and tactics.

In 1990 Bowker published *Online Searching: Principles and Practice*; its authors were Dick Hartley, Andy Large and Lucy Tedd, together with Michael Keen. It is instructive to compare this earlier book with the current one. Several significant differences readily can be identified. Most of *Online Searching* is devoted to traditional online services of which Dialog and Questel-Orbit are typical examples. CD-ROMs are referenced a number of times in the Index, but are discussed as relatively new phenomena: for example, 'Some databases are now becoming available on small very high density optical discs known as CD-ROMs'. Neither the term Internet nor World Wide Web can be found anywhere in *Online Searching*. By the same token, one chapter in *Online Searching* was devoted to Videotex and Teletext systems, no longer considered significant technologies for information storage and retrieval except in the case of France's Minitel. In the chapter 'Beyond Boolean Searching' a discussion can be found of techniques such as output ranking and relevance feedback which were barely beyond the experimental phase in 1990. The major developments that have occurred in information system technologies are reflected, of course, in *Information Seeking in the Online Age*.

The difference in the titles of the two books is also significant: the term 'searching' in the 1990 book has been replaced by 'seeking' in the current one. The choice of the latter term was prompted by the growing acceptance that information stores can be browsed as well as searched, that many users on at least some occasions will opt for the former approach, and that both design and retrieval considerations are different for browsing and searching.

These comparisons between *Online Searching* and *Information Seeking in the Online Age* highlight the changes that have taken place and will continue to take place in information retrieval systems. No author can escape the transitory nature of information technologies. Yet the principles that lie behind searching and browsing strategies, interface design, search evaluation procedures, and so on, are much more consistent. *Information Seeking in the Online Age* stresses the principles and exemplifies them with real examples drawn from a variety of platforms. Its chapter arrangement is not by technological platform but rather opts for a conceptual presentation.

Interestingly, such an approach has been facilitated by the marked convergence between traditional online systems, CD-ROMs, OPACs and the World Wide Web. The online systems are no longer, for example, primarily command driven and connect-time priced. Menus and hypertext links are ubiquitous. OPACs include sophisticated retrieval engines incorporating Boolean, keyword and field searching. Output ranking is found across all platforms. Windows-based, mouse-driven interfaces are becoming standard regardless of the technological platform. In the authors' view, at least, it is no longer helpful to present information seeking in the context of individual kinds of system.

How, then, *have* the authors chosen to present the topics covered in *Information Seeking in the Online Age?* The first three chapters offer an introduction to information seeking. Chapter One gives a general overview of information-seeking systems followed by several sample searches on the World Wide Web, a university Online Public Access Catalogue, an electronic journal, an online bibliographic database, and an online biographical directory. Chapter 2 turns attention to the information seeker. How can seekers and searches be categorized, and what do research studies tell us about information-seeking behaviour? Chapter 3 presents a historical perspective on the development of electronic information resources and services, and describes a selection of such services.

The next four chapters contain the core of the book – they deal with information organization, searching and browsing. Chapter 4 establishes the crucial link between information seeking and language. Both the information stored electronically and the requests from users for information are expressed in language. Commercial systems that can take any natural language expression of information – a phrase or sentence, whether grammatically well formed or otherwise – and match that against a large database to retrieve relevant information continue to elude systems designers. Onus is placed upon the seeker to summarize the information need in one or more concepts and then transform those concepts into possible search terms. Chapter 4 looks at the role of controlled vocabularies – thesauri, classification schemes and subject headings – as one way of representing both information sources and information needs, as well as the tactics that must be employed if instead the source and need are expressed in natural language terms. Chapter 5 turns to the ways in which information is organized in databases and the way database indexes are structured for searching, as well as hypertext structures that facilitate browsing rather than searching. Chapter 6 deals with searching: database selection, term selection and combination, and data outputting. It also discusses various search tactics that can be used to narrow searches that have produced too many results, or to broaden searches that find no or too few results. Chapter 7 considers the alternative information-seeking approach – browsing. How does browsing differ from searching, what kind of browsing strategies are available, and what kinds of browsing tools can be employed?

Chapter 8 offers an overview of interfaces. The interface is the medium through which the user and the information system interact. It determines how users can issue instructions to the system – by commands, menus of various kinds, buttons, icons, and so on – and how the system responses are displayed. It also includes other features such as help and tutorial facilities, and error messages. Screen layout features such as colour, fonts and spacing all play a role in determining overall whether the interface offers a logical, consistent and friendly environment for the user, as against an illogical, inconsistent and hostile environment. The success of a search can depend in no small part upon the quality of the interface: a rich information source and a powerful retrieval engine will be of little avail if the interface presents a barrier to rather than a facilitator for communication between user and system.

Chapter 9 builds on the advice offered in the earlier chapters by presenting a series of searches. It looks at the search process from start to finish – choosing the appropriate source, preparing the search strategy, executing the search, reviewing preliminary results, revising the strategy if necessary in the light of these results, outputting retrieved data, and finally terminating the search. The chapter ends with a brief discussion of end-user searching and its impact on library and information staff.

Chapter 10 deals with search evaluation. How can any search, retrieval system or searcher be evaluated? What is considered a successful search, and how is success measured? The chapter also discusses user studies as an alternative to evaluation experiments, and finishes with a review of database evaluation criteria.

The range of information sources and information systems from which examples could be chosen is enormous. The authors have tried to provide a variety of such examples, but obviously many more are left out than can possibly be included. Where possible an international flavour has been added, but perhaps inevitably, given not only the authors' own experience but also the concentration of the electronic information industry in North America and western Europe, sources and systems from certain regions are more heavily emphasized than others.

The authors would like to acknowledge the cooperation of the search services and information producers whose products are included in the sample searches; their willingness to allow reproduction of search extracts was essential if this book was to see the light of day.

Despite the availability today of so many communication mechanisms – from physical transportation modes such as trains and aircraft to virtual modes such as airmail, telephone, fax and email – it remains a challenge for three authors on two continents to assemble a book such as this. The challenge is the greater as all the authors have had a hand, to a greater or lesser degree, in writing all the chapters. Contemporary technologies notwithstanding, there really is no substitute for old-fashioned face-to-face encounters. The authors have been lucky enough to meet in twos and threes over the last few years in an amazing variety of more or less exotic locations to which their non-book-related plans carried them. To all the individuals and organizations that incidentally made this book happen by arranging these brief encounters, the authors are indebted.

Montreal/Aberystwyth/Manchester
Summer 1998

Contents

About the Authors   v
Preface   vii
List of Figures   xv
Copyright permissions   xx
List of Tables   xxi

CHAPTER 1: GENERAL OVERVIEW   1
   Introduction   1
   Information Search Systems – The Basic Elements   5
   Some Sample Searches   10
   Sources of Further Information   21
   References and Further Reading   25

CHAPTER 2: INFORMATION-SEEKING BEHAVIOUR   27
   The Innateness of Human Information Seeking   27
   Information Seekers   29
   Information Seeking   31
   Types of Searches   35
   Research Findings about Information Seekers   36
   Conclusions   38
   References   39

CHAPTER 3: ACCESS TO ELECTRONIC INFORMATION
RESOURCES: AN OVERVIEW   41
   Introduction   41

Historical Review   43
Electronic Information Resources   45
Online Search Services   49
Online Public Access Catalogues   59
CD-ROM   61
The Internet   65
Summary   69
References   70

CHAPTER 4: LANGUAGE AND INFORMATION
RETRIEVAL   73
Language and Meaning   73
Controlled Vocabularies   77
Controlled Vocabulary in Retrieval   95
Problems with Controlled Vocabulary   98
The Natural Language Alternative   99
Citations for Representation and Retrieval   100
Problems with Proper Names   102
Representing Images for Retrieval   104
Summary   106
References and Further Reading   106

CHAPTER 5: INFORMATION ORGANIZATION   109
Introduction   109
Databases   110
Parsing the Records   120
File Structures   123
Hypermedia   132
Indexing the Internet   136
Metadata   136
References and Further Reading   140

CHAPTER 6: SEARCHING   143
Introduction   143
Basic Boolean Search Facilities   144
Display Facilities   156
Further Search Facilities   159
Command Language Variation   161
Search Strategies   163
Search Tactics   165
Best Match or Ranked Output Retrieval   169
References   177

CHAPTER 7: BROWSING   179
Browsing versus Searching   180
Browsing Strategies   180
Types of Browsing   181
Browsing Tools   182
Advantages of Browsing   192

Browsing Limitations   193
The Best of Both Worlds   194
References   194

CHAPTER 8: INTERFACES   197
The Role of Interfaces   197
Design Criteria   198
The Dialogue Transaction Mode   201
Display Features   221
Output Options   226
Input Devices   226
Output Devices and Quality   228
On-Screen Help   228
Interfaces Today and Tomorrow   231
References   237

CHAPTER 9: INFORMATION SEEKING – SOME PRACTICAL
ISSUES   239
The Search Process   239
General Search Guidelines   253
Search Examples   255
Impact on Library and Information (LIS) Staff of End-User
Searching   269
Training Issues for Searching   273
References   275

CHAPTER 10: SEARCH EVALUATION   277
The Need for Evaluation   277
Recall and Precision Measures   278
Criticisms of Recall and Precision Measures   282
Navigational Retrieval Systems   288
User Studies   289
Database Evaluation   291
Practical Results   293
References   294

List of Acronyms   297
Index   301

List of Figures

1.1   Basic elements of an information search system   6
1.2   University of Wales Aberystwyth home page   11
1.3   Part of Web page display of monthly programme,
      Commodore Cinema, Aberystwyth   11
1.4   Part of display for *Titanic* film at the Internet Movie Database
      Web site   12
1.5   Result of AltaVista search for outback tours in Alice
      Springs   13
1.6   Part of a home page for a tour operator   14
1.7   Search options and Author display for Manchester
      Metropolitan University Library OPAC   15
1.8   List of items by a sought author in the Manchester
      Metropolitan University OPAC   15
1.9   Fuller details of one record from the Manchester
      Metropolitan University OPAC search   16
1.10 Contents page of electronic journal, *D-Lib Magazine*   17
1.11 Typical electronic journal article   18
1.12 Search form for ERIC database on OCLC FirstSearch   19
1.13 Example of an ERIC record on OCLC FirstSearch   20
1.14 Some electronic resources available from the National Library
      of Australia   23
3.1   Example of a BookData record   48
3.2   Part of home page of America Online showing some broad
      subject search categories   50
3.3   Search form for Livewire database on Profound   53

3.4   Home page of Engineering Information Village   55
3.5   Sample search for dinosaur eggs on STNEasy   56
3.6   Result of dinosaur eggs search on STNEasy   57
3.7   Part of a company record displayed through FT Discovery   58
3.8   Social sciences databases available through MELVYL at the
       University of California   60
3.9   Home page of NISS: information for education   61
3.10   Some UK higher education library OPACs available
       through NISS   62
3.11   Home page of webCATS at the University of Saskatchewan   62
3.12   Japanese Web OPACs from webCATS geographical index   63
3.13   Broad subject categories available for browsing on Excite   67
3.14   Power Search form on Excite   68
3.15   Home page of Lycos   69
3.16   Search form for LycosPro   70
4.1   Part of main menu of Yahoo! UK and Ireland   79
4.2   Gardening section of Excite Lifestyle   80
4.3   Subject areas available on the Social Science Information
       Gateway menu   81
4.4   Extract from the *Inspec Thesaurus, 1995*   82
4.5   Extract from *Thesaurus of Psychological Terms, 6th edition*   84
4.6   Extract from rotated descriptor display, *Thesaurus of ERIC
       Descriptors, 13th edition*   85
4.7   Extract from two-way hierarchical term display, *Thesaurus of
       ERIC Descriptors, 13th edition*   86
4.8   Extract from descriptor group display, *Thesaurus of ERIC
       Descriptors, 13th edition*   87
4.9   Use of the online thesaurus on ERIC during a search on
       Dialog   89
4.10   Subdivisions of the main Class 500 Sciences in the Dewey
       Decimal Classification Scheme   90
4.11   Extract from Dewey Decimal Classification Scheme for
       physics   91
4.12   Extract from INSPEC Classification Scheme for physics   92
4.13   Extract from LCSH for physics   93
4.14   Comparison of term display in the 10th and 11th editions of
       LCSH (after Lancaster and Warner)   94
4.15   A record from the INSPEC database on Dialog   96
4.16   Result of a search for cited author on BIDS ISI   101
4.17   Partial display of items citing a particular reference on
       BIDS ISI   102
5.1   Bibliographic record from the ASFA database on Dialog   111
5.2   Amended company record derived from the KOMPASS
       Canada database on Dialog   112
5.3   Amended extract of a chemical record from the ChemTox
       database on Dialog   114
5.4   Full-text record from the *Los Angeles Times* on Dialog   116
5.5   Variation in structure of some databases covering
       biomedicine on Dialog   118

5.6   MARC record for a book   119
5.7   MARC record for a WWW resource   120
5.8   Fictitious bibliographic record   122
5.9   Index terms generated from sample record   123
5.10 Extract from online help available on DialogWeb for the
      ASFA database   124
5.11 Inverted file structure: Index file   128
5.12 Inverted file structure: Postings file   128
5.13 Inverted file structure: Print file   129
5.14 Word positional information in an inverted file structure   130
5.15 Simplified relational model of a library   131
5.16 Sample HTML tags   134
5.17 Sample contents page to demonstrate links within a WWW
      document   135
5.18 The Dublin Core elements   139
6.1   Database selection on Dialog   145
6.2   Database selection on OCLC FirstSearch   146
6.3   Single term selection on AltaVista   147
6.4   The effect of truncation in the PsycInfo database on Dialog   148
6.5   The impact of using parentheses in the Enviroline database
      on Dialog   150
6.6   Word proximity operators as used on Dialog   152
6.7   The impact of field searching on search output exemplified
      using the LISA CD-ROM   154
6.8   Examining the inverted file index for the ERIC database on
      Dialog   155
6.9   Sample search on Pollution Abstracts on Dialog   157
6.10 Search for spoil heaps using Northern Light search engine   158
6.11 Using DialIndex to aid database choice   159
6.12 Examples of command variation for some search functions   162
6.13 Example of search narrowing using CAB International   168
6.14 Search broadening by concept removal on LISA   169
6.15 Search broadening by use of synonyms on LISA   170
6.16 Hypothetical coordination level search   172
6.17 Hypothetical ranking by proximate pairs   176
7.1   Use of thumbnail images on *The Islamic Book* CD-ROM
      (McGill University)   183
7.2   Scrolling menu from the *Microsoft Encarta 98 Encyclopedia*
      CD-ROM   184
7.3   Browse option on main menu of ALEPH Ex-Libris OPAC at
      the South African Library   185
7.4   Browse Start on ALEPH Ex-Libris OPAC at the South African
      Library   186
7.5   Full-screen menu from Yahoo! on the World Wide Web   186
7.6   Hierarchical hypertext links on the WWW – main sports
      index on WebCrawler   187
7.7   Hierarchical hypertext links on the WWW – baseball links on
      WebCrawler   188

7.8   Hierarchical hypertext links on the WWW – Major League
       Baseball links on WebCrawler   189
7.9   Hierarchical hypertext links on the WWW – Montreal Expos
       baseball team   189
7.10   Hierarchical hypertext links on the WWW – Montreal Expos
       baseball team official Web site   190
7.11   Horizontal hypertext links on *Microsoft Encarta 98
       Encyclopedia* on CD-ROM – Penicillin article   190
7.12   Horizontal hypertext links on *Microsoft Encarta 98
       Encyclopedia* on CD-ROM – Sir Alexander Fleming article   191
8.1   Excerpt from Advanced Search Tips on Excite   206
8.2   Full-screen menu on DialogWeb   209
8.3   Full-screen menu from Disney Videos on WWW   210
8.4   Pull-down and pop-up menus, *Microsoft Encarta 98
       Encyclopedia* on CD-ROM   211
8.5   Command menu from SilverPlatter's PC-SPIRS ERIC
       CD-ROM, 1998   211
8.6   Form filling on the DRA Web OPAC at the State Library
       of Florida   213
8.7   Form filling on HotBot   214
8.8   Buttons on *Compton's Interactive Encyclopedia* CD-ROM, 1998   215
8.9   Radio buttons on the *Grolier Multimedia Encyclopedia* CD-ROM,
       1997   216
8.10   Bibliographic Database Applications standard icon set (IFLA)   217
8.11   Time bar on *Compton's Interactive Encyclopedia* CD-ROM,
       1998   218
8.12   *Nature's* graphical index page on the WWW   219
8.13   On-screen form on AltaVista Maps   220
8.14   Point and click navigation on AltaVista Maps   221
8.15   Zoom on AltaVista Maps   222
8.16   The Middle Bailey on DK Multimedia's *Castle Explorer*
       CD-ROM   223
8.17   Screen Layout on *Compton's Interactive Encyclopedia* CD-ROM,
       1998   224
8.18   Help screen from SilverPlatter's WinSPIRS ERIC CD-ROM,
       1998   229
8.19   Opening screen of Merlin OPAC (Best-Seller) at the
       Bibliothèque de Montréal   232
8.20   Z39.50 search interface at the Bibliothèque de Montréal   233
8.21   Z39.50 display interface at the Bibliothèque de Montréal   234
8.22   Virtual tour of the National Library of Canada   235
9.1   Search form for Healthgate   242
9.2   Search form for DialogSelect   243
9.3   Example of PASCAL record on Dialog   245
9.4   Search form for British Library OPAC97   246
9.5   Part of page on search tips for InfoSeek   247
9.6   Search form for Drugs in Development on DialogWeb   248
9.7   Cyberstacks classification for medicine using Library of
       Congress Subject Headings   249

9.8   Alphabetic subject approach to electronic resources described
      on BUBL LINK   249
9.9   Example of relevance ranking help page from OLIB OPAC
      at Harper Adams Agricultural College   250
9.10 Output from five Internet search engines   251
9.11 Display of items from OPAC97   252
9.12 Search form for BIDS   256
9.13 Titles of some retrieved references on BIDS   257
9.14 Part of display of a Science Citation Index record on BIDS   258
9.15 List of possible Arts and Humanities databases on OCLC
      FirstSearch   259
9.16 Search form for MLA Bibliography database on OCLC
      FirstSearch   260
9.17 Some retrieved references from MLA Bibliography   261
9.18 Search on the INNOPAC OPAC at the Australian National
      University   262
9.19 Display of one catalogue record at Australian National
      University Library   263
9.20 Example of ability to search by linking to LC Subject
      Headings   264
9.21 Inputting a search of LISA database on CD-ROM   264
9.22 Results of a search on LISA   265
9.23 Architecture subject categories on Yahoo!   266
9.24 Selection of sites giving information on Frank Lloyd Wright
      on Yahoo!   266
9.25 Frank Lloyd Wright in Wisconsin home page   267
9.26 Search form for Deutsche Bahn timetable   268
9.27 Display of possible train times from Berlin to Warsaw   268
9.28 Part of Edinburgh Engineering Virtual Library (EEVL)
      home page   270
9.29 Part of search form for EEVL   270
9.30 Results of an EEVL search   271
10.1 Recall/precision matrix   280

Copyright Permissions

List of Tables

3.1 Growth in numbers of databases, producers and vendors/
     distributors   46
3.2 Some widely used bibliographic databases   47
4.1 Examples of synonyms and near synonyms   74
4.2 Examples of English and North American spelling variants   75

CHAPTER 1

General Overview

Introduction

Seeking information is an important activity in human society. While it can be argued that this has always been the case, it is even more prevalent now in what is often referred to as the information society. Moore (1997), in writing the chapter on the information society in Unesco's *World Information Report*, notes that societies, in both developing and developed countries, are changing as information plays a crucial part in economic, social and political life at the end of the 20th century. Most members of modern society need to be able to seek and successfully find relevant information.

As is described further in the next chapter on information-seeking behaviour, before the advent of the printing press in the 15th century, information was transmitted orally or through manuscripts (i.e. hand-written documents). Since Gutenberg's invention much information has been created on paper and recorded in various forms such as books, pamphlets, reports, files, catalogues, ledgers and journals. Book publishing continues to be a major industry with some 1,000 books published worldwide each day and this shows little sign of diminishing. In the UK, for instance, 102,000 books were published in 1996 compared to 68,000 in 1991. Printed information can have many advantages for those seeking information: the format is familiar, it is portable, and it can be read or browsed without any specialist equipment. Printed documents are typically stored in libraries, archives, filing cabinets, desks, drawers and bookshelves and often take up a lot of space – large research libraries, for instance, operate in terms of miles of storage shelving. Expanding library buildings is increasingly costly. The University of California at Berkeley spent $46 million in the 1990s on an underground addition to house 1.5 million books – an average cost of $30 per volume, whereas the price of magnetic disc storage, in contrast, has fallen to about $2 per 300-page publication (Lesk, 1997). As well as the expense of providing storage facilities, other disadvantages of printed sources include the cost and slow speed of distribution, the limited retrieval facilities and their linear format.

During the 20th century information has also been transmitted on radio, television and, increasingly, through electronic communications. It is reckoned that more information will be produced between 1970 and 2000 than in the previous 5,000 years. Developments in information and communication technologies (ICT) have been responsible for much of this information 'explosion'. Many of these changes are based upon computer systems' capability to store vast amounts of data, to process those data speedily and to make them available to users all over the world through telecommunications networks. The initial digital computers of the 1940s and 1950s were used for processing numerical data: the so-called number-crunching activities. The ability to store and retrieve textual information developed during the 1960s and 1970s with a variety of search services being made available. Initially these services provided access to abstracting and indexing publications that gave scientists (mainly) information about articles published in the primary journal literature. These systems are typically based on the searcher using terms to express a search query which is then matched with terms that have been used to describe a particular article. During the 1980s the search services developed from providing access to bibliographic databases to allowing searches of full-text material such as newspapers and encyclopaedias, and business information, as described more fully in Chapter 3. Various organizations, such as The Dialog Corporation, Financial Times Information and Reuters, provide access to a number of these types of databases. Searching for information in some of the early search services was a fairly complex process which required understanding the syntax of special command languages and a knowledge of various search techniques. During the late 1980s many databases started to be published on compact disc-read only memory (CD-ROMs). Physically similar to the audio compact disc this medium is particularly appropriate for storing information that is not updated very frequently, such as dictionary and encyclopaedia entries, and retrospective files of bibliographic descriptions. The searching of CD-ROM discs is carried out locally, possibly via a local area network, with no long-distance communication links. By the late 1990s CD-ROM has become a recognized medium for publishing information covering a range of topics including many computer games (with CD-ROMs of games being 'given away' on the front cover of popular computer magazines) and software. For example, a book on intranets has a CD-ROM attached with relevant programs to assist in the creation of intranets (Cimino, 1997). A further development in optical storage technology has been the digital video (or versatile) disc-read only memory (DVD-ROM) which looks similar to a CD-ROM, but which is capable of holding about seven times as much data and was designed from the beginning to deliver high-quality multimedia streams at high data rates.

The emergence of graphical user interfaces, client server technology and, above all, the rapid development of the Internet and the World Wide Web (WWW) during the 1990s have completely transformed the electronic generation, storage and retrieval of information. Initially the Internet, which is essentially a network of networks enabling computers around the world to 'talk' to one another using a special set of commands, was used for communicating via electronic mail (email), transferring files of data or programs (ftp), and accessing remote data (telnet). However, the development in the early 1990s of the WWW, which began as a hypertext publishing system at the European Laboratory for Particle Physics (CERN) in Geneva and enables a searcher to follow links within and between documents, has had immense impact on the use of the Internet for publishing information and thus for searching. Quite frequently the WWW address of the home page of the producer of a product being advertized on a poster, on television or in a printed magazine will be given with the expectation that the reader will access that Web page for further information. Children watching the long-running British television programme 'Blue Peter' are exhorted to look at http://www.bbc.co.uk/bluepeter for further details of a recipe given in the programme, or some further information on an item covered. Even when reading the packet of cereal at the breakfast table one is invited to access the home page (for example http://www.kelloggs.com) for further information.

It is no longer only text which is stored and can be retrieved from the WWW: image, graphic and sound data can also be stored and transmitted. The information may be structured for searching or may be organized for browsing. Certainly seeking information stored on electronic media is no longer the preserve of specialists but is an everyday activity undertaken by millions of professional people as a normal part of their work routine; increasingly, it is also an activity undertaken by children in schools to assist in their learning and understanding and by 'ordinary' people at home, in libraries or cybercafes, who wish to book airline tickets, plan holidays, make contact with long lost friends or just 'surf'.

Access to information, including electronic information, is a fundamental right of citizens in many countries and so national governments are involved. In the 1990s US President Bill Clinton and his Vice-President Al Gore became early advocates of the WWW for disseminating information and enabling 'open' government, allowing virtual access to the White House via the Web site http://www.whitehouse.gov. Their lead has been followed in many other countries such as Japan with its link to its Prime Minister via http://www.kantei.go.jp and the UK with its Government Information Service at http://www.open.gov.uk. In Malaysia the Prime Minister, Dr Mahathir Bin Mohamad, has gone further and developed the idea of a multimedia super corridor (MSC), following discussions with Bill Gates of Microsoft and others. The MSC is a 15 by 50 kilometre zone extending south from Malaysia's capital, Kuala Lumpur, to the new Kuala Lumpur International Airport, and which includes a new information tech-nology city, Cyberjaya. The seven flagship applications in the MSC planned for 1998 include electronic government, a national multipurpose smart card, telemedicine, World Wide manufacturing Webs, borderless marketing centres, a new multimedia university and smart schools.

In the many countries of the world in which English is not the main language there have naturally been worries about the predominance of the English language on the WWW and related cultural issues. On the other hand the WWW is seen by many speakers of minority languages (e.g. Welsh in the UK, Catalan in Spain) as a useful communications medium. In many of the countries of central and eastern Europe, providing access to the Internet from a range of locations, including schools and libraries, has been part of a strategy to open up society following the political changes in the early 1990s.

Setting up the necessary infrastructure by which people can access the Internet is a challenge for organizations, companies, governments and, if being done from home, individuals. In higher education establishments worldwide access to the Internet became commonplace during the 1990s with students being allocated email addresses on enrolment in the same way as they are allocated cards to use the library. In the business workplace many professionals worldwide now have easy access to information from the workstations on their desks. Forrester Research in the US has predicted that corporate end users are likely to grow in the commercial sector from 2 to 40 percent by the year 2001 (Galt, 1997). Many schools have Internet access with students and staff having their own email addresses and access to the Internet from networked workstations. The growth in ICT in schools is likely to increase with many national governments stating their belief in educating their future citizens in the information society. During the 1990s there has been a growth in the number of Internet cafes, or cybercafes, where anyone can surf or search the Internet for a fee (and have a cup of coffee). Even in some airports, such as Changi in Singapore, it is possible for passengers to access the Internet while they await connecting planes. Public libraries are thought by many to be suitable places for general community access to electronic information resources on the Internet. A report published by the Library and Information Commission in the UK argues that libraries, long seen as centres of knowledge and learning, must be repositioned as the communications backbone of the information society and be able to connect everyone who wishes to the Internet, so that the nation is not divided into the information 'haves' and 'have-nots' (New Library: The People's Network,1997). The collaborative approach adopted within the UK public library community to providing access to networked resources and the EARL (Electronic Access to Resources in Libraries) project (http://www.earl.org.uk) is described by Smith *et al.* (1997). In the US public libraries have been providing access to the Internet since the mid-1990s and many believe (e.g. McLure *et al.*, 1996) that public libraries should be at the centre of a coordinated effort in providing public access to the Internet and the National Information Infrastructure. Home computing has mushroomed with the decrease in cost of personal computers (PCs) and the developments in telecommunications technology that enable many home computer users to access the Internet. Home computers are particularly prevalent in the US and Herther (1998) reports that many are being bought to gather and manipulate information.

One inevitable result of such developments is 'information overload'. A survey of 1,300 managers, undertaken by Reuters in 1996, found that information overload (often caused by the Internet) is delaying decision making (Reuters Business Information, 1996). Dealing with email messages, not all of which will prove relevant, took some managers up to an hour a day. Using Internet search engines to retrieve information can sometimes be a slow process (especially at certain times of the day) and can result in far too many 'hits' so that picking out relevant ones can be difficult. It is also natural to browse when carrying out an Internet search so that the time taken is even further increased. In some situations this is not a major problem, but if the searcher is in an organization where 'time = money' then serious repercussions may occur. In such situations, proper training to use the search engines effectively is necessary and an automatic 'information filtering agent' can be used to sift all the information retrieved from a search for that portion which is relevant. However the managers in the survey recognized that the Internet is a vital information resource and that if an organization does not have a Web site then it is regarded as 'behind the times'.

Information Search Systems – The Basic Elements

The systems that have been developed for enabling users to seek information from large electronic information stores may allow 'pulling' information from the store (e.g. What time is the next train from Berlin to Warsaw?, Can I be given details about the astronomer Galileo?, Does the library have the *Rough Guide to Nepal*?) or 'pushing' new information being added to the store (e.g. information from newswires such as Reuters, current details of prices of particular stocks and shares, recently released company reports). This 'pushing and pulling' of information has existed since the early days of information retrieval systems, with the 'pull' type of search sometimes being referred to as a retrospective search and the 'push' type of search being referred to as selective dissemination of information (SDI). The basic elements for either type of search include the searcher, search formulation, workstation, link to computer system, search software, store of information and the retrieved items. This section provides a broad overview of these elements with the intellectual aspects of the information-seeking process being discussed further in Chapter 2, the mechanics of searching in Chapter 6, the process of browsing for information in Chapter 7 and the important issue of interfaces in Chapter 8. These elements are represented in diagrammatic form in Figure 1.1

Searcher

The person who actually carries out the search may be the person with the information need (often referred to as the end user) or it may be an intermediary. Further information on searchers is given in Chapter 2. An intermediary is usually a librarian or information scientist who interprets

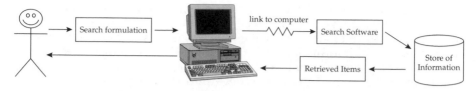

Figure 1.1   Basic elements of an information search system

the request for information and 'translates' it into the necessary language of the search system being used. In the early 1980s much searching used highly structured command languages with a 'pay per minute' tariff which was not hospitable to novices, and so many searches were carried out by such intermediaries. With the development of CD-ROMs, more user-friendly search interfaces and charging mechanisms which were not linked to the time spent searching or browsing, searches began to be carried out by end users during the 1980s. The widespread use of Windows, with the 'point and click' of the mouse, meant that search interfaces seemingly became more friendly for end users during the 1990s and this trend has continued with the search engines developed for use with the Web. However, as stated by Day, 'What end-user interfaces have done is create the illusion that searching (often complex) databases is easy' (Hanson and Day, 1994). More information about the impact of end-user searching on the role of the library and information professionals is given in Chapter 9.

Search formulation

Shneiderman *et al.* (1997) refer to the search formulation as the most complex phase of any search for information as it involves many decisions. The first decision concerns the source which is to be searched; this may be a library catalogue, a 'clump' (physical or virtual) of catalogues, a partic-ular database (e.g. the Medline database of articles from about 3,700 medical journals published in 70 countries with around 400,000 records added each year), a range of databases in a particular subject on one search service, (such as DialogWeb), a local Web site, or the whole of the World Wide Web. The next decision in formulating the search involves deciding which parts of the record (or fields) should be searched. In many cases the searcher may wish to search all parts of the record. However, if the records deal with items that include specified fields such as date information, subject information, producer or provider details, then these attributes may be used in formulating the search. Some search software may require search terms representing the concepts of a search to be linked using the Boolean oper-ators AND, OR, NOT. The search for company directors born in Montreal and educated at McGill University (see next section) shows the use of field searching and Boolean operators. Many of the WWW search engines, such as AltaVista, Infoseek and Lycos, can deal with a list of 'natural language' terms as shown in the search for outback tours in Alice Springs (also in the next section).

Workstation

The workstation used for most searching nowadays is a PC, which normally comprises a high-speed processor, a good-quality monitor, keyboard, a mouse, an integral CD-ROM drive, a modem and a large amount of store. Most PCs will be run under a version of the Windows operating system and offer access to a number of icons depicting various search services. These might include various local databases, networked CD-ROM databases, local online catalogues and access to the WWW via a browser such as Netscape Navigator or Internet Explorer. Each of these search systems will no doubt have its own search software and so will present a number of search interfaces to the users who must remember which system is being used at any one time and, most importantly, what information is being searched.

Workstations might have a number of peripherals attached. It is quite common, especially in the home environment, to have a linked laser printer so that high-quality, often colour, printouts can be produced. Sound players, or speakers, are needed to listen to sound that may be stored on a CD-ROM (e.g. a recording of a Martin Luther King speech on the Encarta CD-ROM) or retrieved via the Internet.

Sometimes special software is needed on the workstation to view files that may have been retrieved from a search. For instance, if accessing Web sites from Japan, China or Korea then software to enable the display of, and ability to enter Kanji-based characters would be necessary. Many publishers of electronic journals, especially those that also produce parallel printed journals, have made these journals available in the portable document format (PDF) which requires the Adobe Acrobat software (freely available on the Internet) for displaying and printing those documents.

The concept of a 'scholar's workstation' was developed during the mid-1990s. The common approach to implementing the scholar's workstation is to enhance and collate local library resources into a single interface. In order to create such an environment computing support must be combined with library resources to generate an appropriate system. For instance, the McGill Interactive Data Access System (MIDAS), is an initiative of the McGill University Libraries in Canada. The objective of MIDAS is to provide the McGill community with a consistent and intuitive user interface to access electronic information and resources located at McGill and elsewhere; details are provided at http://www.library.mcgill.ca/whatismd.htm.

Herther (1998) describes developments in network computers (NCs), developed by firms such as Sun, Oracle and IBM. NCs differ from PCs as they contain no stored applications software and rely on networked servers for computing and access to files and software. NetPCs are also described by Herther; these would give users some control over local processing and storage and are being developed by firms such as Compaq and Microsoft.

Link to computer system

If a search is being carried out on a CD-ROM or DVD-ROM installed in the PC, the link between database and computer system takes place within the PC. Linking workstations and file servers within a given local area (such as an office building or a university campus) can be accomplished using a local area network (LAN) which enables data to be transmitted at high speeds.

The development of the Internet enables remote workstations to access, with comparative ease, computer systems all over the world. Very often the searcher may not be aware of the links – although at some times the networks become very crowded and response time becomes so slow as to make any searching non-viable. To enable all these computers to 'talk' to one another it is necessary that they communicate using a standard procedure – this is known as a *protocol*. The protocol governing the transmission of information over the Internet is known as Transmission Control Protocol/Internet Protocol (TCP/IP). Every computer which is permanently linked to the Internet has its unique IP address in a similar way that all telephones have a unique telephone number.

Many businesses and organizations have realized the popularity of the Internet and the WWW as a communication device and have developed internal networks based on the TCP/IP protocols – these are known as intranets. Intranets are used for internal corporate information sharing rather than for 'public' information. Pelissier *et al.* (1997) describe the use of intranet technology at Unesco for communications between its headquarters in Paris and its information stations in offices in other parts of the world such as Bangkok, Cairo, Caracas, Dakar and Nairobi. They argue that 'it provides a cheap, user-friendly standard interface which is easy to maintain'.

Search software or search engine

The program, or set of programs, which processes a search request, carries out a search of the stored data and reports on the items retrieved is known as the search software or the search engine. Search terms from, say, a title or abstract (in a bibliographic database) or from a Web page are assembled in an index and the search is carried out on this index (described further in Chapter 5). The facilities and functions offered by the search software, which usually include ways of combining search terms and searching in specific parts of a record, are described in more depth in Chapter 6, with some search examples given later in this chapter and more in Chapter 9.

Search software can be used for searching locally held databases, and some of the search engines (e.g. Excite, Harvest, Muscat, Open Text or Verity) can be used to index and therefore provide search facilities to local Web sites. Verity's SEARCH 97 software, for instance, is used by a number of information providers (including the *Financial Times*, Dow Jones and Reuters) to provide search and retrieval solutions for online and CD-ROM products as well as for the Internet and corporate intranets.

Store of information

The store of information which may be searched is sometimes structured into collections (often referred to as databases) of individual items (known as records) which are made up of individual parts (known as fields). When a search of a bank account is carried out using a 'hole in the wall' or automated teller machine (ATM) an individual account (or record) from the whole database of accounts is accessed using a special card and a password or personal identification number (PIN); an individual field, such as the amount held in the account, then can be selected and the contents displayed. Examples of records from a variety of databases are given throughout the book and an overview of the range of electronic information resources is given in Chapter 3.

Sometimes there is no obvious structure to the information which is being searched and the full text is searched. Some Internet search engines index whole Web pages, others just the first few lines and others specialize in providing access to collections of email addresses (this can be useful to genealogists seeking long lost family members). When searching Encyclopedia Britannica Online the search engine searches the 44 million plus words that are included on that Web site.

The information may be physically stored on different types of media. A local database of, say, community information may be stored on the hard disc of a server and then be searchable from various workstations. Alternatively the information may be stored on an optical disc, such as a CD-ROM or DVD-ROM or on a set of networked CD-ROMs. The large online search services, such as DialogWeb, have many disc drives onto which are loaded exchangeable packs of hard discs. In some situations the searcher is not searching a centralized service but accessing computers in various parts of the world as part of a 'distributed' search process. This concept involving the use of the Z39.50 protocol is covered further in Chapter 8.

Retrieved items

When the search software has retrieved some items it is necessary for the searcher to look at them. In bibliographic retrieval systems the 'item' stored, searched and retrieved is a bibliographic citation consisting of various fields such as author, title, journal, descriptors (terms to describe the item), abstract, language and year of publication. When such a record has been retrieved all or part of it may be displayed, downloaded, printed or emailed to the searcher. Increasingly, electronic journal collections provide full-text access to some retrieved references or alternatively article supply agencies or document delivery services can be used to provide them. Some such services are now being 'merged' with bibliographic search services to provide an integrated approach. For instance, the OCLC FirstSearch service has a linked database, Electronic Journals Online, and the Bath Information and Data Services (BIDS) has the linked Journals Online, both of which provide the full text of many articles which might have been first retrieved from a search of the bibliographic databases on these services. Details of OCLC FirstSearch and BIDS are given in Chapter 3.

When carrying out a search on the WWW, sites which hold information that 'matches' with the search request are listed and then the searcher has to 'click' on potentially relevant sites to look further for, hopefully relevant, information. Some Web sites as well as some CD-ROM databases are multi-media, which means that 'items' retrieved can consist not just of text but also audio recordings, video or animation sequences and still images.

The order in which retrieved items is presented to the searcher is important and many search systems, as described further in Chapter 6, employ 'relevance ranking' algorithms to ensure that what are thought to be the most relevant references are displayed first.

Some Sample Searches

The searches included here aim to provide the reader with an overview of the range of search systems and types of information that can be retrieved. Fuller details of general search facilities are given in Chapter 6 and further search examples are given in Chapter 9.

Search 1: Looking at local information via a home page

The home page of any Web site usually provides access to a range of local and remote information sources. Many Web sites which serve a particular locality will include details of current events in that community. An example of the home page of the University of Wales Aberystwyth is shown in Figure 1.2. The address of this Web page, or the uniform resource locator (URL), is http:// www.aber.ac.uk. By working through the menus and choosing appropriate options (Visitors, Entertainments, Cinemas, Commodore Cinema) a list of films currently showing at the Commodore Cinema in Aberystwyth is displayed (Figure 1.3). Alternatively, if the URL for the Commodore cinema (http://www.aber. ac.uk/ cinema/commodore. html) had been known to the searcher it could have been input directly. If the searcher clicks on *Titanic* to find out more information about that film then immediately a link is made to another computer at the Internet Movie Database (http://uk.imdb.com) which provides details of tens of thousands of films, actors, producers, directors and so on. Figure 1.4 shows some of the information about *Titanic*; using the appropriate links further information about the film (such as awards received, plot and reviews) can be displayed. This is basically what searching the Internet is like: you can click from one place to another using the mouse, without necessarily knowing where you are going.

Search 2: General Internet search using a search engine

In this example, a searcher is planning a holiday to Alice Springs and wishes to find an operator offering 'outback' tours. No obvious source of information is known to the searcher and so a decision is made to do a general search of the Internet using the AltaVista search engine and entering a natural language request as 'outback tours in Alice Springs'. This results in a quick response, as shown in Figure 1.5, indicating that there

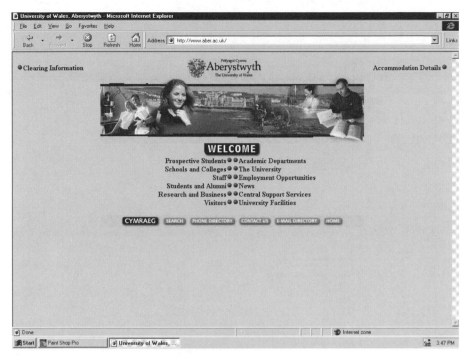

Figure 1.2   University of Wales Aberystwyth home page

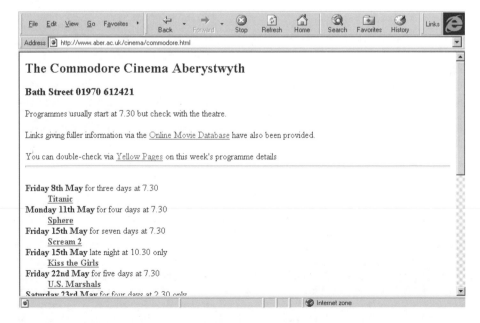

Figure 1.3   Part of Web page display of monthly programme, Commodore Cinema, Aberystwyth

Figure 1.4   Part of display for *Titanic* film at the Internet Movie Database Web site

are over a million matches or 'hits'. In fact, with this search formulation, only one of the main search terms (outback, tours, Alice, Springs) need match an item for its retrieval and so not all the hits will necessarily be relevant. However, the hits which the AltaVista search engine decides most closely match the search request are shown first. Figure 1.5 lists the first items retrieved and clicking on one, Sahara Outback Tours, the searcher is linked directly to the Web site of the tour company (based in Alice Springs), the first page of which is shown in Figure 1.6. If required, an online booking for a tour can be made over the Internet.

Search 3: Search for a particular book in a library

The catalogues of many libraries are now available for online searching via an online public access catalogue (OPAC) as part of the library management system. At the Manchester Metropolitan University a system called Talis, produced by the British firm BLCMP Library Services, is used for library management, and this has a Web-based OPAC. Figure 1.7 shows the range of ways in which a book might be accessed: title, author, keyword and so on, and the first part of an author search for R.J. Hartley. The five references for items by R.J. Hartley are shown in Figure 1.8. Clicking on one of these gives fuller details of the book as well as of copies held at different sites (Figure 1.9); via a link with the issue system, the searcher also can see if a copy is available for loan.

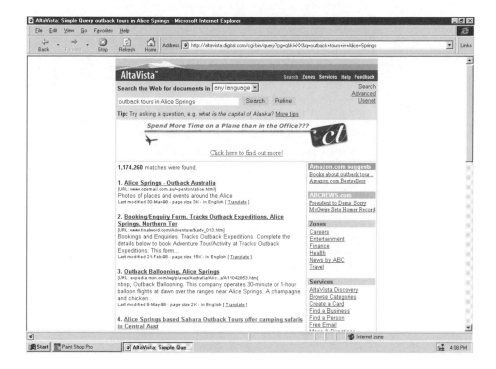

Figure 1.5   Result of AltaVista search for outback tours in Alice Springs

Search 4: Looking at articles published in the latest issue of an electronic journal

By early 1998 an estimated 4,000 electronic 'academic' or scholarly journals on a variety of subjects were available via the Internet. In addition, a large number of electronic 'magazine'-type journals cover popular activities such as golf, photography, skiing or supporting football clubs. *D-lib Magazine* is an academic journal which offers a forum for researchers and developers of advanced digital libraries. It is coordinated by the Corporation for National Research Initiatives in the US as part of the Digital Libraries Initiative. The main host site for the *D-lib Magazine* is at http://www. dlib.org/dlib but to enable easy access in other parts of the world there are 'mirror' sites at the Australian National University (http://sunsite. anu.edu.au/mirrors/dlib) and at the UK Office for Library and Information Networking (UKOLN) (http://mirrored.ukoln.ac.uk/lis-journals/dlib/ dlib). Figure 1.10 shows the first page of the table of contents for the January 1998 issue, which also provides a search facility to look at previous issues, and through Ready Reference links to access a number of digital library projects. Figure 1.11 shows the start of an article about Dublin Core metadata. There is no print equivalent of this journal.

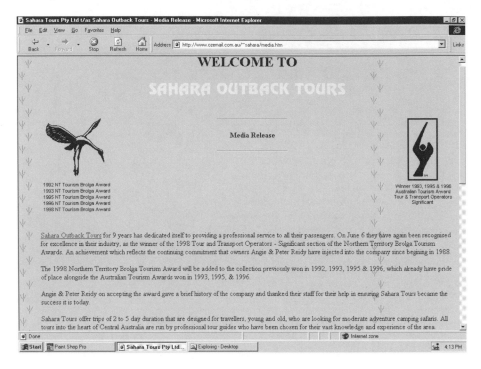

Figure 1.6   Part of a home page for a tour operator

Search 5: Search for articles or reports published on a particular subject

In this search example information is sought on the subject of bilingual education in Canada. A decision is made to use ERIC – an education resources database which covers 800,000 references to books, journal articles, theses, conference proceedings, research reports etc., published since 1966. ERIC is produced by the US Office for Education and is available in many forms including CD-ROM, via online search services such as DialogWeb or via OCLC FirstSearch. The searcher had access to OCLC FirstSearch (which is described further in Chapter 3) and so this was used for the search. Figure 1.12 shows the opening page of ERIC, with the search topic 'Canada and bilingualism' inserted in the search box to be matched with subject keywords. By clicking on one of the 300 plus items retrieved, the full record is displayed as shown in Figure 1.13. The strong structure of this record can be seen, with individual fields for author, title, year, abstract, descriptors and so on.

Search 6: Search for information related to business executives

The searcher, in this example, wishes to find a list of company executives and directors who were born in Montreal and studied for their first degree

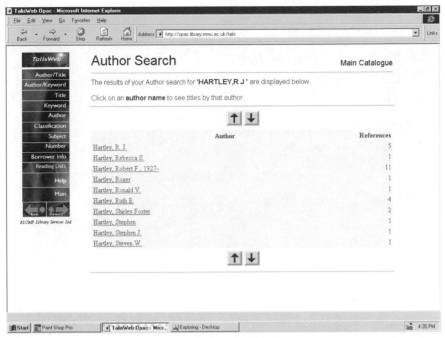

Figure 1.7 Search options and Author display for Manchester Metropolitan University Library OPAC

Figure 1.8 List of items by a sought author in the Manchester Metropolitan University OPAC

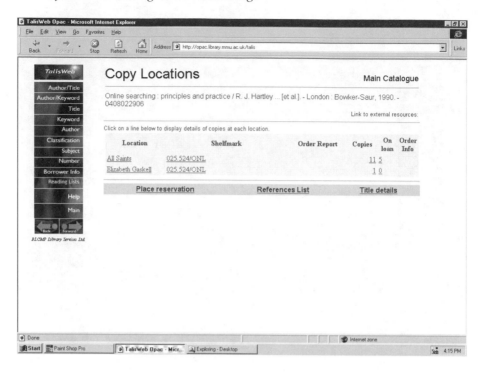

Figure 1.9 Fuller details of one record from the Manchester Metropolitan University OPAC Search

at McGill University. A database, known as Standard and Poor's Register – Biographical, giving information on about 70,000 key business executives in North America, is available for searching as a CD-ROM from Dialog or on DialogWeb. In this case a decision is made to use the command version of DialogWeb. The first step is to select the Standard and Poor's database from among the numerous available on DialogWeb. This is done by using the Begin command followed by the number (526) identifying the specific database required:

BEGIN 526

The database has been indexed to include birth city and a code (BC =) is allocated to that field. Similarly the undergraduate college attended by the executives is indexed using the code UC =. In Dialog the command to choose search terms is SELECT. The search statement:

SELECT BC = Montreal?

results in 397 matches (the ? is called a truncation symbol and ensures that entries listed under Montreal, Montreal Quebec, or Montreal Que. in the BC = field are all found). These 397 items are allocated to set 1, known as S1.

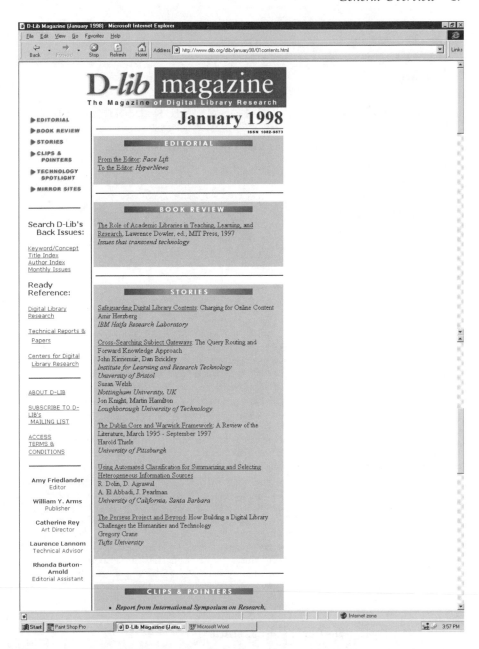

Figure 1.10 Contents page of electronic journal, *D-lib Magazine*

D-Lib Magazine
January 1998

ISSN 1082-9873

The Dublin Core and Warwick Framework

A Review of the Literature, March 1995 - September 1997

Harold Thiele
Department of Library and Information Science
School of Information Sciences
University of Pittsburgh
Pittsburgh, Pennsylvania
hthiele@lis.pitt.edu

Overview

The purpose of this essay is to identify and explore the dynamics of the literature associated with the Dublin Core Workshop Series. The essay opens by identifying the problems that the Dublin Core Workshop Series is addressing, the status of the Internet at the time of the first workshop, and the contributions each workshop has made to the ongoing discussion. The body of the essay describes the characteristics of the literature, highlights key documents, and identifies the major researchers. The essay closes with evaluation of the literary trends and considerations of future research directions. The essay concludes that a shift from a descriptive emphasis to a more empirical form of literature is about to take place. Future research questions are identified in the areas of satisfying searcher needs, the impact of surrogate descriptions on search engine performance, and the effectiveness of surrogate descriptions in authenticating Internet resources.

Introduction

The literature associated with the Dublin Core Workshop Series is of recent origin having started in 1995. It focuses on the development and promotion of metadata elements that facilitate the discovery of both textual and non-textual resources in a networked environment and support heterogeneous metadata interoperability. The object is to develop a simple metadata set and associated syntax that will be used by information producers and providers to describe their networked resources, thereby improving their chance of discovery.

Figure 1.11   Typical electronic journal article

[**Database**= ERIC]

Welcome to *ERIC* ! By doing a search, you agree to the OCLC Terms and Conditions and the ERIC Terms and Conditions.

Word, Phrase (Help)   **Keyword Index** (Help)

Search for `canada and bilingualism` **in** Subject ▼ Browse Index

Start Search   History   Advanced Search ⌄

ERIC   ERiC

Description	References to thousands of educational topics. Includes journal articles, books, theses, curriculi, conference papers, and standards and guidelines.
Records	940 K
Dates Covered	1966 ...
Updated	Monthly
Full Text	No
Periodicals Covered	(information not available)
Producer	Educational Resource Information Center
Date Added	1991-09-01
Optional Features	Interlibrary Loan, Related Subjects
Terms & Conditions	None

Return

[TOP]   Databases   **Search**   Results   Record   News   Text Only   Exit   Help

Figure 1.12   Search form for ERIC database on OCLC FirstSearch

[**Database**= ERIC | **Search**=su:(canada and bilingualism) | **Results**= 339 records | **Record**=4]

Ownership: Check the catalogs in your library.
```
       ERIC NO: ED407837
  AVAILABILITY: EDRS Price - MF01 Plus Postage. PC Not Available from EDRS.
        AUTHOR: Foster, Rosemary
         TITLE: The "Successful" Bilingual Senior High School Student.
          YEAR: 1997
      PUB TYPE: Research/technical report; Speech/conference paper
      LANGUAGE: English
      ABSTRACT: A 1992 Canadian study and 1994 followup investigated the high
                school experience of six Anglophone French immersion students
                who participated in a pilot program in French immersion in
                elementary and junior high school and continued immersion
                study in high school. Data were gathered during the students'
                tenth grade, primarily in semi-structured interviews with
                students and their parents. The students were committed to
                studying core high school courses in French because of
                positive experiences in immersion. Perceived benefits included
                French fluency, ability to think in different ways, close-knit
                peer group, and pride in participation in a challenging
                alternative program. Perceived limitations included a shortage
                of bilingual content area teachers, restricted course
                selection, lack of appealing learning resources, limited
                program support for students having difficulty, and lack of
                recognition of the immersion program. A four-year followup
                revealed that all graduated with a bilingual certificate. One
                was valedictorian of his class and gave his speech in both
                English and French, and was later selected as top high school
                scholar in the province. Results suggest the students'
                "feeling of success" about early immersion experiences and
                family support were significant factors in immersion
                persistence. Parent perceptions of their children are also
                discussed. Contains 14 references. (MSE)
         NOTES: 15p.  Paper presented at the Annual Meeting of the American
                Educational Research Association (Chicago, IL, March 1997).
    MAJOR DESC: Academic Achievement; Academic Persistence; Bilingual
                Students; French; Immersion Programs; Second Languages
    MINOR DESC: Bilingualism; Case Studies; Foreign Countries; High School
                Students; High Schools; Interviews; Language of Instruction;
                Student Attitudes; Student Experience
   IDENTIFIERS: Canada; French Language Schools
CLEARINGHOUSE NUMBER: FL024497
```

[TOP]   Databases   Search   Results   **Record**   News   Text Only   Exit   Help

Figure 1.13   Example of an ERIC record on OCLC FirstSearch

Similarly the search statement:

SELECT UC = McGill

results in 194 matches with records about people whose undergraduate degrees are from McGill. These are allocated to set 2.

Combining the two sets to select only those items that include both BC = Montreal? and UC = McGill is done in the following way:

SELECT S1 AND S2

and results in 106 hits.

These can be displayed using the type command:

TYPE 3/5/1

which results in full details (format 5) being given from set 3 of the first record of the 106. The record would be in the form:

JONES, Robert, F.3
Birth: Montreal, Que., Canada (1943)
Undergrad. College: McGill University (Canada)
Primary Co. Affiliation: Executive V-P (Europe)
Happy Products
1188 McTavish Rd
Montreal H1A 3J2

Sources of Further Information

Printed information

In 1977 two journals, *Online* and *Online Review* (since renamed *Online and CDROM Review*) were launched. Between them these two publications contain many important papers, and recent issues of these journals are now also available on the Internet. Another important event in 1977 was an international meeting on online information held in London, organized by Learned Information. This has become an annual event attracting tens of thousands of (mainly European) participants and its proceedings provide useful papers on access to electronic information. This meeting has spawned other conferences and events around the world (further details can be gained from http://www.learned.co.uk). Another major conference in the US is run by Online Inc., publishers of *Online* and, inter alia, a number of books on searching (further details can be gained from http://www.onlineinc.com).

Journals such as *Database* and *Database Searcher* concentrate more on practical aspects of searching, often including valuable hints on searching particular databases. Newspaper-style publications, such as *Information World Review* and *Information Today*, cover the current news regarding the online industry. Other journals, many now also available in electronic form, containing relevant material include *Electronic Library, Emedia Professional (formerly CD-Professional), Information Technology and Libraries, Journal of Documentation, Journal of Information Science, Journal of the American Society for Information Science, Managing Information, New Review of Information Networking, New Review of Text and Document Management,* and *Program: Electronic Library and Information Systems.*

Various user groups have been set up with the aim of bringing together those involved in searching electronic information resources and related topics in a given region, for example the Aberystwyth Online User Group, UK Online User Group (UKOLUG) and the Southern California Online Users Group. Other groups represent those using a particular service or group of services, such as the Joint Information Systems Committee (assisted) Bibliographic Dataservices User Group (JIBS) in the UK. JIBS acts as a focal point for the many users of search services such as the Bath Information and Data Service (BIDS), Edinburgh Data and Information Access (EDINA) and the Consortium of University Research Libraries' OPAC (COPAC) that are funded by the Joint Information Systems Committee of the Higher Education Funding Councils (JISC). The newsletters of various user groups can also provide useful overviews of developments in specific areas: the *UKOLUG Newsletter,* for instance, has sections covering CD-ROM, Internet and telecommunications developments.

There are a number of general textbooks on searching and a huge number related to Internet developments – a selection has been included in the references at the end of this chapter.

Electronic information sources

A wealth of information is available on the WWW that is of relevance to readers of this book – although knowing where to find it is not always obvious. The online help pages of the various search engines usually provide detailed instructions on how to use their search facilities. Overview information on search engine developments is available through Websites (such as: http://www.searchenginewatch.com). The UKOLUG Web site (http://www.ukolug.demon.co.uk) provides links to the electronic versions of some of the printed online journals just noted as well as to recent relevant electronic or printed articles comparing the performance of search engines. Organizations and groups that are involved in education and training for access to electronic information resources sometimes make information available on the Web. The Netskills team at Newcastle University, for instance, has produced various guides for searching the Internet (http://www.netskills.ac.uk/support/searching). A regular column on search engines appears in the electronic version of the journal *Ariadne.* BUBL is an information service from Strathclyde University in Scotland (and funded by JISC) which gives a lot of information, including tables of contents of both printed and electronic journals, a classified way of accessing Internet resources and details of various mailing lists. BUBL was first developed in the early 1990s and has proved useful to many library and information professionals all over the world. The Thomas Parry Library at the University of Wales Aberystwyth has developed PICK: Quality Internet resources in library and information science (LIS), which provides links to many electronic LIS resources as well as explaining how

Electronic Australiana

The National Library offers access to a range of electronic Australiana resources that are available on the Internet and World Wide Web in addition to the more traditional library materials it holds in its collections.

Content

Guides to Australian Information on the WWW
Online (the Internet with an Australian flavour)
Australia and the Rest of the World
Australian Studies
Finding / Contacting Australians

Culture and Cultural Heritage
Geography
Law
Australian Publishers and Literature

Guides to Australian Information on the WWW

- Australian Governments' Entry Point
- Australian Bureau of Statistics
- This is Australia / Telstra
- About Australia
- The Australian Home Page
- The Australia Index / Charles Sturt University
- OzCool — including Top 100 Ranking Australian Sites for the Week
- Australian Internet Directories
- Beyond the Black Stump Australiana Page
- Australian Directories
- WebSource: Everything Australian on the Internet
- Australia - WWW Virtual Library
- National Library of Australia Internet subject guides

Online (the Internet with an Australian flavour)
For more general access to the Internet, including search engines, discussion lists, etc., see our Internet Resources page.

Figure 1.14 Some electronic resources available from the National Library of Australia

to search such resources (http://www.aber.ac.uk/~tplwww/e). References to other Web resources such as electronic journals, details of research projects, online search service providers, and database producers are included where relevant in the book.

National initiatives related to electronic information resources

In many countries, initiatives are underway to improve access to electronic information resources. Such initiatives are often referred to under the name 'digital libraries'. The Digital Library Initiative (DLI) in the US comprises six federally funded projects in digital library research, with partnerships led by universities such as the University of California at Berkeley, University of California, Santa Barbara, Carnegie Mellon University, University of Illinois at Urbana-Champaign, University of Michigan and Stanford University. More information about DLI is given in links available from the *D-lib Magazine* electronic journal referred to in Search 4.

Similar initiatives are underway in other countries. In Singapore, for instance, Timely Information for All, Relevant and Affordable (TIARA) is a multiagency collaborative effort by the National Library Board, the National Science and Technology Board, participating libraries and the National Computer Board's Digital Library Cluster. TIARA provides access to a range of electronic information services including the several hundred databases on Dialog, some of Elsevier's full-text science journals, some of Cambridge Scientific Abstracts' databases as well as online catalogues of libraries in Singapore (http://www.digilib.org.sg). In Canada, the Canadian Initiative on Digital Libraries (CIDL) is an alliance of Canadian libraries interested in improving communication and coordination in the development of Canadian digital library resources (http://www.nlc-bnc.ca/cidl/). The objectives of CIDL include:

- To formulate and implement strategies toward increased communication, awareness and education on digital library matters.
- To identify and promulgate digital library standards and best practices.
- To define methods to better coordinate digital library activities among institutions and to avoid duplication in the development of digital resources.

National libraries can often be good starting places for finding out about digital library developments in a country. The Digital Library Programme of the British Library is described on the Portico Web server (http://portico.bl.uk) and links are available through the Gabriel gateway to the Web sites of 34 national libraries in west, central and eastern Europe. Many of these are impressive Web sites and give links to many local resources. The National Library of Australia provides access to a range of electronic resources about Australia and some of these are shown in Figure 1.14.

Funding the infrastructure to enable searching of electronic resources is also often undertaken by national bodies. In the UK, this is achieved in the higher education sector by JISC whose mission is: 'To stimulate and enable the cost effective exploitation of information systems and to provide a high quality national network infrastructure for the UK higher education and research councils communities'. JISC is responsible for funding a variety of initiatives, including BUBL and BIDS, as well as a series of projects in the Electronic Libraries (eLib) Programme. Full details of the 58 projects that were funded in 1995–1998 are given at http://www.ukoln.ac.uk/elib. Further work is in progress and many of these projects are influencing electronic library developments in other countries.

As more and more information providers make their information available electronically but not in printed form then the know-how to seek information on these sources will be an essential life skill. The apparent simplicity of information seeking in this new environment is deceptive.

Successful information seeking in reality remains a complex task and the intention of the following chapters is to provide a discussion of that information-seeking process.

References and Further Reading

Armstrong, C.J. and Hartley, R.J. (1997) *Keyguide to Information Sources in Online and CD-ROM Database Searching*. London: Mansell

Armstrong, C.J. and Large, J.A. (1999) *Manual of Online Search Strategies*. 3rd edn. Aldershot: Gower

Berkman, R.I. (1994) *Find It Online*. New York: Windcrest/McGraw-Hill

Bradley, P.(1997) *Going Online, CD-ROM and the Internet*. 10th edn. London:Aslib

Cimino, J.D. (1997) *Intranets: the surf within*. Rockland (Mass.): Charles River Media Inc.

Galt, J.S. (1997) Does the future of the online industry lie in individually customised services? How online hosts are adapting to the future. In D.I. Raitt, P. Blake and B. Jeapes (eds) *Online Information 97: Proceedings of the 21st International Online Information Meeting London 9–11 December 1997*. Oxford: Learned Information, 13–18

Hanson, T.A. and Day, J.M. (1994) *CD-ROM in Libraries: Management Issues*. London: Bowker-Saur

Herther, N.K. (1998) The personal computer: today's workhorse moves into the 21st century. *Online*, **22** (1) 29–38. Also available at http://www.onlineinc.com/online-mag/JanOL98/herther1.html

Lesk, M. (1997) Going digital. *Scientific American*, March 1997. Also available at www.sciam.com/0397issue/0397/lesk.html

McClure, C.R., Bertot, J.C., and Beachboard, J.C. (1996) Enhancing the role of public libraries in the national information infrastructure. *Public Libraries*, **35**(4), 2–8

Moore, N. (1997) The Information Society. In Y. Courrier and A. Large (eds) *World Information Report 1997/8*. Paris:Unesco, 271–84

New Library: The People's Network (1997) London: Library and Information Commission. Also available at: http://www.ukoln.ac.uk/services/lic/newlibrary/

Pelissier, D., Brion, A. and Bara R. (1997) Intranet or client-server: which is the best tool to deliver information within an institution such as UNESCO? In D.I. Raitt, P. Blake and B. Jeapes (eds) *Online Information 97: Proceedings of the 21st International Online Information Meeting London 9–11 December 1997*. Oxford: Learned Information, 139–52

Reuters Business Information (1996) *Dying for Information? An Investigation into Information Overload in the UK and Worldwide*. London: Reuters. Also available at http://www.bizinfo.reuters.com/overload.html

Ridley, D. (1996) *Online Searching: A Scientist's Perspective. A Guide for Chemical and Life Sciences*. Chichester: Wiley

Shneiderman, B., Byrd, D. and Croft, W.B. (1997) Clarifying search: a user-interface framework for text searches. *D-Lib Magazine* available at: http://www.dlib.org/dlib/january97/retrieval/01shneiderman.html

Shuman, B.A. (1993) *Cases in Online Search Strategy*. Englewood, Colorado: Libraries Unlimited

Smith, P., Stone, P., Campbell, C., Marks, H. and Copeman, H. (1997) EARL: collaboration in networked information and resource sharing services for public libraries in the UK. *Program*, **31**(4), 347–63

Tseng, G., Poulter, A. and Hiom, D. (1997) *The Library and Information Professional's Guide to the Internet.* 2nd edn. London: Library Association Publishing

Vickery, B. and Vickery, A. (1993) Online search interface design. *Journal of Documentation*, **49**(2), 103–87

Winship, I. and McNab, A. (1996) *The Student's Guide to the Internet.* London: Library Association Publishing

CHAPTER 2

Information-Seeking Behaviour

The Innateness of Human Information Seeking

Seeking information is a fundamental human function, vital to survival. As Marchionini (1995) explains, life requires us to plan and execute actions, and to do this we need to have plausible mental models (understandings) of the world. In order to generate such mental models, information is required – that is, anything with the potential to change a mental state. For Marchionini, 'information-seeking is a process driven by life itself'. In pre-literate eras, humans were already seeking information on a wide range of subjects of crucial importance to their daily lives: the most suitable locations to establish their settlements, the best ways to hunt and catch their prey, ways to cure sickness and heal wounds, astronomical signs that might portend good or bad fortune, and so on. Once information had been collected by the senses – sight, hearing and touch – it could be stored in human memory and passed orally from generation to generation. With the development of writing systems, such stores of oral information were supplemented by visual information – writing and images – maintained on stone, clay, papyrus and ultimately paper, that could be searched to answer specific questions. Documents were collected by rulers, nobles and priests, and stored in organized collections – libraries. With growing leisure time and expanding literacy, wider sections of society could supplement information gathered personally or gleaned from listening to elders, by consulting written information sources. As these documentary sources grew ever bigger, it became necessary to employ more sophisticated organizational methods to ensure that sought information was found, including library catalogues, indexes and abstracts. Technological developments eventually introduced additional media: records, tapes, broadcast television programmes, film and video. The development of digital information storage media, capable of holding very large quantities of text, images and sounds that can be searched using sophisticated retrieval software, offers yet a further extension of the apparatus to facilitate information seeking.

Technological developments have also transformed access to information. Although the same system of bones, muscles and ligaments gives us personal mobility as for our ancestors, we can now travel with minimal delay to an information source (documentary, digital or personal) whether it be the other side of town or the other side of the world. The train, ship, automobile and aeroplane have radically reduced distances from the days when a faraway library might be reached only on foot or horseback. Even more dramatically, the telephone, television, fax and now computer enable us to access remote information without the need to relocate physically.

Despite such enormous technological developments, our ability to process retrieved information has not evolved similarly. Our optical and audio networks that allow us to read texts, view images and hear sounds (for some of us now enhanced by optical and audio devices to correct sight and hearing defects), and the olfactory organs that enable us to detect smells (the least developed human sense mechanism) are the same as those employed by Roman senators, medieval scholars or Victorian novelists. Above all, the same human brain continues to direct all these operations as well as processing the resulting sensory data that have been collected. Our cognitive processors continue to employ the same basic strategies to store, filter, retrieve and compare collected data, and then to draw inferences from them.

Although information seeking is innate to human beings, never before have we been called upon to manage so much stored information. Technological support, and especially the appearance of computers and data communication networks, is both a response to this information explosion and a cause of it. There are now larger volumes of information than ever before, new ways of collecting information, new information containers and new tools for working with information. Such manipulation of information, whether in the workplace, the home or a place of entertainment, increasingly signifies computer manipulation of digitized information. Information is generally and overtly recognized, as never before, for its economic, social and political importance, recognition encapsulated in phrases such as 'the information society', 'information rich versus information poor' and 'the information highway'. Increasingly, the wealth both of individuals and of nations is generated not by their ability to farm, mine or even manufacture, but by their control over information resources. The ability to identify, acquire and use information is vital to all inhabitants of 'information societies'.

Information Seekers

There is a tendency to discuss the seekers (or users) of information as if they are a homogeneous group. This is, of course, far from the truth. In reality, seekers differ from one another in a number of respects. It is important to realize this as the ways in which they search for information, and the kind of information system that can best serve them in this quest (as well as the kind of information sought) will be influenced by their profiles.

The most commonly applied characteristic relates to the seekers' level of experience in information retrieval. Applying this measure, seekers can be categorized as novice or experienced. Considerable research has been undertaken to establish how experienced searchers differ in their strategies from novice searchers, and to establish whether experienced users are indeed more successful searchers than novices (see below). There is no working definition, however, of what constitutes an experienced searcher: what knowledge must the experienced searcher possess? Allen (1991) for example, identifies four types of knowledge: general world knowledge, knowledge of the information retrieval system being used, knowledge of the information-seeking task being undertaken, and knowledge of the topic being searched. Michel (1994) identifies 11 sources of information used during searching, listed under three headings.

Those internal to the searcher

- The reason for the search – the broader situation prompting the search.
- Beliefs about the information retrieval system that are logical pre-conditions for a search, such as that the system is a possible place to find what is wanted.
- The object of the search – the seeker's notion of what is being looked for.
- The object specifications – the actual criteria that must be met to satisfy the search.
- Domain knowledge – knowledge relating to the general area of the search objective.
- Search knowledge – about information systems in general and the specific system in particular.

Those created by the searcher

- The linguistic expression of the objective in one or more words.
- The actual search terms selected by the seeker to express the objective.

Those external to the information seeker

- Guidance devices that assist the user, such as help screens or manuals.
- System terms – searchable terms in the records such as controlled terms.
- The actual organized collection of data available on the information system.

Borgman (1996), viewing the knowledge required by a searcher in some-what narrower terms than Allen and Michel, suggests just three layers of knowledge:

- Conceptual – to convert an information need into a searchable query.
- Semantic – to construct a query for a given system.
- Technical – to enter queries as specific search statements.

Hsieh-Yee (1993) is one researcher who has tried to define 'novice' and 'experienced' searcher, albeit still in rather general terms. Novice searchers for her are non-professional searchers who have little or no search experi-ence and have not taken courses in online searching or attended relevant workshops provided by librarians or system vendors. Experienced searchers are professional searchers who have at least one year of search experience and have either taken courses on online searching or attended workshops provided by system vendors.

A related distinguishing characteristic is between an information pro-fessional (or information intermediary) – the person who conducts a search on behalf of a client – and an end user – the person who actually wants the information to answer a specific need. This distinction was especially valid when most online searching was conducted by intermediaries – librar-ians or other information specialists – rather than by the actual information requester. Information professionals were considered to be experienced users, as was generally the case, and end users were seen as being novices who conducted searches rarely and with little or no preliminary training (often also true). Much searching is now undertaken by end users, although intermediaries certainly still have an important role to play.

Information seekers can be categorized by a variety of other criteria. Does the seeker bring to the search a thorough knowledge of the subject in which that search is to be conducted, or is the seeker a comparative beginner in the field? The subject specialist's search is likely to be different from the non-specialist's because, for example, the former will have a greater aware-ness of the subject's terminology, and therefore be better placed to select suitable search terms, including, where necessary, synonyms (automobile/ car) and terms at different hierarchical levels (engine – cylinder – piston); these linguistic skills are important in searching and are discussed more fully in Chapter 4. The specialist should be more skilled at selecting the most suitable source or sources for the search, increasingly difficult as elec-tronic information resources proliferate. The specialist should also be able to judge the relevance of information as it is being retrieved during a search, a skill that can help the searcher to re-define the strategy if it is failing to produce relevant materials (the concept of relevance is discussed more fully in Chapter 10).

Until quite recently, most user studies have confined their attention to young adults; the majority have been undertaken in university libraries whose patrons are mainly undergraduate students, with smaller numbers of graduate students and teachers. The explanation for this is quite simple: most researchers are located in university departments, and the most obvious and accessible source for their investigations is to be found on their own doorsteps. It would be difficult to argue, however, that such seekers represent a cross-section of information system users in general. Now more interest is being shown in other user groups (see later). A prime example is children, who increasingly use online information systems both in school and at home. Do systems that have been designed for adults work just as effectively for children, or do the different cognitive skills and knowledge bases of children demand information systems that have been especially designed with this specific user group in mind? The same might be said of users at the opposite end of the age spectrum. Elderly citizens are likely (for the time being, at least) to be less familiar with computers, to have poorer eyesight and less precise hand movements than their juniors. Should this make a difference, for example, to the kinds of input and output devices provided at an OPAC or an Internet workstation (see Chapter 8)?

Seekers might also be differentiated by their search objective. A user might on one occasion be trying to find absolutely everything that is available on a topic, whether it is directly or only tangentially linked to it; another seeker (or the same one on a different occasion) may only want to find a little information, but that information must be directly on the topic. These distinctions will almost certainly affect the way in which the search should ideally be conducted (see Chapter 6) as well as the sources chosen to be searched.

Finally, psychological factors such as attitude, motivation and cognitive style can differentiate users (or even the same user on different occasions).

As a shorthand, the terms 'users', 'searchers' and 'seekers' are frequently to be found throughout this book, without necessarily specifying any particular kind and as if they belong to one homogeneous group. This should not conceal the fact that each user is an individual, and that each search conducted is a unique experience.

Information Seeking

In order to carry out a search for any kind of information, it is necessary to progress through a series of steps, typically called the search process. This is the case regardless of whether the information seeker is a novice or has experience, is an information intermediary or an end user, is young or old, a subject expert or a beginner, and so on. It also holds true for any type of computerized information system. Marchionini (1993) characterizes information seeking as a problem-solving activity dependent on: the seeker, the problem, the search system and the outcomes. It involves interaction among a number of sub-processes: problem recognition, problem definition, search system selection, query conceptualization, query formulation, query execution, examination of results, and iteration of some or all of these sub-processes if the results suggest this is necessary.

The first step is to recognize that a problem exists which requires the collection of information for its resolution. That is to say, a gap is identified between what is understood and what is necessary to understand. Belkin, Oddy and Brooks (1982) constructed a model of information seeking based on the information seekers' anomalous states of knowledge (ASK).

The information seekers have a problem, but neither that problem nor the information needed to solve the problem are clearly understood (they are anomalous). In this model, information seekers must go through a process of clarification to articulate a search request. Taylor (1962) defined four levels of information needs: visceral, conscious, formalized and compromised. At the visceral level the user recognizes a need for information but it may be nothing more than a vague sort of dissatisfaction. At the conscious level the searcher can characterize the need but only through an ambiguous and rambling statement. At the formalized level the need can be clearly articulated in a rational and unambiguous statement. Finally, at the compromised level the problem can be recast as a formalized statement in terms acceptable to the search system. In a search the task is to convert a visceral, conscious or formalized need into a compromised need. To achieve this compromised level may require considerable effort on the user's part. Failure to formulate a 'correct' search statement is likely to lead to search failure. Recognition of the difficulties information seekers have in identifying their needs precisely has focused attention on browsing as an alternative strategy to searching (see Chapter 7).

The information-seeking process

The following steps – constituting the information-seeking process – are intended to establish a formalized search statement.

What information?

Exactly what information is required? The answer to this question includes not only as precise a formulation as possible of the subject matter being sought, but also decisions on a series of non-subject criteria. Should the information be restricted to one language? Some databases, such as the OPAC of a large university library, may contain information in many languages, and many bibliographic databases contain references to journal articles, conference papers, reports, and so on, in numerous languages. Must the information be current, or are older data relevant? In the case of bibliographic databases, are only references to documents available locally of interest? What level of exposition is being sought? The seeker may want detailed, scholarly information or a popular overview of a subject. In practice, it will not always be possible to give a precise answer to the question of what information is required: first, because the information seeker cannot formulate a sharply defined expression of the required information; and second, in the case of the search being undertaken by an information intermediary rather than the seeker, because the intermediary has not been able to understand the information seeker's need. In such cases, browsing rather than searching may prove more productive, if also more time consuming.

Information need

The importance of establishing as precisely as possible the information need is crucial when the search itself will be conducted by an intermediary rather than by the end user (who may not even be present when the intermediary carries out the search). For this reason an intermediary must always conduct a pre-search interview with the end user prior to the search, and during this interview establish exactly what information is required to meet the user's need. Several authors have offered guidance for conducting this interview, emphasizing its importance; for example, Quint (1991) believes that 'without doubt, the most critical area of the entire search process . . . is the reference interview'. In such interviews, there is a tendency for the user to begin by expressing the information need broadly; Eichman (1978) discusses reasons for this phenomenon. The skilful intermediary must be able to winkle out the real (and more precise) need by careful questioning. If the end user is also the searcher, the requirement to establish the information need remains just as important. Otherwise, a search can begin without any clear direction, and the result may be that relevant information is missed, as well as irrelevant information being collected – especially unfortunate if the user must pay directly for the amount of information retrieved (for example, per record displayed or downloaded).

Sources of information

Once the information need has been understood, it is possible to select the information source or sources to be searched. This book is more concerned with searching electronic information sources than with the sources themselves – an attempt to list them all would take numerous volumes. Many guides and directories are now available, both electronically and in print, to online databases, CD-ROMs, and Internet resources. It is clearly important to select a source that is relevant to the information need – the most accomplished search strategy realized in the wrong place will reveal little of interest. Selection of a source also implies selection of a technological platform, although in a growing number of cases, a source is available on more than one platform. For example, an OPAC can be searched in the library, but it may also be possible to access it via the Internet – through Telnet or increasingly the World Wide Web; a bibliographical database may be available on CD-ROM or via one or more online vendors such as STN or Dialog.

Conversion of need into concepts

The next step in the search process is to convert the information need into one or more concepts. A user may want to find information about the kinds of clothing that knights wore in the medieval period. This contains three discrete concepts: clothing; knights, and medieval. Each of these concepts in turn can be expressed by one or more terms that can be employed in the subsequent search. For example, clothing, clothes or garments are synonyms for the same concept; and tunics or cloaks, as kinds of clothing, are linked hierarchically to that broader concept. Information may be located under both the singular and plural forms of nouns, and therefore it is necessary to think of knight as well as knights. The terms medieval, mediaeval and middle ages represent both spelling variants and synonyms.

Some information sources are indexed using the actual language found in them – natural language indexing – and in such cases the user must consider all the terms that conceivably might be used in the source to represent any one concept; failure to do this may result in some information not being retrieved (see Chapter 4). Other information sources have been indexed using a controlled vocabulary taken from a thesaurus – in such cases it is necessary to find the precise term in the controlled vocabulary that has been used to express each concept. One role of a thesaurus is to eliminate the need to think of synonyms or variant spellings: the thesaurus will select one term only to represent each concept. A thesaurus should also link broader and narrower concepts, for example clothes and tunics (see Chapter 4).

Search strategy

A search strategy must next be formulated that will retrieve information containing the selected search terms, and leave aside all other information in the database. The kind of strategy will depend upon the type of dialogue transaction mode employed by the interface to the information system (see Chapter 8). It may involve choosing the right commands to use along with the search terms (see Chapters 6 and 9). In this case the initial strategy often is worked out by the user before the search begins (offline). It may involve navigating through a series of menus or on-screen forms, at certain stages being prompted to enter the search terms (see Chapter 8). In a direct manipulation interface, the strategy may involve activating windows, buttons and icons (see Chapter 8). Many information systems use Boolean logic to combine terms, allow the search to be restricted to certain parts of a record (such as only its title), allow searches to be conducted on phrases (middle ages) as well as individual words, permit the user to specify within how many words two terms must appear in a record, allow a truncation symbol after a word stem to find all variants of this stem, and so on (see Chapter 6). All these facilities must be incorporated, where appropriate, into the strategy.

Strategy implementation and review

The most obvious step in the search process is to enter the information system and implement the chosen strategy. It is important to review the results – the retrieved information – as they emerge to establish early in the search that the strategy is on the right track. A long and complex strategy should not be undertaken without viewing sample items that are being retrieved, unless the user is extremely confident that the strategy is good. It is sensible to correct a faulty strategy as early as possible in the search. A major virtue of an online information system is its interactivity – search results can be evaluated online and the strategy adjusted if the initial information needs are not being met. Such an evaluation is more difficult for an intermediary to make than an end user. The searcher should always be ready to evaluate results and iterate through a revised strategy if this seems necessary.

Types of Searches

Searches can be divided into three broad categories: known-item searches, factual searches and subject searches. They impose different demands upon the searcher and involve different strategies.

In a known-item search, as its name suggests, the user is trying to locate information about something that is already known. The most typical example is a search in a bibliographical database or a library OPAC to find additional bibliographical details or the library location number of a publication which is already known to the searcher. As long as the searcher has sufficient bibliographic information to pinpoint the item (in the case of a book, for example, the name of the author, the title and the year of publication), the search should be short and straightforward. Two kinds of problem are encountered in this kind of search. First, the searcher may fail to invert the author's surname (normally a requirement when searching in the author field of a bibliographic record); that is, the search is carried out on Charles Dickens rather than Dickens Charles or Dickens C (according to the rules applied by the specific information system). Searching on names is discussed in Chapter 4. Second, the searcher has incorrect bibliographic information; for example, it is especially easy when searching for a title to make one or two mistakes in the actual wording – searching for 'Oliver Twist' instead of the correct title, 'The Adventures of Oliver Twist' (this problem can be avoided where the system permits searching on keywords (searching on a single term or phrase within a longer string such as a title) rather than searching the title field in its entirety as one phrase).

A second type of search is one that seeks to establish or confirm a specific fact: what is the capital of Turkey; when was the Liberal Party in Canada founded; in what year did the American author, James, die? In these kinds of searches, the most important factor in finding the answer is not the strategy but rather choosing a suitable source – the search is normally quite simple. The biggest retrieval problem is likely to be location of irrelevant information – on the turkey fowl, the British Liberal Party or one of the English King James'. This is especially prevalent when the information source is very large and therefore has greater potential to include such red herrings, as with large full-text databases or the World Wide Web.

Known-item and specific fact searches have one thing in common: there is an obvious termination point for the search. Once the item or the fact has been found the search is at an end. Of course, the retrieved information may not always be factually correct, but this is another issue (see Chapter 10). The retrieval process has been successful even if the actual data are incorrect.

A decision as to when to end the third type of search – the subject search – is less straightforward. This search type attempts to locate information about a subject. It is open ended because normally the searcher has little or no idea at the outset of what may be retrieved from the information store, or when everything of relevance has been found. Should the search be terminated because all possibilities have been exhausted, or should the strategy be amended because it is not finding everything there is to find? Many searches are subject oriented. They may be bibliographic (for example, find references to articles on nuclear power) or they may be searches of the information itself (find descriptions of nuclear power generation, or as many statistical data as possible on the quantities of nuclear power generated around the world in 1998). These kinds of searches typically demand greater searching skills than the other two search types. They are more fully discussed in the following chapters.

Research Findings about Information Seekers

Many studies have been conducted to answer questions such as: What characteristics make a successful information seeker, and does an experienced seeker perform more successful searches than a novice seeker? Here it is possible to report only briefly upon a small sample of such studies. The difficult issue of what constitutes a successful search, and how best to measure success, is discussed in Chapter 10.

In the early years of online searching, several authors proposed various personal characteristics that were necessary in an accomplished seeker (in those days they were discussing intermediaries, not end users). These included such worthy traits as intelligence, an analytical mind, enthusiasm, courage, self-confidence and perseverance. These studies are reviewed by Bellardo (1985a) who concludes, politely, that not all of them were designed and executed perfectly. Fidel (1987) is also critical of the experimental methodologies adopted in the searching behaviour studies she had examined, primarily because they involved too many variables; Fidel and Soergel (1983) in fact list over 200 variables that can apply to searching. Too often the results have shown bigger differences between searching proficiency among the individual searchers in any one group than can be found between the different searcher groups representing controlled variables, suggesting that factors other than the variables under investigation are accounting for searching performance (or, of course, that the groups themselves have been wrongly identified).

Some studies have even failed to find a clear, positive relationship between search experience and search results. Lancaster *et al.* (1994), for example, compared CD-ROM searches on a bibliographic database by graduate student end users and skilled university librarian intermediaries. The librarians were able to find in total more relevant records on the database than the students, but a higher percentage of the records retrieved by the students were judged relevant by them. The greatest problem encountered by the students was failure to identify and use all the terms needed to perform a more complete search; they were less successful in identifying synonyms than the librarians. Hsieh-Yee (1993) found in her study, however, that search experience positively affected search behaviour, especially when the experienced searchers had some subject knowledge relevant to the topic of the search. They used more synonyms and tried more combinations of search terms than novices.

Many studies have commented upon the positive evaluations typically made by end users of their own search results, and questioned whether such optimism is really justified (see, for example Martin and Nicholas,

1993; Lancaster *et al.*, 1994). Sanderson (1990) considers that no matter how user friendly the system, end users need clear directions to help them get the best results; training programmes should emphasize system capabilities and the kind of information that can be obtained, and should include hands-on sessions in which users are taught how to do basic searches.

Bellardo (1985b) explored a possible link between searching performance, on the one hand, and creativity (as measured by the Khatena-Torrance Creative Perception Inventory) and academic ability (as measured by the Graduate Record Examination (GRE)) on the other. She concluded that 'the differences in performance among individuals with the same level of experience and type of training can be attributed, to a small degree only, to their general verbal and quantitative aptitude, and to their inclination toward critical and analytical creative thinking.' Saracevic *et al.* (1988) concentrated on four cognitive traits of searchers: language ability (the ability to make inductive inferences through word association); logical ability (the ability to make deductive inferences); preferred style of learning (concrete experience, reflective observation, abstract conceptualization and active experimentation); and searching experience (in this case, on the Dialog online system). They found that the records retrieved by those with greater language ability and an abstract conceptualization mode of learning were more likely to be on target – that is, relevance scores were higher (see Chapter 10). Searchers who scored high on logical reasoning were not so favoured, nor were those with greater searching experience (although it should be emphasized that none of the searchers was a novice). Searchers for whom abstract conceptualization was the preferred learning mode were better at finding a high percentage of the records on the database that were relevant to the search query – high recall (see Chapter 10). No other characteristic affected recall. This study found (as indeed have many others) marked differences in individual performances that cannot be explained by the controlled variables. Allen (1993) found that logical reasoning ability positively influenced end users of a bibliographical CD-ROM in identifying potentially useful citations from among those retrieved and in selecting search terms. Nevertheless, he failed to find any significant relationship between reasoning ability and search quality as measured by the traditional evaluation tools – precision and recall (see Chapter 10).

Toronto Public Library conducted focus groups for users with low or limited literacy skills to investigate if they could locate library materials using the OPAC (White, Deane and Livingston, 1996). These users encountered difficulties in a number of areas. They were unfamiliar with library terminology and did not always understand terms such as 'fiction', 'author' or 'title', employing instead the alternatives 'stories', 'the person who wrote the book' and 'the name of the book'. They also had problems with the keyboard, the confusing amount of detail displayed on screens and OPAC jargon such as 'call number', 'truncated', 'format', 'select' and 'display'.

Children have received attention from several researchers. Marchionini (1989) gave primary school students two search tasks to be undertaken on a CD-ROM encyclopaedia. The first was a factual search – in what year was speed skating introduced into the Olympic Games? The second was an open-ended subject search – find information about women who have travelled in space. Most of these novice users were successful in finding the required information, but the children from the higher grades were more successful than their younger counterparts and took less time. The children were equally successful at the factual and the subject searches, but the latter took longer and required more steps in the search strategy. Marchionini comments that further research is needed to establish whether the differences in performance between the older and the younger students are explained by knowledge of the subject domains, general information-seeking experience, or system manipulation skills. He was impressed by the students' high level of performance in using the various retrieval features offered by the CD-ROM, and their searches were highly interactive rather than being carefully planned before beginning the search. Large, Beheshti, Breuleux and Renaud (1994) also investigated primary school students' retrieval skills from an electronic encyclopaedia. Like Marchionini, they were impressed by the searching abilities demonstrated by these young novices. The complexity of the strategy and the success of the search was related to the complexity of the search query, as measured by the number of individual concepts involved. As more concepts were introduced, the students encountered more problems in selecting suitable search terms and combining them in an effective strategy. Solomon (1993) investigated OPAC searching by elementary school students. He comments 'It was startling to see how even the smallest first graders achieve some success.' Nevertheless, he recommends the addition to the OPAC of specific user tools that would help the children, including displays of relationships between subject headings and automatic addition of cross references. Borgman, Hirsh, Walter and Gallagher (1995) found that elementary school students prefer OPACs to card catalogues although they encounter some difficulties, including spelling, typing, alphabetizing, vocabulary selection and Boolean logic. Like Solomon, they propose special features to be included in OPACs intended for children.

Conclusions

End-user seeking is becoming increasingly common as the population at large becomes more used to computerized applications in many domestic, leisure and work domains, as interfaces become more tolerant of novice users, as the amount and variety of digital data grows and as new delivery platforms such as the World Wide Web are developed. Undoubtedly, end users still encounter problems: selection of unsuitable information sources to answer the information need, inability to identify the concepts embedded in that need and to convert them into suitable search terms, misspelling of search terms, a reluctance to use all the search facilities available on the system, and over-confidence in their abilities and their search results. At the same time, studies demonstrate time and again that end users are enthusiastic about doing their own searching. It may be that intermediaries can do a better job, but the research studies have failed to demonstrate this conclusively. It seems probable that information professionals will continue to execute searches for their patrons: not all information seekers want to spend time doing a search even if they know how, and intermediaries may be called upon to implement searches that the end user has found too difficult to accomplish. Important training and troubleshooting roles also remain for the intermediary. But end-user searching does seem here to stay.

References

Allen, B. (1991) Cognitive research in information science: implications for design. In M.E. Williams, (ed) *Annual Review of Information Science and Technology* **26**. Medford, NJ: Learned Information, 3–37

Allen, B. (1993) Logical reasoning and retrieval performance. *Library and Information Science Research*, **15** (1), 93–105

Belkin, N.J., Oddy, R.N. and Brooks, H.M. (1982) ASK for information retrieval. Part 1: background and theory. *Journal of Documentation*, **38** (2), 61–71

Bellardo, T. (1985a) What do we really know about online searchers? *Online Review*, **9** (3), 223–39

Bellardo, T. (1985b) An investigation of online searcher traits and their relationship to search outcome. *Journal of the American Society for Information Science*, **36** (4), 241–50

Borgman, C.L. (1996) Why are online catalogs still hard to use? *Journal of the American Society for Information Science*, **47** (7), 493–503

Borgman, C.L., Hirsh, S.G., Walter, V.A. and Gallagher, A.L. (1995) Children's searching behavior on browsing and keyword online catalogs: the Science Library Catalog Project. *Journal of the American Society for Information Science*, **46** (9), 663–84

Eichman, T.L. (1978) The complex nature of opening reference questions. *Research Quarterly*, **17** (3), 212–22

Fidel, R. (1987) What is missing in research about online searching behavior. *Canadian Journal of Information Science*, **12** (3/4), 54–61

Fidel R. and Soergel, D. (1983) Factors affecting online bibliographic retrieval: a conceptual framework for research. *Journal of the American Society for Information Science*, **34** (3), 163–80

Hsieh-Yee, I. (1993) Effects of search experience and subject knowledge on the search tactics of novice and experienced searchers. *Journal of the American Society for Information Science*, **44** (3), 161–74

Lancaster, F.W., Elzy, C., Zeter, M.J., Metzler, L. and Low, Y.M. (1994) Searching databases on CD-ROM: comparison of the results of end-user searching with results from two modes of searching by skilled intermediaries. *RQ*, **33** (3), 370–86

Large, J.A., Beheshti, J., Breuleux, A. and Renaud, A. (1994) A comparison of information retrieval from print and CD-ROM versions of an encyclopedia by elementary school students. *Information Processing and Management*, **30** (4), 499–513

Marchionini, G. (1989) Information-seeking strategies of novices using a full-text electronic encyclopedia. *Journal of the American Society for Information Science*, **40** (1), 54–66

Marchionini, G. (1995) *Information Seeking in Electronic Environments*. Cambridge: Cambridge University Press

Marchionini, G., Dwiggins, S., Katz, A. and Lin, X. (1993) Information seeking in full-text end-user-oriented search systems: the roles of domain and search expertise. *Library and Information Science Research*, **15** (1), 35–69

Martin, H. and Nicholas, D. (1993) End-users coming of age? Six years of end-user searching at the Guardian. *Online & CDROM Review*, **17** (2), 83–9

Michel, D. (1994) What is used during cognitive processing in information retrieval and library searching? Eleven sources of search information. *Journal of the American Society for Information Science*, **45** (7), 498–514

Quint, B. (1991) Inside a searcher's mind: the seven stages of an online search – Part 1. *Online*, **15** (3), 13–18

Sanderson, R.M. (1990) The continuing saga of professional end-users: law students search Dialog at the University of Florida. *Online*, **14** (6), 64–9

Saracevic, T., Kantor, P., Chamis, A.Y. and Trivison, D. (1988) A study of information seeking and retrieving. *Journal of the American Society for Information Science*, **39** (3), 161–76, 177–96, 197–216

Solomon, P. (1993) Children's information retrieval behavior: a case analysis of an OPAC. *Journal of the American Society for Information Science*, **44** (5), 245–64

Taylor, R. (1962) The process of asking questions. *American Documentation*, **13** (4), 391–6

White, M.A., Deane, L. and Livingston, B. (1996) Toronto Public Library's Online Public Access Catalogue Project. *Feliciter*, **42** (4), 30–31

CHAPTER 3

Access to Electronic Information Resources: An Overview

Introduction

Seekers can access electronic information resources via a variety of means or technologies. Before outlining these, a brief review of the history of accessing electronic information resources is given, along with a short overview of the types of information available. Individual sections then cover online search services, online public access catalogues (and systems), CD-ROMs and the Internet, with further examples of searches being given in Chapter 9.

Any seeker needs to decide which is the appropriate access method to use for a particular search – in many cases this obviously depends on what is available and the relative costs, and this is described further in Chapter 9. Many options are often possible: stand-alone CD-ROMs, networked CD-ROMs, locally loaded databases, remote online search services, databases loaded on specific Web sites and general Internet access. Electronic information providers may also make their products available in different ways – and it is often difficult to decide which is the most appropriate and cost effective. Chadwyck Healey (http://www.chadwyck.co.uk), for instance, produces many electronic information resources. One example is English Poetry, covering the works of more than 1,250 poets from 600 to 1900 and containing over 165,000 poems. Chadwyck Healey makes English Poetry available as a CD-ROM as well as part of its Literature Online (LION) search service available via the Internet. The Institution of Electrical Engineers (http://www.iee.org.uk) has been involved in providing information services to scientists since 1898 and its INSPEC database provides access to the world's scientific and technical literature in physics, electrical engineering, electronics, communications, control engineering, computers and computing, and information technology. The INSPEC database is available from a range of online services (including Dialog, OCLC, and STN), as a CD-ROM database (using UMI ProQuest software) and for loading on a local computer system. Quint (1998) describes how the range of databases available for searching on particular platforms is not static and the vigilant searcher needs to be aware of changing access possibilities. Tenopir and Barry (1997), in the first of a planned annual analysis of the database marketplace, report on responses from 25 companies that provide access to electronic information resources via online search services, the Web and CD-ROM. They conclude that 'the database marketplace is rife with chaos because there is no one dominant technology and pricing policy.'

Some companies offer services which provide access to electronic information resources via a number of methods. SilverPlatter (http://www.silverplatter.com), for instance, provides access to bibliographic and full-text databases via local, network, CD-ROM, DVD-ROM, Internet or intranet access. SilverPlatter works with about 120 information providers to offer over 300 electronic databases in a wide range of subjects. Initially, in the mid-1980s, SilverPlatter was mainly involved in publishing databases on CD-ROM and developed its SilverPlatter Information Retrieval System (SPIRS) for this purpose. During the 1990s, with the growth in the need to network CD-ROMs, SilverPlatter developed its Electronic Reference Library (ERL) technology as a client/server solution for delivering integrated access to bibliographic and full-text databases as well as electronic journals through its SilverLinker service. SilverPlatter is working in partnership with a number of international electronic information companies, including Ameritech Library Services, Academic Division and VTLS, to integrate access to databases with library management systems and OPACs. Another example of such a company is Ovid Technologies (http://www.ovid.com) which provides access to 80 full-text and bibliographic databases of relevance to the academic, biomedical and scientific communities. The Ovid interface was developed as a way of providing easy access for both novice and experienced searchers to health-based CD-ROM databases. In 1994 the company, then known as CD Plus Technologies, acquired the long-standing US online search service – BRS Online. Thus, access to the 80 or so bibliographic databases and electronic journals is possible via single-user CD-ROM, locally networked CD-ROM, locally networked hard discs with Ovid databases or via the online service. The Health Sciences Library System of the University of Pittsburgh is one example of an Ovid user. It has an 80-user licence to Ovid Client/Server and Ovid Web Gateway software for the Sun Solaris platform which provides access to a range of medically related databases as well as to the full text of some core medical journals.

Historical Review

The early electronic computers developed during and soon after World War II were used primarily for 'number crunching' or code breaking. However, Vannevar Bush, a former president of the Massachusetts Institute of Technology (MIT) and Director of the US Wartime Office of Scientific Research and Development, published an article in 1945 in which he urged scientists to turn their energies into making the vast store of human knowledge accessible and useful (Bush, 1945). The techniques suggested by Bush included developing a system which would store information (such as books, pictures, articles, newspapers and business correspondence) and could be searched, from a scientist's desktop, using a series of personal links for navigation. Although Bush had a microfilm-based system in mind, his ideas have finally come to fruition with the developments first of hypertext systems and then the Web.

Bourne (1980) cites the first investigation of searching for text-based information on a computer as that carried out by Bagley in 1951 at MIT. Bagley attempted to program an early computer to search encoded abstracts and found that, although it might technically be possible, it was not feasible due to problems with the existing technology and the cost. In 1960 the System Development Corporation (SDC) in Santa Monica, California, publicly demonstrated an interactive system known as Protosynthex which searched the entries of an encyclopaedia and used many of the techniques now available to searchers. In 1961 Luhn of IBM developed programs for generating keyword indexes to the titles of articles appearing in *Chemical Abstracts* produced by the American Chemical Society. *Chemical Abstracts* is an example of a paper publication which was first started in the early 20th century and aimed to provide chemists with an index and abstracts to the increasing amount of published articles in the field of chemistry. Printed indexing and abstracting journals were an attempt to cope with what was perceived as 'information overload' of scientific, technical and medical (STM) publishing around the turn of the last century. There were similar publications in other fields: *Engineering Index*, *Index Medicus* and *Science Abstracts* are some examples. By the late 1990s the electronic databases of bibliographic information linked to these printed products (COMPENDEX, Medline and INSPEC respectively) are still major sources of STM information. The Chemical Abstracts database included some 13 million records of chemically-related and patent literature in 1998.

In the 1960s other organizations in the US developed online search systems for bibliographic information. In 1964 the Lockheed Missiles Corporation of Palo Alto, California, demonstrated an online system known as CONVERSE to search its in-house library database. Following this, Lockheed was awarded a contract to develop an online retrieval system for the US National Aeronautics and Space Administration (NASA) – this software became known as Dialog. In 1965 SDC, in a project funded by the Advanced Research Projects Agency (ARPA) of the US Department of Defense, was involved in developing a system which allowed 13 government and private organizations access, via a telephone, to a file of 200,000 bibliographic records on foreign technology. Also around this time the

National Library of Medicine (NLM) in the US investigated using a computer to assist in the production of its printed index to the medical literature, *Index Medicus*. It was soon realized that, having prepared all the necessary information in machine-readable form, it would be possible to search the records using a computer.

During the early 1970s some of the experimental online systems were being translated into working systems. At the NLM, the Abridged Index Medicus by Teletypewriter Exchange (AIM/TWX) provided access to 100 journals in clinical medicine. In 1972 Lockheed began its Dialog system as a commercial service offering access to six bibliographic databases. Access to such online search services became feasible through the rise of packet-switched networks which were the forerunners of the Internet. However, searching these systems was not particularly easy, was quite expensive and the services aimed to provide access mainly to STM information. The community of searchers, producers and providers of electronic information services was still small.

Many developments in the 1980s led more people to search for information stored electronically. In libraries, Online Public Access Catalogues (OPACs) began to replace card catalogues. They were used to look for a particular item held in the library or for items on a particular subject. OPACs were designed to be used by any searcher with no previous training or experience. The coverage of other publicly available databases grew to include business information, social sciences information, humanities information, news and current events. There were also developments in new types of 'source' databases which included directory information, financial information, statistics, chemical structure information and the full text of documents. Another development was in the 'workstation' used for carrying out the search – the 'dumb' terminals of earlier days were replaced by PCs which provided for faster and more user-friendly search interfaces. However, many of the online search services still operated a pay-by-use scheme. The advent of databases on CD-ROM had a dramatic impact on searching as many more end users were able to search them (using improved interfaces) in a manner that was 'free at point of search', as payment for using the CD-ROM was in the form of an annual licence fee.

The phenomenal spread of the Internet in the 1990s has had a major influence on access to electronic information sources for large numbers of people worldwide. O'Leary (1997), in a paper which describes the developments in the online industry since the 1970s, notes that the low cost of current access to many information sources is a major reason for their adoption by an increasing number of end users, thus making the Internet, and especially the Web, the 'de facto communications plain of the future'. Arnold and Arnold (1997) look at the factors (or vectors of change) that have affected electronic information provision in the last 20 years and how these can be examined for the future. These factors include:

- The business climate which is seen as having moved from a 'visionary' approach in 1977 to being a 'good thing' in 1997 and will be 'hard to escape' in 2007.

- The electronic information environment which was 'cryptic, complex and limited' in 1977, is a 'must-have service for the affluent and forward-looking' in 1997 and will have almost total penetration of the educated segments of the population by 2007.
- The markets which were 'severely limited' in 1977 but have now expanded into new consumer markets.
- The computer infrastructure which has moved from 'time-sharing', large, centralized computers in the 1970s to client/server PC networks.
- Staffing which has moved from scientists to librarians to 'anyone with a computer'.

Electronic Information Resources

Dempsey and Russell (1997) note that the phrase 'information resources' is often used to refer to books, images, bibliographic records, Web pages, journal articles or other types of resource which often exist in collections that might be databases, Web sites, document supply centres, multimedia documents or libraries.

Printed directories of publicly available databases have been produced since the 1970s. For instance, in 1979 Cuadra Associates started the *Directory of Online Databases* which identified two classes of database available for searching:

- Reference – i.e. these databases refer or point the user to another source (e.g. a document, organization or an individual) for additional information or the full text.
- Source – i.e. these databases contain the original source data such as numeric information (original survey data or statistically manipulated representations of data), textual-numeric information (such as company annual reports, handbook-type data or chemical and physical properties), full text (such as a full newspaper item, a journal article, a court decision or a technical specification) and software which can be downloaded for use on a local computer.

The 1997 edition of the *Gale Directory of Databases* provides an overview of the growth in the number of databases, the number of database producers and the number of vendors/distributors of these databases. Table 3.1 includes some figures taken from this analysis (Lopez Nolan, 1997).

Details of some of the widely used bibliographic databases are given in Table 3.2. These are mainly in the STM area and comprise vast numbers of records of published works. Records in these databases generally contain abstracts as well as bibliographic details of the articles and subject terms which have usually been allocated by trained indexers. Most of these databases are available via a number of online search services as well as on CD-ROM and possibly via Web sites on the Internet. Such details of databases in a range of subjects , along with qualitative commentaries, are given in the *World Database* series of directories (e.g. Armstrong, 1993).

Table 3.1   Growth in numbers of databases, producers and vendors/ distributors

Year	No. of databases	No. of producers	No. of vendors /distributors
1980	411	269	71
1985	2,247	1,316	414
1990	3,943	1,950	645
1994	5,307	2,220	812
1997	10,000	3,400	1,800

With such large databases subsets are often made available, and so when searching it is important to be aware of the time frame or subject sub-topic covered. For instance, the Commonwealth Agricultural Bureaux (CAB) databases are available on CD-ROM and on various online services as subject subsets covering CAB:Tourism and Leisure, CAB: Veterinary Science and Medicine, and CAB Health, among others. Figure 1.13 in the first chapter shows an example of a record in the ERIC database as displayed on the OCLC FirstSearch service, and further examples of different types of records are given in Chapter 5.

A particular type of bibliographic database is the book database which usually gives details of books currently in print or listed in national bibliographies. The national bibliographies of many European countries including France, Germany, Italy, Portugal, Spain and the UK are published by Chadwyck Healey. The format used for describing books in national bibliographies is often based on some form of the machine-readable catalogue (MARC) format that was developed by the Library of Congress in the US and the British National Bibliography in the 1960s. Data from databases of MARC records are often used as the basis of records in OPACs. Figure 5.6 gives an example of a MARC record. MARC provides good facilities for describing the physical attributes of books but is not so appropriate for providing subject information. To overcome this, some agencies are developing book databases which include more information. Figure 3.1 contains a record for a biography of Vera Brittain from the BookData database of two million or so records (http://www.bookdata.co.uk). Information about other book-related Web resources (publishers, bookshops, etc.) is provided by the Bookseller Web site (http://www.the bookseller.com).

There have been many developments during the 1990s in electronic publishing and supplying of articles to users. Many publishers are looking to CD-ROMs and the Web to publish their materials. In 1994 Britannica Online became available on the Internet (http://www.eb.com) and so users can search for information in the 66,000 encyclopaedia articles as well as be linked to 5,000 or so worldwide Web sites of relevance to particular search topics. Many newspapers are now published both in electronic and paper format. The 1990s also saw an increase in the number of electronic

Table 3.2 Some widely used bibliographic databases

Name	Subject area	Producer	Approx. no. of records (in millions)	Start date
ABI/Inform	Business/management	University Microfilms International	1.3	1971
BIOSIS	Biology	BIOSIS	10.5	1969
COMPENDEX	Engineering	Engineering Information Inc.	4	1970
EMBASE	Medicine	Elsevier Science Publishing	7	1974
ERIC	Education	US Office for Education	0.8	1966
INSPEC	Physics, electro-technology,computers	Institution of Electrical Engineers	5	1969
Medline	Medicine	US National Library of Medicine	8	1966
PsycInfo	Psychology	American Psychological Association	1	1967
Science Citation Index	General science	Institute for Scientific Information (ISI)	14	1974

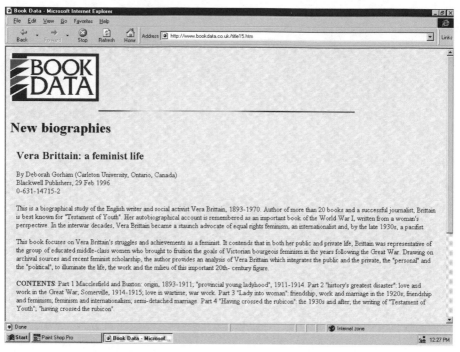

Figure 3.1   Example of a BookData record

journals and newsletters published. Hitchcock *et al.* (1997) provide an overview of UK developments in journal publishing on the Web with descriptions of the Pilot Site Licence Initiative (PSLI) and some of the eLib projects. The PSLI involves various publishers (Academic Press (AP) and the Institute of Physics were the first) which make available electronic versions of issues of every journal title in their catalogues to participating universities. The PSLI model is being used in other countries too: AP, for instance, has set up an arrangement in the state of Ohio which provides access to AP journals from each college library in the state. Other publishers are providing direct access via the Web to their journals: Elsevier Science-Direct, for instance, provides access to some 1,200 STM journals. Electronic publications can add value, compared to a print publication, by including colour, high-quality graphics, searching facilities, multimedia presentations and direct links to other related material, including electronic 'skywriting' such as comments from readers. An example of one electronic journal, *D-lib Magazine*, is given in Figures 1.10 and 1.11 with a second example, *Nature*, in Figure 8.12. Machovec (1997) describes some of these electronic journal developments in more detail. There has been considerable research in electronic journal publishing and major advances in this area are likely to affect anyone involved in searching electronic information sources for academic research purposes. A further development of the 1990s has been the growth of current awareness services-instant article supply (CAS-IAS), with a description of 30 such services being given by

Davies and Boyle (1998). CAS-IAS products are available from a number of types of supplier which include publishers (e.g. AP, Blackwells), existing information providers (e.g.ISI), professional/learned societies (e.g. Royal Society of Chemistry), national organizations (e.g. British Library Document Supply Centre), subject-based organizations (e.g. BIOSIS, Ei), CD-ROM full-text producers (e.g. UMI and Business Periodicals Online) and subscription agencies (e.g. Dawson and Swets).

During the 1990s many librarians and information scientists became concerned about the quality of information contained in public databases. In Finland a working group was formed from the Finnish Society for Information Services to study and evaluate the quality of Finnish databases. At about the same time the Southern California Online Users Group became interested in this area and identified various criteria for defining quality (see Chapter 10). This work, and the work of others involved in quality issues, has been developed at the Centre for Information Quality Management (CIQM) in the UK. CIQM was originally set up by the UK Library Association (LA) and the UK Online User Group to act as a clearing house to which database users may report problems relating to the quality of any aspect of a database (search software, data, indexing, documentation, training). CIQM collects statistics on database quality issues which are fed back into the information industry and it also has implemented a system of database quality labels (Armstrong, 1996). CIQM and the LA continue to develop techniques for applying 'quality' labelling of Internet resources.

Online Search Services

Saffady (1996) defines a remote online search service as 'a publicly available, fee-based information service that provides online, time-shared access to one or more computer databases' and provides a detailed review of services available in 1996 and the costs associated with searching such services. For many years the online search services were the main means of providing access to a range of publicly available electronic information resources.

Initially these services were used to provide access to bibliographic databases in the STM fields using quite complex command languages. Over the years there have been many developments in creating user-friendly interfaces (as described in Chapter 8) as well as increasing the breadth of information contained in these databases 'hosted' or made available by the search services.

One major development was the advent of consumer services such as America Online (AOL), Prodigy, Genie and CompuServe in the US in the 1980s. Such services cover information on general issues such as health, finance, education, sports events, weather and news as well as information for more specialist groups. They can be accessed via simple search systems, they provide email and electronic shopping facilities, are targeted at individual users with no previous experience of using online services, involve a monthly subscription and use mass marketing techniques to advertize their products. White (1996) provides an overview of these services in the

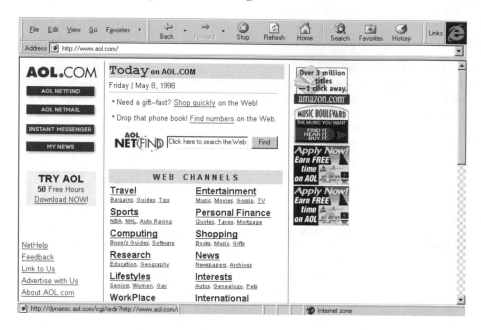

Figure 3.2   Part of home page of America Online showing some broad subject search categories

mid-1990s. By 1998 AOL had some 11 million members worldwide in Canada, France, Germany, Japan and the UK, as well as the US. Figure 3.2 shows part of the opening page of AOL which indicates the breadth of its coverage.

The online search service industry is a volatile one and there have been many births, marriages, divorces and deaths of services over the years. The impact of the Internet with its more anarchic approach to the storage and retrieval of information is still to be fully realized. It provides a very different model to that offered by the traditional online services with their precise numbers of databases that have typically been prepared by professionals and so have a 'stamp' of authority attached to the information contained. A description of a selection of services available in 1998 is included here to provide the reader with an idea of their scope. Some of the services are general (or 'supermarket') in nature, others are more specialized.

General

Bath Information and Data Services (BIDS) http://www.bids.ac.uk

BIDS is a provider of networked information for the higher education and research communities in the UK. It operates from the University of Bath and offers access to a fairly select range of bibliographic databases from major suppliers covering subjects such as science, engineering, medicine, social sciences, education, arts and humanities plus worldwide access to full-text electronic journals. BIDS was set up in 1991 by JISC and is believed to be the world's first national service providing widespread access to commercially supplied bibliographic databases free at point of delivery. Organizations pay a fixed annual fee to access each database, which can then be made available 'free at point of use' to all searchers in that organization. The complementary BIDS JournalsOnline service provides Web access to a range of full-text electronic journals from leading academic publishers, including Academic Press, Arnold, Blackwell Publishers and Blackwell Science (Morrow, 1997). JournalsOnline allows any user, anywhere in the world, to search or browse the article database free of charge; full-text documents are available to subscribers or can be purchased individually. At the beginning of 1998 BIDS was used by about 12,000 people per day. A search of the ISI Science Citation Index database on BIDS is given in Chapter 9.

The Dialog Corporation http://www.dialog.com

The Dialog Corporation offers one of the most comprehensive and authoritative sources of electronic information with, in late 1997, a combined database estimated to be 50 times the size of the Web. The Dialog Corporation was formed in late 1997 when Market Analysis and Information Database (MAID) plc acquired search services such as Dialog and DataStar from Knight Ridder which, in turn, had acquired Dialog from Lockheed and DataStar from Radio Suisse during the 1980s. The Dialog Corporation's strategy is to deliver information using the platforms and output formats required by customers. It sees the Internet as a major communications medium and aims to offer a seamless interface from a customer's intranet to the many terabytes of text and images held within its collections. By 1998 there were some 200,000 customers in 150 countries using services or products from The Dialog Corporation. Two major services from The Dialog Corporation are now described.

DIALOGWEB

The DialogWeb service provides electronic access to a range of materials including:

- 470 databases containing over 330 million articles, abstracts, and citations.
- The complete text of articles from 7,000 journals, magazines, and newsletters.
- The complete text of over 100 leading US and international newspapers.
- Wire service stories from Knight Ridder/Tribune Business News etc.
- Financial profiles and background information on more than 12 million US and one million international companies.
- Details on over 15 million patents from 56 patent-issuing authorities worldwide.
- Data on more than 10 million chemical substances.

Fifty of these databases are also available on CD-ROM as part of the Dialog OnDisc Collection, and a selection of 200 or so databases are available for searching on the DialogSelect service. This service has been designed to address the specific information needs of professional end users in the pharmaceutical, legal, consumer product and media industries. During the 1980s most of Dialog's databases provided biblio-graphic details of STM articles. However, in the 1990s the number of business-related databases on Dialog has grown and now represents a major subject area. A number of searches using DialogWeb are shown in Chapter 6.

MAID PROFOUND

MAID plc has provided business intelligence services, including market research reports, real time and archived business news, company statistics, broker reports and up-to-date stock market and commodity prices to busi-ness professionals worldwide since it was founded in London in 1985. MAID's aim at that time was to develop and operate the first specialized online database of market research reports in response to the needs of the advertizing and marketing industries. The company's online service, Profound, includes information from more than 4,000 publishers around the world. Profound incorporates an enhanced version of Adobe Acrobat portable document format (PDF) capabilities, allowing users while online to import charts and other graphical data in their original formats directly into popular business software applications. An example of the search form for the LiveWire database is shown in Figure 3.3. Profound LiveWire is a news alerting service which applies InfoSort technology to 25 newswire feeds allowing news, matching with predefined criteria, to be delivered automatically to a user's desktop computer.

OCLC FirstSearch http://www.oclc.org

The Online Computer Library Center (OCLC) Inc. of Dublin, Ohio, entered the online search service field in 1991 with OCLC FirstSearch. OCLC has been providing a variety of services to libraries throughout the world since the 1970s and its WORLDCAT bibliographic database on books contains over 37 million records from about 63 countries in 370 diffe-rent languages. OCLC FirstSearch offers about 60 databases (including popular databases such as Medline, ERIC, BIOSIS and ABI/Inform) for searching. Some of these databases enable links to be made to the Electronic Collections Online database of scholarly journals where the full text of articles retrieved from a search can be obtained. Examples of searches using OCLC FirstSearch are given in Figures 1.12, 9.15 and 9.16.

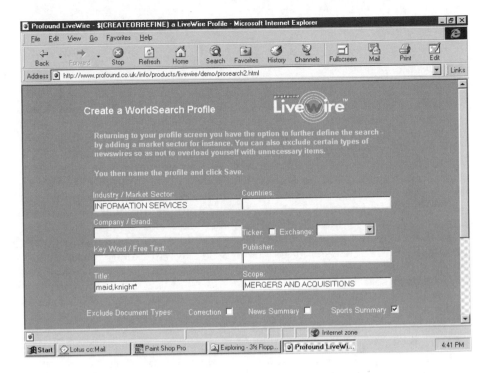

Figure 3.3   Search form for Livewire database on Profound

Questel-ORBIT http://www.questel.orbit.com

Questel-ORBIT is part of France Telecom Multimedia and provides access to about 250 databases covering patent, trademark, chemical, scientific, technical, business and news information. Online Retrieval of Bibliographic Information Timeshared (ORBIT) is the name for the original software developed by SDC for the US National Library of Medicine in the early 1970s. Since then the ORBIT service has changed ownership and emphasis many times (including, for a time, being part of Robert Maxwell's empire in the 1980s when the service was known as Pergamon ORBIT Infoline). In 1994 the service was acquired by France Telecom, which also owned the Questel service. Questel has operated as an online search service in France since the 1970s using software which is designed to be adaptable for various types of searcher from medical professionals to stock brokers. Questel-ORBIT is one of the main services providing access to French-language material. Questel-ORBIT also offers access, via the Internet, to the QPAT-US patent database covering 20 years of US patents There are 35,000 worldwide users of this service.

Scientific

Deutsches Institut für Medizinische Dokumentation und Information (DIMDI)
http://www.dimdi.de

DIMDI is a government institution within the scope of the German Federal Ministry of Health and is based in Cologne, Germany. DIMDI's main task is to provide quick and easy access to the latest information in all fields of the life sciences. After initially concentrating on healthcare and medicine with the provision of access to the Medline database in the 1970s, DIMDI now offers a broad collection of databases covering the entire spectrum of both the life and social sciences. DIMDI is an important European search service as it provides access to about 100 databases comprising 70 million records in various languages including a number of German-language databases that deal with biomedicine and related disciplines. DIMDI developed a general relational-based information processing system known as GRIPS to search its databases. As with many other search services, GRIPS had a command-based interface initially but now also has a Web-based search interface.

Elsevier Engineering Information Inc. http://www.ei.org

In early 1998 the publishing and information service assets of Engineering Information (Ei) Inc. were acquired by Elsevier Science, and Elsevier Engineering Information Inc. was formed. Ei had been involved with processing and publishing engineering information since 1884 and started production of the COMPENDEX database in the mid-1960s. As with similar scientific database producers, Ei made its COMPENDEX database available via a number of online search services as well as on different CD-ROM systems. In the 1990s it developed its Ei Village for providing access to relevant engineering information resources and services on the Web. Some of the links possible through Ei Village are shown in Figure 3.4; these include access to COMPENDEX and a document delivery service. Regionalized editions of Ei Village are being produced: one is for the German-speaking European community which will be hosted by FIZ Karlsruhe, and another is planned for the Philippines. Ei Village is an example of a database producer, search service provider and a provider of links to quality Internet resources in a particular subject area.

STN International http://www.fiz-karlsruhe.de

Scientific and Technical information Network (STN) International is the name given to a service operated cooperatively by three organizations (in Japan, Germany and the US) for the international scientific community. It offers information services mainly in chemistry and engineering. The Japanese partner is the Japan Information Centre of Science and Technology (JICST). JICST has been operating an online information system in Japan since 1976, and since 1985 overseas searchers have been able to access its databases in Tokyo. JICST is involved in preparing abstracts, in Japanese, of

Figure 3.4   Home page of Engineering Information Village

STM articles published in Japan. The German partner is FIZ-Karlsruhe (Fachinformations Zentrum Energie, Physik, Mathematik) and the American partner is the Chemical Abstracts Service, a division of the American Chemical Society. Messenger, the command language interface to STN databases, was designed for fast and efficient information retrieval and incorporates the general features of any search language as well as the ability to search for chemical structures. The graphical input of chemical structures is supported by STN's front-end software, STN Express. A Web-based interface to the STN files has also been developed known as STN Easy. The form for seeking information is shown in Figure 3.5 with a search for dinosaur eggs, and the display of some retrieved references can be found in Figure 3.6.

News/business

Dow Jones Interactive Publishing http://bis.dowjones.com

Dow Jones & Company set up its Dow Jones News/Retrieval (DJNR) information service for US stockbrokers in 1974. Dow Jones Interactive, the current version of DJNR, is aimed at meeting the diverse information needs of every employee in a company and so can be customized as appropriate for that company. The service integrates a wide range of information from current news in national newspapers and Dow Jones Newswires to

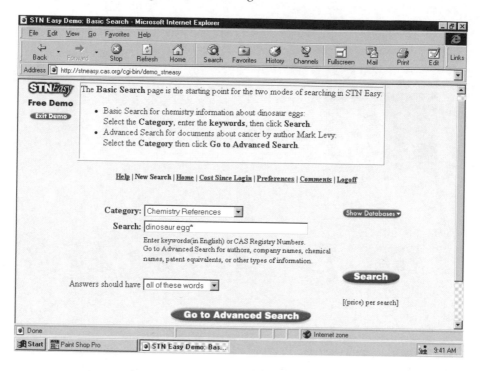

Figure 3.5   **Sample search for dinosaur eggs on STNEasy**

in-depth background information from market research and investment analyst reports. Information from Dow Jones Interactive can be incorporated into a company's intranet, formatted for any local computing environment, or is accessible from one site on the Internet. Dow Jones now offers a wide range of business news and information, including *The Wall Street Journal*, to corporations and consumers around the world. The services are aimed at end users and the software incorporates features to enable business people to manipulate the information retrieved.

Financial Times http://www.info.ft.com/

The *Financial Times* (FT) offers a range of electronic information products including CD-ROMs of the newspaper, of company and industrial information (FT McCarthy) and share prices (FT Prices). FT Profile is one of Europe's leading online business information services providing data from thousands of sources including newspapers (such as the *Financial Times, Washington Post* and *Le Monde*), magazines (such as *The Economist* and *Business Week*), news agencies (such as Reuters News, Press Association and TASS), newswires, company information (such as FT McCarthy, FT Extel and Dun & Bradstreet), market research (from leading providers such

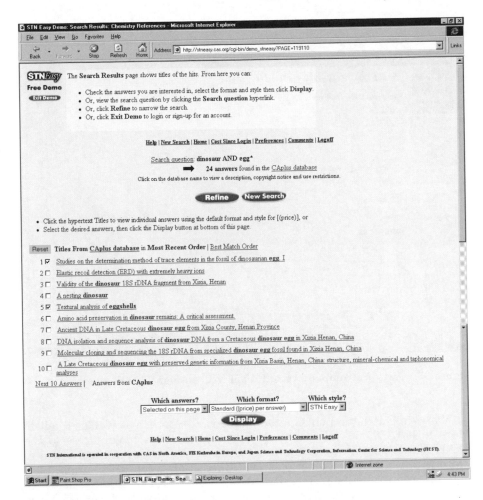

Figure 3.6   Result of dinosaur eggs search on STNEasy

as Mintel, and Frost & Sullivan), and country profiles and risk analyses (such as reports from the Economist Intelligence Unit). FT Discovery is described as a 'desktop briefing tool' which aims to bring business and company information to users. Figure 3.7 shows some company information (for Laura Ashley plc.) from the FT Discovery service.

LEXIS-NEXIS http://www.lexis-nexis.com

The LEXIS service began in 1973 to help legal professionals research the law more efficiently by providing them with access to full texts of legal information. NEXIS began as a news service in 1979. LEXIS-NEXIS is now a major service of news, business and political information, and there are

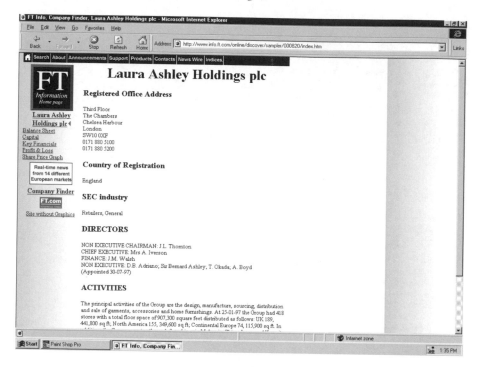

Figure 3.7   Part of a company record displayed through FT Discovery

databases in Dutch, French, German, Italian and Spanish as well as English. More than 1,250,000 subscribers in over 60 countries have access to the LEXIS-NEXIS services and about 300,000 searches a day are carried out. More than 9.5 million documents are added each week to the more than one billion documents online. The LEXIS-NEXIS Tracker service provides daily alerts via company email or intranet to users. LEXIS-NEXIS was acquired by Reed Elsevier in 1994.

Reuters http:// www.reuters.com

Reuters was founded in 1849 and is one of the biggest and oldest news-gathering services with bureaux in many parts of the world. As a database producer Reuters over the years has supplied information to many online search services including Dialog, America Online and LEXIS-NEXIS. In 1986 Reuters bought Textline, an online business search service set up in 1980 by a British firm, Finsbury Data Services. Ojala (1996) provides an overview of Reuters involvement in information provision as well as describing briefly the Textline service. Reuters has also developed stand-alone systems for end users, including Reuters Business Alert, Reuters Business Briefing, and Reuters Insurance Briefing. Reuters also provides information on the Internet – for instance, Reuters NewMedia reports on breaking news stories through filtered current-awareness services. In addition, Reuters is linked with Internet services such as Yahoo! and Infoseek. As well as being a major supplier of news information, Reuters is involved in financial information services. For instance it owns I.P.Sharp, a Canadian-based economics and statistics database company and online service provider.

Online Public Access Catalogues

OPACs have always been designed with end users in mind and so the interfaces that have developed over the years from the early command- and menu-based systems to the current form filling on Web pages are intended to be straightforward for library patrons. However, the information that is searched, i.e. the records in the catalogue database, are often stored in the MARC format which has little information to support elaborate subject searching.

Online public access catalogues (OPACs) first appeared in the late 1970s and provided searchers with search facilities similar to those of a traditional card catalogue, i.e. access by author, title (as a phrase), class mark or call number (as a phrase), and possibly subject headings (as a phrase). During the 1980s some suppliers of integrated library management systems started to enter the market with products incorporating OPACs based on the information retrieval techniques developed by the online search services. These OPACs included as access points individual words from titles, subject headings, authors or other names, and search statements could be constructed by linking search terms using Boolean operators.

As with any other search system a distinction can be made between *query searching*, where the user has a clear idea of the document or information required, and *browsing* where the user examines some of the range of search vocabulary and documents available. Most OPACs provide for phrase and keyword searching and some perform a keyword search if the phrase search fails. Phrase searching usually consists of implicitly ANDing words in the phrase and matching them with the index.

In the 1990s OPACs began to provide access to other local and remote electronic information resources: these are sometimes referred to as online public access systems. Boss (1993) describes this in more depth and reports that some libraries include individual journal citations in their OPAC, with several database producers such as Information Access Company, the Institute for Scientific Information and Wilson providing site licences for local loading of databases. This is usually achieved by loading the databases into the local library system and applying the local system's indexing and search commands, thus allowing users to search for journal articles in the same way as they might search for monographs. For many years the University of California (UC) has provided access in this way to bibliographic databases for users from UC establishments (such as UC Berkeley, UC Los Angeles, UC San Diego) through a system called MELVYL. Figure 3.8 shows details of some social sciences databases available on MELVYL. This approach of individual organizations providing

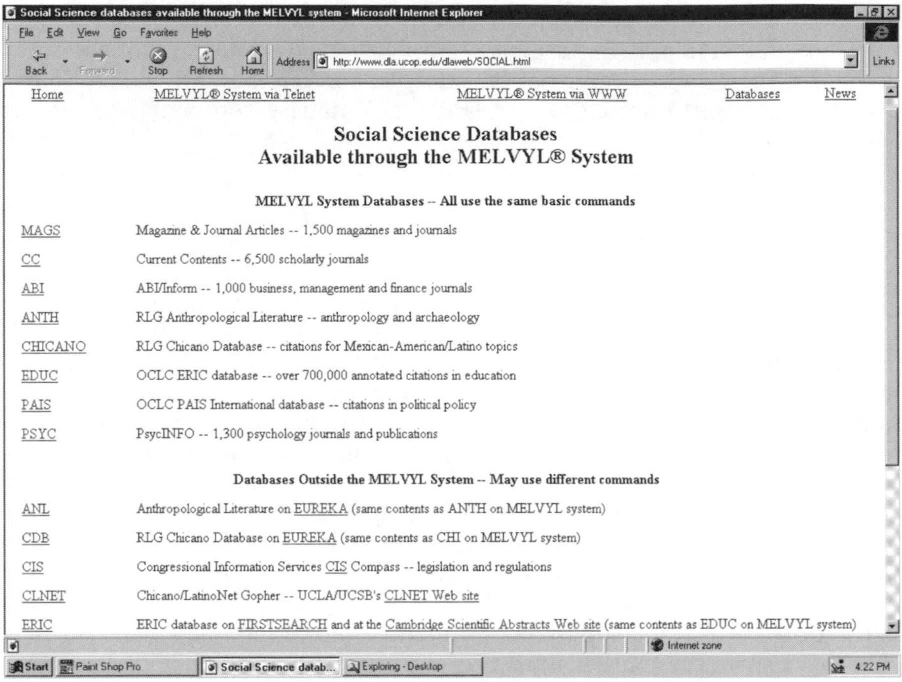

Figure 3.8   Social sciences databases available through MELVYL at the University of California

access to locally loaded databases for a 'cooperative' or 'consortium' of libraries has been adopted elsewhere when a country-wide collective approach to providing electronic information services (as undertaken in the UK) is not in operation. In 1997 UC became one of the libraries participating in OCLC's FirstSearch Electronic Collections Online service which aims to link searchers directly to the full text of items retrieved via an initial search of a bibliographic database.

Many OPACs can now be accessed via the Internet, and can therefore be a useful resource for distant researchers and scholars to identify and locate texts. Some specialized services can direct users to relevant OPAC information relating to texts which tend to be located at universities or national libraries. In the UK for instance, National Information Services and Systems (NISS) provides a gateway service to a range of electronic information resources as seen in Figure 3.9 (http://www.niss.ac.uk). Figure 3.10 shows a listing of some of the UK higher education library OPACs that can be accessed – the *Info* link provides details of the holdings of the library, passwords (if necessary) and the library management system used. At the University of Saskatchewan in Canada the webCATS service provides a link to library catalogues all over the world searchable via the Web. Figure 3.11 shows the home page of webCATS (http://www.lights.com/webcats/). WebCATS lists OPACs under: geographical location, vendor and library type; Figure 3.12 shows an excerpt from the location index under Japan.

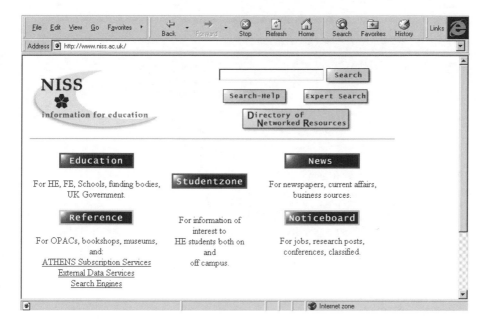

Figure 3.9 Home page of NISS: information for education

Many OPACs now use a variety of interaction methods such as commands, menus, form filling and function keys. In spite of attempts to make the OPAC interaction self-explanatory, users still encounter problems, so online assistance or printed leaflets are generally provided. Most users are more successful at 'known item' searching rather than subject searching (see Chapter 2). An example of an OPAC search for an author's name was given in Figures 1.7, 1.8 and 1.9, and a subject search of an OPAC is given in Figures 9.18, 9.19 and 9.20.

CD-ROM

The use of optical technology for information storage and retrieval had its first application in publishing and distributing music when CD-Audio was launched in 1982. CD-ROMs appeared commercially in 1985 and were initially used to store text-based data. CD-ROMs hold about 650 Mb (650,000 bytes) of information and were quickly accepted in the library and information community for the storage and retrieval of bibliographic records. The typical CD-ROM interface, when compared to the interfaces of the online search services, were more user friendly and by the mid-1990s were being widely used by the general public. Other reasons for this were:

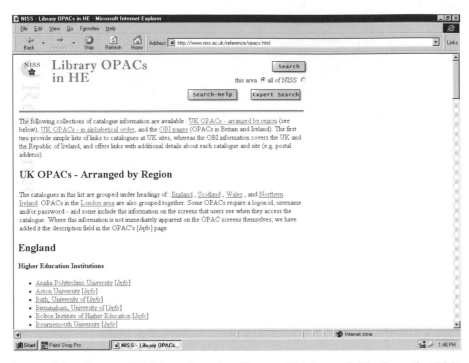

Figure 3.10   Some UK higher education library OPACs available through NISS

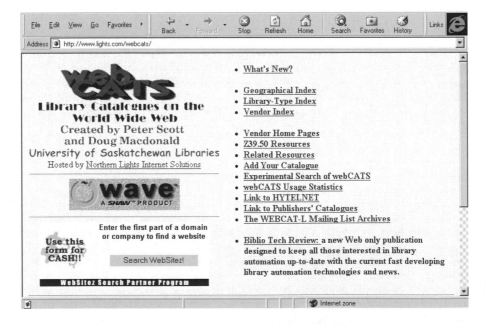

Figure 3.11   Home page of webCATS at the University of Saskatchewan

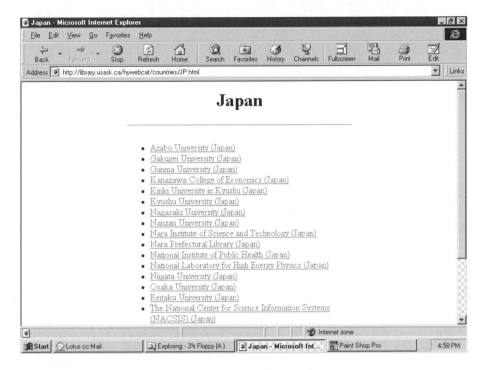

Figure 3.12   Japanese Web OPACs from webCATS geographical index

- CD-ROMs could incorporate a variety of media (text, animation, graphics, sound and video) on a single device.
- CD-ROM drives with quality sound and video features had become standard features on desktop computers.
- The price for these workstations fell during the 1990s.
- The number of CD-ROM titles expanded rapidly, with many devoted to the home consumer market.

The development of multimedia technology has prompted many CD-ROMs aimed at the education market including encyclopaedias such as *Microsoft Encarta Encyclopedia*, *Comptons Interactive Encyclopedia* and the *Grolier Multimedia Encyclopedia*, and dictionaries, such as *My First Amazing Dictionary*. These, along with CD-ROMs covering national newspapers and specialized educational titles, have proved very popular in schools and public libraries.

CD-ROM is seen by some as a transient technology. McSean and Law (1990) outline the key features of a database distribution technology as being:

- inexpensive;
- high capacity (accommodates entire databases or families of databases);

- multiuser (can be networked in the same way, locally, as an OPAC);
- common and intuitive search interface across all databases;
- crossfile searching so a search statement matches with several databases simultaneously;
- powerful retrieval;
- multimedia capabilities;
- robustness (workstations and associated technologies stand up to vandalism, theft and carelessness).

They felt in 1990 that CD-ROM technology, while being a reasonable first attempt to distribute electronic information resources to end users, ultimately would be 'a step on the road to somewhere else'. In the intervening years, however, CD-ROM has proven a popular technology for providing access to a range of different electronic information resources in many settings and so cannot really be described as a 'transient technology'. Guenette (1996), in attempting to answer the question 'will online replace CD-ROM?', notes that for some applications 'such as storing data at incredibly low cost in a broadband playback mechanism accessible and usable worldwide' CD-ROM is an appropriate technology, whereas in other areas ' such as making up-to-the minute information and communication available to users', online services and the Internet are appropriate technologies. A number of CD-ROMs are now being produced as 'hybrid' products that include links to Web sites. Hybrid CD-ROMs can overcome many problems inherent in searching the Internet for information, while eliminating the static nature of CD-ROM. The number of hybrid CD-ROM titles has grown from 756 in 1996 to over 3,000 in 1997. Many electronic publishers such as DK Multimedia, Hutchinson's and Microsoft are developing hybrid CD-ROMs.

One reason for the initial rapid acceptance in the 1980s of CD-ROM technology was agreement on the international standard (ISO 9660) for storage and indexing of data. However, with multimedia CD-ROMs the situation is more complicated as there are now many formats, for instance CD-ROM XA (eXtended architecture), Photo CD and Video CD as well as many different hardware and software platforms through which the information on the CD-ROM is accessed. The Multimedia PC (MPC) standard defines the requirement of a Windows-based PC to process multimedia CD-ROMs, but has been widely criticised. In many workplaces CD-ROMs are networked so that searchers have access to a range of CD-ROM products from their workstations. Networking can pose many challenges both in terms of the technology to be used and in acquiring an appropriate licence from the CD-ROM producer to allow access from multiple workstations. Ma (1998) outlines various CD-ROM network solutions that were investigated by a Californian college library wishing to provide its users with access to electronic information on CD-ROMs and the Web.

A new form of optical technology is the digital video (or versatile) disc (DVD) which is capable of holding 4 to 19 gigabytes of information. It has been predicted that by the year 2000 more optical disc drives sold will be using DVD technology than CD technology (although these drives will also be capable of reading CD-ROMs). With the ability to hold much more information on one disc, say the whole of the Medline database, this will no doubt be an attractive option to some searchers who have currently switched from searching Medline on CD-ROM to searching on the Internet.

A number of interface examples from CD-ROM databases are provided in Chapter 8 and a search of the LISA database on CD-ROM is shown in Figures 9.21 and 9.22.

The Internet

The Internet developed from an early distributed network known as ARPA Network (ARPANET), designed by the US Department of Defense in the late 1960s, whose main aim was to link academic, research and military establishments in the US. ARPANET was based on packet-switching technology and by the mid-1970s a new set of protocols based on packet switching had been developed which enabled a number of networks to be linked to ARPANET. This protocol is known as TCP/IP where transmission control protocol (TCP) handles the conversion of messages into packets at source and their re-assembling in the correct order at the destination, and Internet Protocol (IP) handles addressing the packets to their final destinations.

Many countries adopted packet-switching technology in the 1980s and developed networks to link various computers and workstations; examples include the Australian Academic Research Network (AARNET), CA*NET (in Canada), Nordunet (in Scandinavia) and the Joint Academic Network (JANET) in the UK. Davies (1996) outlines recent growth in the use of the Internet in Asia with government initiatives such as JARING in Malaysia and similar developments in Singapore, Thailand, Indonesia and Japan.

By the 1990s the Internet was being used for a variety of purposes such as:

- sending electronic mail (email);
- transferring files of data or programs from one computer to another (this is achieved using file transfer protocol (FTP);
- gaining access to other computers which store relevant information (using the telnet protocol);
- joining USENET discussion groups (there are over 15,000 different subject-based public discussion groups covering pop groups, writings of particular authors, gardening, food, films, education etc.).

In 1993 a method was developed at the high energy research centre (CERN) in Geneva for disseminating and finding information on the Internet. This is known as the World Wide Web, or the Web, and makes use of hypertext to establish links within or between electronic information resources. The Web has made the Internet very accessible and easy to search using navigational, or browser software such as Netscape Navigator and Internet Explorer.

Information is found on the Web by using a search engine of which a number now exist. Comparisons of search engines regularly appear in sources such as those noted in Chapter 1, and criteria used to compare them include collection methods, indexing techniques, abstracting policy and search facilities – more details of these are given in Chapter 9. Brief details of a few search engines are included here.

AltaVista http://www.altavista.digital.com

Digital Equipment Corporation, a large computer corporation in the US, developed AltaVista in 1995 in its Palo Alto research laboratories with the aim of providing an indexing and search tool for USENET discussion groups and the Web. Every word is indexed from every Web page; if searching for a very precise unusual term, this is advantageous. However, the corollary is that sometimes very large numbers of items can be retrieved from a search. AltaVista provides a 'simple' search mode where terms can be entered in a list (in this case they are automatically ORed); also terms can be prefixed with a + (to indicate that the terms *must* be present), or a – (to indicate that the term must *not* be present). Phrases can be searched by including the phrase in quotes (e.g. "New South Wales"). A simple search on AltaVista is shown in Figures 1.5 and 1.6. In the 'advanced' search mode on AltaVista users can combine terms using Boolean operators as well as other operators. A search can be restricted only to those Web sites in a particular language, reflecting the growing amount of non-English information on the Web (in 1998 this covered Chinese, Czech, Danish, Dutch, English, Estonian, Finnish, French, German, Greek, Hebrew, Hungarian, Icelandic, Italian, Japanese, Korean, Latvian, Lithuanian, Norwegian, Polish, Portuguese, Romanian, Russian, Spanish and Swedish). AltaVista also provides an automatic translation service (using the SYSTRAN software); search statements and/or Web sites can be translated from English into French, German, Italian, Portuguese and Spanish or vice versa. AltaVista has proved to be a popular Internet search service and there are many affiliated sites around the world to serve Asia, Latin America, Australia, Northern Europe and Southern Europe in addition to the original site in Palo Alto.

Excite http://www.excite.com

Excite was developed by six graduates from Stanford University in California who decided to 'create a software tool to manage the vast amount of information available on the Internet'. The resulting software combines search and retrieval with automatic hypertext linking, subject grouping and automatic abstracting, and was officially launched in late 1995. By the end of 1996 almost 400 firms were advertizing on Excite (advertizing of products seems to be the inevitable way of raising revenue on these free search engines) and Excite had acquired two of its search and navigation competitors: Magellan and WebCrawler. Excite provides access to a wide range of information through subject directories, a search engine, current news etc., and uses the concepts of 'channels' to search for types of information: autos, careers and education, entertainment, lifestyle, sports, travel. Each channel contains similar features such as topical news, a directory of relevant sites, bulletin boards and chat facilities as well as a search box. The developers of Excite have produced a special search facility known as intelligent concept extraction (ICE) to analyze a particular Web site and determine relevant keywords that might be used for its indexing. When a query is entered, Excite searches the entire Web for documents containing related concepts and not just the keywords entered. Excite's combination of subject tree and keyword approach is indicated in Figure 3.13, which shows the broad subject categories, and Figure 3.14 which shows the search facilities.

Lycos http://www.lycos.com

Lycos, one of the first search engines for the Web, was developed at Carnegie Mellon University in Pittsburgh in 1994. Besides providing a search facility, Lycos now provides a subject directory, and information on cities, stocks, individuals, sounds and pictures, and companies – see the home page in Figure 3.15. Lycos indexes the title, headings, subheadings, first 20 lines and the 100 most 'weighty' words (i.e. not stopwords) from Web sites. An example of the Lycos Pro search form is shown in Figure 3.16.

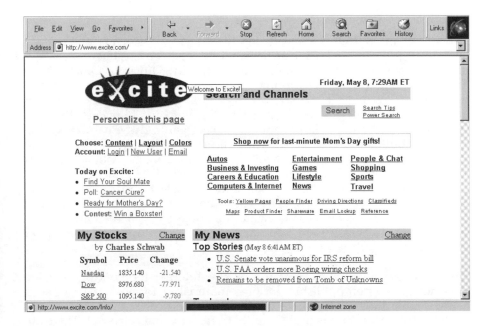

Figure 3.13   Broad subject categories available for browsing on Excite

Figure 3.14   Power Search form on Excite

Yahoo! http://www.yahoo.com

Yahoo! began in 1994 as a way for two doctoral students at Stanford University to keep track of their personal interests on the Internet. Yahoo! originally stood for Yet Another Hierarchically Officious Oracle. Now Yahoo! contains organized information on tens of thousands of computers linked to the Web and is managed by Netscape. The *San Jose Mercury News* noted that 'Yahoo is closest in spirit to the work of Linnaeus, the 18th century botanist whose classification system organized the natural world.' Yahoo! is built around a subject tree directory which also has links to AltaVista. The home page of Yahoo! is given in Figure 7.5 with an example of a search using Yahoo! being shown in Figures 9.23 and 9.24. Yahoo's strengths lie in the fact that human indexers select and describe (using appropriate subject headings) entries selected for the Yahoo! database, and that searchers can browse or navigate the subject tree if they are not too sure of how to phrase their information need in an appropriate manner for a search.

Since anyone can publish anything on the Internet the controls that are often in place when publishing printed material or formal databases such as those found on CD-ROMs or online search services are not evident and so there can be variations in the quality of information retrieved. There are various projects to provide access to 'quality' electronic information resources on the Internet and details of some of these are included in

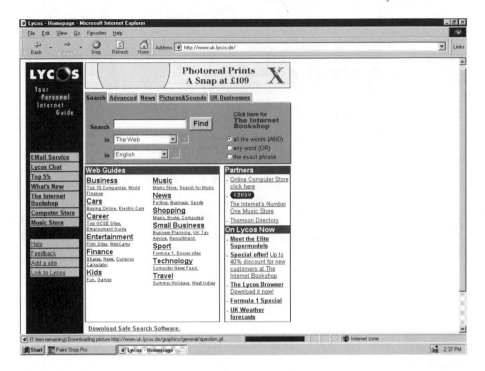

Figure 3.15   Home page of Lycos

Chapter 9. Many libraries and information centres provide this sort of 'vetting' of sites for their users and will point to sites that have passed the criteria for approval.

Printed guides, such as that by Turecki (1996) which provides standardized descriptions of some 2,750 sites, can be used. Inevitably, there are also Web-based guides such as that produced by EARL (Electronic Access to Resources in Libraries) which includes links to a number of sites of interest to the 'general public' and, for those in higher education, the Internet Scout Report (http://www.cs.wisc.edu/scout/report/) with a written description by Calcari(1997).

Summary

In summary, a vast number of electronic information resources are available – some highly structured and compiled by professionals and others unstructured and made available by anyone. The ways of accessing such resources can be either via an online search service (which usually costs money), via an OPAC developed by a library or information service (which is usually free), via a CD-ROM database (for which an annual licence fee will probably need to be paid) or via the Internet (which may or may not be free).

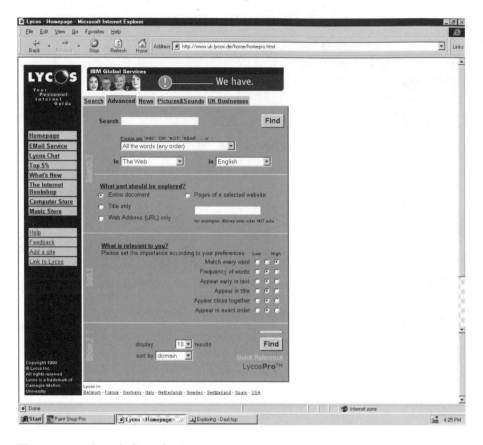

Figure 3.16   Search form for LycosPro

References

Armstrong, C.J. (1993) *World databases. Vol. 1 Medicine.* London: Bowker-Saur

Armstrong, C.J. (1996) Questions of quality. *New Review of Information Networking,* **2,** 249–53.

Arnold, S.E. and Arnold E.S. (1997) Vectors of change: electronic information from 1977–2007. *Online,* **21**(4), 19–33. Also available at http://www.onlineinc.com/ onlinemag/JulOL97/arnold7.html

Boss, R.W. (1993) Online catalog functionality in the 1990s: vendor responses to a model RFP. *Library Technology Reports,* **29**(5), 587–785

Bourne, C.P. (1980) Online systems history, technology and economics. *Journal of the American Society for Information Science,* **31**(3), 155–60

Bush, V. (1945) As we may think. *Atlantic Monthly,* also available at: http:// www.theAtlantic.com/atlantic/atlWeb/flashbks/computer/bushf.htm

Calcari S. (1997) The Internet Scout Project. *Library Hi Tech,* **15**(3–4), 11–18

Davies M. and Boyle, F. (1998) CAS-IAS services: where are we now? *Electronic Library,* **16**(1), 37–48

Davies, R. (1996) The Internet as a tool for Asian libraries. *Asian libraries,* **5**(1) 43–52

Dempsey, L. and Russell, R. (1997) Clumps or . . . organised access to printed scholarly publications: outcomes from the 3rd MODELS workshop. *Program*, **31**(3), 239–50

Fecko, M.B. (1997) *Electronic Resources: Access and Issues*. London: Bowker-Saur

Guenette, D. (1996) The CD-ROM online connection. *CD-ROM Professional*, **9**(3), 30–44

Hitchcock, S., Carr L., and Hall, W. (1997) Web journals publishing: a UK perspective. *Serials*, **10**(3), 285–99

Lopez N.K. (1997) *Gale Directory of Databases. Vol. 1 Online Databases* and *Vol.2 CD-ROM, Diskette, Magnetic Tape, Handheld and Batch Access Database Products.* Detroit, MI: Gale Research Inc.

Ma, W. (1998) The near future trend: combining Web access and local CD networks. Experience and a few suggestions. *Electronic Library*, **16**(1), 49–54

Machovec, G.S. (1997) Electronic journal market overview. *Serials Review*, **23**(2), 31–44

McSean T. and Law D. (1990) Is CD-ROM a transient technology? *Library Association Record*, **92**(11), 837–41

Morrow, T. (1997) BIDS and electronic publishing. *Information Services and Use*, **17**(1), 53–60

Ojala, M. (1996) Reuters profile: an online hall of mirrors. *Database*, **19**(4), 12–19

O'Leary, M. (1997) Online comes of age. *Online*, **21**(1), 10–20. Also available at http://www.onlineinc.com/onlinemag/JanOL97/oleary1.html

Quint, B. (1998) The mounting death toll: "dead" databases revisited. *Database*, **21**(1), 14–22

Saffady, W. (1996) The availability and cost of online search services. *Library Technology Reports*, **32**(3), 337–456

Tenopir, C. and Barry, J. (1997) Database marketplace 97: the data dealers. *Library Journal*, **122**(9) 28–36

Turecki G. (1996) (ed.) *Cyberhound's Guide to Internet Databases*. Detroit, MI: Gale Research Inc.

White, M. (1996) The market prospects for consumer online services in Europe. *The Electronic Library*, **14**(6), 503–508

CHAPTER 4

Language and Information Retrieval

Language and Meaning

The fundamental aim of information retrieval is to match an information need against a file or database with the intention of retrieving from the database those items which match the information need. In this context, a database is a collection of information of some kind, organized in such a way that discrete elements can be retrieved. Thus a database might contain the full text of documents such as newspaper or encyclopaedia articles. It might contain document representations (surrogates) such as entries in a library catalogue, or factual data such as physical or chemical properties, commodity prices or train times. The database might include not only text but also images and sound as found on both multimedia CD-ROMs and the World Wide Web.

It is crucial to realize that computers process strings of characters. They cannot 'understand' text except in very restricted subject domains such as gardening and even in those restricted domains complex semantic information must be stored in the system. Thus computers do not recognize synonyms such as those noted later in this chapter. Furthermore unless they have been programmed to do so they cannot recognize spelling mistakes or the similarity between variants such as singulars/plurals or British/North American variants (Vickery and Brooks, 1987). Finally they cannot disambiguate multiple meaning words such as mercury (planet or metal?) and certainly cannot cope with ambiguous statements such as 'You would not recognize Johnny since he has grown another foot.'

Table 4.1   **Examples of synonyms and near synonyms**

Word	Synonym/near synonym
Cars	Automobiles, motor cars
Elderly	Senior citizens, aged, old
Remuneration	Pay, salary, wages
Aeroplanes	Aircraft, airplanes, planes
Rubella	German measles
Boats	Ships
Shoes	Footwear
Farming	Agriculture
Pavement	Sidewalk

Given the complexity of language and the fact that computers only match characters, the retrieval process is far more complex than simply entering a few keywords and then waiting for the computer to respond with everything it holds that the searcher requires. It is the purpose of this chapter to explore linguistic diversity and its implications for retrieval, and to examine approaches which have been taken to overcome the problems this diversity causes for retrieval systems.

Bryson (1990) tells us that the English language has a particularly rich vocabulary because it has evolved from Anglo-Saxon but with considerable inputs from Norse, Norman French, Latin and Greek. He comments that the *Oxford English Dictionary* has some 615,00 entries to which must be added a large technological vocabulary. Thus it is not surprising that there are many examples of different words which mean exactly or nearly the same thing, for example the word *rule* emanates from Anglo-Saxon while a synonym, *regulation*, comes from Norman French. Table 4.1 provides a small number of examples of synonyms and near synonyms to illustrate this point.

It can be seen from this table that there are several types of synonym: changes in terminology which occur over time (elderly, senior citizen), technical and everyday terms for the same thing (rubella, German measles) and different terms from different English-speaking countries (pavement, sidewalk). Strictly speaking some of these terms are not exact synonyms (e.g. shoes, footwear), but rather, are near synonyms. Whether or not such occurrences can be treated as synonymous for retrieval purposes will be context dependent and will be explored later in the chapter. Many pairs of words have opposite meanings: sharp and blunt, light and dark, peaceful and violent. These are antonyms. When searching for information, an antonym may serve as a search term. For example, a search on causes of family stability may also usefully take into consideration causes of family instability. Additionally there are numerous irregular plurals (e.g. goose, geese) which can cause problems for retrieval. The English language has the additional complication of spelling differences, for example, between English and American usage as illustrated in Table 4.2.

Table 4.2   Examples of English and North American spelling variants

UK spelling	US spelling
aluminium	aluminum
axe	ax
cataloguing	cataloging
cheque	check
colouring	coloring
defence	defense
haemorrhage	hemorrhage
mould	mold
oesophagus	esophagus
plough	plow
sceptic	skeptic
sulphur	sulfur
theatre	theater
traveller	traveler
tyre	tire
whisky	whiskey
woollen	woolen

Bryson suggests that the vocabularies of other languages are less rich than English. He illustrates this argument by suggesting that there are about 200,000 words in common usage in English while he puts the number of words in common use in German at about 180,000 and in French at about 100,000. Nevertheless, even in languages with smaller vocabularies, there are numerous examples of synonyms. For example, in French, a TV channel might be either *canal* or *chaîne* while the notion of a ghost might be expressed by any of *revenant, fantôme* or *spectre*. In German the words *Wagen* or *Auto* both mean car while either *Orange* or *Apfelsine* can be used to mean orange, and a castle could be either *Burg* or *Schloss*. The notion of the reunification of Germany can be referred to by either the word *Wende* or the word *Wiedervereinigung*. Finally, in Greek, the notion of a car is conveyed by either the word αυτοκίνητο or the word αμάξι, and the words χρόνος and έτος both mean year.

The examples to date have concentrated upon single words but when those words are combined into phrases or sentences then the possibility of expressing the same idea in many ways becomes even more problematic. Lancaster (1979) illustrates the point perfectly with his example of the levels of a chemical substance in the blood which might be expressed as any of the following:

- blood levels
- serum levels
- blood concentration
- serum concentration

- concentration of . . . in the blood
- concentration of . . . in the serum
- level of . . . in the blood
- level of . . . in the serum.

As examples of different sentences, it should be apparent that the following each have approximately the same semantic value while there is considerable syntactic variation:

- Colin wore a green shirt.
- Colin's shirt was green.
- The green shirt was worn by Colin.
- Colin, the one with the green shirt. . . .
- The only green shirt in the entire crowd was Colin's.

Additionally, those with the appropriate contextual knowledge would know straight away from the sentence:

- Colin was walking down the street in his Hibernian shirt

that his shirt was green. Thus the richness and diversity of the language enable the same idea to be conveyed in a variety of ways.

In addition, of course, it is not simply that a concept can be expressed in more than one way, but that words can have more than one meaning. The meaning of a sign outside a newsagent's shop a few years ago which read 'Mid-Wales airport takes off' would have been clear to shoppers. Taken literally, however, the sentence has quite a different meaning and presumably one which the headline writer came to regret. A more serious example adapted slightly from Meadow is the sentence 'He covered the field.' This has a considerably different meaning depending upon whether the context is literature searching, crop spraying or the conduct of a particularly energetic sportsman (Meadow, 1973). Multiple meaning is not confined to sentences: many words have more than one meaning. An example in English is the word *play* which can be both a verb (when it is either an activity undertaken by children or something which sports people seek to do) or a noun (when it is a theatrical performance). Another example is the noun *mercury* which can mean either a planet in the solar system or a metal. Once again this is not a phenomenon confined to the English language. The French word *volant* might mean any one of the following: steering wheel, flywheel, shuttlecock, flounce (of a dress) and flying. While *jet* can be any of the following: casting (of metal), jet of a liquid, a throw or the weathering of buildings as well as a jet aircraft. In German *Bank* might mean either a bench or a (financial) bank and *Base* could be either a chemical base or (female) cousin or aunt. Finally in Greek, the word, πίνακας, has several meanings including a blackboard, a control panel or a table of information (such as the medals table displayed at the Olympic Games).

Controlled Vocabularies

Given this diversity of language it is not surprising that the creators of information retrieval systems have long sought to impose some standardization of vocabulary on the retrieval process. A hypothetical example may serve to illustrate the point. Let us suppose that a German bibliographic database covering the subjects of food and agriculture included 39 items dealing with oranges. Without any form of vocabulary standardization, 22 of these items might contain the term *Apfelsinen* but not the term *Orangen*. Thus the searcher using only one search term would not retrieve all 39 items. Effective and complete retrieval places upon the searcher (or possibly the system), the burden of being aware of both synonyms used in the database. The general argument, which this example illustrates, is that retrieval will be adversely affected by linguistic diversity unless there is some form of language standardization within the database. The contention is that the use of a standardized vocabulary will promote retrieval by reducing the demand upon the searcher to know and use all possible synonyms. Such standardization is achieved by choosing one of the synonyms as the approved term. So returning to the example, it might be that all items are indexed under the term *Apfelsinen*. The choice of *Apfelsinen* instead of *Orangen* is an illustration of using a standardized vocabulary to promote retrieval. Another example is provided by the way in which most libraries group together books on similar subjects to promote searching and browsing. Every book is assigned an alphanumeric code to represent its subject content and the code is selected from a standardized vocabulary called a classification scheme. The books can then be arranged on the shelf in alphanumeric sequence grouping together books on the same topic. The use of a standardized vocabulary has been a feature of information retrieval since well before computers were applied to the task.

This standardization has been achieved by using what is known as a controlled vocabulary. Controlled vocabularies emerged in two differing bibliographic environments which has resulted in two differing types of vocabularies and approaches to their use. One of these environments was library cataloguing where the tradition emerged of using a controlled vocabulary to present a summarizing statement or representation of the overall content of the document, usually a single controlled vocabulary statement. The controlled vocabularies developed in this arena include classification schemes such as the Dewey Decimal Classification Scheme and subject headings such as Library of Congress Subject Headings (LCSH). The second environment resulted from the indexing of scientific, technical and medical (STM) research papers and reports, either for internal collections or for the major printed abstracting and indexing publications which were the forerunners of the STM bibliographic databases. Here, the approach to representation was one of indexing the documents in depth by representing each of the major concepts in the document by a term from the controlled vocabulary. All the terms in such a controlled vocabulary typically are listed in what is called a thesaurus (see later).

The result of these two approaches has been two different types of vocabulary and thus concept representation. In the summarizing approach, the vocabulary is at a more general level and the representation of content is by a single term or at most a small number of terms from the vocabulary. In the depth-indexing approach the vocabulary contains much more specific terminology and usually far more terms are assigned to each item. Thus McClure (1976), for example, has pointed out that while the typical entry in an STM database might have ten to 12 terms assigned to it the average number of terms assigned to items in a library catalogue is 1.3.

A controlled vocabulary can be defined as an artificial language which has been created for a particular information retrieval system or group of related systems. Like other languages, a controlled vocabulary has its own vocabulary and syntax. In theory the use of a controlled vocabulary should promote the retrieval process by ensuring that there is consistent representation of concepts, both when the database is created and when it is being searched. A controlled vocabulary should promote retrieval by bringing together in some way terms which are semantically related (Lancaster, 1977). This is achieved by controlling the occurrence of synonyms, near synonyms, quasi-synonyms (that is words meaning the same or very nearly the same thing), perhaps also antonyms (words meaning the opposite), and differentiating between homonyms (the same word with different meanings). In addition a controlled vocabulary indicates the relationships between terms, whether these are invariant relationships such as genus-species or temporary relationships which apply only in the situation of the particular retrieval system.

While the notion of a controlled vocabulary occurs most widely in the field of bibliographic databases, there are controlled vocabularies in other spheres. For example, the North American Industrial Classification System (NAICS), which has been devised as a part of the North American Free Trade Agreement (NAFTA), is a classification scheme for industrial organizations (see http://www.ntis.gov/business/sic.htm). The Standard Industrial Classification (SIC) Scheme is a similar system in the UK. Tools such as NAICS and SIC were created to categorize industrial data such as trade statistics and production statistics.

A second example is provided by the Chemical Abstracts Service (CAS) Registry Numbers developed to overcome the problem that there is more than one convention for the formal naming of the several million chemicals in existence. In addition, many widely used chemicals often have common, or so-called trivial names, which are widely used but do not follow any formal naming scheme. If trade names of products such as agrochemicals and pharmaceuticals are added, it can be appreciated that there is a need for a means of uniquely identifying chemical compounds. Both SIC codes and CAS Registry Numbers have become vital tools for information retrieval in their respective subjects.

The language problems discussed earlier in this chapter are just as prevalent, if not more so, in the rapidly evolving electronic information environment of the Web. It is interesting to note the beginnings of the use of vocabulary control through the categorization offered on search engines. The menu of a search engine such as Yahoo! UK and Ireland, shown in Figure 4.1, is simply a form of vocabulary control. Sites dealing with, for example, 'movies' will be grouped under this heading within the broader

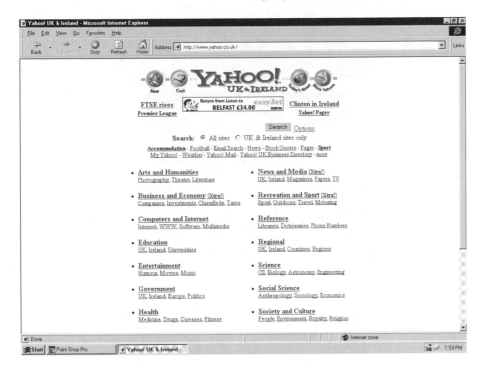

Figure 4.1 Part of main menu of Yahoo! UK and Ireland

'entertainment' section even if they have rather used the term 'film' or 'motion picture'. Figure 4.2 is taken from the gardening section of Excite Lifestyle, part of the subject categorization offered from the Excite search engine home page as shown in Figure 3.13. It shows various sub-topics (composting, ponds, for example) as well as recommended Web sites. This is really a simple form of classification. Figure 4.3 shows a list of subject areas available on the Social Science Information Gateway (SOSIG), a UK gateway to evaluated resources in the social sciences on the Internet which enables users to browse subject areas. Once again this is a simple form of vocabulary control.

Thesauri

At its simplest a thesaurus is a list of approved terms, descriptors or controlled terms as they are variously called, that can be used by indexers to represent the content of information-bearing items. Usually, though, the term thesaurus implies more than a list of approved terms. Rather, there is an expectation that the thesaurus will indicate any semantic relationships between the approved terms and provide pointers from non-approved terms to approved terms.

Synonyms and near synonyms are controlled by deciding that one term is to be the approved term and will always be used to express the concept

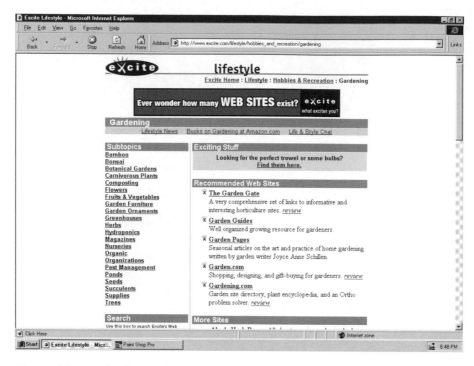

Figure 4.2   **Gardening section of Excite Lifestyle**

when it occurs in the database. A reference is then made in the thesaurus from any synonym(s) to that term. For example:

pupils
use students

indicates that 'students' has been chosen as the preferred term rather than 'pupils'. The reciprocal relationship should always be provided. Thus:

students
UF pupils

where UF means use for. The decision about whether or not two terms can be treated as synonymous is not solely a matter of their semantic value. An important consideration is also the context in which the thesaurus is to be used. For example, if a thesaurus is to be used in a database dealing with 20th-century life it might be decided to include index items about footwear. As this is not a major topic in the database, it might well be acceptable to treat the near synonyms 'shoes' and 'footwear' as synonymous and simply use one of the terms as a controlled term. If, however, the subject of the database is fashion then it might well be decided that as there will be many items about different types of footwear in the database, the interests of precise retrieval are best served by the inclusion in

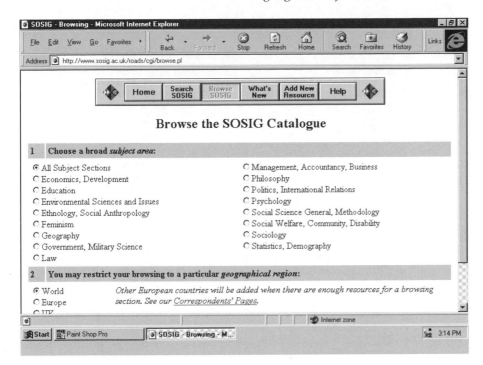

Figure 4.3 Subject areas available on the Social Science Information Gateway menu

the thesaurus of separate terms for each different type of footwear. Thus while the semantic value of the two terms is unchanged, the context of use is significantly different and it is the context which has influenced the decision about inclusion of controlled terms in the thesaurus.

Homonyms are generally distinguished either by use of scope notes or by a simple explanatory statement in brackets, for example:

mercury (metal)
mercury (planet)

Many relationships can exist between approved terms but generally they are of two types: hierarchical or associative. As the name implies, hierarchical relationships are best thought of as a tree structure of terms. Typically they might be genus-species relationships or whole-part relationships. The relationships are conventionally indicated by BT for broader term and NT for narrower term. Thus:

computers
NT microcomputers

and the reciprocal

microcomputers
BT computers

data recording cont.
TT   recording
RT   data acquisition
     digital storage
     magnetic recording
CC   B3120B; C5520
DI   January 1985
PT   magnetic recording

data reduction
BT   data handling
TT   data handling
RT   curve fitting
     data acquisition
     data analysis
     recording
     spectral analysis
CC   C6130; C7000; C7410H
DI   January 1985
PT   data reduction and analysis

data reduction and analysis
     heading was preferred term until January 1985
     USE data analysis
          data reduction

data representation
     USE data structures

data security
     USE security of data

data structures
UF   data abstraction
     data models
     data representation
NT   abstract data types
     spatial data structures
     tree data structures
BT   file organisation
TT   file organisation
RT   program control structures
     relational databases
     search problems
     trees (mathematics)
     type theory
CC   C6120
DI   January 1969

data tables
     USE collections of physical data

data transfer formats
     USE electronic data interchange

data transmission equipment
     USE data communication equipment

data transmission systems
     heading was preferred term until January 1977
     USE data communication

data visualisation
UF   data visualization
     scientific visualisation
     visualisation of data
BT   computer graphics
TT   computer graphics
RT   surface fitting
     user interfaces
CC   C6130B; C7300; C7400
DI   January 1993
PT   computer graphics

data visualization
     USE data visualisation

database languages
UF   data manipulation languages
NT   query languages
BT   programming languages
TT   languages
CC   C4250; C6140D; C6160
DI   January 1995
PT   query languages

database machines
BT   database management systems

database machines cont.
     special purpose computers
TT   computer applications
     computers
     file organisation
CC   C5400; C6160
DI   January 1995
PT   database management systems
     special purpose computers

database management systems
UF   data dictionaries
     data models
     databases
     DBMS
     fourth-generation languages
     hierarchical databases
     network databases
NT   active databases
     database machines
     deductive databases
     distributed databases
     object-oriented databases
     relational databases
     statistical databases
     temporal databases
     very large databases
     visual databases
BT   file organisation
     information systems
TT   computer applications
     file organisation
RT   application generators
     concurrency control
     data integrity
     database theory
     decision support systems
     geographic information systems
     group decision support systems
     hypermedia
     integrated software
     multimedia systems
     query languages
     query processing
     systems re-engineering
     transaction processing
CC   C6160; C7250L; D2080
DI   January 1977
PT   file organisation
     management information systems

database querying
     USE query languages
          query processing

database theory
RT   database management systems
     distributed databases
     programming theory
     query processing
     relational algebra
     relational databases
     search problems
     temporal logic
CC   C4250
DI   January 1985
PT   database management systems

databases
     USE database management systems
          information services

databases, online
     USE information retrieval systems
          information services

DATALOG
BT   logic programming languages
     query languages
TT   languages
     logic
RT   deductive databases
     query processing
CC   C6110L; C6140D; C6160K
DI   January 1995
PT   query languages

dating, Earth
     USE geochronology

Figure 4.4   Extract from the *Inspec Thesaurus, 1995*

A small number of thesauri indicate the term which is at the top of a hierarchy of terms with the designation TT (top term). For example, Figure 4.4 shows an extract from the 1995 edition of the *Inspec Thesaurus*. Under the controlled vocabulary term *'database management systems'* appears the entry:

TT computer applications
  file organization

This indicates that the term appears in two different hierarchical structures of which the two top terms are *'computer applications'* and *'file organization'*.

Associative relationships are those which have no hierarchical relationship or indeed permanent relationship but are clearly related in the context for which the thesaurus will be used. Examples might be the relationship between an activity and the agent of that activity such as:

programming
RT computers

or between a raw material and something produced from that raw material:

grapes
RT wine

Obviously the relationship should be shown in both directions. Thus the entries:

computers
RT programming

wine
RT grapes

would be expected.

Figure 4.5 contains an extract from the alphabetical listing of the sixth edition of the *Thesaurus of Psychological Terms*, the thesaurus used with the PsycInfo database. It shows more clearly a range of term relationships. In addition it demonstrates the use of scope notes (SN) such as those for the terms ethnography and etymology. Scope notes are used to define the exact meaning of the term for the purposes of the particular retrieval system.

All thesauri will contain an alphabetical listing of terms but many of the larger and well-established thesauri also display the terms in a variety of other ways to help the user. For example, the ERIC thesaurus, in addition to its alphabetical display of terms, has three other forms of term display: a rotated descriptor display, a two-way hierarchical term display and descriptor groups. These forms of display are illustrated in Figures 4.6, 4.7 and 4.8. These additional displays are not essential to the functioning of the thesaurus; rather they act as indexes to the main alphabetical display and are intended to facilitate the use of the main alphabetical sequence.

Estimation [67]
PN 1091   SC 17980
SN Subjective judgment or inference about the character, quality, or nature of a person, process, or thing which may or may not involve the inspection or availability of data or pertinent information.
N ↓ Statistical Estimation [85]
 Time Estimation [67]

Estradiol [73]
PN 769   SC 18000
B Estrogens [73]
 Hormones [67]
 Sex Hormones [73]

Estrogen Antagonists
Use Antiestrogens

Estrogens [73]
PN 517   SC 18010
B Hormones [67]
 Sex Hormones [73]
N Estradiol [73]
 Estrone [73]
R Antiandrogens [82]
 Antiestrogens [82]

Estrone [73]
PN 8   SC 18020
B Estrogens [73]
 Hormones [67]
 Sex Hormones [73]

Estrus [73]
PN 427   SC 18030
R ↓ Animal Biological Rhythms [73]
 Animal Sexual Receptivity [73]
 ↓ Menstrual Cycle [73]
 ↓ Menstruation [73]

Ethanal
Use Acetaldehyde

Ethanol [73]
PN 2213   SC 18040
UF Ethyl Alcohol
B Alcohols [67]
R Fetal Alcohol Syndrome [85]

Ether (Anesthetic) [73]
PN 34   SC 18050
UF Ethyl Ether (Anesthetic)
B Anesthetic Drugs [73]
 General Anesthetics [73]

Ethics [67]
PN 658   SC 18060
N Experimental Ethics [78]
 Personal Values [73]
 Professional Ethics [73]
 Social Values [73]
 ↓ Values [67]
R Euthanasia [73]
 Morality [67]
 ↓ Religious Beliefs [73]
 ↓ Social Influences [67]

Ethiopia [82]
PN 31   SC 18064
B Africa [67]

Ethnic Differences
Use Racial and Ethnic Differences

Ethnic Disorders
Use Ethnospecific Disorders

Ethnic Groups [73]
PN 2327   SC 18080
N American Indians [67]
 Anglos [88]
 Arabs [88]
 Asians [82]
 Eskimos [73]
 Gypsies [73]
 ↓ Hispanics [82]
 Mexican Americans [73]
R Blacks [82]
 Ethnic Values [73]
 Ethnology/ [67]
 Ethnospecific Disorders [73]
 Minority Groups [67]
 ↓ Racial and Ethnic Attitudes [82]
 Racial and Ethnic Differences [82]
 Tribes [73]
 Whites [82]

Ethnic Identity [73]
PN 934   SC 18090
SN Feelings, ties, or associations that an individual experiences as a member of a particular ethnic group.
B Sociocultural Factors [67]
R ↓ Social Identity [88]

Ethnic Values [73]
PN 208   SC 18100
B Social Influences [67]
 Sociocultural Factors [67]
 Values [67]
R ↓ Ethnic Groups [73]

Ethnocentrism [73]
PN 139   SC 18110
SN Exaggerated tendency to identify with one's own ethnic group, or the inclination to judge others in terms of standards and values of one's own group.
B Racial and Ethnic Attitudes [82]
R ↓ Social Identity [88]

Ethnography [73]
PN 249   SC 18120
SN Descriptive study of cultures and societies. Used for the scientific discipline or the descriptive analyses themselves. Consider also ETHNOLOGY/.
R Anthropology [67]
 Ethnology/ [67]
 Kinship Structure [73]
 Race (Anthropological) [73]
 ↓ Rites of Passage [73]
 ↓ Sociocultural Factors [67]

Ethnolinguistics [73]
PN 133   SC 18130
SN A part of anthropological linguistics concerned with the interrelation between a language and the cultural behavior of those who speak it.
B Linguistics [73]
R ↓ Dialect [73]
 Ethnology/ [67]
 Psycholinguistics [67]
 Slang [73]
 Sociolinguistics [85]

Ethnology/ [67]
PN 1504   SC 18140
SN Conceptually broad array term referring to the study of the origin, distribution, characteristics, and relations of the cultures or ethnic groups of the world. Also, a branch of anthropology dealing with the comparative or analytical study of human culture or societies. Use a more specific term if possible. Consider also ETHNOGRAPHY.

Ethnology/ — (cont'd)
R Animism [73]
 Cultism [73]
 ↓ Culture (Anthropological) [67]
 Culture Shock [73]
 ↓ Ethnic Groups [73]
 Ethnography [73]
 Ethnolinguistics [73]
 Ethnospecific Disorders [73]
 Folk Medicine [73]
 Kinship Structure [73]
 Myths [73]
 Race (Anthropological) [73]
 Shamanism [73]
 ↓ Sociocultural Factors [67]
 Taboos [73]
 Transcultural Psychiatry [73]
 Witchcraft [73]

Ethnospecific Disorders [73]
PN 16   SC 18150
UF Ethnic Disorders
R ↓ Ethnic Groups [73]
 Ethnology/ [67]
 Mental Disorders/ [67]
 ↓ Personality Disorders [67]
 Transcultural Psychiatry [73]

Ethology (Animal)
Use Animal Ethology

Ethyl Alcohol
Use Ethanol

Ethyl Ether (Anesthetic)
Use Ether (Anesthetic)

Ethylaldehyde
Use Acetaldehyde

Etiology [67]
PN 5830   SC 18190
SN Study of the causes and origins of disorders. Used for the science itself or the specific etiological findings and processes.
UF Aetiology
 Pathogenesis
R Disorders/ [67]
 Patient History [73]

Etymology [73]
PN 44   SC 18200
SN Branch of linguistic science which traces the origin of words and morphemes to their earliest determinable base in a given language group and describes historical changes in words. Used for the discipline or specific etymological aspects of given words.
UF Word Origins
B Linguistics [73]
R Words (Phonetic Units) [67]

Eugenics [73]
PN 21   SC 18210
SN Applied science or the biosocial movement which advocates the use of practices aimed at improving the genetic composition of a population. Usually refers to human populations. Compare ANIMAL BREEDING, ANIMAL DOMESTICATION, and SELECTIVE BREEDING.
R ↓ Family Planning [73]
 Genetic Counseling [78]
 Genetics/ [67]
 Reproductive Technology [88]
 Selective Breeding [73]
 ↓ Sterilization (Sex) [73]

Figure 4.5 Extract from *Thesaurus of Psychological Terms*, 6th edition

```
                            PROGRAMS
              ACCELERATED  PROGRAMS (1966 1980)   Use ACCELERATION (EDUCATION).
                    ADULT  PROGRAMS
          ADULT EDUCATION  PROGRAMS (1966 1980)   Use ADULT EDUCATION and ADULT PROGRAMS
           ADULT READING  PROGRAMS
                ADVANCED  PROGRAMS (1966 1980)
      ADVANCED PLACEMENT  PROGRAMS
            AFTER SCHOOL  PROGRAMS
            ANTI POVERTY  PROGRAMS   Use POVERTY PROGRAMS
         ANTI SEGREGATION  PROGRAMS (1967 1980)   Use RACIAL INTEGRATION
                ASSEMBLY  PROGRAMS
                ATHLETIC  PROGRAMS (1966 1980)   Use ATHLETICS
              AUDIOVISUAL  PROGRAMS (1966 1980)   Use AUDIOVISUAL INSTRUCTION
        AUTOINSTRUCTIONAL  PROGRAMS (1966 1980)   Use PROGRAMMED INSTRUCTION
       BILINGUAL EDUCATION  PROGRAMS
                 BRACERO  PROGRAMS (1966 1980)   Use BRACEROS
               BREAKFAST  PROGRAMS
                BUILDING  PROGRAMS   Use CONSTRUCTION PROGRAMS
                  CHURCH  PROGRAMS
               CITY WIDE  PROGRAMS (1967 1980)   Use URBAN PROGRAMS
                   CIVIC  PROGRAMS   Use COMMUNITY PROGRAMS
      CLASSROOM GUIDANCE  PROGRAMS (1968 1980)
                   CO OP  PROGRAMS   Use COOPERATIVE PROGRAMS
                 COLLEGE  PROGRAMS
         COLLEGE LANGUAGE  PROGRAMS (1967 1980)
  COLLEGE SECOND LANGUAGE  PROGRAMS
       COLLEGE WORK STUDY  PROGRAMS   Use WORK STUDY PROGRAMS
               COMMUNITY  PROGRAMS
                   ACTION  PROGRAMS (COMMUNITY) (1966 1980)   Use COMMUNITY ACTION
        COMMUNITY CONSULTANT  PROGRAMS (1966 1980)   Use CONSULTATION PROGRAMS
      COMMUNITY RECREATION  PROGRAMS
          COMMUNITY SCHOOL  PROGRAMS   Use SCHOOL COMMUNITY PROGRAMS
         COMMUNITY SERVICE  PROGRAMS (1966 1980)   Use COMMUNITY SERVICES
    COMPENSATORY EDUCATION  PROGRAMS (1966 1980)   Use COMPENSATORY EDUCATION
           COMPREHENSIVE  PROGRAMS
                COMPUTER  PROGRAMS (1966 1984)   Use COMPUTER SOFTWARE
        COMPUTER ORIENTED  PROGRAMS
            CONSTRUCTION  PROGRAMS
            CONSULTATION  PROGRAMS
             COOPERATIVE  PROGRAMS
  COOPERATIVE WORK EXPERIENCE  PROGRAMS   Use COOPERATIVE EDUCATION
              COUNSELING  PROGRAMS (1966 1980)   Use COUNSELING SERVICES
  COUNSELING INSTRUCTIONAL  PROGRAMS (1967 1980)
                  COUNTY  PROGRAMS
                     DAY  PROGRAMS
                DAY CAMP  PROGRAMS
                DAY CARE  PROGRAMS (1966 1980)   Use DAY CARE
                 DAYTIME  PROGRAMS (1967 1980)   Use DAY PROGRAMS
           DEMONSTRATION  PROGRAMS
           DEVELOPMENTAL  PROGRAMS
     DEVELOPMENTAL STUDIES  PROGRAMS
              DISCUSSION  PROGRAMS (1966 1980)   Use DISCUSSION
                DOCTORAL  PROGRAMS
                 DROPOUT  PROGRAMS
             EDUCATIONAL  PROGRAMS (1966 1980)
               EMERGENCY  PROGRAMS
     EMPLOYEE ASSISTANCE  PROGRAMS
             EMPLOYMENT  PROGRAMS
                 ENGLISH  PROGRAMS (1966 1980)   Use ENGLISH CURRICULUM
             ENRICHMENT  PROGRAMS (1966 1980)   Use ENRICHMENT ACTIVITIES
                 EVENING  PROGRAMS
       EVENING COUNSELING  PROGRAMS (1966 1980)   Use COUNSELING SERVICES and EVENING PROGRAMS
               EXCHANGE  PROGRAMS
               EXEMPLARY  PROGRAMS   Use DEMONSTRATION PROGRAMS
            EXPERIMENTAL  PROGRAMS
  EXTENDED TEACHER EDUCATION  PROGRAMS
         EXTERNAL DEGREE  PROGRAMS
       EXTRAMURAL ATHLETIC  PROGRAMS (1966 1980)   Use EXTRAMURAL ATHLETICS
                  FAMILY  PROGRAMS
                 FEDERAL  PROGRAMS
                  FEEDER  PROGRAMS (1966 1980)   Use FEEDER PATTERNS
         FIELD EXPERIENCE  PROGRAMS
  FIVE YEAR TEACHER PREPARATION  PROGRAMS   Use EXTENDED TEACHER EDUCATION PROGRAMS
                    FLES  PROGRAMS (1967 1980)   Use FLES and SECOND LANGUAGE PROGRAMS
               FOLLOWUP  PROGRAMS   Use FOLLOWUP STUDIES
        FOREIGN LANGUAGE  PROGRAMS   Use SECOND LANGUAGE PROGRAMS
             FOUNDATION  PROGRAMS
     FREE CHOICE TRANSFER  PROGRAMS
                    GED  PROGRAMS   Use HIGH SCHOOL EQUIVALENCY PROGRAMS
  GENERAL EDUCATIONAL DEVELOPMENT  PROGRAMS   Use HIGH SCHOOL EQUIVALENCY PROGRAMS
                GUIDANCE  PROGRAMS
                  HEALTH  PROGRAMS
  HIGH SCHOOL EQUIVALENCY  PROGRAMS
                    HOME  PROGRAMS
        HUMAN RELATIONS  PROGRAMS
              IMMERSION  PROGRAMS
            IMMUNIZATION  PROGRAMS
           IMPROVEMENT  PROGRAMS
          INDIVIDUALIZED  PROGRAMS
  INDIVIDUALIZED EDUCATION  PROGRAMS
                 INPLANT  PROGRAMS
               INSERVICE  PROGRAMS (1966 1980)   Use INSERVICE EDUCATION
     INSERVICE EDUCATION  PROGRAMS   Use INSERVICE EDUCATION
```

Figure 4.6   Extract from rotated descriptor display, *Thesaurus of ERIC descriptors, 13th edition*

RESOURCE TEACHERS
SCIENCE TEACHERS
SECONDARY SCHOOL TEACHERS
SPECIAL EDUCATION TEACHERS
STUDENT TEACHERS
SUBSTITUTE TEACHERS
TEACHER INTERNS
TELEVISION TEACHERS
TUTORS
VOCATIONAL EDUCATION TEACHERS
BUSINESS EDUCATION TEACHERS
DISTRIBUTIVE EDUCATION
  TEACHERS
TRADE AND INDUSTRIAL TEACHERS
WRITING TEACHERS
THERAPISTS
OCCUPATIONAL THERAPISTS
PHYSICAL THERAPISTS
VETERINARIANS

EVALUATION
RECOGNITION (ACHIEVEMENT)
PROFESSIONAL RECOGNITION

SERVICES
PROFESSIONAL SERVICES

TRAINING
PROFESSIONAL TRAINING

GROUPS
PERSONNEL
SCHOOL PERSONNEL
GROUPS
PERSONNEL
PROFESSIONAL PERSONNEL
FACULTY
COLLEGE FACULTY
PROFESSORS

DATA
PROFILES

MEASURES (INDIVIDUALS)
TESTS
PROGNOSTIC TESTS

GOVERNANCE
ADMINISTRATION
PROGRAM ADMINISTRATION

ATTITUDES
PROGRAM ATTITUDES

PLANNING
BUDGETING
PROGRAM BUDGETING

PROGRAM CONTENT

COSTS
PROGRAM COSTS

PROGRAM DESCRIPTIONS

DESIGN
PROGRAM DESIGN

DEVELOPMENT
PROGRAM DEVELOPMENT

PROGRAM EFFECTIVENESS

EVALUATION
PROGRAM EVALUATION

PUBLICATIONS
REFERENCE MATERIALS
GUIDES
PROGRAM GUIDES

PROGRAM IMPLEMENTATION

IMPROVEMENT
PROGRAM IMPROVEMENT

PROGRAMING PROBLEMS (1966 1980)

PROGRAM LENGTH

METHODS
EDUCATIONAL METHODS
TEACHING METHODS
PROGRAMMED INSTRUCTION
COMPUTER ASSISTED INSTRUCTION
INTELLIGENT TUTORING SYSTEMS
PROGRAMMED TUTORING

EDUCATIONAL MEDIA
INSTRUCTIONAL MATERIALS
**PROGRAMMED INSTRUCTIONAL
MATERIALS**

INSTRUCTION
INDIVIDUAL INSTRUCTION
TUTORING
METHODS
EDUCATIONAL METHODS
TEACHING METHODS
PROGRAMMED INSTRUCTION
PROGRAMMED TUTORING

GROUPS
PERSONNEL
PROGRAMMERS

DEVELOPMENT
MATERIAL DEVELOPMENT
COMPUTER SOFTWARE
  DEVELOPMENT
LIBERAL ARTS
SCIENCES
INFORMATION SCIENCE
COMPUTER SCIENCE
PROGRAMMING

PROGRAMMING (BROADCAST)

LANGUAGE
PROGRAMMING LANGUAGES

PROGRAM PROPOSALS
RESEARCH PROPOSALS

PROGRAMS
ADULT PROGRAMS
ADULT READING PROGRAMS
HIGH SCHOOL EQUIVALENCY
  PROGRAMS
ADVANCED PLACEMENT PROGRAMS
AFTER SCHOOL PROGRAMS
ASSEMBLY PROGRAMS
BILINGUAL EDUCATION PROGRAMS
CHURCH PROGRAMS
COLLEGE DAY
COLLEGE PROGRAMS
DOCTORAL PROGRAMS
EXTERNAL DEGREE PROGRAMS
MASTERS PROGRAMS
COMMUNITY PROGRAMS
COMMUNITY RECREATION
  PROGRAMS
SCHOOL COMMUNITY PROGRAMS
COMPREHENSIVE PROGRAMS
COMPUTER ORIENTED PROGRAMS
CONSTRUCTION PROGRAMS
CONSULTATION PROGRAMS
COOPERATIVE PROGRAMS
COUNTY PROGRAMS
DAY PROGRAMS
DEMONSTRATION PROGRAMS
DEVELOPMENTAL PROGRAMS
DEVELOPMENTAL STUDIES
  PROGRAMS
EMERGENCY PROGRAMS
EMPLOYEE ASSISTANCE PROGRAMS
EMPLOYMENT PROGRAMS
EVENING PROGRAMS

EXCHANGE PROGRAMS
STUDENT EXCHANGE PROGRAMS
TEACHER EXCHANGE PROGRAMS
EXPERIMENTAL PROGRAMS
FAMILY PROGRAMS
FEDERAL PROGRAMS
FIELD EXPERIENCE PROGRAMS
SUPERVISED OCCUPATIONAL
  EXPERIENCE (AGRICULTURE
FOUNDATION PROGRAMS
GUIDANCE PROGRAMS
HEALTH PROGRAMS
BREAKFAST PROGRAMS
IMMUNIZATION PROGRAMS
LUNCH PROGRAMS
MENTAL HEALTH PROGRAMS
HOME PROGRAMS
HUMAN RELATIONS PROGRAMS
IMPROVEMENT PROGRAMS
SELF HELP PROGRAMS
INDIVIDUALIZED PROGRAMS
INPLANT PROGRAMS
INSTITUTES (TRAINING PROGRAMS)
INTERCULTURAL PROGRAMS
INTERGENERATIONAL PROGRAMS
INTERNATIONAL PROGRAMS
INTERNSHIP PROGRAMS
INTERSTATE PROGRAMS
MIGRANT PROGRAMS
NATIONAL PROGRAMS
NONSCHOOL EDUCATIONAL
  PROGRAMS
OUTREACH PROGRAMS
PILOT PROJECTS
POVERTY PROGRAMS
PRETECHNOLOGY PROGRAMS
READING PROGRAMS
ADULT READING PROGRAMS
RECREATIONAL PROGRAMS
COMMUNITY RECREATION
  PROGRAMS
DAY CAMP PROGRAMS
PHYSICAL RECREATION PROGRAMS
RESIDENT CAMP PROGRAMS
SCHOOL RECREATIONAL PROGRAMS
REGIONAL PROGRAMS
REHABILITATION PROGRAMS
DROPOUT PROGRAMS
REMEDIAL PROGRAMS
RESEARCH PROJECTS
RESIDENTIAL PROGRAMS
RESIDENT CAMP PROGRAMS
SCIENCE COURSE IMPROVEMENT
  PROJECTS
SCIENCE PROGRAMS
SUMMER SCIENCE PROGRAMS
SECOND LANGUAGE PROGRAMS
COLLEGE SECOND LANGUAGE
  PROGRAMS
IMMERSION PROGRAMS
SPECIAL PROGRAMS
INDIVIDUALIZED EDUCATION
  PROGRAMS
INDIVIDUALIZED FAMILY SERVICE
  PLANS
RESOURCE ROOM PROGRAMS
SPECIAL DEGREE PROGRAMS
STATE PROGRAMS
STUDENT LOAN PROGRAMS
SUMMER PROGRAMS
SUMMER SCIENCE PROGRAMS
TEACHER EDUCATION PROGRAMS
EXTENDED TEACHER EDUCATION
  PROGRAMS
TESTING PROGRAMS
TRANSFER PROGRAMS
FREE CHOICE TRANSFER PROGRAMS
TRANSITIONAL PROGRAMS
TUTORIAL PROGRAMS
URBAN PROGRAMS
VACATION PROGRAMS
VALIDATED PROGRAMS
WEEKEND PROGRAMS
WORK EXPERIENCE PROGRAMS
WORK STUDY PROGRAMS
YOUTH PROGRAMS

PROGRAM TERMINATION

PROGRAM VALIDATION

EDUCATION
PROGRESSIVE EDUCATION

PROJECT APPLICATIONS (1967 1980)

VISUAL AIDS
EQUIPMENT
PROJECTION EQUIPMENT
FILMSTRIP PROJECTORS
MICROFORM READERS
OPAQUE PROJECTORS
OVERHEAD PROJECTORS
TACHISTOSCOPES

MEASURES (INDIVIDUALS)
PROJECTIVE MEASURES
ASSOCIATION MEASURES

PROJECTS (1966 1980)

PROMOTION (OCCUPATIONAL)
FACULTY PROMOTION
TEACHER PROMOTION

METHODS
PROMPTING

LINGUISTICS
DESCRIPTIVE LINGUISTICS
GRAMMAR
SYNTAX
FORM CLASSES (LANGUAGES)
PRONOUNS

LANGUAGE ARTS
SPEECH
PRONUNCIATION

INSTRUCTION
SPEECH INSTRUCTION
PRONUNCIATION INSTRUCTION

STANDARDS
CRITERIA
EVALUATION CRITERIA
VALIDITY
LIBERAL ARTS
HUMANITIES
PHILOSOPHY
LOGIC
MATHEMATICAL LOGIC
PROOF (MATHEMATICS)

PROOFREADING

SERVICES
INFORMATION SERVICES
INFORMATION DISSEMINATION
COMMUNICATION (THOUGHT TRANSFER)
PROPAGANDA

MATHEMATICAL CONCEPTS
PROPERTIES (MATHEMATICS)

TECHNOLOGY
ACCOUNTING
PROPERTY ACCOUNTING

EVALUATION
PROPERTY APPRAISAL
ASSESSED VALUATION

TAXES
PROPERTY TAXES

LITERACY
LANGUAGE ARTS

Figure 4.7   Extract from two-way hierarchical term display, *Thesaurus of ERIC descriptors, 13th edition*

Descriptor Group Display

The Descriptor Groups offer a "table of contents" to the *Thesaurus*. A Descriptor Group Code appears within the main entry of each term in the Alphabetical Display of the *Thesaurus*. See the preceding Descriptor Groups section for Scope Notes about the various Descriptor Groups. Below is an alphabetical listing of all the Descriptors assigned to each Descriptor Group.

110 LEARNING AND PERCEPTION

ABILITY IDENTIFICATION
ABSTRACT REASONING
ACTIVE LEARNING
ADULT LEARNING
AROUSAL PATTERNS
ASSOCIATIVE LEARNING
ATTENTION
ATTENTION CONTROL
AUDIENCE RESPONSE
AUDITORY DISCRIMINATION
AUDITORY PERCEPTION
AUDITORY STIMULI
AURAL LEARNING
BEHAVIOR CHAINING
BEHAVIOR MODIFICATION
CLASSICAL CONDITIONING
COGNITIVE MAPPING
COGNITIVE PROCESSES
COGNITIVE PSYCHOLOGY
COGNITIVE RESTRUCTURING
COGNITIVE STRUCTURES
COGNITIVE STYLE
COMPENSATION (CONCEPT)
COMPREHENSION
CONCEPT FORMATION
CONCEPTUAL SCHEMES (1967 1980)
CONCEPTUAL TEMPO
CONDITIONING
CONSERVATION (CONCEPT)
CONSTRUCTED RESPONSE
CONSTRUCTIVISM (LEARNING)
CONTINGENCY MANAGEMENT
CONVERGENT THINKING
COVERT RESPONSE
CREATIVE THINKING
CRITICAL THINKING
CUES
DECISION MAKING
DECISION MAKING SKILLS
DEDUCTION
DEPTH PERCEPTION
DIMENSIONAL PREFERENCE
DISCOVERY LEARNING
DISCOVERY PROCESSES
DISCRIMINATION LEARNING
DIVERGENT THINKING
EIDETIC IMAGERY
ELECTRICAL STIMULI
ENCODING (PSYCHOLOGY)
EPISTEMOLOGY
EVALUATIVE THINKING
EXTINCTION (PSYCHOLOGY)
EYE FIXATIONS
EYE MOVEMENTS
FAMILIARITY
FIELD DEPENDENCE INDEPENDENCE
FIGURAL AFTEREFFECTS
FORMAL OPERATIONS
FUNDAMENTAL CONCEPTS
GENERALIZATION
HABIT FORMATION
HABITUATION

HEARING (PHYSIOLOGY)
IMITATION
INCIDENTAL LEARNING
INDUCTION
INFERENCES
INFORMATION SEEKING
INTELLECTUAL EXPERIENCE
INTENTIONAL LEARNING
INTUITION
KINESTHETIC METHODS
KINESTHETIC PERCEPTION
LEARNING
LEARNING EXPERIENCE
LEARNING MODALITIES
LEARNING MOTIVATION
LEARNING PLATEAUS
LEARNING PROBLEMS
LEARNING PROCESSES
LEARNING STRATEGIES
LISTENING COMPREHENSION
LOGICAL THINKING
LONG TERM MEMORY
MEDITATION
MEMORIZATION
MEMORY
METACOGNITION
MISCONCEPTIONS
MNEMONICS
MULTISENSORY LEARNING
NEGATIVE REINFORCEMENT
NONVERBAL LEARNING
NOVELTY (STIMULUS DIMENSION)
OBEDIENCE
OBJECT PERMANENCE
OBSERVATIONAL LEARNING
OPERANT CONDITIONING
OVERT RESPONSE
PAIRED ASSOCIATE LEARNING
PATTERNED RESPONSES
PERCEPTION
PERCEPTUAL MOTOR LEARNING
PICTORIAL STIMULI
PLANNING
POSITIVE REINFORCEMENT
PRAISE
PRESCHOOL LEARNING (1966 1980)
PRIMACY EFFECT
PRIOR LEARNING
PROBLEM SOLVING
PRODUCTIVE THINKING
PUPILLARY DILATION
READER RESPONSE
RECALL (PSYCHOLOGY)
RECOGNITION (PSYCHOLOGY)
REFERENCE GROUPS
REINFORCEMENT
REMINISCENCE
RETENTION (PSYCHOLOGY)
REVIEW (REEXAMINATION)
ROLE MODELS
ROTE LEARNING
SCHEMATA (COGNITION)
SELECTION
SENSORY DEPRIVATION

SENSORY EXPERIENCE
SENSORY INTEGRATION
SEQUENTIAL LEARNING
SERIAL LEARNING
SERIAL ORDERING
SHORT TERM MEMORY
SOCIAL COGNITION
SOCIAL REINFORCEMENT
STIMULATION
STIMULI
STIMULUS GENERALIZATION
SUGGESTOPEDIA
SYMBOLIC LEARNING
TACTILE STIMULI
TACTUAL PERCEPTION
THINKING SKILLS
TIME FACTORS (LEARNING)
TIME PERSPECTIVE
TIMEOUT
TOKEN ECONOMY
TRANSCENDENTAL MEDITATION
TRANSFER OF TRAINING
VALUE JUDGMENT
VERBAL LEARNING
VERBAL OPERANT CONDITIONING
VERBAL STIMULI
VISION
VISUAL ACUITY
VISUAL DISCRIMINATION
VISUAL LEARNING
VISUAL LITERACY
VISUAL PERCEPTION
VISUAL STIMULI
VISUALIZATION

120 INDIVIDUAL DEVELOPMENT

ABILITY
ACADEMIC ABILITY
ACADEMIC APTITUDE
ACADEMIC ASPIRATION
ACHIEVEMENT
ACHIEVEMENT NEED
ACTIVITIES
ADOLESCENT DEVELOPMENT
ADOLESCENTS
ADULT DEVELOPMENT
ADULTS
ADULTS (30 TO 45)
AFFECTION
AFFECTIVE BEHAVIOR
AFFILIATION NEED
AGE
AGE DIFFERENCES
AGE GROUPS
AGING (INDIVIDUALS)
ALTRUISM
ANDROGYNY
ANIMAL BEHAVIOR
APATHY
APTITUDE
ASPIRATION
ASSERTIVENESS
ASSOCIATION (PSYCHOLOGY)

Figure 4.8 Extract from descriptor group display, *Thesaurus of ERIC descriptors,* **13th edition**

In some retrieval situations the thesaurus is accessible online. It is possible to see how many times a term has been used in the database and how the term is related to other terms. Figure 4.9 shows a display of the ERIC thesaurus on Dialog. Examination of the term "educational planning" in the index (Expand educational planning) displays both the numbers of postings (11,495) and the number of related terms in the thesaurus (17). Use of the command Expand again, this time with the reference number (E3) for "Educational planning", (R2–R12) causes the related terms to be displayed. This display shows the terms' relationships to "educational planning" and their number of occurrences. In many online thesauri no link is provided from non-approved to approved terms, but the thesaurus may be used 'behind the scenes' in electronic products in a way which is impossible with their print equivalents. Considerable experimental work has been undertaken by Pollitt and colleagues, who have demonstrated how a thesaurus can be used in the search interface to provide a 'view' of the database and thus guide searchers in the development of searches. Their work involved creating search interfaces to the Medline and INSPEC databases using associated controlled vocabulary. They have also provided multilingual access to the documents of the European Parliament using a thesaurus-based interface (Pollitt, Ellis and Hosch, 1994; Pollitt, *et al.*, 1994). In the commercial environment, the Mintel CD-ROM incorporates a form of vocabulary control in its user interface so that a search term such as *'European Union'* is automatically linked with synonyms such as *'EU'*, *'EEC'*, *'Common Market'*, and items containing any of these terms are retrieved.

Classification schemes

Grouping together objects on the basis of some similar attribute is a widespread human activity. It has probably been undertaken since the earliest days of human life. The importance of classification can be illustrated by imagining the near impossibility of shopping at the local supermarket if the goods were not so arranged that similar products were found close together. As far as information retrieval is concerned, classification by subject has been a basic principle of *organization* in libraries since their earliest days. This *organization* is achieved using a classification scheme, of which the best known is the Dewey Decimal Classification (DDC) mentioned earlier in the chapter.

So-called enumerative classification schemes, such as Dewey and the Library of Congress Classification (LCC), seek to organize the whole world of knowledge into a hierarchy of subjects. Each subject is given a notation, which indicates its place in the hierarchy. Thus in the Dewey scheme, the whole spectrum of knowledge is divided into ten main classes and each of these is divided into narrower subjects. For example, one main class is science to which the notation 500 has been allocated and which is shown in Figure 4.10. As the process of subdivision is continued, more complex notations are used to represent more detailed subjects, as can be seen in the brief extract from the schedules of the Dewey Scheme for physics, in Figure 4.11. Documents and other information-bearing items are then assigned the notation which most accurately summarizes their content.

? expand educational planning

Ref	Items	RT	Index-term
E1	2		EDUCATIONAL PLAN GAME
E2	1		EDUCATIONAL PLANNING
E3	11495	17	*EDUCATIONAL PLANNING (PROCESS OF DETERMINING THE OBJECTIVES OF EDU...)
E4	1		EDUCATIONAL PLANNING COMMITTEES
E5	0	1	EDUCATIONAL PLANS
E6	2		EDUCATIONAL PLURALISM
E7	4		EDUCATIONAL POLICIES COMMISSION
E8	15019	18	EDUCATIONAL POLICY
E9	1		EDUCATIONAL POLICY INFORMATION CENTRE (UK)
E10	5		EDUCATIONAL POLICY RESEARCH CENTER
E11	1		EDUCATIONAL POLICY RESEARCH CENTERS
E12	1	1	EDUCATIONAL POLITICS

Enter P for PAGE for more

?e e3

Ref	Items	Type	RT	Index-term
R1	11495		17	*EDUCAIONAL PLANNING (PROCESS OF DETERMINING THE OBJECTIVES OF EDU...)
R2	0	U	1	ACADEMIC PLANNING
R3	0	U	1	EDUCATIONAL PLANS
R4	3790	N	10	COLLEGE PLANNING
R5	721	N	32	EDUCATIONAL FACILITIES PLANNING
R6	77793	B	46	PLANNING
R7	3190	R	16	ARTICULATION (EDUCATION)
R8	650398	R	146	EDUCATION
R9	8084	R	10	EDUCATIONAL ADMINISTRATION
R10	10443	R	27	EDUCATIONAL ASSESSMENT
R11	3699	R	18	EDUCATIONAL COOPERATION
R12	6549	R	19	EDUCATIONAL DEVELOPMENT

Enter P for PAGE for more

Figure 4.9   Use of the online thesaurus on ERIC during a search on Dialog

```
500  general sciences
510  mathematical sciences
520  astronomy and allied sciences
530  physics
540  chemistry
550  geology
560  palaeontology
570  life sciences
580  botany
590  zoology
```

Figure 4.10   Subdivisions of the main Class 500 Sciences in the Dewey Decimal Classification Scheme

Given the origins of classification as a means of keeping together in a library books on similar subjects rather than as an information retrieval device per se, this summarizing approach is understandable.

In addition to these general classification schemes which organize the whole sphere of knowledge into a hierarchy, many bibliographical database producers have developed highly specific classification schemes which cover only the field of knowledge of their database(s). Originally these were intended to enable the document representations to be grouped together by subject in a printed abstracting journal. In the electronic environment, however, they can be used as search aids to provide accurate retrieval. An item in a bibliographic database such as EMBASE or INSPEC might well have several classification codes assigned to it rather than a single summarizing classification code. Such database-specific classification schemes often provide very specific subject codes, thereby permitting the subject field of the database (medicine in the case of EMBASE and physics, computing and electrical and electronic engineering in the case of INSPEC) to be represented exhaustively. This can be seen by comparing the specificity of the vocabulary in the extract from the 1995 INSPEC classification scheme (Figure 4.12) with the more general vocabulary of the library classification schemes such as Dewey (Figure 4.11). The NAICS and SIC codes discussed earlier in the chapter are further examples of complex specific classification schemes.

Subject headings

Subject headings provide another alphabetical form of vocabulary control. Traditionally, lists of subject headings have been used to provide subject access to documents in a library catalogue. The most widely used subject headings scheme is the Library of Congress Subject Headings (LCSH). As its name implies, it was developed at the US Library of Congress initially for internal use in cataloguing books but has been widely adopted by many other libraries to provide vocabulary control and subject access in their catalogues. Like library classification schemes, a small number of subject statements, often only one, summarizes the entire content of a book. Thus

.382   Elasticity

                                 Variant names: elastic, temporary deformation

                                 Including elastic limit, coefficient of restitution

                                 Class here Hooke's law

                                 Class elastic vibrations in 531.32

.385   Plasticity

                                 Variant names: permanent, plastic deformation

.4   **Friction and viscosity of solids**

                      Standard subdivisions are added for either or both topics in heading

.5   **Mass and gravity of solids; projectiles**

                      Including laws of falling bodies

.54   Density and specific gravity

                                 Standard subdivisions are added for either or both topics in heading

.55   Projectiles

                                 Including trajectories [*formerly* 531.31]

                                 Class here ballistics

.6   **Energy**

                      Including momentum, work

                      Class comprehensive works on energy in physics in 530; class interdisciplinary works on energy in 333.79

.62   Conservation of energy

                                 Conservation of mass-energy relocated to 530.11

                                 See also 333.79 16 for programs to conserve energy

.68   Transformation

                                 Change in form of energy

                                       For a specific transformation, see the resultant form, e.g., transformation of light to heat 536

532   **Fluid mechanics   Liquid mechanics**

                      Class here hydraulics (hydromechanics)

                      For pneumatics, see 533

    .001-.009   Standard subdivisions

➢   532.02-532.05   Fluid statics and dynamics

                      Class comprehensive works in 532

.02   Statics

                      Including buoyancy

Figure 4.11   Extract from Dewey Decimal Classification Scheme for physics

A6770	**Films of quantum fluids and solids** *(inc. physical adsorption)* *1973-.*
A6780	**Solid helium and related quantum crystals**
A6780C	Lattice dynamics and sound propagation (solid helium/quantum crystals) *1973-. Before, use A6780*
A6780G	Thermal properties (solid helium/quantum crystals) *1973-. Before, use A6780*
A6780J	Magnetic properties and NMR (solid helium/quantum crystals) *1973-. Before, use A6780*
A6780M	Defects, impurities, and diffusion (solid helium/quantum crystals) *1977-. Before, use A6780*
A6790	**Other topics in quantum fluids and solids (e.g. neutron-star matter)** *1977-.*
A6800	**Surfaces and interfaces; thin films and whiskers** *for impact phenomena, see A79...; for physics of crystal growth, see A6150C;* *for corrosion, oxidation, and surface treatments, see A8160...*
A6810	**Fluid surfaces and interfaces with fluids** *(inc. surface tension, capillarity, wetting and related phenomena)* *1973-.*
A6810C	Fluid surface energy (surface tension, interface tension, angle of contact, etc.)
A6810E	Fluid interface elasticity, viscosity, and viscoelasticity *1977-.*
A6810G	Fluid interface activity, spreading *1977-.*
A6810J	Fluid kinetics (evaporation, adsorption, condensation, catalysis, etc.) *1977-.* *(see also A8265... Surface processes)*
A6815	**Liquid thin films** *1973-.*
A6817	**Monolayers and Langmuir-Blodgett films** *1992-. Before, use A6845..., A6855* *for adsorbed layers, see A6845...*
A6820	**Solid surface structure**
A6822	**Surface diffusion, segregation and interfacial compound formation** *1988-. 1973-87, use A6820, A6848*
A6825	**Mechanical and acoustical properties of solid surfaces and interfaces** *1973-.* *for tribology, see A6220P and A8140P*
A6830	**Dynamics of solid surfaces and interface vibrations** *1973-.*
A6840	**Surface energy of solids; thermodynamic properties**
A6842	**Surface phase transitions and critical phenomena** *1988-. Before, use A6820*
A6845	**Solid-fluid interface processes** *(see also A8265M Sorption and accommodation coefficients)*
A6845B	Sorption equilibrium at solid-fluid interfaces *1977-. Before, use A6845*
A6845D	Evaporation and condensation; interface adsorption and desorption kinetics *1977-. Before, use A6845*

Figure 4.12   Extract from INSPEC Classification Scheme for physics

Physicians, Muslim   *(May Subd Geog)*
  UF Islamic physicians
      Muslim physicians
Physicians, Occupational
  USE Occupational physicians
Physicians, Rating of
  USE Physicians—Rating of
Physicians, Ukrainian American
  USE Ukrainian American physicians
Physicians, Women
  USE Women physicians
Physicians (General practice)
  (May Subd Geog)
  ⌐R729.5.G4⌐
  UF General practice (Medicine)
      General practitioners
  BT Medicine—Practice
  RT Family medicine
      Medicine—Specialties and specialists
  — **Attitudes**
  — **Supply and demand**   *(May Subd Geog)*
      ⌐RA410.6-RA410.9⌐
Physicians (Roman law)
  BT Roman law
Physicians as artists   *(May Subd Geog)*
  BT Artists
      Medicine and art
Physicians as authors   *(May Subd Geog)*
  BT Authors
Physicians as musicians
  ⌐R707.3⌐
  BT Musicians
Physicians' assistants   *(May Subd Geog)*
  ⌐R697.P45⌐
    Here are entered works on personnel qualified to
  perform diagnostic and therapeutic procedures under
  the responsibility and supervision of a physician.
  Works on personnel who perform administrative and
  clerical duties in a physician's office and may assist
  in routine clinical procedures are entered under
  Medical assistants.
  UF Assistant medical officers
      Clinical assistants
      Feldshers
      Medex
      Physician extenders
      Physician support personnel
      Physicians' associates
      Physicians' extenders
  BT Allied health personnel
  NT Nurse practitioners
  — **Education**   *(May Subd Geog)*
      ⌐R847-R847.7⌐
      BT Paramedical education
  — **Supply and demand**   *(May Subd Geog)*
Physicians' associates
  USE Physicians' assistants
Physicians' bookplates   *(May Subd Geog)*
  UF Book-plates, Physicians'
      ⌐Former heading⌐
  BT Medical bookplates
Physicians' children
  USE Children of physicians
Physicians' extenders
  USE Physicians' assistants
Physicians in art
  USE Medicine and art
Physicians in literature   *(Not Subd Geog)*
  SA *subdivision* Characters—Physicians
      under names of authors, e.g.
      Shakespeare, William, 1564-1616—
      Characters—Physicans
Physicians in motion pictures
  BT Motion pictures
Physicians in television   *(May Subd Geog)*
  UF Physicians on television
  BT Television
Physicians' insurance
  USE Physicians—Insurance requirements
Physicians' liability insurance
  USE Insurance, Physicians' liability

Physicians' literary writings
  USE Physicians' writings
Physicians' literary writings, American
  USE Physicians' writings, American
Physicians' literary writings, Brazilian
  USE Physicians' writings, Brazilian
Physicians' literary writings, English
  USE Physicians' writings, English
Physicians' offices
  USE Medical offices
Physicians on postage stamps
  ⌐HE6183.P5⌐
  BT Postage stamps
Physicians on television
  USE Physicians in television
Physicians' spouses   *(May Subd Geog)*
  UF Physicians' wives
      ⌐Former heading⌐
  BT Spouses
Physicians' Strike, Israel, 1982
  BT Strikes and lockouts—Physicians—
      Israel
Physicians' wives
  USE Physicians' spouses
Physicians' writings
  UF Physicians' literary writings
      ⌐Former heading⌐
  BT Literature
Physicians' writings, American
  (May Subd Geog)
  UF American physicians' writings
      Physicians' literary writings, American
      ⌐Former heading⌐
  BT American literature
Physicians' writings, Arab
  USE Physicians' writings, Arabic
Physicians' writings, Arabic
  (May Subd Geog)
  UF Arabic physicians' writings
      Physicians' writings, Arab
      ⌐Former heading⌐
  BT Arabic literature
Physicians' writings, Brazilian
  (May Subd Geog)
  UF Brazilian physicians' writings
      Physicians' literary writings, Brazilian
      ⌐Former heading⌐
  BT Brazilian literature
Physicians' writings, English
  (May Subd Geog)
  UF English physicians' writings
      Physicians' literary writings, English
      ⌐Former heading⌐
  BT English literature
Physicians' writings, Spanish
  (May Subd Geog)
  UF Spanish physicians' writings
  BT Spanish literature
Physicists   *(May Subd Geog)*
  ⌐QC15-QC16⌐
  BT Scientists
  NT Astrophysicists
      Nuclear physicists
      Women physicists
  — **Biography**
Physics   *(May Subd Geog)*
  ⌐QC⌐
  UF Natural philosophy
      Philosophy, Natural
  BT Physical sciences
  RT Dynamics
  NT Agricultural physics
      Archaeological physics
      Astrophysics
      Ballistics
      Biophysics
      Capillarity
      Classification—Books—Physics
      Communication in physics
      Compressibility
      Conservation laws (Physics)

      Constraints (Physics)
      Cosmic physics
      Critical phenomena (Physics)
      Diffusion
      Electricity
      Evaporation
      Expansion (Heat)
      Field theory (Physics)
      Fluids
      Force and energy
      General relativity (Physics)
      Geophysics
      Gravitation
      Heat
      Information theory in physics
      Ions
      Lasers in physics
      Magnetism
      Mathematical physics
      Matter
      Mechanics
      Medical physics
      Mesoscopic phenomena (Physics)
      Microphysics
      Motion
      Motion pictures in physics
      Music—Acoustics and physics
      Nanostructures
      Nuclear physics
      Open systems (Physics)
      Optics
      Permeability
      Phenomenological theory (Physics)
      Physical metallurgy
      Pneumatics
      Psychophysics
      Quantum theory
      Radiation
      Radiology
      Relaxation phenomena
      Similarity (Physics)
      Solid state physics
      Sound
      Statics
      Statistical physics
      Sum rules (Physics)
      Superposition principle (Physics)
      Surfaces (Physics)
      Symmetry (Physics)
      Thermodynamics
      Viscosity
      Weights and measures
  — **Apparatus and instruments**
      USE Physical instruments
  — **Bibliography**
      RT Physics literature
  — **Congresses**
  — — **Attendance**
  — **Experiments**
      ⌐QC33⌐
      NT Electricity—Experiments
          Magnetism—Experiments
          Physics projects
  — **Formulae**
  — **Graphic methods**
  — **Information services**
  — Instruments
      USE Physical instruments
  — **Laboratory blanks**
      ⌐QC36⌐
  — **Laboratory manuals**
      ⌐QC35-QC37⌐
  — Mathematics
      USE Mathematical physics
  — **Philosophy**
      ⌐QC6⌐
      NT Causality (Physics)
  — **Religious aspects**
      ⌐BL265.P4⌐
  — — **Buddhism, ⌐Christianity, etc.⌐**
  — **Research**   *(May Subd Geog)*

Figure 4.13   Extract from LCSH for physics

the vocabulary of subject headings tends to be more general than that of thesauri. The vocabulary is presented as a set of terms, or headings, which might be qualified with a sub-heading. Unlike classification schemes, the vocabulary is not represented by a notation. Figure 4.13 shows a brief extract from LCSH, which illustrates the general nature of the vocabulary. The history of subject headings in general and LCSH in particular is beyond the scope of this book. Chan (1995) provides a full discussion.

While thesaurus creation is usually undertaken as a one-off activity with possibly some periodic updating, subject headings lists normally have developed over a period of time and with much less consistency. Consequently there is less predictability about the approved terms within the vocabulary as the following examples from LCSH illustrate. Some multi-word terms occur in natural language word order such as:

10th edition	11th edition
Child psychiatry (indirect)	Child psychiatry (may subd geog)
Here are entered works on the clinical and therapeutic aspects of mental disorders in children. Descriptive works on mental disorders of children are entered under Child psychopathology. Work on mentally ill children themselves are entered under Mentally ill children	Here are entered works on the clinical and therapeutic aspects of mental disorders in children. Descriptive works on mental disorders of children are entered under Child psychopathology. Work on mentally ill children themselves are entered under Mentally ill children
ss Adolescent psychiatry	
Autism	UF Children—Mental disorders
Child development deviations	Pediatric psychiatry
Child guidance clinics	Psychiatry, Child
Child mental health	BT Child mental health services
Child psychology	Pediatric neurology
Child psychopathology	Psychiatry
Child psychotherapy	RT Child mental health
Children of the mentally ill	Child psychology
Cognition disorders in children	Child psychopathology
Hysteria in children	NT Adolescent psychiatry
Infant psychiatry	Child development deviations
Mentally handicapped children	Child psychotherapy
Mentally ill children	Children of the mentally ill
Psychomotor disorders in children	Cognition disorders in children
Psychoses in children	Hysteria in children
Schizophrenia in children	Infant psychiatry
School phobia	Interviewing in child psychiatry
Sleep disorders in children	Mentally handicapped children
x Children—Mental disorders	Mentally ill children
Pediatric psychiatry	Psychomotor disorders in children
Psychiatry, Child	Psychoses in children
xx Child mental health	Schizophrenia in children
Child mental health services	Sleep disorders in children
Child psychology	
Child psychopathology	
Pediatric neurology	
Psychiatry	

Figure 4.14   Comparison of term display in the 10th and 11th editions of LCSH (after Lancaster and Warner)

Norwegian children's literature

while others involve some form of inversion for example:

Children's literature, Norwegian

The lack of a consistent inversion policy made the vocabulary unpredictable. Not only was the vocabulary in LCSH less consistent than in a typical thesaurus but relationships between terms were shown in a different manner from thesauri. Since its 1986 edition LCSH has replaced its traditional means of indicating relationships between subject headings with the BT, NT and RT method of cross-referencing which has been adopted from thesauri. The impact of this change is demonstrated in Figure 4.14, based upon Lancaster and Warner (1993); entries for child psychiatry are presented as subject headings in the left-hand column, and as thesaural term relationships in the right-hand column. The Library of Congress has now embarked upon considerable changes to its vocabulary with the intention of making it much more consistent. Thus it is reasonable to suppose that the differences between thesauri and subject headings will become less and less apparent in the future. Nevertheless the searcher needs to be aware of the inconsistencies in terminology associated with subject headings, since there will be many millions of items in library catalogues around the world which were created using the inconsistent terminology.

Controlled Vocabulary in Retrieval

It is possible now to examine how controlled vocabularies are used in the retrieval process.

Figure 4.15 shows a typical bibliographical record from the INSPEC database on Dialog. It includes two forms of controlled vocabulary: terms from the INSPEC thesaurus, which appear in the descriptor field, and the classification codes from the INSPEC classification scheme which appear in the class codes field. The database producer adds both these forms of subject representation to the record. It is a way of adding value to the data by making them more searchable through the presence of terms from the controlled vocabularies. As a result of adding these terms to the records in the database, the searcher can search either using natural language or controlled vocabulary or indeed a combination of the two. While the whole search process is considered in greater detail in Chapter 6 and the advantages of searching natural language are considered in the next section of this chapter, it is useful to consider the value of exploiting controlled vocabulary searching in retrieval.

It was noted earlier in this chapter that controlled vocabularies are intended to aid retrieval by providing consistency of representation. Thus, the theory goes, since the database producer has represented concepts in the predictable terminology of the controlled vocabulary then the searcher can look in that controlled vocabulary, discover the terms chosen to represent sought concepts and then use those terms in a search. This obviates the need

? t s3/9/1

3/9/1
DIALOG(R)File   2:INSPEC
(c) 1998 Institution of Electrical Engineers. All rts. reserv.

5816599 INSPEC Abstract Number: C9803-6130B-015
  Title: Selective culling of discontinuity lines
  Author(s): Hedley, D.; Worrall, A.; Paddon, D.
  Author Affiliation: Dept. of Comput. Sci., Bristol Univ., UK
  Conference Title: Rendering Techniques '97. Proceedings of the Eurographics Workshop.
Eurographics   p.69-80, 329
  Editor(s): Dorsey. J.; Slusallek, P.
  Publisher: Springer-Verlag, Wien, Austria
  Publication Date: 1997 Country of Publication: Austria ix+342 pp.
  ISBN: 3 211 83001 4   Material Identity Number: XX98-00033
  Conference Title: Rendering Techniques '97. Proceedings of the Eurographics Workshop.
Eurographics
  Conference Date: 16-18 June 1997 Conference Location: St. Etienne, France
  Availability: Zinna Castro, ACM, 1515 Broadway, New York, NY 10036-9998, USA
  Language: English   Document Type: Conference Paper (PA)
  Treatment: Practical (P)
  Abstract: In recent years discontinuity meshing has become an important part of mesh based solutions
to the global illumination problem. Application of this technique accurately locates all radiance
function discontinuities in the scene and is essential for limiting visual artifacts. In an environment
containing m edges there are $O(m/sup\ 2)$ D/sup 1/ and D/sup 2/ discontinuities. With a typical scene
this can result in many thousands of discontinuity lines being processed. We review existing methods
for reducing these lines and introduce an improved, perception based metric for determining which
discontinuities are important and which can safely be ignored. Our results show that a 50% or more
reduction in the number of discontinuity lines can be achieved with a corresponding reduction in
general mesh complexity, with little or no perceptible change to the rendered result. (21 Refs)
  Descriptors: brightness; computational complexity; lighting; mesh generation; rendering (computer
graphics)
  Identifiers: selective culling; discontinuity lines; discontinuity meshing; mesh based solutions; global
illumination problem; radiance function discontinuities; visual artifacts; perception based metric;
general mesh complexity; rendered result
  Class Codes: C6130B (Graphics techniques); C4240C (Computational complexity); C4260
(Computational geometry)
  Copyright 1998, IEE

Figure 4.15   A record from the INSPEC database on Dialog

to think of all the potential synonyms, near synonyms, quasi-synonyms or
word variants that might be present in the database. It is this consistency of
representation that is seen as the greatest advantage of controlled vocabularies. An additional advantage is that term relationships can be displayed to
aid the development or amendment of a search, for example by suggesting
terms which can be used to broaden or narrow the search (see Chapter 6).

In practice, restricting a search to controlled terms from the thesaurus
rather than using natural-language terms found anywhere in the database
is likely to reduce the number of items retrieved and almost certainly also
to increase the precision of the search. These notions are considered in
greater depth in Chapter 6 and the question of search precision is developed more fully in Chapter 10.

Research by Markey, Atherton and Newton (1980) indicates that the use of a thesaurus has a significant influence on the outcome of a search in the ERIC database containing bibliographic information about education publications. They investigated the use of the ERIC thesaurus in some 650 searches by experienced searchers. They noted that the thesaurus was used in about 68 percent of searches. Analysis of these searches suggested the thesaurus increased the precision performance of the search and natural language improved the recall performance. Fidel (1991) has undertaken a lengthy study which indicates that *experienced* searchers make considerable use of controlled vocabulary in their searches. They do so according to a small number of rules of thumb of which examples are:

If the sought term maps directly to a descriptor then use that descriptor
If the concept has many synonyms then use a descriptor
If the concept is not clear to the searcher then use a descriptor

These rules of thumb, together with several relating to the use of natural language and indeed the combination of the two language types, have been merged into a search term selection routine. However, it must be emphasized that there is no proven relationship between these rules of thumb and search outcome or search effectiveness.

Most research into the relative advantages of controlled vocabulary and natural language has been undertaken with bibliographic databases. Such databases include only a limited amount of natural language – typically a title and a short abstract. Little is known about the value of controlled vocabularies for retrieval from full-text databases. It was generally supposed that the large number of natural-language terms available for searching would lead to successful retrieval. However, Duckitt (1981) has marshalled arguments in favour of the use of controlled vocabularies in full-text databases. Gillaspie (1995) has undertaken a preliminary analysis of retrieval failure in full-text legal retrieval systems and ascribes retrieval failure to the complexity of language. For example 'false drops' were frequently caused by either homonyms or by 'correct meaning, wrong context', such as a judge mentioning a case or an issue in the negative to state that the court did not intend to discuss it. The failure to retrieve relevant material was frequently caused by linguistic phenomena such as the presence of synonyms or the occurrence in texts of anaphora (a later abbreviated reference to an earlier occurring entity). Furthermore, the use of terminology of a different specificity adversely affects retrieval. So, for example, a document which referred solely to a specific life-saving technique such as dialysis would not be retrieved if the searcher used only the more general term 'life sustaining'. The ease with which irrelevant material is retrieved with Internet search engines suggests the need for the use of controlled vocabularies. However, suggestions and arguments are no substitute for facts; there is a need for further research to build on Gillaspie's initial efforts to ascertain whether or not controlled vocabularies aid full-text retrieval.

Classification schemes are used in retrieval in a number of ways. Many library OPACs offer classification codes as one search option. In practice, however, this option is not often used by library patrons, probably because they do not understand either the notation or its potential for retrieval.

In a large bibliographic database such as INSPEC, classification codes are useful to restrict the scope of the search. INSPEC covers several disciplines: physics, electronics, computer science and information science. The last comprises only a small proportion of the items in the database. A search for items within information science can include as one of the search criteria the classification code C72#. C72 is the main classification code for information science and the truncation symbol # enables the search to retrieve any of the subdivisions of class C72. Other search criteria can then be combined with this classification code to find items dealing with, say, interfaces but only in the information science literature and not the computer science literature.

Problems with Controlled Vocabulary

The notion that controlled vocabulary improves retrieval by imposing a consistent representation of subjects sounds fine in theory. Considerable experimental investigation (see Chapter 10) has, however, failed to demonstrate this improved retrieval performance in practice. There are several reasons for this.

First, by restricting the vocabulary to one or several approved terms, the specificity of natural language is lost. In practice concepts are represented by the most appropriate term in the controlled vocabulary. As a consequence items might be indexed by a term which does not exactly match the concept. For example, in a thesaurus for a database on the subject of leisure the most precise term might be football. This term would then have to be used to index items about American football, Australian rules football, soccer and possibly rugby football too. Inevitably there would be considerable loss in specificity and increased opportunities for retrieval of unwanted information. Furthermore antonyms, such as roughness and smoothness, might be indexed under the same term thus leading to loss of precision.

Second, even the exhaustive indexing referred to earlier (that is, at least ten terms per item) results in a dramatic reduction in terms compared with the hundreds or thousands of natural language words found in many database records. All of these terms are available for searching when natural rather than controlled language is used.

Third, controlled language is not the language of discourse within the subject field. It is an artificial language created by information specialists. As such, it can never reflect completely the current terminology in the field. By its very nature a controlled vocabulary cannot be continuously amended but only occasionally updated or else control is jeopardized. A term must be accepted into the discipline before it is added to the controlled vocabulary. Research has shown that the controlled languages of retrieval systems are not necessarily understood or used effectively by experts within the given fields (Bates, 1977).

Fourth, it is difficult to determine the subject of a document and to assign several controlled terms to represent that subject. In practice indexers are not always consistent in assigning the same controlled terms to the represent the same concept. This is known to occur both between different indexers and the same indexer on different occasions (Cooper, 1969).

Finally, Oppenheim (1993) notes that thesauri are expensive to create and maintain. Furthermore the subject analysis necessary to assign controlled terms to a document is slow work and must be undertaken by specialists with the appropriate subject knowledge. For such reasons, they are only used in a minority of commercially available databases. It is interesting to note, however, that the expansion of the Web has been accompanied by numerous attempts, not confined to the information community, to introduce controlled vocabulary to improve search performance. One example is the use of the well-established *Art and Architecture Thesaurus* by the developers of the ADAM gateway to art, design and media sources on the Internet.

The Natural Language Alternative

The alternative to controlled vocabulary for searching is natural language. However, the unfettered combination of natural language terms can lead to the retrieval of unexpected and unwanted items. To take a frequently used example, the combination of the words *venetian* and *blind* could lead to the retrieval of documents about coverings for windows or about sight-less inhabitants of an Italian city. While this example is clever and may be amusing, in reality, of course, few commercial databases contain material about both interior decoration and ophthalmology. Therefore both possible interpretations are unlikely to exist in the one database. However, this example does illustrate the problem of terms occurring in a document with ambiguous semantic relationships. More realistic examples might be the terms *school library* and *table water*, both of which have rather different meanings when the word order is reversed. Such potential problems in natural language searching occur especially in databases with comprehensive subject coverage such as many OPACs or Web search engines.

Natural-language searching requires effort on the part of the searcher to think of likely synonyms, near synonyms, antonyms and spelling variants. Failure to do so is likely to result in the search failing to retrieve many relevant items.

Notwithstanding these arguments, natural language has its obvious advantages. First and foremost, it is the language of communication of searchers within the subject. Searchers can use the nuances of meaning which are found in natural language. Natural language enables greater specificity in searching. It is also more adaptable to change as new words and phrases emerge in the specialist vocabulary of a discipline. Using natural language saves the searcher the need to access and understand the function and operation of a thesaurus. Natural language enables the searcher to use more search terms and the database producer is spared the expense of thesaurus creation and maintenance.

It is interesting to carry out a search for the terms *blind* and *venetian* on three very different electronic information sources. A search on the large COPAC database which contains the details of books in some of the major university libraries in the UK (http://copac.ac.uk/copac/) and the OPAC of a typical public library service (http://libcat.suffolkcc.gov.uk) produced no postings for the combination of the terms *blind* and *venetian*. However, a search on

Infoseek (http://ultra.infoseek.com) produced several hundred items. These included information about venetian blinds, disability research units, blind people regaining sight and even the history of information retrieval. These findings could be used by both the proponents of natural language and of controlled vocabularies to argue the merits of one approach over the other. Thus it is perhaps no surprise that in the practical world of information retrieval, information specialists have reacted pragmatically and used a mixture of both natural language and controlled vocabulary in their searching.

Citations for Representation and Retrieval

One attempt to overcome the retrieval problems caused by the complexity of language, both natural and controlled, uses citations. The Institute for Scientific Information (ISI) in Philadelphia has compiled a series of data-bases: Science Citation Index, Social Science Citation Index, and Arts and Humanities Citation Index. Most academic writings contain references (that is citations) to other academic publications. This might be to indicate where more detailed information can be located on the topic, to support the choice of methodology or equipment, to refer to a theory, or to challenge an argument presented in another publication. ISI databases take advantage of this fact by using such citations as indexes to that writing. Citation indexing is based upon the idea that the searcher can start with a known publication which is relevant to an information need and then search for those items which have cited (i.e. quoted) the known item. That is to say, the searcher can pose the query 'which papers have cited paper x that I know to be relevant to my work'. In practice it is possible to search for items which have cited all the works of a known author, or all the works of a known author published in a particular year or which have cited a particular paper. It is also possible to attempt to seek more precision by retrieving items which have cited relevant paper *a* and relevant paper *b*. One example of a citation search statement is:

cited reference = beheshti_j 1996,15, 231

that is to say which papers have cited a paper whose first-named author is J. Beheshti and which was published in 1996 in volume 15 of a journal and which started on page 231. ISI has taken the view that it is so unlikely that there would be more than one occurrence of author's name, year, volume and starting-page number but in different journals, that it is unnecessary to include the journal name in a cited reference search. Figure 4.16. shows the 44 items retrieved when the Science Citation Index was searched on the BIDS service for those items which cite the author Gary Marchionini. Figure 4.17 shows the first few of the 17 items which cited Marchionini's 1995 book *Information Seeking in Electronic Environments*.

Problems with Proper Names

So far this discussion of language and retrieval has concentrated on subject searching. However, variations in the way in which proper names may be

BIDS ISI Citation Display

| Easy Search | Advanced Search | Citation Search | Display Current Result Set | Display Marked List | Save/Retrieve Searches | Help! | News & Info |

Logout

The search found 44 cited references.

| Retrieve articles which cite checked references | Retrieve articles which cite any of these refs. |

displaying the fields from articles retrieved

Copyright 1998, Institute for Scientific Information Inc.

```
MARCHIONINI_G, IN PRESS J AM SOC IN   (2 refs )
MARCHIONINI_G, IN PRESS MAKING TRAN  (1 refs )
MARCHIONINI_G, 1985, ED258585  (1 refs )
MARCHIONINI_G, 1987, Vol.30, CACM  (1 refs )
MARCHIONINI_G, 1987, Vol.12, CAN J INF SCI   (1 refs )
MARCHIONINI_G, 1987, Vol.12, CANADIAN J INFORMATI   (5 refs )
MARCHIONINI_G, 1988, COMPUTER   (4 refs )
MARCHIONINI_G, 1988, Vol.21, COMPUTER   (13 refs )
MARCHIONINI_G, 1988, Vol.3, COMPUTER   (1 refs )
MARCHIONINI_G, 1988, ED TECHNOLOGY    NOV   (2 refs )
MARCHIONINI_G, 1988, EDUC TECHNOL  (1 refs )
MARCHIONINI_G, 1988, Vol.28, EDUC TECHNOL   (6 refs )
MARCHIONINI_G, 1988, Vol.19, IEEE COMPUT   (2 refs )
MARCHIONINI_G, 1988, Vol.20, IEEE COMPUT   (1 refs )
MARCHIONINI_G, 1988, Vol.21, IEEE COMPUT   (17 refs )
MARCHIONINI_G, 1988, Vol.19, IEEE COMPUTER   (1 refs )
MARCHIONINI_G, 1988, IEEE COMPUTER    JAN   (9 refs )
MARCHIONINI_G, 1988, IN PRESS CANADIAN J   (1 refs )
MARCHIONINI_G, 1988, IN PRESS INT J MAN M   (1 refs )
MARCHIONINI_G, 1989, 5 HARV U PERS PROJ W   (2 refs )
MARCHIONINI_G, 1989, Vol.30, INT J MAN MACH STUD   (6 refs )
MARCHIONINI_G, 1989, Vol.40, J AM SOC INFORM SCI   (9 refs )
MARCHIONINI_G, 1989, Vol.29, J EDUC LIBR INF SCI   (1 refs )
MARCHIONINI_G, 1989, REPORT PERSEUS PROJE   (1 refs )
MARCHIONINI_G, 1990, 53RD P ANN M AM SOC   (1 refs )
MARCHIONINI_G, 1990, DESIGNING HYPERMEDIA   (2 refs )
MARCHIONINI_G, 1990, Vol.23, P 53 AM SOC INF SCI   (1 refs )
MARCHIONINI_G, 1990, PERSEUS ANN REPORT E   (1 refs )
MARCHIONINI_G, 1991, Vol.16, CAN J INFORM SCI   (1 refs )
MARCHIONINI_G, 1991, Vol.16, CANADIAN J INFORMATI   (2 refs )
MARCHIONINI_G, 1991, INTERFACES INFORMATI   (1 refs )
MARCHIONINI_G, 1991, Vol.28, P ASIS ANNU MEET   (1 refs )
MARCHIONINI_G, 1991, Vol.24, SIGCHI B   (1 refs )
MARCHIONINI_G, 1992, Vol.43, J AM SOC INFORM SCI   (5 refs )
MARCHIONINI_G, 1993, Vol.15, LIBR INFORM SCI RES   (2 refs )
MARCHIONINI_G, 1993, SPARKS INNOVATION HU   (3 refs )
MARCHIONINI_G, 1994, Vol.12, ACM T INFORM SYST   (2 refs )
MARCHIONINI_G, 1994, CHALLENGES INDEXING   (1 refs )
MARCHIONINI_G, 1994, CR4569 NASA   (1 refs )
MARCHIONINI_G, 1994, Vol.45, J AM SOC INFORM SCI   (2 refs )
MARCHIONINI_G, 1995, CAMBRIDGE SERIES HUM   (1 refs )
MARCHIONINI_G, 1995, Vol.38, COMMUN ACM   (4 refs )
MARCHIONINI_G, 1995, INFORMATION SEEKING   (14 refs )
MARCHIONINI_G, 1996, P 59 ANN M AM SOC IN   (1 refs )
```

Figure 4.16   Result of a search for cited author on BIDS ISI

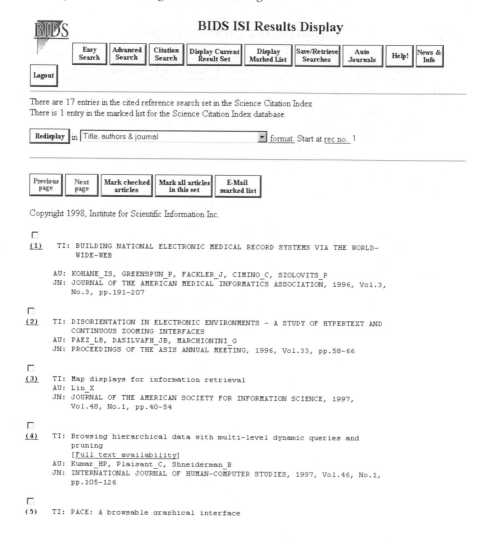

Figure 4.17   **Partial display of items citing a particular reference on BIDS ISI**

expressed can also cause problems for retrieval. Recalling that retrieval operates by matching character strings, it is easy to appreciate that there can be problems in retrieval by name. For example, the names of the authors of this book might be found in several forms, such as:

Hartley, Dick
Hartley, R. J.
Hartley, Richard J.
Hartley, Richard John

Large, Andrew
Large, Andy
Large, J. A.
Large, J. Andy
Large, J. Andrew
Tedd, L. A.
Tedd, Lucy
Tedd, Lucy A.

It should be noted that these variants have been presented with consistent use of punctuation and spacing. If the possible variations of these are taken into account, there is scope for even greater variety in the ways that names occur in databases.

The potential for retrieval failure caused by name variants becomes more complex when pseudonyms, compound surnames, saints, rulers and romanized versions of names from non-Roman scripts are taken into account. A few examples will suffice to indicate the scope for retrieval failure. The artist known throughout most of the world as El Greco has the proper name Domenikos Theotokopoulos. The correct name of the well-known composer is Ludwig van Beethoven, and the proper name of the author Lewis Carroll is Charles Lutwidge Dodgson. There is considerable opportunity here for the unwary searcher to fail to retrieve required material. Cornell (1989) reports that with variations in transliteration into the Roman alphabet the famous Greek poet C.P. Cavafy appears in a file intended to standardize names in no fewer than nine different guises:

Cavafy, C. P. (Constantine P.)
Kabaphes, Konstantinos Petrou
Cavafy, Constantine P.
Kavafis, Konstantin
Cavafis, Constantinos
Kavaphes, Konstantinos Petrou
Kavafis, Konstantinos Petrou
Kavafis, Constantino
Kavafis, Konstandinos

There is a similar problem with the names of organizations and their abbreviations. The structure of government departments changes regularly to reflect both societal developments and differing political priorities. To take an example from the UK, in the summer of 1997 the Department of National Heritage became the Department of Culture, Media and Sport. In a similar manner the names of companies frequently change to reflect changes in ownership and/or direction. For example, the well-known search service Dialog has been known as Lockheed Dialog, Dialog and KR Dialog. Since its acquisition by MAID it is now The Dialog Corporation. Finally, place names might occur in many variants. A good example is the relationship between England, Britain, Great Britain, GB, G.B., British Isles, United Kingdom, U.K. and UK. A further complication is that place names may occur either in the form by which they are known in a particular country or by their English name. The north European country may be known as Finland or Suomi. The River Danube is known as the Donau in Germany and Austria, as the Dunaj in the Czech Republic and Slovakia, the Duna in Hungary, the Dunerea in Romania and the Dunay in Russia. The capital of Greece might be referred to as Athens or Athinai (a search on AltaVista produced 57,360 occurrences of the English-language spelling and 636 of the transliterated Greek spelling). While the English-language version of the Athens search retrieved far more items than the Greek version, many were irrelevant since they were items about Athens (Georgia) in the US.

Some software systems help the searcher in this. The CDS/ISIS package, for instance, has a facility known as ANY which enables a collective name to be assigned to a group of search terms, e.g. ANY UK could be used to match with U.K., G.B., Great Britain, etc.

While some database creators impose some control over the way in which author names are presented, it is by no means the case that different database producers will apply exactly the same rules. Accordingly there is considerable onus on the searcher to think about possible name variants which may occur in a given resource. Wherever possible, it is advisable to check any available print or electronic guidance for information on the manner in which proper names are presented and to search accordingly. It may be necessary to accept the retrieval of some irrelevant material in order to retrieve the relevant. Wherever possible it may be sensible to combine a name with some other retrieval criteria such as subject, date or language.

Representing Images for Retrieval

In many fields, images are very important: obvious examples are architecture, art history, journalism and medicine. Thus it is no surprise that there is a long history of indexing images in slide libraries, newspaper libraries and picture research companies. Traditionally this has been achieved using conventional controlled vocabularies such as the *Art and Architecture Thesaurus* or the ICONCLASS classification scheme. While these schemes can do an acceptable job, there is a need for considerable human effort in the assignment of index terms. For example, Davis (1998) of Corbis Corporation, a leading provider of images to a wide range of clients, reported that Corbis cataloguers could process only 50 to 180 images per day. The figure depends upon the complexity of the images. Given that their collection contains 1,500,000 images, the cost of cataloguing them was enormous.

The advent of images on CD-ROM and particularly on the Web has stimulated considerable interest in image retrieval and the information needs of image users. Given the considerable cost of human indexing and cataloguing of images referred to above, researchers have investigated automatic means of image retrieval and thus the field of content-based image retrieval (CBIR) has developed. CBIR systems have been developed which retrieve images on the basis of colour or texture or shape and present the images in a ranked order to the user. Colour and texture can be remarkably useful in retrieval and systems such as VIRAGE are now available (http://www.virage.com). Experiments have been conducted into the viability of retrieving art images using these techniques (Holt and Hardwick, 1994).

Shape too has been shown to be effective in retrieval. For example, Eakins, Boardman and Shields (1996) have developed ARTISAN, a system which matches a candidate trademark against a database of trademark shapes and ranks the images in the database by similarity with the candidate image. ARTISAN represents a trademark by a mixture of shape features such as boundaries and the presence of various shapes such as straight lines and curves.

There have been impressive achievements in content-based image retrieval (CBIR). However, there remains a large gap between the retrieval achievable by CBIR and the sort of retrieval which users wish to undertake. Enser (1993) and Armitage and Enser (1997) have investigated users' image information needs by investigating the queries posed to a range of image collections. Examples of complex queries which they noted include:

the depiction of vanity in painting
Victorian paintings on, or incorporating the subject of 'invention'
people who are phobic about new technology
industrial health

However, many queries are much more straightforward such as requests for pictures of named people, places or types of buildings. Nevertheless, there remains a considerable gap between the ability of CBIR systems to retrieve by similarity of colour or shape or texture and the expressed needs of image users.

Eakins (1996) has described this problem by referring to three levels of image retrieval. He refers to level 1 as retrieval by primitive features such as colour or shape or texture or spatial location of image elements (e.g., find all items with a yellow star in a ring on a blue background). Level 2 can be thought of as retrieval by attributes of the image such as the objects depicted in the image (e.g. find pictures of a train crossing a bridge). Level 3 would involve retrieval based on abstract attributes or on a high degree of reasoning about the meaning of an image (e.g. find pictures of English folk dancing). This would require considerable interpretation about what the figures in an image are doing. Arguably, the problem is even more complex in the art world where many images are used to depict such intangibles as emotions.

The challenge for image retrieval is to develop means of bridging the gap between retrieval at level 1 by automatic means and retrieval at levels 2 and 3, which is what users require. Until CBIR can deal with the higher level queries then the costly human indexing of images will be necessary.

A particular problem for CBIR is that, despite Enser's work, there is little or no understanding of how users wish to put queries to an image retrieval system. While researchers can develop and test retrieval algorithms without attention to user presentation of information needs, this latter work must be undertaken before usable systems can be developed. Preliminary work is underway in the design of interfaces to CBIR systems (Venters, Eakins and Hartley, 1997).

Summary

This chapter has sought to demonstrate the complexity of text-based retrieval caused by linguistic diversity, as well as the complexity of representing images. Some of the most important approaches taken to overcome the problems caused by this complexity have been explained. The process of searching will be examined in greater detail in Chapter 6.

References and Further Reading

Armitage, L.H. and Enser, P.G.B. (1997) Analysis of user need in image archives. *Journal of Information Science*, **23**(4), 287–99

Bates, M.J. (1977) Factors affecting subject catalog search success. *Journal of the American Society for Information Science*, **28**(3), 161–9

Bryson, B. (1990) *Mother Tongue the English Language*. London: Penguin

Chan, L.M. (1995*) Library of Congress Subject Headings: Principles and Applications* 3rd edn. Englewood, CO: Libraries Unlimited

Cooper,W.S. (1969) Is interindexer consistency a hobgoblin? *American Documentation*, **20**(3), 266–78

Cornell, E. (1989) Greek, computers and libraries. *Library Review*, **38**(5), 7–13

Davis, I. (1998) Corbis: a new way of looking at the world. Paper presented at The Challenge of Image Retrieval. Newcastle upon Tyne, United Kingdom, 5–6 February 1998

Duckitt, P. (1981) The value of controlled indexing systems in online full text databases. *Proceedings of the 5th International Online Information Meeting*. Oxford: Learned Information, 447–53

Eakins, J.P. (1996) Automatic image content retrieval – are we getting anywhere? *Proceedings of the 3rd International Conference on Electronic Library and Visual Information Research (ELVIRA3). De Montfort University, Milton Keynes, May 1996.* London: Aslib, 123–35

Eakins, J.P., Boardman, J. and Shields K. (1996) Retrieval of trademark images by shape feature. The ARTISAN project. *IEE Colloquium on Intelligent Image Databases*. London: IEE (Institution of Electrical Engineers)

Enser, P.G.B. (1993) Query analysis in a visual information retrieval context. *Journal of Document and Text Management*, **1**(1), 28–52

Fidel, R. (1991) Searchers' selection of search keys: II. Controlled vocabulary or free-text searching. *Journal of the American Society for Information Science*, **42**(7), 501–14

Gillaspie, D.L. (1995) The role of linguistic phenomena in retrieval performance. *Proceedings of the 58th Annual Meeting of the American Society for Information Science.* **32**. Medford, NJ: Information Today. 90–96

Holt, B. and Hardwick L. (1994) Retrieving art images by image content: the UC Davis QBIC project. *Aslib Proceedings*, **46**(10), 243–8

Lancaster, F.W. (1977) Vocabulary control in information retrieval systems. *Advances in Librarianship*, **7**, 1–40

Lancaster, F.W. (1979) *Information Retrieval Systems Characteristics, Testing and Evaluation* 2nd edn. New York: John Wiley

Lancaster, F.W. (1986) *Vocabulary Control in Information Retrieval* 2nd edn. Arlington,VA: Information Resources Press

Lancaster, F.W. and Warner, A.J. (1993) *Information Retrieval Today*. Arlington,VA: Information Resources Press

McClure, C. (1976) Subject and added entries as access to information. *Journal of Academic Librarianship*, **2**(1), 9–14

Markey, K. Atherton, P. and Newton, C. (1980) An analysis of controlled vocabulary and free text search statements in online searches. *Online Review*, **4**(3), 225–36

Meadow, C.T. (1973) *The Analysis of Information Systems* 2nd edn. Los Angeles: Melville Publishing

Mischo, W. (1982) Library of Congress subject headings: a review of the problems and prospects for improved subject access. *Cataloging and Classification Quarterly,* 1(2/3), 105–124

Oppenheim, C. (1993) Has free text searching rendered the thesaurus redundant? *Journal of Document and Text Management,* 1(2), 115–23

Pollitt, A.S., *et al.* (1994) Peek-a-boo revived – end-user searching of bibliographic databases using filtering views. *Online Information 94: Proceedings of the 18th International Online Information Meeting.* Oxford: Learned Information, 63–74

Pollitt, A.S., Ellis, G.P. and Hosch, I. (1994) Improving search quality using thesauri for query specification and the presentation of search results. In H. Albrechtsen and S. Oernager (eds) *Knowledge Organization and Quality Management. Proceedings of the 3rd ISKO conference, 20–24 June 1994 Copenhagen, Denmark.* Frankfurt/Main: Indeks Verlag, 382–9

Venters, C.C., Eakins, J.P. and Hartley, R.J. (1997) The user interface and content-based image retrieval systems. In D. Harper and J. Furner (eds) *Proceedings of the 19th BCS-IRSG Colloquium on Information Retrieval Research Aberdeen, April 1997.* London: Springer Verlag. Also available at http://www.springer.co.uk/ewic/workshops/IRR97/

Vickery, A. and Brooks H.M. (1987) PLEXUS: the expert system for referral. *Information Processing and Management,* 23(2), 97–117

CHAPTER 5

Information Organization

Introduction

A distinction is drawn in this book between searching for information, which is discussed in Chapter 6, and browsing for information, which is discussed in Chapter 7. Some electronic information sources are organized and store information to aid searching while others store information in a manner which aids browsing. An appreciation of how information is organized in databases can help information-seeking strategies by showing what goes on 'behind the scenes' when, for example, a Boolean matching operation is executed. Generally, the more structured the information the more amenable it is to searching while less structured information can be presented in a manner which promotes browsing. This chapter provides a non-technical overview of how databases are structured to promote searching and how hypermedia structures, which promote browsing, operate. While multimedia information sources abound, currently the searching and browsing facilities normally are based upon textual information contained in those products and not on the sound or images. The role of metadata for electronic resource description and discovery is increasingly important and so the final part of the chapter examines metadata and its potential.

An important part of organizing information for retrieval is the creation of the index. In this book, the verb 'to index' is used in different ways. In the previous chapter, it was used to mean the selection of terms by a human indexer to represent the subject content of an item. In this chapter, it refers to the automatic creation of entries in an index to enable a database to be searched.

Databases

The textual information found on a CD-ROM or a search service, such as Dialog or Questel, is stored as a database: that is as an organized collection of data. The database consists of the data themselves and a series of associated indexes which exist to make those data readily searchable. As described in Chapter 3 a database will generally be of a particular type, namely source (numeric, full text or text numeric) or reference (bibliographic or directory). However, some databases contain a mixture of bibliographic data and the full text. One example is the ABI/Inform database which comprises 1.3 million bibliographic records and the full text of papers from about 1,000 business journals.

The basic unit of a database is the record. Each record in a database contains all the information about a single item. For example, each record in a patents database contains all the information about a single patent. Similarly each record in an online encyclopaedia contains one article, and the information about each chemical product in a database of agrochemicals is contained in a single record. Records, therefore, contain a different set of data depending on the type of information being stored.

Records are divided into a number of separate fields, each field containing one element of information in the record. For example, in a database of company information the name of the company, its address, its directors, products and turnover would each be stored in different fields. While there may be minor variations in the information stored about different items in the same database, the structure in which that information is stored will normally be the same. For example, some records in a company information database may include the details of the parent company which owns the company in question, whereas in other records these data will be inappropriate because the company concerned does not have a parent company. Nevertheless the structure of the different records would be the same.

There can be considerable differences between record structures in various databases although these databases are found on the same search service. This is demonstrated in Figures 5.1 to 5.4 which show four types of record taken from different databases available from The Dialog Corporation. Figure 5.1 shows a typical record from Aquatic Sciences and Fisheries Abstracts (ASFA), a database concerning the science, technology and management of the aquatic environment. It includes many fields which are typical of STM bibliographic databases, namely, title (TI), author (AU), corporate source (CS), source (SO), publication year (PY), language (LA), document type (DT), abstract (AB) and descriptor (DE). Additionally it includes some fields which are unusual, such as summary language (SL) and section heading (SH). Finally, it includes a small number of fields which are probably unique to this database. The environment field (EN) is used to indicate the aquatic environment (e.g. freshwater, marine etc.) under consideration while the CI field is used to indicate which of the many cooperating centres created the record.

Figure 5.2 is an example of a record in a company information database based upon KOMPASS Canada, which provides business information,

Field label	Field
AA=	ASFA Accession Number: 4066242
TI=	Sea cucumbers: Current fisher and prospects for aquaculture
AU=	Hamel, J.-F.; Mercier, A.
CS=	Societe d'Exploration et dFe valorisation de l'Environnement, 90 Notre-Dame Est, Rimouski (Quebec), Canada G5L 1Z6
SO=	Aquaculture Magazine "AQUACULT.MAG.", vol. 23, no. 1, p. 42–53
PY=	1997
SN=	ISSN: 0199–1388
LA=	Language: English
SL=	SUMMARY LANGUAGE: English
DT=	DOCUMENT TYPE: JOURNAL ARTICLE
CI=	ASFA INPUT CENTER NUMBER: CS9713350
AB=	Even though sea cucumbers have been harvested commercially for at least 1000 years, the current fisheries pertaining to the product remain scarcely documented and, in general, poorly managed. Close parents of sea stars and sea urchins, sea cucumbers are quite common on sand, silt and rocky bottoms around the world. A lot of species colonize the intertidal zone and sublittoral while others are found in deeper trenches of the ocean floor. Of the hundreds of species listed, only a few dozens are harvested for commercial purpose; the others are usually too small or their flesh toxic. Like those of most echinoderms, sea cucumber fisheries are generally developed on a small scale and cater to the Asian countries. Sea cucumber meat is said to contain beneficial chemicals that many believe to have healing properties which may cure certain forms of cancer, and be used in anti-bacterial and anti-fungal treatments.
DE=	DESCRIPTORS: aquaculture development; echinoderm fisheries; fishery products; Holothuroidea
EN=	ENVIRONMENT: MARINE
SH=	SECTION HEADING: 01584 Aquaculture: Culture of other aquatic animals
FS=	FILE SEGMENT: ASFA 1: Biological Sciences & Living Resources

Figure 5.1   Bibliographic record from the ASFA database on Dialog

Field label	Field
CO	Cassco Machines 4 William Morgan Drive
CY=,ZP=	Toronto M4H 1E6
CU=	Ontario
CN=	Canada
TE=	(416)4254140 TELEX: 06219888 FAX: (416)4256196
DE= (description of business)	Manufacturer and Exporter of Hot stamping machines, decorating equipment, marking machines, embossing machines, and dies and assembly machines
EM= (NUMBER OF EMPLOYEES)	85
FT= FOREIGN TRADE STATUS	Producers, Manufacturers
NA=	Chairman: Carl Thuro Vice President Export: Ken Thuro
IC= (Industry code)	28 Printing and publishing Prod 44 Pulp and Paper Industry. Printing Office Machinery and Equipment Prod 47 Metal and Woodmaking Machines, Machine Tools and Accessories, Special Purpose Machines. Industrial Robots Prod
PC= (Product code) PN= (Product name)	28100 Typesetting, Photocomposition, Moveable Type, Accessories Prod 2810011 Typesetting on Photopaper or Film Prod 2810017 Typesetting, Computer Controlled, for Correction Prod 2810018 Typesetting, Computer Controlled, for Line Justification Prod 2810019 Typesetting, Computer Controlled, for Conversion Prod 28140 Printing Blocks and Plates, Engraving, Photo-Engraving, Reprography, Colour Separation Prod 2814003 Photo Engraving, One-Colour Zinc and Copper Prod 44900 Small Office Equipment Prod 4490002 Date Stamps Prod 4490003 Numbering Stamps Prod 47850 Machine Tools other than for Metal and Wood Prod
TN= (Tradename)	Cassco Casscosil

Figure 5.2   Amended company record derived from the KOMPASS Canada database on Dialog

including name, address, telephone number, executive names, and industry and product listings, for approximately 30,000 Canadian companies. The record has been simplified, nevertheless it clearly illustrates this type of database. This record is structured with fields for the company name (CO) and address, management, number of employees (EM), its region (CU) and country (CN) together with information about the company's products, relevant product codes and affiliated companies.

Figure 5.3 shows a small part of a record from the ChemTox database and contains some physical and chemical properties of the chemical methyl mercaptan together with a small number of variants on its name. It contains detailed information on its toxicity and detailed regulations governing its handling including transportation. This extract demonstrates the highly structured nature of some electronic data with a large number of short fields.

Many databases contain full-text articles from newspapers, journals and encyclopaedias. These records are much less structured than those discussed so far, as is demonstrated in Figure 5.4 which contains an amended version of an article from the *Los Angeles Times*. It can be seen that there are fewer fields and that most of the data in the record appear in the single field which contains the text of the article.

As the electronic information market has matured, the same database may be available from several sources and it is important for the searcher to be aware that different database suppliers may have made the database available in slightly different ways. There might be slightly different data elements present and they might be labelled slightly differently. Additionally, the records may be parsed slightly differently (see later) and this will have implications for retrieval.

Different databases of a similar type will have some commonality in record structure. For example, Figure 5.5 has been produced by taking some of the data elements from four major bibliographic databases (Science Citation Index (SCI), Biosis, Medline and Embase) that contain biomedical information, as they are available from The Dialog Corporation. Each row of the table represents a particular field and each column represents a particular database. An 'x' in the appropriate cell of the table indicates the presence of a field in a particular database. While no claim is made for its complete accuracy, the table indicates both that there is considerable similarity in the structure of the databases but also some subtle variations.

Standards and rules have played an important part in the production of databases for information searching. Database producers have their own internal rules about the ways in which data are to be entered into their databases. The objective is to ensure uniformity of, for example, author names and corporate names. Given the commercial nature of these operations, these rules are rarely accessible. However, the library community has developed similar rules for the cataloguing of books which are widely available. In the English-speaking world, the Anglo-American Cataloguing Rules (AACR2) is the most widely known of these standards and certainly more complex than the in-house rules adopted by bibliographic database producers. From the user's perspective it has produced some, but certainly not complete, uniformity in library catalogues. AACR2 consists of two

Field label	Field
XN= NA= (Chemical Name)	METHYL MERCAPTAN
SY= (synonyms)	MERCAPTAN METHYLIQUE
	(plus many more not displayed)
RN= CAS Registry Number	74–93–1
RR= RTECS Number	PB4375000
MF= Molecular Formula	CH4S
MW= Molecular Weight	48.11
Wisswesser Line Notation	SH1
UP= Record Last Updated	03/28/94
	PHYSICAL PROPERTY INFORMATION
Physical Description	CLEAR LIQUID OR COLORLESS GAS WITH ODOR OF ROTTEN CABBAGE
BP= Boiling Point in C	6C
Boiling Point in F	42.9 F
Boiling Point in K	279.21 K
MP= Melting Point in C	–119.9 C
FP= Flash Point in C	–18.15 C
Vapor Specific Gravity	1.66 (air = 1)
Heat of Vaporization (J/Kg)	$5.112 \times$ E5 J/kg
Heat of Combustion (J/Kg)	$-257 \times$ E5 J/kg
Critical Pressure in kN/M2	1050 psia
Critical Temperature in C	196.85 C
UE= Upper Explosive	21.8%

Figure 5.3   Amended extract of a chemical record from the ChemTox database on Dialog

Limit	
LE= Lower Explosive Limit	3.9 %
Ionization Potential	9.44
SG= Specific Gravity	0.892 @ 6C
Water Solubility (mg/L)	2.4%
Absorbance Units	0.016 at PEL of (C) 10 ppm
Absorbance Wavelength	3.4
Linearity Term (Foxboro) :	796.2
Foxboro Pathlength/Multi	20.25
Incompatibilities	STRONG OXIDIZERS, BLEACHES; MERCURY (II) OXIDE SAX
Reactivity w/ Water	REACTS TO PRODUCE TOXIC AND FLAMMABLE VAPORS (STEAM ALSO) SAX
Reactivity w/ Common Mtl	REACTS WITH ACIDS TO PRODUCE TOXIC AND FLAMMABLE VAPORS SAX
Stability Dur. Transport	No Data
Polymerization Possible	NOT PERTINENT HCDB
Minimum Detectable Conc	1.3
Toxic Fire Gases	HIGHLY TOXIC FUMES OF OXIDES OF SULFUR
Odor Description	Garlic; foul; strong offensive
Odor Detection Limit	No data
Odor (100% Detection)	0.0021 ppm
Uses	Synthesis, especially of methionine, jet fuel additives, fungicides; also as catalyst. Condensed Chemical Dictionary, 10th ed (and several more pages ot data)

Figure 5.3   (cont.)

Field Label	Field
TI	Mars Surveyor Spacecraft Blasts Off Science: NASA mission will map the planet's surface, identifying landing sites for future journeys. It is the first of three expeditions leaving for Mars in the next two months.
JN	Los Angeles Times (LT)
PD	FRIDAY November 8, 1996
AU	K. C. COLE; TIMES SCIENCE WRITER
ED	Edition: Home Edition Page: 26 Pt. A
AT (Story type)	Wire
TX	NASA's Mars Global Surveyor blasted off from Cape Canaveral, Fla., on Thursday atop a Delta rocket en route to the Red Planet – the initial step in an attempt to eventually probe Mars for further evidence of life. Surveyor, which is managed by the Jet Propulsion Laboratory in Pasadena, is the first of three missions to Mars expected during a two-month launch window this fall, when Mars and Earth are favorable aligned. The window won't open again for more than two years. "We're on our way!" NASA space science chief Wesley Huntress Jr. said of the first U.S. mission to Mars since the Viking missions of the 1970s. "These are the kinds of days you kind of live for in space science and space exploration." After Surveyor reaches Mars next fall, it will be joined by the Russian spacecraft Mars 96, which will drop two landers onto the planet's surface. Surveyor's instruments will scrutinize the entire planet from space while the Russian probes provide an on-site reality check from the surface. Ironically, the final mission to be launched to Mars this year, NASA's Pathfinder, will blast off in December but is due to arrive first, on July 4. None of the missions is expected to directly shed much light on the question most on peoples' minds since the National Aeronautics and Space Administration released images of fossil-like forms on a Martian meteorite two months ago: Did ancient life exist on Mars? Definitive answers will have to wait for future missions that can bring back Martian rocks for analysis in Earth laboratories. But Surveyor will pave the way by thoroughly mapping the planet's surface, identifying promising landing sites. Once it is captured by Martian gravity, Surveyor will spread its solar panel wings and glide into a nearly circular 235-mile-high orbit, then loop around the planet every two hours taking detailed pictures of its

Figure 5.4   Full-text record from the *Los Angeles Times* on Dialog

	enormous mountains and volcanoes, ancient river channels and frozen poles. On-board instruments will gather clues about the planet's atmosphere, surface chemistry, magnetic fields and radiation, and beam daily weather reports back to Earth. Its cameras can pick up objects as small as a minivan. Above all, it will look for signs of water – a requirement for life as we know it. The smallish Surveyor is a hastily assembled successor to the billion-dollar Mars Observer, which arrived at Mars in August 1993 but then disappeared from NASA's radar screens, never to be heard from again. According to NASA chief Daniel Goldin, Surveyor carries 80% of Observer's instruments at one-quarter the cost. Over the next 10 years, NASA plans to launch a pair of spacecraft to Mars every 26 months, during each launch window. The only snag in the $230-million mission Thursday appeared to be a solar panel on the spacecraft that did not extend properly. NASA expects it to straighten out eventually. Photo: A Delta rocket carrying NASA's Mars Global Surveyor lifts off Thursday from Cape Canaveral, Fla. Spacecraft is expected to arrive next fall.
DE (Descriptors)	MARS (PLANET); SPACE EXPLORATION; SPACE PROGRAMS – UNITED STATES

Figure 5.4   (cont.)

	SciSearch	Biosis	Medline	Embase
abstract	X (some)	X	X	X
accession number	X	X	X	X
author	X	X	X	X
author affiliation	X	X	X	X
CAS Registry Number		X	X	X
cited references	X			
country of publication			X	
descriptor	X	X	X	X
descriptor code		X (Concept Codes)		
document type	X	X	X	
identifier	X		X	
ISBN				X
ISSN		X	X	X
journal name	X	X	X	X
language	X	X	X	X
manufacturer's name				X
publication year	X	X	X	X
publisher				X
section heading				X
section heading code				X
series				X
subfile	X		X	X
summary language				X
title	X	X	X	X
trade name		X		X
update	X	X	X	X

Figure 5.5   Variation in structure of some databases covering biomedicine on Dialog

sections. The first is a set of rules which provides guidance in bibliographic description. The second provides guidance on the choice of headings so that, in theory, the problems of the names Beethoven, El Greco and Lewis Carroll, referred to in Chapter 4, should be solved by accurate application of AACR2. Thus the rule for headings for persons indicates that they should be catalogued under the name by which they are known. While this should ensure the use of the pseudonyms El Greco and Lewis Carroll rather than their proper names, it does not make it unambiguously clear how to

MARC tag	Data
010	95–4331
040	DLC $c DLC $d AGL
020	082631595X
043	n–us–nm $a n–usu–
050 00	SB407 $b .M875 1994
082 00	635.9/09789 $2 20
072 0	F110
090	$b
049	ORDE
100 1	Morrow, Baker H., $d 1946–
245 10	Best plants for New Mexico gardens and landscapes : $b keyed to cities and regions/$c Baker H. Morrow.
260	Albuquerque : $b University of New Mexico Press, $c [1994?]
300	xii, 267 p. : $b ill. (chiefly col.), maps ; $c cm.
504	Includes bibliographical references (p. 244–248) and index.
650 0	Plants, Ornamental $z New Mexico. Landscape gardening $z New Mexico.

Figure 5.6   MARC record for a book

deal with a composer such as Ludwig von Beethoven. Indeed the treatment may well vary from country to country.

Database producers frequently store data in a record structure which conforms to the International Standards Organization standard ISO 2709. One example of a structure which meets this standard is machine readable cataloguing (MARC), which was developed during the 1960s and the 1970s as a structure for bibliographic records and as a way of promoting the exchange of bibliographic data. Since the mid-1970s many national libraries throughout the world have adopted a form of the MARC format for bibliographic descriptions. OCLC's WORLDCAT database of some 36 million items also uses this format. An example of a record representing a book is presented in Figure 5.6. The numeric field tags are in the left-hand column and the data in the right-hand column. While the MARC structure is perceived as being principally for data about books, it can also be used for other print-based media, such as serials and music and indeed can be used to store information about electronic resources. OCLC, for instance, uses the MARC format to describe Internet resources in its databases. An example of a bibliographic description of an Internet resource within the MARC format is shown in Figure 5.7: note the use of the 856 field to store the

MARC tag	Data
040	UOK $c UOK
006	[a 001 0]
007	c $b r $d a $e n
041 1	eng $h grclat
050 4	PA3621 $b .I48
082 04	880/.09 $2 20
090	$b
049	ORDE
245 04	The Internet Classics Archive $h [computer file].
256	Computer text data
260	[Cambridge, Mass.] : $b The Archive, $c c1995–
538	Mode of access: Internet.
500	Title from title screen.
508	"Credit, Daniel C. Stevenson."
520	Includes full text HTML versions in English of Greek and Latin classics, plus links to other related sites, some with texts also in the original languages. Online index available
650 0	Classical literature $x Translations into English $x Databases.
700 1	Stevenson, Daniel C
710 2	Internet Classics Archive.
856 7	$u http://the-tech.mit.edu/Classics/ $2 http

Figure 5.7   MARC record for a WWW resource

Internet location. Further details about MARC and AACR2 can be found in Hunter and Bakewell (1991).

Parsing the Records

The database producer must decide how the information in each field is to be processed to generate the index. This process is known as parsing. The decisions, taken by the database producer/service supplier, cannot be altered by the searcher but it is valuable for the searcher to be aware of these decisions and their potential to affect retrieval.

The individual fields can be indexed in various ways. For each database, the database designer decides how to index every field and the indexing is undertaken automatically by the software whenever new records are added to the database. The available choices are word indexed, phrase indexed, word and phrase indexed or no indexing.

For some fields each significant individual word in the field might be useful for retrieval and so the field will be word indexed, that is to say each individual word is identified and checked against a stopword list. The stopword list contains words which occur frequently and have no value in retrieval and so are not indexed. Examples are *in, of, and, but*. All the remaining words are added to the index. Thus, in a database of books, it is likely that the decision would be taken to word index the title field. Thus, for John Freely's book *Strolling through Athens*, this would mean that each of the three words, *strolling, through* and *Athens* would be added to the index.

Other fields might best be treated as phrases rather than individual words. One example is the names of authors: Richard J. Hartley, J. Andrew Large and Lucy A. Tedd are most sensibly treated as three phrases, each of which consists of the name of one of the authors of this book. The benefit of this is that the constituent parts of the names are kept together. Thus there is no chance, for example, that a search for items by Lucy Large would retrieve any books written by the authors of this book. In some situations, fields are best indexed by both individual words and by phrases, for instance, with the controlled vocabulary field of a bibliographic database or the product name field in a company database. So, in Figure 5.1 the terms in the descriptor field: aquaculture development, echinoderm fisheries, fishery products and Holothuroidea would be both word and phrase indexed. This would lead to the three phrases, aquaculture development, echinoderm fisheries, fishery products being indexed along with the seven individual words, aquaculture, development, echinoderm, fisheries, fishery, Holothuroidea and products.

Some fields contain data that are most unlikely to be useful in the search process although it is important that the data be displayed in any retrieved record (for example pagination details in a bibliographic database). Such fields will not be indexed at all.

This type of indexing is carried out automatically by the computer-without any human intervention.

Figure 5.8 shows a possible record, containing bibliographic information about a journal article, in an imaginary database on medical informatics. The record is divided into 11 fields: accession number, authors, authors' affiliation, title, source, volume, issue, pages, year, controlled terms and abstract. A word is defined here as any alphanumeric string bounded on either side by a space or by the end of the field. A phrase is defined as being marked by a semi-colon followed by a space or by the end of field marker. A decision is made that certain fields will not be indexed at all because no-one is likely to want to search them; in this case, volume (vo), issue (is) and pagination (pg).

All other fields from the record in Figure 5.8 are indexed as follows and are therefore searchable:

Word indexed – ab, an, ti, yr
Phrase indexed – aa, au, so
Word and phrase indexed – ct

The abstract, accession number, title and year fields are word indexed since each individual word might be useful for retrieval. The individual words

an:	1245
au:	Jones, Jean; Wilkinson, Michael
aa:	Department of Electronic Communication Studies; University of Widgettown
ti:	Developments in medical information on the Internet and its use by nurses
so:	Journal of Medical Internet Applications
vo:	6
is:	3
pg:	129–137
yr:	1998
ct:	information seeking; medical informatics; World Wide Web
ab:	A study of the growth of medical information on the Web and its effect on the information seeking behaviour of nurses, particularly in community health centres

Figure 5.8   Fictitious bibliographic record

from the title and abstract are identified and then checked against the list of stopwords, which in this case include a, and, but, by, in, its, of, on, the and to. Words that are not included in the stopword list are added to the index.

The author, author's affiliation and source fields are phrase indexed to keep each phrase intact. The importance of this decision for searching should be noted. For instance, a search for the author Wilkinson using only the surname will not find the record because only part of the whole phrase has been used in the search instead of the complete phrase. (The searcher can overcome the problem of not knowing the first name or initial by using a truncation symbol after the surname to search for a phrase beginning with 'Wilkinson' – see Chapter 6.) A search for the single word 'Widgettown' similarly will not retrieve this item since the index entry is for the phrase 'University of Widgettown'.

The controlled term field, which contains phrases chosen by a human indexer from a thesaurus (as described in Chapter 4), is both word and phrase indexed. The individual words *information* and *seeking* are entered into the index as well as the phrase *information seeking*. It should be noted here that in most search systems upper and lower case letters are treated as identical. The resulting index entries, generated from the whole record, are shown in Figure 5.9.

The searcher cannot alter the database structure or indexing but should become familiar with the features of individual databases which are to be searched frequently as well as the retrieval facilities which the search engine

```
1245(an)
1998(yr)
Behaviour(ab)
Centres(ab)
Community(ab)
Department of Electronic Communication Studies(aa)
Developments(ti)
Effect(ab)
Growth(ab)
Health(ab)
Informatics(ct)
Information(ti,ab,ct)
Information seeking(ct)
Internet(ti)
Jones, Jean(au)
Journal of Medical Internet Applications(so)
Medical(ti,ab,ct)
Medical informatics(ct)
Nurses(ti,ab)
Particularly(ab)
Seeking(ab,ct)
Study(ab)
University of Widgettown(aa)
Use(ti)
Web(ab,ct)
Wide(ct)
Wilkinson, Michael(au)
World(ct)
World Wide Web(ct)
```

Figure 5.9   Index terms generated from sample record

offers. Online help is usually available to the searcher. Figure 5.10 shows an extract from the information provided by The Dialog Corporation on its Web site for the ASFA database. There is a description of the database subject coverage together with details of the various indexes available for searching (see later in the chapter) and limits which can be applied (see Chapter 6).

File Structures

Normally a searcher can retrieve information from an online database very quickly – whether this is a search of a database on a CD-ROM database or a remote service such as Dialog or LEXIS. Ten seconds is considered a long time to wait for a response, even though the database might contain, as does Medline, about eight million records. Although this is undoubtedly due to the hardware and software used, it is also considerably influenced by the file structure. An inverted file structure is often used to ensure speedy retrieval times. Searchers need not be familiar with the

AQUATIC SCIENCES AND FISHERIES ABSTRACTS (ASFA)

Last Loaded On Web: Monday, Feb 9 1998
Last Update To Bluesheet: September 20, 1996

File Descriptions
Aquatic Sciences and Fisheries Abstracts (ASFA) is a comprehensive database
on the science, technology, and management of marine, brackishwater, and
freshwater environments and resources. The database corresponds to the
printed publications Aquatic Sciences and Fisheries Abstracts, Part 1: Biological
Sciences and Living Resources; Part 2: Ocean Technology, Policy, and Non-
Living Resources; Part 3: Aquatic Pollution and Environmental Quality; ASFA
Aquaculture Abstracts; and ASFA Marine Biotechnology Abstracts. The
database also contains records that have not appeared in the ASFA print
publications. ASFA's international editorial staff monitors over 5,000 primary
journals and a wide variety of other source documents including books,
monographic series, conference proceedings, and technical research reports.

Aquatic Sciences and Fisheries is a collaborative effort of the Food and
Agriculture Organization (FAO) of the United Nations (Rome), the
Intergovernmental Oceanographic Commissions of UNESCO (Paris), the
Division for Ocean Affairs and the Law of the Sea of the United Nations (New
York), the Ocean and Coastal Areas Programme Activity Centre of the United
Nations Environment Programme (Nairobi), the International Council for the
Exploration of the Sea (Copenhagen), the World Conservation Union (Gland),
and national agencies in twenty-three countries.

Dialog File Data
Dates Covered:	January 1978 to the present
File Size:	Over 586,000 records as of October 1997
Update Frequency:	Monthly (approximately 2,4000 records per update)

Database Content Bibliographic Records

**Figure 5.10   Extract from online help available on DialogWeb for the ASFA
database**

SEARCH OPTIONS
BASIC INDEX SEARCH DISPLAY

Suffix code	Field name	Indexing	Examples
None	All Basic Index	Word	S AQUACULTURE
/AB	Abstract	Word	S SEA(W)CUCUMBER/AB
/DE	Descriptor	Word and Phrase	S FISHERY(W) PRODUCTS/DE
/ID	Identifier	Word and Phrase	S PLASMIDS/ID
/TI	Title	Word	S FISHERY/TI

ADDITIONAL INDEXES

Prefix code	Field	Indexing	Search Example
AA=	ASFA Accession Number	Phrase	S AA=4066242
AU=	Author	Phrase	S AU=MERCIER, A?
BN=	Standard Book	Phrase	S BN=0–08–042530–5 S BN=0080425305
CI=	ASFA Input Center Number	Phrase	S CI=CS9713350
CL=	Conference Location	Word	S CL=INDIA
CS=	Corporate Source	Word & Phrase	S CS=(EXPLORATION AND VALORISATION S CS=SOCIETE D?EXPLORATION ET DE VALOR?
CT=	Conference Title	Word	S CT=(GLOBAL(W)CLIMATE)
CY=	Conference Year	Phrase	S CY=1997
DT=	Document Type	Phrase	S DT=JOURNAL ARTICLE
EN=	Environment	Phrase	S EN=MARINE
FS=	File Segment	Phrase	FS=ASFA 1: BIOLOGICAL SCIENCES?
JN=	Journal Name	Phrase	S JN=AQUACULTURE MAGAZINE

Figure 5.10 (cont.)

LA=	Language	Phrase	S LA=ENGLISH
PD=	Publication Date	Phrase	S PD=970000
PU=	Publisher	Word	S PU=(OCEANOGRAPHIC (W)RESEARCH
PY=	Publication Year	Phrase	S PY=1997
RN	Report Number	Word & Phrase	S RN="FAO BGD/89/012' S RN=FAOBGD89012
SC=	Section Heading Code	Phrase	S SC=01584
SH=	Section Heading	Phrase	S SH=AQUACULTURE: CULTURE OF OTHER AQ?
SL=	Summary Language	Phrase	S SL=ENGLISH
SN=	International Standard Serial Number (ISSN)	Phrase	S SN=0199–1388 S SN=01991388
SO=	Source Information	Word	S SO=(AQUALCULT? AND 42 AND 1997)
UD=	Update	Phrase	S UD=199709:9999

LIMITING

Sets and terms may be limited by Basic Index suffixes, i.e., /AB, /DE, /DF, /ID, /IF, /TI (e.g., S S4/DE).

SUFFIX	FIELD NAME	EXAMPLES
/ABS	Abstract present	S S3/ABS
/ENG	English Language	S S4/ENG
/NOABS	No Abstract	S S6/NOABS
/NONENG	Non-English	S S7/NONENG
/YYYY	Publication Year	S S3/1996:1997

Figure 5.10   (cont.)

intricacies of inverted file structures but a grasp of the principles behind them can help to understand the searching process.

Inverted file structure

A simple inverted file consists of three related files. In this book, they are referred to as the index file (see Figure 5.11), the postings file (see Figure 5.12) and the print file (see Figure 5.13). The index file contains all the terms, in alphabetic sequence, which have been taken from the various records in the database according to the parsing rules. An excerpt from an index file, based upon some of the words in the record in Figure 5.8, appears in Figure 5.11. It contains three items of information: the term, the number of postings (i.e. the number of records in which the term occurs) and a pointer to the location in the postings file (postings file address) where more information is stored. It is the index file which enables the software to make a very rapid response when a search term is entered into the system. Whenever new records are added to the database, the index-able terms are added to the index file. If the term is not already in this file, it is added in its appropriate alphabetical sequence and a posting number of '1' is given; that is to say the term occurs in one record on the database. If the term already exists in the index file then the postings number is increased by one. Thus the addition of another record including the term Internet would cause the number of postings to increase from 2,345 to 2,346. If a term occurs more than once in a record (as does the term information in Figure 5.6) then the number of postings is still only increased by one as the index file lists the number of individual records in which the term is found and not the total number of occurrences of that term throughout the database. It must be emphasized that this indexing process is implemented by the search system at every database update and does not require the attention of the human indexer.

The postings file (see Figure 5.12) has a location number for every term in the index file. Linked to this number are the record numbers of all the records which include that term. Thus the postings file links the index file with the print file. For example, the term *Internet* has the postings file address 5478 (Figure 5.11) and occurs in records 1, 2, 3, 4, 7, 8 and so on (Figure 5.12). Finally the print file (see Figure 5.13) consists of the records in the database maintained in accession number order.

A consideration of how a search is processed may help explain the importance of the file structure. If a searcher enters a single term then the software checks for the presence of the term at the appropriate point in the alphabetical sequence of the index file. If the term is not in the index file then a message is displayed to the searcher indicating that the term does not occur in the database. If the searcher enters a term which is present in the database then the software responds by indicating the number of postings. So if the searcher enters the term 'nurses' then the software would respond by indicating that there were 21 records in the database containing this term – these are known as hits. The searcher might conclude that 21 items is a reasonable number to deal with and instruct the software to display the items on the screen. If so, the software retrieves the accession numbers

TERM	No. of postings	Postings file address
. . . . .		
Browsers	27	1233
Centres	23	3245
Community	6	6100
Developments	14	1456
Doctors	29	2378
Effect	234	65
Email	145	6740
Engine	26	2354
Engineers	35	4356
Growth	153	3297
Health	635	8234
Informatics	23	3298
Information	347	2682
Internet	2345	5478
Learning	156	6390
Medical	89	7789
Nurses	21	8256

Figure 5.11   Inverted file structure: Index file

Address	Record numbers
1233	88,91,427 . . . . .
1456	18,98,1245 . . . . .
2378	5,6,7,8,1455 . . . . .
2682	23,45,561,678, ... 1245
3448	666,783,1011
5478	1,2,3,4,7,8,9,23,45,56,67 1245
6100	456,789,987,1034,1123,1245
6390	45,47,269,345,589
6740	2,3,5,18,34,56,269,345,589 . . . . .
7789	36,47,59,63,269 . . . . .
8256	1,3,578,892,1245 . . . . .

Figure 5.12   Inverted file structure: Postings file

Record No 1244 . . . . .

Record No 1245

Jones, Jean; Wilkinson, Michael.

Department of Electronic Communication Studies; University of Widgettown.

Developments in medical information on the Internet and its use by nurses

Journal of Medical Internet Applications 6 3 129–137 1998

Controlled terms: information seeking; medical informatics; World Wide Web

A study of the growth of medical information on the Web and its effect on the information seeking behaviour of nurses, particularly in community health centres.

Record No 1246 . . . . .

Figure 5.13   Inverted file structure: Print file

of the records at location 8,256 in the postings file, finds these records in the print file and displays them in reverse record number order 1,245, 892, 578, and so on.

The postings file plays a more crucial role if the searcher requires more than a single term search. Let us suppose that the searcher is looking for items about the use of the Internet by nurses. The searcher enters the terms 'nurses' and 'Internet' linked by the Boolean operator AND. The search software goes to the index file and notes the postings of each of the terms and their associated locations in the postings file. The software examines the postings file at location number 5,478 (Internet) and location number 8,256 (nurses) and compares the record numbers. Every time a record is found in both locations (1, 3, 1,245 and so on), then a record has been identified that contains *both* terms. The user is then told how many such matching records have been found. If the user wishes to display some of the hits these may be located using the record numbers in the print file. A similar three-stage process involving an initial check in the index file, a matching algorithm in the postings file and a final retrieval from the print file is employed when users have input a search request with a Boolean OR operator (e.g. email OR Internet). In this case all the record numbers at both postings file locations will need to be retrieved. When search terms are linked by Boolean NOT, the procedure is similar with an algorithm that checks for record numbers appearing in the list of accession numbers for the first term but not the second term.

In practice, inverted file structures are more complex than Figures 5.11 to 5.13 imply, since they record not simply the presence of a term in a record as explained above but, crucially, the position of the term within the record. There are numerous ways in which this can be achieved, one of which is presented in Figure 5.14. In this example, the word-indexed data from the

Term	Record number	Field	Position
behaviour	1245	ab	19
centres	1245	ab	26
community	1245	ab	24
developments	1245	ti	1
effect	1245	ab	14
growth	1245	ab	5
health	1245	ab	25
informatics	1245	ct	4
information	1245	ab	8
information	1245	ab	17
information	1245	ct	1
information	1245	ti	4
internet	1245	ti	7
medical	1245	ab	7
medical	1245	ct	3
medical	1245	ti	3
nurses	1245	ab	21
nurses	1245	ti	12
particularly	1245	ab	22
seeking	1245	ab	18
seeking	1245	ct	2
study	1245	ab	2
use	1245	ti	10
web	1245	ab	11
web	1245	ct	7
wide	1245	ct	6
world	1245	ct	5

Figure 5.14   Word positional information in an inverted file structure

title, controlled terms and abstract fields of record 1,245 in Figure 5.8 have been presented as a table which enables the exact position of the word in the record to be preserved. The words appear in the left-hand column, the record number in the next column and this is followed by columns containing the field label and the position of the word within the field. As would be expected, the stopwords do not appear in the inverted index but are still taken into account when counting the position of words in the record. Some operational systems count stopwords in this manner while others do not. Recording the precise position of a term in a record enables searching by field and by word proximity as described in Chapter 6.

Borrower Table

Borrower Number	Name	Address	Expiry Date
001234	Joe Bloggs	Plymouth	31.12.99
002345	Arthur Brown	Exeter	31.12.99

Book Table

Book Number	Author	Title	Publisher	Date	Classification Number
01234567	Jones	Beginner's fluid mechanics	Cambridge	1996	532
01234449	Smith	Chemistry	Oxford	1995	540

Loans Table

Transaction	Borrower Number	Book Number	Date due
0000024	002345	01234449	27.07.98
0000025	005678	00034468	28.07.98

Orders Table

Order number	Book number	Supplier number	Date ordered	Copies
002349	00337788	0023	14.03.98	2
002350	00556677	0056	17.03.98	1

Suppliers Table

Supplier number	Supplier name	Address
0023	Arkwrights Books	Banbury
0024	Barkers Software	Andover

Figure 5.15   Simplified relational model of a library

Relational databases

A different file structure, namely the relational database and the associated software, i.e. a relational database management system (RDBMS), is typically used for OPACs, which are part of an integrated library management system. An RDBMS requires information to be stored in a series of linked tables, the columns of which correspond to fields in conventional records and the rows of which are the records themselves. The relational model was developed to combat data redundancy and data inconsistency in complex multifile applications. A very simplified relational model of a library is presented in Figure 5.15. It can be seen that the application consists of a series of tables for borrowers, books, loans, orders and suppliers. Examination of the data stored in the tables demonstrates the way data redundancy is avoided. For example, there is no record indicating that book order number 002349 has been ordered from Arkwrights Books nor is there a record that Arthur Brown has a book on chemistry on loan. The RDBMS software enables queries to be answered with a series of operations which enable tables to be created 'on the fly'. Thus, for example, data elements from the loans table can be combined with those from the books table and the borrower table to create overdue notices. Data from the orders table and suppliers table can be put together to show what has been ordered from Arkwrights Books. Similarly data from the loans table, borrowers table and books table can be combined to show that Arthur Brown has a chemistry book on loan. It is not the purpose of this book to discuss the relational model in detail. Interested readers are referred to books on the topic such as that by Martin (1980).

There are a number of RDBMS packages available; for example the BLCMP Talis OPAC (as used in Figures 1.7–1.9) is based on the Sybase RDBMS and the OLIB OPAC (with details of its relevance ranking algorithm shown in Figure 9.9) is based on the ORACLE RDBMS. A description of the OLIB system (known as Oracle Libraries at the time the cited article was written) has been provided by Verity (1993). The system is especially interesting because it incorporates a number of features to improve searching including:

- a stemming algorithm (automatic truncation by the system);
- subject searching using text retrieval and term weighting (see Chapter 6);
- subject search expansion using a thesaurus;
- hypertext-style browsing;
- graphical user interface;
- multimedia support.

Hypermedia

The concept of hypermedia has its origins in the notion that people often use books, and certainly libraries, in a non-sequential way while the text in books and other print-based media is organized sequentially. Sequential organization is fine for developing an argument or expounding a theory but, it is argued, information seekers follow up clues in their information hunt in a non-sequential manner (this point is developed further in Chapter 7).

For example, a piece of academic writing might include a sentence such as:

Jones has frequently argued that ... (Jones, 1987)

where the full bibliographic details of Jones' 1987 publication are given in the bibliography. In a hypertext system the searcher might be able to click on the in-text reference and be taken immediately to the citation in the bibliography. Another use might be to move from a term in a text to its definition in an associated glossary. It is a small logical step, although admittedly a much larger technological step, to move from a system permitting linkages between text sequences to hypermedia where sound and images as well as text can all be linked.

Many multimedia CD-ROM products enable the information seeker to browse in a non-sequential manner using hypermedia links. The Microsoft Music Central CD-ROM provides a guide to popular music from around the world. It brings together photographs of artists, biographies, videoclips of live performances, photographs of album covers and a discography which lists the tracks on particular albums. By clicking on the appropriate links, it is possible to move between media and to move around the information in a non-sequential manner. Thus, to take an example, the entry for Dire Straits includes a photograph of the group and a video clip of a live performance of the well-known song 'Sultans of Swing'. There are links to the entries for some individual members of the group, so it is possible to click on a link to a biography of Mark Knopfler, the mainstay of the group. Clicking on the appropriate links provided, it is possible to move to many more entries including the entry for the group, the Notting Hillbillies, in which Knopfler has played, or to the legendary rock guitarist Eric Clapton with whom Knopfler has performed. Obviously, this process could be continued further, so enabling the user to browse through large volumes of multimedia information by following links between related chunks of information. Browsing in this manner, rather than by either reading sequentially or by searching with given search criteria, is a realistic information-seeking strategy in hypermedia documents. However, it must be appreciated that the user does not have the freedom to move anywhere in the hypermedia product. It is only possible to follow the links established when the product was created.

The World Wide Web is best thought of as a series of hypermedia items, which have been created across the Internet. In the case of the Web, links can be made between files on any computers which are connected to the Internet. It is this linking and the consequent ability to move between data around the world which has been a crucial feature of the success of the Web. Thus while the links in Music Central enable the user to move non-sequentially to information on the CD-ROM, the Web enables the user to move to information which has been linked across many host computers. Many individuals who maintain their own Web pages include links to numerous other sites which they use frequently.

The Web is also used as a vehicle for making electronic journals available to users (see Chapter 3). In its turn this is leading to an extension of the use of hypermedia links. Rather than links between citations within a text of a paper to the full reference in the bibliography of the paper, it is possible to make links to the full text of the cited paper in another journal, possibly on a different site on the Web. Demonstration services in the three disciplines of biology, cognitive science and computer science have been developed in the Open Journal Project at Southampton University in the UK (Hitchcock *et al.*, 1997a, 1997b). This approach has the potential significantly to improve access to primary literature.

A major factor in the widespread success of the Web has been the markup language HTML (Hypertext Markup Language). HTML is simply one type of document structure within the broader framework of the standard generalized markup language (SGML). SGML is significant because it concentrates on document structure and attributes rather than layout. Although its influence is still confined to pockets of the publishing industry, SGML may turn out to have more widespread and significant value than its sibling, HTML. A full discussion has been provided by Goldfarb (1990), one of its originators.

HTML provides a series of tags which are used to markup important features of a document. Some of the most important HTML tags are shown in Figure 5.16. The meaning of many of the tags is quite straightforward. Thus, the tag <P> is used to mark the start of a paragraph and the tag <L> is used to label each individual item in a list. Normally a tag should be accompanied by its equivalent 'end of structure' tag such as </P> to mark the end of a paragraph.

Sometimes tags have one or more attributes which further define the characteristics of the text or are used to specify sources of data, for example the <IMG> tag is used to define an image. This will take attributes which define how the image will appear (aligned to the left and so on). This tag also uses the attribute SRC to specify the source of the image. This might be locally held or indeed might be anywhere on the Web. Thus:

<IMG SRC = "c:\images\filename.gif">

indicates a local filename with the name 'filename.gif' which is stored in the images directory on the C drive. While

HTML tag	Tag Name	Comments
<HTML>	HTML	Marks start of an html document
<HEAD>	HEAD	Marks start of a document Head
<BODY>	BODY	Marks start of the body of document
<TITLE>	TITLE	Marks start of title of document
<P>	Paragraph	Marks start of a paragraph
<HI>	Level 1 head	Marks start of a first level heading
<A>	Anchor	Marks start of an anchor: the fundamental hypertext link
<IMG>	Image	Marks the insertion of a referenced image
<OL>	Ordered list	Marks start of an ordered list
<UL>	Unordered list	Marks start of an unordered list
<L>	List item	Marks a member of a list

Figure 5.16   Sample HTML tags

<IMG SRC = "http://www.somewhere.com/images/piccy.gif">

indicates an image with the filename 'piccy.gif' stored in the images directory of a remote Web site known as 'somewhere.com'.

The anchor tag (<A>) is the vitally important tag which enables both
interdocument and intradocument links to be created. This is achieved
using the attributes HREF and NAME, as follows. A link to another Web
site can be created in a document with an anchor, the HREF attribute and
an appropriate URL. Thus:

<A HREF = "http://www.northernlight.com">

creates a link to the Web site of the Northern Light search engine. Such a
link might be used as follows:

If you are interested in searching the Internet, you might use

<A HREF = "http://www.northernlight.com"> the Northern Light Search
Engine</A> as well as others

This results in the text the Northern Light Search Engine being turned into
a link on which the user can click. The result of that clicking is to move
to the specified URL, in this case the Northern Light home page.

Figure 5.17 demonstrates how links can be created within a large Web
document. It shows the links both from a contents page to various parts
of the text of a document and the links back from the various parts of the
document to the text. The crucial tag is the anchor tag <A> and its attributes NAME and HREF. The HREF attribute is used to indicate a place to
which a link has been made while the NAME attribute is used to create a
point to which an HREF link can be made. Many books are available to

```
<A NAME="TOC">Table of contents</A>
<P>
<A HREF="#PART1">Part 1 </A> <BR>
<A HREF="#PART2">Part 2 </A> <BR>
<A HREF="#PART3">Part 3 </A> <BR>
</P>

<A NAME="PART1"><H1>Part 1</H1></A>
<P> The text of part 1 would be here and is followed by a link back to the
table of contents using an anchor
<A HREF="#TOC">Return to table of contents</A>
<P>

<A NAME="#PART3"><H1>Part 3</H1></A>
<P> The text of part 3 would be here and is followed by a link back to the
table of contents using an anchor
<A HREF="#TOC">Return to table of contents</A>
<P>
```

**Figure 5.17   Sample contents page to demonstrate links within a WWW
document**

explain HTML in the detail necessary to enable the reader to develop Web pages: the purpose here has been only to demonstrate how links are made to facilitate browsing.

Indexing the Internet

As the Web has grown, so the number of search engines, which provide one means of locating information on the Internet, has also increased. The search engines include a component known as a Web spider or Web crawler. This is a piece of software which regularly trawls the Web, visiting sites, 'reading' them, following up links both within the site and to other sites. The crawler then 'reports back' the information from a site to the search engine. A spider will revisit sites on a regular basis and report back changes. The data, reported back to the search engine, are used to create huge indexes maintained by the search engines. These form the basis for the search engines to offer both ranked output and Boolean searching to find information on the Internet (see Chapter 6). McMurdo (1995) notes that the Lycos search engine collects the following details from each web site:

- URL;
- title;
- headings and subheadings;
- 100 most 'weighty' words (defined using the product of term frequency and inverse document frequency as described in Chapter 6);
- first 20 lines;
- size in bytes;
- number of words;
- all its http, ftp and gopher URL references.

One development to save crawlers from the burden of scanning every Web site in its entirety is a program, known as Harvest, developed at the University of Boulder, Colorado. Harvest incorporates an automatic indexing program which picks up terms that have been generated (either manually or automatically) to describe a particular Web site. In an article on searching the Internet, Lynch (1997) comments that 'the librarian's classification and selection skills must be complemented by the computer scientist's ability to automate the task of indexing and storing information. Only a synthesis of the differing perspectives brought by both professions will allow this new medium to remain viable.'

Metadata

No discussion of the organization of electronic information resources would be complete without a consideration of metadata. However, apart from a very general statement, namely that metadata are data about data, it is very difficult to find a definition of metadata with which all agree. It easy to see why this should be the case; metadata can mean different things to different people because they use the term in very different contexts and have rather different requirements. Furthermore, it is an evolving concept. Among others, metadata are of interest to computer scientists, librarians and information scientists, archivists, museums curators, social scientists and users of geospatial data. The applications for which various metadata are used vary, as does the relative importance attached to different elements of metadata. It is important for geospatial data to include clear information regarding access to the data, transfer of the data and use of the data as well as information about the 'fitness for use' of a dataset. These are notions which would have little meaning to the cataloguer engaged upon the creation of a library catalogue and producing records such as those in Figure 5.6.

Before considering metadata formats, it is useful to have a clear view of the functions of metadata. Following Heery, Powell and Day (1997), the six functions of metadata can be viewed as:

- Searching, that is, identifying the existence of a resource.
- Location, that is, finding a particular instance of a resource.
- Selection, that is, analysis and evaluation of a resource based upon a description provided.
- Semantic interoperability, that is, enabling searching across domains by means of equivalent elements.
- Resource management, that is, collection and database management.
- Availability, that is, information about the availability of a resource.

In given situations, the particular functions of the metadata will influence the format. For example, metadata used principally in the selection function might require richer data than metadata used for some of the other functions noted.

While recognizing the varying functions for metadata and different needs of metadata users, it should be borne in mind that this book is about information seeking. Thus, the concern is particularly about searching and location functions and to a lesser extent the selection and availability functions. Additionally, it is important to note that metadata researchers have in mind that metadata users may be pieces of software as well as humans.

Some writers categorize metadata into three types: unstructured, structured and semi-structured (Heery, Powell and Day, 1997; Dempsey and Heery, 1998). At present, the predominant resource discovery mechanism for electronic information resources on the Internet is the search engine, several of which are discussed throughout this book. While these tools perform satisfactorily when used to *locate* known resources on the Internet, they are less successful for resource *discovery*. One problem, which soon becomes visible, is their propensity to retrieve large numbers of items. All too often the number retrieved is unmanageably large and the proportion of retrieved items which are relevant is all too small. Furthermore, there is no way of knowing how many relevant items have not been retrieved. Given the completely automatic means by which these search engines have been created, this is perhaps unsurprising.

At the other end of the scale are the highly structured data in library catalogues and other bibliographic tools. These are expensive to produce since they require both a form of quality control, something which is notably absent from search engines, and the use of skilled human indexers and cataloguers to produce structured records.

Given the sheer volume of resources available on the Internet, it is inevitable that resource discovery tools must be developed which can be created automatically. However, the use of structured records and standards has its advantages and so some effort has been expended on the development of semi-structured metadata. The objective is to develop data structures that have some of the advantages of highly structured data but which can be created without the need for the knowledge and skills necessary to create bibliographic databases. Several such formats, or templates, exist which provide some of the features of the structured, evaluated bibliographic database but without the need for input by trained users. One template, the Internet Anonymous Ftp Archive (IAFA) template, was developed by a working group of the Internet Engineering Task Force (IETF) to enable file transfer protocol (ftp) archive administrators to describe their various resources. It has been extended to enable the description of Web resources. Another template, WHOIS++, was developed as a protocol for providing distributed information about people (email addresses, telephone numbers, etc.) on the Internet when ftp was the main method of Internet communication.

The IAFA and WHOIS++ templates formed the basis of the Resource Organization and Discovery in Subject-based Services (ROADS) templates for resource description. ROADS is a UK eLib project which has developed resource discovery software. This software and the ROADS metadata template is used by several of the UK subject-based gateways to Internet resources. These services provide access to networked resources, which have been evaluated by subject specialists and then described by human-created metadata. These include:

- ADAM: Art, Design, Architecture and Media Information Gateway.
- Biz/ed: Business Education on the Internet.
- EEVL: Edinburgh Engineering Virtual Library.
- IHR-Info: Institute of Historical Research.
- RUDI: Resources for Urban Design Information.
- SOSIG: Social Science Information Gateway.

However, a different metadata template, namely the Dublin Core metadata model, is attracting considerable interest. The Dublin Core consists of 15 data elements, which have been agreed through a series of international meetings, the first of which was held in Dublin, Ohio. It is intended to meet the varying needs of experts within different disciplines dealing with different types of data available over the Internet. These data elements are set out in Figure 5.18, which is taken from the work of Weibel (1997), the leading proponent of the Dublin Core. More information about this evolving area can be acquired from the Web (http://purl.org/meta-data/dublin_core_elements). The elements are sufficiently generic to enable adoption for a variety of applications.

Element name	Element purpose
Title	The name given to the resource by the creator or publisher
Creator	The person(s) or organisation(s) primarily responsible for creating the intellectual content of the resource
Subject	The topic of the resource: keywords or phrases that describe the subject or content of the resource, including controlled vocabularies or classification schemes
Descriptions	A textual description of the content of the resource, including abstracts in the case of document-like objects or content descriptions in the case of visual resources
Publisher	The entity responsible for making the resource available in its present form, such as publisher, a university department or a corporate identity
Contributor	Person(s) or organisation(s) in addition to those specified in the Creator element who have made significant intellectual contributions to the resource but whose contribution is secondary to the individuals or entities specified in the Creator element (for example, editors, transcribers and illustrators)
Date	The date the resource was made available in its present form
Type	The category of the resource, such as home page, novel, poem, working paper, technical report, essay, dictionary. It is expected that type will be chosen from an enumerated list of types
Format	The data representation of the document such as text/html, ASCII, Postscript file, executable application or JPEG image
Identifier	String or number used to uniquely identify the resource. Examples are URLs for networked resources, globally unique identifiers such as International Standard Book Number
Source	The work, either print or electronic, from which this resource is derived, if applicable
Language	Language(s) of the intellectual content of the resource
Relation	Relationship to other resources. The intent of specifying this element is to provide a means to express relationships among resources that have formal relationships to others, but exist as discrete resources themselves
Coverage	The spatial and temporal characteristics of the resource. Formal specification of Coverage is currently under development
Rights	The content of this element in intended to be a link to a copyright notice, a rights-management statement or perhaps a service that would provide such information dynamically

Figure 5.18 The Dublin Core elements

The hope is that the Dublin Core elements will become widely accepted and that creators of resources will include a metadata description of the item in the header of an HTML document using the HTML META tag. Modified 'harvesting' software would then look for Dublin core metadata rather than the entire document and search engines could be created only from metadata rather than, as often occurs, an entire Web resource.

The Dublin Core is already being used in several developmental projects. For example the EU-funded BIBLINK project, which is being undertaken by several national libraries, is investigating the use of the Dublin Core as a minimum for data exchange. The Nordic Metadata Project is using the Dublin Core metadata framework for its examination of a means of sharing data about electronic resources. Since early 1997 Dublin Core has also been used by the MathN Broker service, which offers access to Postscript versions of pre-prints of papers stored on the Web servers of about 40 departmental Web servers. OCLC NetFirst, with some 55,000 evaluated records of Internet resources, provides a further example of attempts to combine human and automatic approaches to electronic resource discovery (http://www.oclc.org/oclc/netfirst/netfirst.htm).

It seems clear that metadata will play an increasingly important part in improving effective access to electronic resources and that Dublin Core is emerging as the favoured metadata structure. Nevertheless, there remains much work to be done before access to electronic resources is as effective as access to print-based materials. Given the short history of the Internet this is not surprising, and the progress which has been made in a short time should be seen as very impressive.

References and Further Reading

Dempsey L. and Heery, R. (1998) Metadata: a current view of practice and issues. *Journal of Documentation*, **54**(2), 145–72

Goldfarb, C.F. (1990) *The SGML Handbook*. Oxford: Clarendon Press

Harter S. P. (1986) *Online Information Retrieval: Concepts, Principles and Techniques*. London: Academic Press (especially Chapter 3)

Heery, R., Powell A. and Day, M. (1997) Metadata. *Library & Information Briefings*, **75**, 1–19

Hitchcock, S., Quek, F., Carr, L. Witbrock, A. and Tarr, I. (1997a) Linking everything to everything: journal publishing myth or reality? Paper presented at the ICCC/IFIP conference of electronic publishing 1997 New Models and Opportunities, Canterbury, UK, April 1997. Also available at http://journals.ecs.soton.ac.uk/IFIP-ICCC97.html

Hitchcock, S., Carr, L., Harris, S., Hay I.M.N. and Hall, W. (1997b) Citation linking: improving access to online journals. In R. B. Allen and E. Rasmussen (eds) *Proceedings of the 2nd ACM International Conference on Digital Libraries*. New York: Association of Computing Machinery, 115–22. Also available at http://journals.ecs.soton.ac.uk/acdml97.html

Hunter, E. J. and Bakewell, K.G.B. (1991) *Cataloguing*. 3rd edn. London: Library Association Publishing Ltd

Lynch C. (1997) Searching the Internet. *Scientific American*, available at http://www.sciam.com/0397issue/0397.lynch/html

Martin, J. (1980) *An Endusers Guide to Database.* Carnforth: Savant Research Studies

McMurdo, G. (1995) How the Internet was indexed. *Journal of Information Science*, **21**(6), 479–89

Verity G. (1993) Relational database management systems and open systems used in the development of Oracle Libraries. *Program*, **27** (1), 73–82

Weibel S. (1997) The Dublin Core: a simple content description model for electronic resources. *Bulletin of the American Society for Information Science*, **24**(1), 9–11

CHAPTER 6

Searching

Introduction

Information seeking can be viewed as either information searching or information browsing (see Chapter 7), although information seeking is often, in practice, a combination of these two activities. In this chapter basic approaches to searching are discussed. Thus there is an assumption that the information seeker is able to define the information need sufficiently well to proceed with an information-searching strategy rather than a browsing approach. The various types of search (known item, factual and subject) were outlined in Chapter 2. Subject searches are the most difficult to complete successfully because the searcher rarely knows when all the relevant information has been extracted from a particular source.

The aim of any searcher is to achieve the best possible outcome for a search. In general it can be said that searchers seek the following objectives:

- to retrieve approximately the desired number of relevant items (i.e. to avoid retrieving too many items on the one hand or too few or none on the other);
- to avoid retrieving too many irrelevant items;
- to avoid missing too many (or any) relevant items.

They also want to conclude the search as quickly and cheaply as possible.

These objectives must be viewed flexibly depending upon the circumstances of the search. There will be occasions when the searcher's primary objective is to retrieve everything relevant to the search no matter how many items that might be. Examples are a search of a legal database for case law or a search of a medical database for details of the toxic effects of a chemical. At other times the searcher will be satisfied by the retrieval of some but not all of the available information. For example someone searching for hotels in Barcelona may only want a selection of those available. Someone looking for recipes involving eggs and chocolate may want a selection from which to choose, but is most unlikely to require every recipe in which eggs and chocolate are used. There may be rare occasions when the searcher hopes that the number of items retrieved is zero. Examples might be the inventor searching a patents database to check the originality of an invention or the designer of a new trademark who hopes that the new design is not similar to one already in existence.

There are two different approaches to information retrieval: partial match and best match. In partial match, the searcher specifies search criteria and the search engine examines the database and retrieves those items which match the search criteria without any attempt to indicate that one retrieved item is more relevant than another. In the second approach, the searcher presents a search to the search engine, which responds with items ranked by their relevance to the query.

This chapter begins with an explanation of search facilities available in Boolean-based systems, followed by a discussion of search strategies and tactics using these systems. Ranked output retrieval is discussed in a later part of the chapter.

Basic Boolean Search Facilities

In Boolean searching, the searcher presents one or more search statements to the search engine. Each search statement may consist of a single search criterion or a number of search criteria. Usually these criteria are terms or phrases representing subjects but they may also be the names of authors or criteria such as the language of publication or the source of the information. The search engine retrieves from the database those items which match the search terms and allocates a set number to each search statement. Thus the database is partitioned into two: those items which match the search criteria and so are retrieved and those which are not retrieved. Effective manipulation of the created sets to maximize search performance requires the use of a range of strategies and tactics which are discussed later in the chapter.

A variety of retrieval system interfaces exists using command languages, forms and menus. The interface is very important to the search process and interfaces are discussed fully in Chapter 8. Here, searching is discussed in general terms using examples taken from a variety of interfaces and search systems. Where a command language has been used the Dialog command language has been chosen. This does not imply endorsement of this particular command language.

Database selection

Many online search services offer access to dozens or even hundreds of databases (see Chapter 3). In such cases, the first step in the search is to instruct the search system which database(s) to use. This is achieved in a command-driven system with the relevant command and the appropriate database label or name. In Dialog, for example, the command is BEGIN and most databases are referred to by a database number. So to start a search in the PsycInfo database the command:

BEGIN 11

is entered, while the command:

BEGIN 48

would be used by the searcher to choose the SportDiscus database. The system responds by confirming which database has been chosen and indicating the time period for which the database is available. Figure 6.1 gives an example of choosing the SportDiscus database with the user input presented in bold type. In systems that do not employ a command language, the available databases are typically displayed in a table and the searcher selects from that table. For example, Figure 6.2 shows database selection from a table on OCLC FirstSearch. Database selection is also shown in Figure 3.8 (from the University of California's MELVYL), Figure 9.2 (from Dialog's Web interface) and Figure 9.4 (from the British Library's OPAC).

There is no direct equivalent when using an Internet search engine; however, it is possible with some search engines to restrict the search to either Web pages or Usenet. Furthermore, it may also be possible to restrict the Web pages to those occurring on servers in a given country or in a given language.

> **?begin 48**
>
>   02mar98 12:11:00 User711255 Session D619.2
> $0.03   0.002 Hrs File11
> $0.03 Estimated cost File11
> $0.03 Estimated cost this search
> $0.53 Estimated total session cost   0.036 Hrs.
>
>   File 48:SPORTDiscus   1962–1998/Mar
>   (c) 1998 Sport Information Resource Centre
>
>   Set Items Descriptions
>   ─── ──── ────────
>
> ?

Figure 6.1   Database selection on Dialog

database   search   results   record   news   exit   help
[Last Area= (None) | **Last Database**= (None)]

Database Areas	**All Databases**
Arts & Humanities	(Click a database name to search it)

All Databases
(Click a database name to search it)

Database Areas

Arts & Humanities
Business & Economics
Conferences & Proceedings
Consumer Affairs & People
Education
Engineering & Technology
General & Reference
General Science
Life Sciences
Medicine & Health Sciences
News & Current Events
Public Affairs & Law
Social Sciences

All Databases

General Databases
WorldCat   Books and other materials in libraries worldwide. (Info)
Article1st   Index of articles from nearly 12,500 journals. (Info)
Contents1st Table of contents of nearly 12,500 journals. (Info)
NetFirst   OCLC database of Internet resources. (Info)
UnionLists OCLC Union Lists of Periodicals. (Info)

Specialized Databases
ERIC   Journal articles and reports in education. (Info)
GEOBASE Worldwide literature on geography and geology. (Info)
GeoRefS Guide to materials in geology and earth sciences. (Info)
GPO   U.S. government publications. (Info)
MEDLINE Abstracted articles from medical journals. (Info)

MLA   Literature, languages, linguistics, folklore. (Info)
PapersFirst An index of papers presented at conferences. (Info)
Proceedings An index of conference publications. (Info)

[TOP]   **Databases** Search   Results   Record   News   Text Only   Exit   Help

Figure 6.2   Database selection on OCLC FirstSearch

Term selection

Having chosen the database, the searcher enters a search term either in a search box or, if using a command-driven system, by entering the command and search term. In Dialog, the command is SELECT. Thus, to find all the items that include the single term 'children', the searcher enters:

SELECT CHILDREN

The system will then respond by indicating how many records in the database contain the term children. An example of term selection using a dialogue box on AltaVista is shown in Figure 6.3 where the single term, Laugharne, matches with 223 references.

Term truncation

With most search systems, the searcher is able to truncate terms. Thus:

CHILD?

223 documents match your query.
Check out our **Editors Picks** of related sites.
Search **Amazon.com** for top-selling titles about **laugharne.**

Real Name^{SM} Address - laugharne
Subscribe your company, brands and trademarks to the Real Name System.

1. Dylan Thomas and Laugharne
Dylan Thomas and Laugharne. Dylan Thomas. Dylan Thomas (Warrick D.G. Whatman, Canberra) Dylan Thomas
Poetry Index. Dylan Thomas Readers' Home Page (Peter..
http://www.swan.ac.uk/german/ballad/thomas.htm - size 3K - 8-Mar-98 - English - Translate

Figure 6.3   Single term selection on AltaVista

will retrieve all those records containing a word beginning with the stem
'child', such as childish, childlike and children as well as child.

Many but by no means all retrieval systems enable the searcher to place
the truncation symbol within a word. This is called a wild card or embedded truncation. For example:

ORGANI?ATION

would retrieve both the American and the British spelling of the word, and
the search term:

WOM?N

would retrieve occurrences of both the singular and the plural spellings.

In some search services such as DIMDI and the European Community
Host Organization (ECHO), left-hand truncation is possible, that is to say,
terms can be sought with variant prefixes. This can be particularly useful
in searching for complex chemical names. A search for '?dimethylbenzoic
acid' would retrieve items about either 2, 3-dimethylbenzoic acid or
3,4-dimethylbenzoic acid. A less technical example is:

?NQUIRY

that would retrieve occurrences of either 'enquiry' or 'inquiry'.

Truncation can have a significant impact on retrieval. This is demonstrated in Figure 6.4 where, using the PsycInfo database, several ways of
truncating the term 'computer' or 'computation' are presented together
with their associated postings (that is, the number of occurrences of the
term). Generally speaking, the stronger the truncation and the broader the
subject coverage of the database, the greater the possibility for the retrieval
of unwanted material. For example, in a database about animals, 'cat?' will
retrieve items containing cat or cats or cattle or caterpillar. If the database

truncated term	postings
COMPUTER?	25785
COMPUTAT?	2567
COMPUT?	35183
COMP?	357140

Figure 6.4   The effect of truncation in the PsycInfo database on Dialog

were not restricted to material about animals but included other subjects then there are many more words whose presence would cause items to be retrieved. Examples include catastrophe, catering or catalogue. Accordingly truncation should be used with caution.

There is considerable variation in the truncation symbols used by different search engines. Commonly occurring symbols include *, ?, #, :, $, !, and +. Furthermore, some search services use more than one symbol to indicate different sorts of truncation. Thus, for example, STN International uses ! to restrict truncation to a single character within or at the end of a search term, # at the end of a search term to indicate that the stem itself (that is, zero truncation) or the stem followed by a single character are to be retrieved and ? at the end of a term to indicate the stem can be extended by any number of characters.

Boolean term combination

It is frequently necessary to combine more than one term in a search statement. This is achieved using Boolean operators. Most search systems use the three common operators AND, OR and NOT, while some of them offer more possibilities.

AND is used to create a search statement where all the terms must be present in any retrieved items. An example is a search for items containing the terms:

OIL AND POLLUTION

which retrieves those items containing both the terms oil and pollution. Thus use of the AND operator normally reduces the number of items that would have been retrieved using only one of the terms in the search statement since its use establishes more exacting search criteria (all terms must be present).

The second Boolean operator is OR. This operator requires that any one or more of the terms in a search statement must be present in retrieved items but no more than one of them need be present. Typically OR is used when the searcher is not certain which of several synonyms, near synonyms, spelling variants or word forms might be used in the database. Thus the search for:

GREEK OR GREECE OR HELLENIC

will find those items that include one or more of these terms. Normally use of the OR operator will increase the number of items retrieved compared with a search for any one of the terms.

The third operator is NOT. This is used to specify that a term should not be present. Generally its use reduces the number of items retrieved. Thus the search statement:

POLLUTION NOT WATER

will retrieve those items containing the term pollution but only if the term water is not present. There is the possibility with the NOT operator that potentially useful material will not be retrieved. For example a document containing the sentence 'The document discusses the presence of lead compounds in soil in urban areas but specifically excludes any discussion of water pollution' would not be retrieved because of the presence of the term water in the sentence. Yet the meaning of the sentence implies that the document might indeed be very relevant to the search. Thus the NOT operator should be used with considerable care. Some search engines such as AltaVista and LEXIS/NEXIS use AND NOT rather than NOT, while WILSONLINE, another online search service, permits either NOT or AND NOT.

When two or more different Boolean operators are present in a single search statement, for example:

KENT AND APPLES OR PEARS

there is ambiguity in the meaning. Most, if not all, humans would interpret such a search statement as meaning those items which contain the term Kent and either the term apples or the term pears. That is to say, that the OR operator would be processed before AND. However, computers do not interpret; they process according to rules. If the AND operator is processed before the OR, then in this example items would be retrieved that contain both the terms Kent and apples, together with all items containing the word pears whether or not the term Kent was present. Each search engine has rules for the sequence in which the operators are processed and unfortunately these rules vary among search engines.

Fortunately, the search systems provide a way for ensuring that the retrieval engine will execute a statement using more than one different operator in the way that the user desires. Typically, parentheses can be used to override the system's default sequence for executing the operators. For example, if the default sequence for operator execution is AND before OR then the search statement should be presented as:

KENT AND (APPLES OR PEARS)

to override the AND priority and ensure that the OR operation is done first.

Similarly, a search for items on water pollution or soil pollution might be entered as:

(SOIL OR WATER) AND POLLUTION

```
Database:   Enviroline(R) 1975–1997/Nov
            (c) 1997 Congressional Information Service


            Search statement               Postings

            (soil or water) and pollution  21304
            soil or (water and pollution)  39887
```

Figure 6.5   The impact of using parentheses in the Enviroline database on Dialog

which would be considerably different from:

SOIL OR (WATER AND POLLUTION)

Figure 6.5 shows the postings for these two search statements when they were tried on the Enviroline database. The difference in the number of items retrieved is easy to see and emphasizes the importance of correct use of parentheses.

Parentheses should also be used to ensure that complex search statements are processed as intended. For example, a search on the newspaper *Le Monde* on CD-ROM for items about the relationship between Greece and the Former Yugoslav Republic of Macedonia (FYROM) might use a search statement such as:

(SKOPJE OR MACEDOINE OR FYROM)
AND (GREECE OR ATHENES)

where the use of the parentheses makes the search intention unambiguous.

Word proximity

There are occasions where it is not sufficient to specify a search requirement as merely the retrieval of items containing two or more given terms, that is to say, linked by an AND operator. In very large databases, for example, there are many opportunities for two terms to be present in such a way as to have a different meaning from that intended by the searcher. For example the search statement:

NUCLEAR AND POWER

would retrieve a document which contained the following sentence: 'The article discusses the dominant power of males in the nuclear family in Western society'. Assuming that the search statement was intended to retrieve items about nuclear power, this particular item would not be relevant. To avoid such 'false drops', it is necessary to use more restrictive search criteria. Many search engines offer what is known as word proximity or word adjacency searching. Proximity operators enable the positional (but not semantic) relationship between sought terms to be specified. Dialog offers a range of word proximity operators, the most restrictive of which is (W). Thus the search statement:

SELECT INFORMATION(W)RETRIEVAL

requires that the two terms appear next to each other in the specified word order. That is to say, only those items containing the phrase 'information retrieval' will be retrieved. It is possible to be less restrictive by specifying a number of intervening terms which may be present between the sought terms. For example:

SELECT TERM1(nW)TERM2

where n specifies the maximum permitted number of intervening words.
For example:

SELECT GONE(2W)WIND

will retrieve all occurrences of the term gone where there are zero, one or two terms before the term wind appears. In practice it will rarely, if ever, be worth having a value of n which is greater than ten and in most cases it is likely to be considerably smaller.

A less restrictive word proximity operator is (N). The form of use resembles that of the (W) operator except that (N) will retrieve occurrences of the terms in either order, not just in the specified order. So for example the search statement:

SELECT INFORMATION(2N)RETRIEVAL

will retrieve items containing the phrase 'information retrieval' as in the earlier example but will also retrieve occurrences of a phrase such as 'the retrieval of chemical information', which would not be retrieved by the more restrictive (W) operator.

It is also possible to specify that items retrieved contain the sought terms in the same field, thus:

SELECT INFORMATION(F)RETRIEVAL

will retrieve records only where the terms information and retrieval occur, say, in the title field or the descriptor field. The full range of word proximity operators available with Dialog is presented in Figure 6.6.

Some systems enable the use of NOT proximity. Thus the search statement:

SELECT INFORMATION(NOT W)RETRIEVAL

would match only against those occurrences of the term information where it does not occur in the phrase information retrieval.

It should be noted that while most, if not all, search services offer word proximity searching, the precise manner in which they do so varies. The facilities available and their exact implementation are closely linked to the manner of operation of the inverted file system, discussed in Chapter 5. Many search engines have a less comprehensive range of word proximity features than those described here. While this makes the searchers' task less complex, it also reduces the searchers' ability to specify search requirements

Symbol	Example	Function
(W)	S FISH(W)FARMING	Requires that the items retrieved contain the terms in the specified order and adjacent to each other
(nW)	S FISH(2W)FARMING	Requires that the items retrieved contain the specified terms within n words of each other (in this example there can be a maximum of two intervening words) and in the specified order
(N)	S FISH(N)FARMING	Requires that the items retrieved contain the specified terms next to each other but in either order
(nN)	S FISH(3N)FARMING	Requires that the items retrieved contain the specified terms within n words of each other (in this example there can be a maximum of three intervening words) and the sought terms can appear in either order
(F)	S FISH(F)FARMING	Requires that the items retrieved contain the sought terms in the same field
(L)	S FOOT(L)DISEASE	Requires that the items retrieved contain the terms in the same descriptor as defined by the database
(S)	S FOOT(S)DISEASE	Requires that the items retrieved contain the sought terms in the same sub-field unit as defined by the database

Figure 6.6   Word proximity operators as used on Dialog

exactly. More examples of proximity operator use will be found later in this chapter.

Entering phrases

Rather than individual words, many search engines permit the searcher to enter a phrase. Thus it is perfectly possible to enter a search such as:

INTERNET SEARCH ENGINES

However, this must be used with caution as different search engines may process the search very differently. Many search engines treat this search statement as an implied Boolean statement and supply the operators auto-matically. Unfortunately, some search engines may supply Boolean AND so that it is equivalent to:

INTERNET AND SEARCH AND ENGINES

while others may supply Boolean OR so that the search is:

INTERNET OR SEARCH OR ENGINES

Clearly the meaning of these two statements is very different and thus the number of items retrieved is likely to be very different. A third interpre-tation might be:

INTERNET (next to) SEARCH (next to) ENGINES

In this case the entire phrase is treated as one search term. Traditional online services only search for such phrases in fields which have been phrase indexed (see Chapter 5). In practice this often means that the search engine defaults to a search only of the field which contains the terms from the controlled vocabulary.

Field searching

It is frequently useful to specify that the sought term appears in a partic-ular field. For example, this would enable the ready distinction between items written by a particular author and items written about a particular author. In a bibliographical database, it may be important to distinguish between items of which Racine is the author and items which are about Racine and his literature. In schematic terms the difference is between:

author = racine, jean

and:

subject = racine

The precise facilities available will depend upon the particular retrieval software but, for example, might enable the searcher to specify that the personal name appear either in the author field or in one of the subject fields such as title, abstract or descriptor field. Figure 5.10 showed the range of field labels that could be used when searching the ASFA database on Dialog.

The significant impact on search outcome of the decision about which field to search is illustrated by the different postings for the same search term in four different fields in the LISA CD-ROM database as shown in Figure 6.7. The difference between the postings for ft and kw is accounted for by the fact that ft defaults to implicit proximity in expressed order while kw defaults to implicit Boolean AND which is slightly less restrictive and hence retrieves more items. Options available for field searching vary between search engines and databases. The searcher is advised to consult appropriate online or print documentation.

Search criterion	Postings
ti = transaction log$	04
su = transaction log$	38
ft = transaction log$	93
kw = transaction log$	99

where $ is a truncation symbol and the prefix labels refer to title, subject, fulltext and keyword respectively.

Figure 6.7   The impact of field searching on search output exemplified using the LISA CD-ROM

Limiting searches

Many search engines allow users to set limits on the search. These might be global limits which are applied at the beginning of a search, such as an Internet search where the user specifies that only a particular kind of site be searched. Alternatively it may be possible to apply limits to a set which has already been created using an instruction of the form:

LIMIT SET N (LIMIT CRITERIA)

Typical criteria by which a search can be restricted are:

- By date, e.g. only documents published in a given date range.
- By document type, e.g. only books, only journal articles.
- By language, e.g. only items in French.
- By field(s).
- By source, e.g. WWW or UseNet.

Index inspection

It is frequently advantageous to examine the inverted index to discover exactly how a term appears in a given database. For example, it can be very useful to check the precise form in which a sought author's name appears in the phrase-indexed author field (as most databases do not impose any standardization in the case of authors who publish under various forms of their name). It may also be wise to check for the use of singular or plural forms of a word or the use of British or American spellings. Such index consultation is achieved on Dialog by the command EXPAND and is best illustrated with an example.

In Figure 6.8, the searcher has entered the command EXPAND TELEVI-SION. Dialog has responded with a table of 12 terms (Index-term) together with their postings (Items) and the number of related terms (RT). The EXPANDed term appears as the third item in the list. The searcher is able to display the next 12 terms in the alphabetically arranged index by entering P for PAGE. The searcher can then choose any term from the list by use

File 1:ERIC 1966–1997/Dec
   (c) format only 1998 The Dialog Corporation

Set Items Descriptions
── ──── ────────

?**expand television**

Ref	Items	RT	Index-term
E1	35		TELEVISING
E2	1		TELEVISIO
E3	18977	44	*TELEVISION (SYSTEM WHEREBY VISUAL IMAGES, WITH OR WITHOU . . .)
E4	16		TELEVISION ACCESS
E5	6		TELEVISION ADVERTISING AND CHILDREN PROJECT
E6	6		TELEVISION AESTHETICS
E7	3		TELEVISION AND BEHAVIOR (NIMH)
E8	2		TELEVISION ANNOUNCERS
E9	1		TELEVISION AS BABYSITTER
E10	1		TELEVISION AWARENESS TRAINING
E11	1		TELEVISION CAMERAS
E12	2		TELEVISION CHARACTERS

   Enter P or PAGE for more
?**p**

Ref	Items	RT	Index-term
E13	716	8	TELEVISION COMMERCIALS
E14	1		TELEVISION CREATORS
E15	64		TELEVISION CRITICISM
E16	383	8	TELEVISION CURRICULUM (CURRICULUM CONCERNED WITH TELEVISION, TELEVI . . .)
E17	1		TELEVISION DECODER CIRCUITRY ACT 1990
E18	1		TELEVISION DIRECTORS
E19	2		TELEVISION DOCUMENTARIES
E20	2		TELEVISION EDUCATION
E21	0	1	TELEVISION EQUIPMENT
E22	1		TELEVISION FILMSTELEVISION FOCUSED SOCIAL INTERA
E23	1		TELEVISION FOR EFFECTIVE PARENTHOOD
E24	3		

   Enter P or PAGE for more
? select **e16**

	S1	383 "TELEVISION CURRICULUM"

?**select e4–e6**

		16 TELEVISION ACCESS
		6 TELEVISION ADVERTISING AND CHILDREN PROJECT
		6 TELEVISION AESTHETICS
	S2	28 E4–E6

Figure 6.8   Examining the inverted file index for the ERIC database on Dialog

of the reference E numbers rather than by re-typing the terms. This is demonstrated in Figure 6.8 where the phrases "television curriculum", "television access", "television advertising and children project" and "television aesthetics" have been chosen by use of the E numbers (e16 and e4–e6). Once again the point must be made that while this is how the index is examined on Dialog, other search services use rather different commands to offer similar functionality.

Where an online thesaurus is included in the database, inspection of the index may reveal that there are terms related to those displayed. Usually it will be possible to follow up these term relationships and this can be very useful for search development. An example of this was provided in Figure 4.9.

Given the vast size of the databases created by some of the Internet search engines, it is often sensible to take advantage of the equivalent facility which most of them provide. For example, AltaVista and Open Text Index permit a search to be restricted to words in an abstract and most of the major search engines enable a search to be restricted to a specific host. Full details can be found in a survey of search engines (Catching Sites, 1997).

Display Facilities

Given the interactive nature of retrieval from electronic information sources, it is often useful to display the preliminary items retrieved and to amend the search strategy. Most search systems allow user output in a brief format which might consist of the display of a number of items with a single line of information per item. The searcher can evaluate the relevance of the item as well as mark those items for which fuller information is required. Some search services may offer as many as eight or nine predetermined output formats. These formats will offer the searcher different combinations of fields for display. For example Dialog offers:

- accession number;
- bibliographic citation;
- bibliographic citation plus indexing;
- full record including abstract;
- title and indexing;
- title;
- full record (full-text records);
- database label format (for company directories).

Finally, many online search services and some CD-ROM products enable the searcher to define the format in which output will be displayed by indicating, usually by use of labels, those fields which are to appear in the output display.

Many systems also allow the user to review the search strategy by displaying the search history to date. This is achieved in Dialog with the command Display Sets.

?begin *41*

File 41:Pollution Abs 1970±1998/Jan
   (c) 1998 Cambridge Scientific Abstracts

   Set Items Description
   +++ ++++ ++++++++
?select soil or soils
      16086 SOIL
      11213 SOILS
  S1 18607 SOIL OR SOILS
?select urban

  S2 7809 URBAN
?select heavy(w)metal?

      11363 HEAVY
      18438 METAL?
  S3 9572 HEAVY(W)METAL?
?select s1 and s2 and s3

      18607 S1
      7809 S2
      9572 S3
  S4 105 S1 AND S2 AND S3
?limit unit 4/eng

  S5 101 4/ENG
?select s5 and py=199?

      101 S5
    73521 PY=199?
  S6 52 S5 AND PY=199?
?display 6/2/1

Display 6/2/1
DIALOG(R)File 41:Pollution Abs
(c) 1998 Cambridge Scientific Abstracts. All rts. reserv.

240988 97±07731
  Soil characteristics of oak stands along an urban-rural land-use gradient
  Pouyat, R. V.; McDonnell, M. J.: Pickett, S. T. A.
  USDA-Forest Serv., Northeastern Forest Exp. Stn., c/o Inst. Ecosystem
Stud., P.O. Box AB, Millbrook, NY 12545, USA
  J. ENVIRON. QUAL VOL. 24, NO. 3, pp. 516±526, Publ.Yr: 1995
  SUMMARY LANGUAGE ± ENGLISH
  Languages: ENGLISH
  Journal Announcement: V28N8
  Descriptions: soil; forests; land use; Quercus; USA, New York, New York;
heavy metals; rural areas; urban areas
                ±end of record±

?

Figure 6.9   Sample search on Pollution Abstracts on Dialog

Figure 6.10   Search for spoil heaps using Northern Light search engine

In Figure 6.9 a complete search is shown illustrating the use of several search facilities in combination. The search, for information about heavy metals in urban soils, was carried out on the Pollution Abstracts database on Dialog. Several different commands are demonstrated:

Begin (to choose database 41, Pollution Abstracts)
Select (to search for terms)
Display (to view retrieved records, in this case record 1 of the 52 retrieved in set 6)

Record 1 is displayed in pre-defined format 2 which consists of the bibliographic description of the item and the controlled terms assigned to this record. It also contains examples of truncation(?), word proximity(W), Boolean operators(OR,AND) and the use of non-subject search criteria (PY= to search for publication years) and limiting an existing set (limit 4/eng to limit the items in set 4 to just those in the English language).

Figure 6.10 shows a search on Northern Light for information about spoil heaps, by entering the phrase in quotation marks. Organization of the retrieved items into the folders indicated down the left hand side of the figure provides the searcher with a means of limiting the search by using one of the folders which was created 'on the fly' by the search engine.

The facilities mentioned so far can be considered basic facilities available on CD-ROM products and commercial online search services. Many of them are also found on Internet search engines and library OPACs. However, because Internet search engines and OPACs are more obviously designed for end users, these facilities may be built into the retrieval mechanism and not explicitly offered to the searcher.

Further Search Facilities

In addition to the basic search facilities, a number of further retrieval facilities are available on many search services.

Database selection aids

Many search services host multiple databases and selection of the best database(s) to meet a particular information need is often difficult. They may therefore offer some aid to database selection by enabling a comparison of the number of postings attached to a term or a combination of terms within the various databases. This can be achieved through an index of indexes such as Dialog's DialIndex. The searcher can either choose a pre-determined broad subject category, such as social sciences, in which all the databases on Dialog dealing with this subject are included, or pick

?begin 411

File 411:DIALINDEX(R)

?set files socsci

You have 16 files in your file list.
(To see banners, use SHOW FILES command)

?select smoking and policy and workplace

Your SELECT statement is:
select smoking and policy and workplace

Items	File
8	1: ERIC_1966–1997/Dec
41	7: Social SciSearch(R)_1972–1998/Mar W1
17	11: PsycINFO(R)_1967–1998/Feb
3	46: A–V Online_1997/Dec. Q4
5	49: PAIS INT._1976–1998/Jan
435	88: IAC BUSINESS A.R.T.S._1983–1998/Mar 02
7	142: Social Sciences Abstracts_1983–1998/Jan
1	468: Public Opinion_1940–1998/Feb W4
5	21: NCJRS_1972–1998/Jan
3	35: Dissertation abstracts Online_1861–1998/Mar
10	37: Sociological Abst._1963–1998/Feb

11 files have one or more items; file list includes 16 files.

Figure 6.11   Using DialIndex to aid database choice

out individual databases of probable relevance to the search. The search statement can then be tried out in this index of indexes; the resulting postings will show the searcher exactly how many hits will be found in each database should the search be executed in the database file itself rather than merely in DialIndex. Thus, the assumption is that the searcher can choose the most productive database(s) in which to carry out the search. An example is provided in Figure 6.11. The searcher starts by choosing DialIndex, which like regular databases is identified by a number (begin 411). The searcher decides that the best databases are likely to be in the social sciences category and therefore chooses it using the appropriate command together with the Dialog subject category (set files socsci). Dialog responds by indicating that 16 databases (files) belong to its social sciences category. The search terms are then entered as they would be with a regular Dialog database (select smoking and policy and workplace). Dialog responds indicating that 11 databases contain the required combination of terms and indicating the number of items in each database with the required term combination. Thus File 88 IAC Business A.R.T.S. has the most with 435 and File 468 has the least with just a single item. The next step would be to leave DialIndex and perform the search proper using one or more of the 11 databases; DialIndex contains only the index and post-ings files but not the print files which hold the records themselves (see Chapter 5).

Multifile searching

A logical step beyond examining the inverted indexes of several data-bases in a single operation as an aid to database choice is the ability to execute a search across more than one database, so-called multifile searching. Multifile searching is usually undertaken using groups of data-bases within a particular broad subject area such as social sciences or engineering. Such multifile searching is a powerful tool saving the need to execute a search in several databases one after the other. Unfortunately, it also has one major downside. It is no longer possible to exploit some features, such as specific fields or search facilities, unless they are avail-able on all the databases being searched. For example, not all the databases may allow limiting by, say, language. Furthermore although all the data-bases may (they may not of course) include controlled vocabulary terms in a Descriptor field, each database most probably has its own terms listed in its own thesaurus to describe the same concept. The lack of common controlled terms across databases effectively precludes multifile searches on controlled vocabulary terms – natural language searching is the only option.

Since there is often overlap in database content, it is no surprise that multifile searching can result in the retrieval of duplicate citations within a single search. Many of the search services have developed routines for the detection and subsequent removal of these duplicate records from the retrieved sets. This is especially important if a charge is made for viewing retrieved records.

Saving searches and selective dissemination of information

Many search services allow a search strategy to be stored, either for a fixed period of time or permanently, so that it can be reused at a later date without the need to re-enter it. Search statements may be stored temporarily to enable a short period offline to reflect on how to develop the search. Search statements may be stored permanently to enable the search to be run regularly to retrieve material newly added to the database. Many online services have taken this a step further and provide automatic updating of a search by running a stored search against a database whenever new material is added to it. This is usually referred to as selective dissemination of information (SDI).

SDI has existed for many years but has been given a new lease of life through the introduction of products which 'push' selected information to users automatically. Variously referred to as 'intelligent agents', 'filtering agents' or 'push technology', the new products enable a stored search profile to be matched on a regular basis against a wide range of sources such as newswires. The information which matches the profile, is 'pushed' straight to a user's desktop. Thus a highly personalized information service is provided. Since they are so new, the importance of push technologies is not yet clear but it is reasonably certain that customization of information products for groups, organizations and even individuals will play an increasingly important part in the information industry of the future (Galt, 1997; Lawlor, 1997).

Search output processing

Many search services and some CD-ROM products offer additional facilities which strictly speaking are not concerned with effective retrieval but nevertheless are valuable to the searcher. For example, many CD-ROM products and some search services have a downloading format which enables the searcher to create output which is tagged with field labels for incorporation into reference management software such as ProCite or Endnote Plus. Some CD-ROM products may include with the data and search software further software for statistical analysis of the retrieved data.

Command Language Variation

The variation in available commands has been alluded to at various points in this chapter. Figure 6.12 has been drawn from several sources but especially the UKOLUG *Quick Guide to Online Commands* (Webber *et al.*, 1994).

The various commands available to execute the same operation and the variations in the use of symbols underlines the complexity of searching. The row showing Boolean operators indicates the various symbols which are used to represent each of the operators. So Boolean AND might be any of AND, + and * while Boolean OR might be OR or +. Thus the symbol +

Search function	Possible commands	
Database selection	BEGIN x	(x is a number)
	. . C/xxxx	(xxxx is a file label)
	FILE xxx	(xxx is a file name)
	FILE xxxx	(xxxx is a file name)
	FILES xxxx	(xxxx is a file label)
	BAS xxxx	(xxxx is a file label)
	BASE x	(x is a number)
	SEL xxx	(x is a file code)
	select from a prompt list	
Entering search terms	FIND	
	GET	
	PICK	
	SELECT	
	SELECT STEPS	
	or enter term directly at prompt	
Truncation	*	
	?	
	#	
	:	
	$	
	!	
Boolean operators	AND + *	
	OR , +	
	NOT – AND NOT	
	XOR	
Proximity operators	ADJ	
	WITH	
	SAME (F)	
	(W), (N), (L), (S)	
	, # $? / / /	
Specify index or field	xxxx.FI.	
	SELECT FI=xxxx	
	SELECT=xxxx/FI	
	xxxx@FI	
Index display	EXPAND xxxx	
	. . ROOT xxxx	
	NBR xxxx	
	N xxxx	
	. . IND xxxx	
Reviewing search statements	. . D ALL	
	D HIS	
	DISP	
	DISPLAY SETS	
	HIS	
	RECAP	
	REVIEW	
	V	
Online display of retrieved material	. . L	
	. . P	
	PRT	
	TYPE	
Multi-file searching	BEGIN	
	SBAS	
	STARSEARCH	

Figure 6.12   Examples of command variation for some search functions

is used by some services to mean Boolean OR while others use it to mean
Boolean AND. Furthermore the symbol # is a truncation symbol with some
services and a proximity operator with others.

It is not surprising that there have been attempts to implement a common
command language. What is perhaps more surprising is that such attempts
have met with only limited success. Some European search services such
as DIMDI and ECHO have implemented the European Common Command
Language, but most have ignored it. Considerable effort under the auspices
of the US National Information Standards Organization (NISO) has resulted
in the publication of a standard (National Information Standards
Organization, 1994). Whether such a standard will have much influence,
given the increasing dominance of graphical user interfaces, is open to
doubt.

Search Strategies

The importance of language was examined in Chapter 4 and retrieval facilities were reviewed in the previous section of this chapter. It is now possible to see how these can be combined and exploited to achieve the search objective outlined at the beginning of this chapter.

The evaluation of retrieval effectiveness is considered fully in Chapter 10 but it is useful here to introduce the important concepts of recall and precision. Formally, the terms are defined as follows:

$$recall = \frac{\text{number of relevant items retrieved}}{\text{total number of relevant items in database}}$$

$$precision = \frac{\text{number of relevant items retrieved}}{\text{total number of items retrieved}}$$

It has become conventional to multiply each of the ratios by 100 and express them as percentages. The reason for introducing the concepts here is that research has shown that the two ratios are usually inversely proportional for a given database over a number of searches. While it does not automatically follow from this finding, it is often the case that an attempt by a searcher to increase the precision ratio will reduce the recall ratio and vice versa.

While discussion of search strategy mostly refers to subject searches, there will be occasions when the search has to trade accuracy of results against comprehensiveness of search in other types of search. Thus a search to retrieve a small number of items authored by Professor Joan Day might well be undertaken adequately using the search criterion:

AU = DAY, JOAN

However, such a search would not retrieve those items in which she is styled as Joan M. Day or J.M. Day. Thus if the objective of the search is a comprehensive list of items by this author (that is, high recall) in all probability it will be necessary to use the more general search criterion:

AU = DAY, J?

This more general search is likely to retrieve the items by the required author but also items by John Day and indeed any other Day whose first name begins with J. Thus the information seeker will find it necessary to browse through the retrieved items searching for the required items. Recall will have been improved but at the expense of precision.

Observation, interviews with experienced searchers and exchange of experience between searchers in the early days of online searching have led to the development of a range of general approaches to searching which are generally referred to as search strategies. It should be noted that these strategies evolved in the early days of online searching when the sources were essentially bibliographic and the retrieval facilities found on the search services were generally more complex than today's end-user-oriented search engines.

Furthermore the following discussion of search strategies presumes that the searcher has undertaken a careful analysis of the subject of the search and has a clear understanding of the information required. While this matter is glossed over in a single sentence, the reader should not ignore its importance: it has been the subject of many papers and much debate within the information community. An excellent starting point for the interested reader is to be found in Chapter 6 of Harter (1986).

The approach referred to as briefsearch or by some people as 'quick and dirty' is probably the most widely practised. In a briefsearch the individual concepts in the search are not exhaustively represented by all possible synonyms; instead each concept might be represented by only one search term regardless of the number which may be available. In principle this can be thought of as:

Term A AND Term B = search result set

For example, a search for material on the European Union's Common Fisheries Policy might be undertaken by simple term combination as follows:

European (next to) Union
AND
Fisheries (next to) Policy

This approach might be acceptable when the searcher requires only a few items but is much less likely to produce acceptable results if the searcher requires the search to be at all comprehensive (high recall). Nevertheless there is considerable evidence from transaction logs that this is the approach used by many users.

The approach referred to as building blocks is more appropriate for searches where higher recall is sought. A building blocks strategy differs from a briefsearch in that the searcher now uses synonyms and near synonyms for one or more of the sought concepts. Thus it can be thought of as:

Concept A   TermA1 OR TermA2 OR TermA3 etc.
Concept B   TermB1 OR TermB2 etc.
Concept C   TermC1 OR TermC2 OR TermC3 etc.

The search would become:

(A1 OR A2 OR A3)
AND
(B1 OR B2)
AND
(C1 OR C2 OR C3)

Application of the building blocks approach to the previous search example might lead to the following search:

COMMON FISHERIES POLICY
OR
CFP

OR
((EU OR EEC OR COMMON MARKET OR EUROPEAN UNION OR
EUROPEAN ECONOMIC COMMUNITY OR EUROPEAN COMMISSION)
AND (FISHERY OR FISHERIES) AND (POLICIES OR POLICY))

The successive fractions search strategy is a method of cutting down a large
set which has already been created by the use of Boolean AND or Boolean
NOT. Thus in general terms:

Term A AND Term B = Set 1 (a large set)
Term A AND Term B AND Term C = Set 2 (a fraction of Set 1)
(Term A AND Term B AND Term C) NOT Term D = Answer set

An example of this would be:

SWIMMING AND (FEMALE OR WOM?N)

which might produce 318 postings. Then a new term is added, so the search
becomes:

SWIMMING AND (FEMALE OR WOM?N) AND FIT?

which might produce only 29 postings, that is, a fraction of the previous
search. A final fraction is produced by adding one more search term:

(SWIMMING AND (FEMALE OR WOM?N) AND FIT?)
NOT ADVANCED

which might reduce the retrieved set to eight postings.

Citation pearl growing takes as its starting point a very small initial set,
possibly just one item, known to be relevant to the search. This one 'pearl'
is then inspected for suitable new terms which can be used to build the
blocks of the search. This process can be repeated as items retrieved by
the revised search in their turn are examined for further suitable
terms which can be added to the search. These various search strategies
are examined in greater detail by Harter (1986).

Search Tactics

Whatever search strategy might be adopted for a search, the search may not
succeed first time. In this situation the searcher has to interact with the system, examine the retrieved items and subsequently amend the search in such
a way as to improve the search results. There are two basic approaches available to the searcher: reduce the search output by employing tactics to narrow the search; or, if insufficient material has been retrieved, to increase the
search output by employing search broadening tactics. In using these tactics the searcher should remember that while there is no automatic relationship between narrowing and broadening a search and precision and
recall respectively, there is a tendency to increase precision and decrease
recall by narrowing a search, i.e. by reducing the number of items retrieved.
The reverse is also true; namely there is a tendency that increasing the number of items retrieved will increase recall and decrease precision.

Search-narrowing tactics

The aim of search-narrowing tactics is to reduce the output of the search. Ideally this is achieved by reducing the number of non-relevant items retrieved, thereby improving the precision of the search, while at the same time not removing too many of the relevant items. It must be emphasized that the tactics discussed in this and the next section must be used with caution. They are possibilities that the searcher can apply in a given search, but it is crucial to remember what is being sought and not to allow the application of particular search tactics to warp the search objective.

The first tactic which can be applied is to replace one of the existing search terms with a narrower term. But it is important to differentiate between semantic breadth and retrieval breadth. By semantic breadth is meant the breadth of the meaning of the term. For example, it is readily apparent that the term pollution has greater breadth than the term water pollution since the latter is but one branch of the former. By retrieval breadth is meant the capacity to retrieve items or the number of postings associated with a term in a given retrieval system. While logically it might be assumed that the two are the same, this is not necessarily the case. Indeed, in some situations they might be quite the reverse. This is because database producers often instruct their indexers to use the most specific term possible when they are assigning terms to document descriptions. For example, in the ERIC database, the descriptor 'grammar' has been assigned to more than 2,970 documents, while its broader term 'descriptive linguistics' has only been used some 740 times.

One important and obvious way to employ a narrower term is to replace a natural language term with the most appropriate descriptor, assuming that one exists.

A similar tactic is to require that the sought term appears in a particular field. In general, the presence of the term in a title field or a descriptor field is likely to maximize the chances of retrieving relevant material. While there are exceptions, it is generally true that titles are informative of the content of a paper and if a human indexer has assigned a term to a record to represent the content of the original document then it seems reasonable to assume that the document deals with the particular concept. On the other hand there are many opportunities for terms, especially single words, to appear in the abstract field or full text without having the required meaning. Thus replacement of:

TELEVISION

by:

TELEVISION restricted to title or descriptor field

is likely to reduce the number of items retrieved and is also likely to increase the precision of the search. For example, in the CAB Abstracts database restricting the term cattle to the descriptor field rather than anywhere in the record reduces the number of postings from 220,160 to 190,674.

It was noted earlier in the chapter that Boolean AND reduces the number of items retrieved and so if a searcher can add further search criteria linked by Boolean AND then the amount of material retrieved must inevitably decline.

Boolean NOT will have the same effect, although as noted earlier, this approach must be used carefully or there is a chance for the search to exclude relevant material.

If a search statement contains terms linked by Boolean AND which might sensibly be replaced by the terms linked by a form of word proximity operator then this might be a better means of narrowing the search. For example the search statement:

INFORMATION AND RETRIEVAL

might be replaced by the more precise:

INFORMATION(2N)RETRIEVAL

It is easy to see that replacing one form of word proximity with another which is more restrictive will reduce the search output. For example the replacement of:

INFORMATION(2N)RETRIEVAL

by the more restrictive:

INFORMATION(W)RETRIEVAL

will almost certainly reduce the number of postings associated with the particular concept.

A final tactic which might be applied to reduce the output of a search is to add some limits to the search. The options available depend to some extent on the individual database which might have particular features that can be exploited. However, many databases permit some restrictions by language, date of publication or document type.

The searcher has the option of using more than one of these tactics in combination to try to reduce the output of a given search. However, it is sensible to use the tactics in a step-by-step approach and not to change too many features of a search formulation at the same time. Figure 6.13 shows several search narrowing tactics applied to the agricultural database, CAB International, in a search for items about foot and mouth disease. Initially a quick and dirty search is undertaken using the natural language terms foot and disease. This retrieves too large a number of postings (6157). The next step is to try the controlled vocabulary term "foot and mouth disease". The phrase is entered in quotation marks so that the search software treats it as a single term. Without quotation marks the software would recognise *and* as a Boolean operator and treat the search as one for items in which the term foot and the descriptor phrase mouth disease appear. Use of the controlled vocabulary term has reduced the output, but at 3048 items it is still too large. The next tactic is to add a new concept, cattle (set number 3). Again the output is about halved. In set 4 the output is further reduced by restricting the presence of the term cattle to the descriptor field. Imposing the restriction that all items must be published in 1990 or later (set 5) and the restriction that all retrieved items must be in the English language (set 6) again reduces

Database = CAB International 1972 to January 1998

set number	search statement	postings
1	foot and disease	6157
2	"foot and mouth disease"	3048
3	"foot and mouth disease" and cattle	1555
4	"foot and mouth disease" and cattle/de	1267
5	set 4 and py=199*	348
6	set 5 and language=english	270

* = truncation

Figure 6.13   Example of search narrowing using CAB International

the number of items retrieved. This combination of narrowing tactics, then, has reduced the output from over 6,000 items initially to just 270 items at the end.

Search-broadening tactics

There will be occasions when the search formulation does not retrieve sufficient material for the purposes of the search. If this occurs then the searcher can apply a number of search-broadening tactics to increase the output. The objective is to increase the number of items retrieved without retrieving an unacceptably high number of irrelevant items. The tactics available to increase search output are the reverse of the tactics available to reduce search output.

One option is to reduce the number of terms which are combined using Boolean AND. Inevitably, this must increase the number of items retrieved, though there is a danger that in adopting this approach the search formulation no longer matches the information sought and so there may well be an unacceptably high number of irrelevant items retrieved. For example, in Figure 6.14, the search is for material about the use of expert systems as front ends to information retrieval systems. The initial output was deemed not high enough (set 4) and so the decision was taken to remove the concept of front ends (set 3). This has resulted in an increased number of postings but too many of the retrieved items are not about front ends and so do not meet the search requirements.

A second tactic is to introduce a number of synonyms for one or more of the concepts in the search. Using the same search as in Figure 6.14, synonyms have been introduced for all of the concepts when the search was repeated in Figure 6.15; this increased the number of items retrieved from 22 in Figure 6.14 (set 4) to 85 in Figure 6.15 (set 13).

A variant on this tactic might be to replace one or more of the search terms by a term which is related in meaning but has a higher number of postings.

Database Library and Information Science Abstracts 1969 to Feb 1998

set number	search statement	postings
1	expert(adjacent)system*	1163
2	front(adjacent)end*	331
3	information(adjacent)retrieval	14761
4	sets 1 and 2 and 3	22
5	sets 1 and 3	292

* = truncation

Figure 6.14   Search broadening by concept removal on LISA

Greater use of truncation will increase the number of items retrieved although again this needs to be applied with caution since the more severe the truncation the greater the possibility of retrieving irrelevant material.

The less restrictive use of proximity operators, for example, the replacement of (W) by (N) in a search statement or even the replacement of a word proximity operator by Boolean AND will increase the number of items retrieved.

The number of items retrieved also can be increased by the removal of restrictions such as the language, document type, date.

The removal of the requirement that a sought term must appear in a specified field is a final way by which the number of items retrieved can be increased.

As with the narrowing of a search, these tactics can be used in combination but they should be used with caution and the searcher needs to ensure that the meaning of the query is not changed too much in the attempt to retrieve more material. It may be more sensible to repeat the search in a number of databases rather than contort the meaning of the search formulation too much in an attempt to increase the number of items which the search retrieves.

Best Match or Ranked Output Retrieval

It has long been argued by information retrieval researchers that the Boolean retrieval model discussed so far in this chapter is flawed, and considerable effort has been spent on the development of alternative models. However, until recently, the impact of research on practical information retrieval has been minimal. The emergence of Internet search engines, together with an increasing number of alternative retrieval mechanisms for CD-ROMs, OPACs and online search services, has changed the situation.

```
Database Library and Information Science Abstracts 1969 to Feb 1998

set number        search statement                                    postings
1                 expert(adjacent)system*                             1163
2                 knowledge(adjacent)based(adjacent)system*           505
3                 kbs                                                 33
4                 ikbs                                                2
5                 sets 1 or 2 or 3 or 4                               1572
6                 front(adjacent)end*                                 331
7                 interface*                                          3190
8                 sets 6 or 7                                         3414
9                 information(adjacent)retrieval                      14761
10                online(adjacent)searching                          560
11                online(adjacent)retrieval                          160
12                sets 9 or 10 or 11                                  15042
13                sets 5 and 8 and 12                                 85

* = truncation
```

Figure 6.15   Search broadening by use of synonyms on LISA

Problems with Boolean retrieval

The Boolean retrieval model has been criticized for a number of reasons. First, the partitioning of the database into two sets, retrieved and not retrieved, is often not very helpful to the searcher. It presumes that all items in the database are equally irrelevant (and therefore not to be retrieved) or equally relevant (and therefore to be retrieved). This contradicts a common sense observation that relevance is likely to be a matter of degree. Some items may be highly relevant, some quite relevant, some marginally relevant and some irrelevant. Boolean logic does not recognize such shades of grey, but only black and white. Normally, the only ordering of the retrieved set is by reverse date order, and so in terms of subject matter the last item presented and the first item presented are equally likely to be relevant to an information need. No attempt is made to rank retrieved output by its perceived importance to the user.

Furthermore, it is only possible to represent Boolean relationships between terms but there are other types of relationship such as causal relationships. For example, the Boolean combination BITE AND MAN AND DOG may not be ambiguous to the reader who understands that dogs generally bite people rather than the converse; in a Boolean world, however, the causal relationship – who bites whom – cannot be specified. Also, the searcher does not have any control over the number of items retrieved; the searcher cannot specify that only ten items are wanted, but they must be the best ten. Finally, the searcher must understand the use of Boolean operators that quite often function in a manner which is the reverse of their use in everyday speech, especially in the confusion in the use of AND and OR. Someone walking into a music store and asking for information about "trumpets and trombones" probably means, in a logical Boolean statement, "trumpets or trombones."

The response to these problems has been the development of numerous retrieval algorithms which seek to present the user with an output ordered by decreasing relevance to the query. Intuitively, it seems more sensible to provide search output so that those items most likely to meet the information needs of the searcher are presented first. Not only does this approach overcome the need to search through all the items retrieved, it also deals with the criticism that the searcher has no control over the volume of output. With a ranked output system the searcher simply stops working down the ranked list when it is felt that sufficient items have been examined to answer the information need. The basic assumption of all these approaches is that the searcher presents a search statement to the system, which operates as a retrieval black box and presents its output to the searcher. Various approaches to ranked output are presented in a non-technical manner in the rest of this chapter. The interested reader who wishes to gain a more detailed understanding is directed towards Brenner (1996), Ellis (1996) and Salton and McGill (1983).

Coordination level retrieval

Quorum function, or coordination level searching, is one simple alternative to Boolean retrieval. This was developed by Cleverdon and is described in Cleverdon (1984). Coordination level searching can best be explained with an example. Imagine a simple retrieval situation as follows:

	Index Terms
Document 1	A B C D E F
Document 2	A B C D
Document 3	A C
Search	(A or B) and (C or D or E or F)

The basis of coordination level searching is that it seems logical that Document 1 would be more relevant to the searcher than Document 2, which would in turn be more relevant than Document 3. The explanation is that Document 1 contains all six of the terms in the search while Document 2 contains 4 of the 6 and Document 3 contains only two of the terms. Yet a Boolean-based search would retrieve all three items and make no distinction between them in terms of probable relevance. Coordination level searching ignores the use of Boolean term combination and returns items in response to a query as a series of levels. Those items returned at coordination level one contain all the search terms while those at level two contain all but one of the search terms and those at level three contain all but two of the search terms, and so on. Coordination level searching has found application in the QUESTQUORUM search facility which was introduced by the

ESA-IRS search service in 1985 (Muhlhauser, 1985). It has also been used in the experimental OPAC OKAPI and from there was implemented in the Libertas OPAC.

A hypothetical example of a coordination level search is presented in Figure 6.16. The searcher is invited to enter the search terms without any use of Boolean or proximity operators. In an operational system, the system might simply respond by indicating that there are nine highly relevant items and 59 less relevant items. However, coordination level searching can be understood in terms of Boolean searching. It can be seen as the implicit use of Boolean AND and Boolean NOT.

In the figure additional information is present so that the processing of coordination level retrieval can be followed. The six terms are treated as though they were linked by Boolean AND. This is presented in the figure as set seven and leads to the nine items which are deemed to be relevant. Sets eight to 13 each contain five of the six sought terms. Examination of these sets will reveal that the term with the most postings is dropped first (so that set eight does not contain the term 'system'). The term with the second most postings is removed from the next set so that the term 'infor-

---

Please enter the terms which describe the subject of your search
TERMS: EXPERT SYSTEM FRONT END INFORMATION RETRIEVAL

Searching

Set number	Items	Terms
1	11342	expert
2	595796	system
3	18688	front
4	43926	end
5	173372	information
6	17468	retrieval

Creating co-ordination levels

set number	postings	sets
7	9	1 and 6 and 3 and 4 and 5 and 2
8	8	1 and 6 and 3 and 4 and 5 not 7
9	2	1 and 6 and 3 and 4 and 2 not (7 or 8)
10	1	1 and 6 and 3 and 5 and 2 not (7 or 8 or 9)
11	23	1 and 6 and 4 and 5 and 2 not (7 or 8 or 9 or 10)
12	11	1 and 3 and 4 and 5 and 2 not (7 or 8 or 9 or 10 or 11)
13	14	6 and 3 and 4 and 5 and 2 not (7 or 8 or 9 or 10 or 11 or 12)

9 relevant items have been retrieved and
59 less relevant items have been retrieved

Figure 6.16   Hypothetical coordination level search

mation' is not present in set nine and so on. The assumption is that the higher the postings of a term the less value it has as a discriminator between relevant and non relevant. There is increasing use of Boolean NOT through the sets simply to ensure that no items are retrieved more than once. The 59 unique items which are retrieved in sets eight to 13 each contain five of the six sought terms and are presented to the user as items of less relevance. Clearly it would be possible to continue the process so that the searcher is presented next with those items which contain any four of the six search terms and so on.

Term weighting

While coordination level searching presents items to the searcher in a series of levels, this is a limited form of ranking since there could well be many items presented at each level. What is required is a more complete ranking which gives the searcher a fully ranked output in response to a query. A variety of other methods of ranking retrieved items have been attempted. One method is to give a weight to each of the terms in a record; then the total weight which is given to each record in response to a query is the sum of the weights of all the query terms. The highest weighted are ranked highest. The simplest means of weighting terms is to give a weighting based upon the number of times a term occurs in a given record; thus the term which occurs ten times in a record has a weighting of ten while the term which appears only four times has a weighting of four. The argument is, of course, that if a term appears say 10 times in an item then the item is more strongly about that term than if it appears once. This is illustrated in the following example:

Term	A	B	C	D
Document 1	5	6	2	3
Document 2	4	1	7	6
Document 3	3	2	4	2

This shows that Term A occurs five times in Document 1, four times in Document 2, three times in Document 3 and so on.
Thus in a search for terms ABCD the weightings would be:

	Weighting
Document 1	16
Document 2	18
Document 3	11

and so clearly the ranked output would be:

Document 2
Document 1
Document 3

An alternative argument is that the weighting should reflect the frequency of occurrence of the term in the database rather than in the individual record. The rationale for this is that terms which appear with great frequency in a database are not good discriminators between individual records with respect to a given query. The sanity of this approach can be understood by noting the rather limited value of the term 'education' when searching an educational database or the term 'chemical' when searching a chemistry database. A means of weighting terms to give a low weighting to commonly occurring terms and to give a higher weighting to terms which do not occur with such great frequency is to use the reciprocal of the frequency of occurrence in the database. While the value of giving a lower weighting to the commonly occurring terms is interesting, it cannot be used as a sole measure since it will be unable to give different weights and hence rankings to records which contain the same terms. If the terms A, B, C, D in the above example occured 50, 30, 200 and 60 times respectively in the database then the weighting for each document is:

$$1/50 + 1/30 + 1/200 + 1/60$$

that is 0.065.

A commonly occurring weighting mechanism is to use the combination of the frequency of occurrence of term in record and the reciprocal of the frequency of occurrence in the database. The rationale for this approach is that it gives a positive weighting to terms which occur frequently in each individual document, while giving a lower weight to those terms which occur frequently in the whole database. Thus the weights for each of the terms and hence the total weights of the documents in the previous example would be:

Document 1

Term A	5/50	=	0.1
Term B	6/30	=	0.2
Term C	2/200	=	0.01
Term D	3/60	=	0.05
Total weight		=	0.36

Document 2

Term A	4/50	=	0.08
Term B	1/30	=	0.033
Term C	7/200	=	0.035
Term D	6/60	=	0.100
Total weight		=	0.248

Document 3

Term A	3/50	=	0.06
Term B	2/30	=	0.067
Term C	4/200	=	0.02
Term D	2/60	=	0.033
Total weight		=	0.18

Thus the documents would be ranked:

    Document 1
    Document 2
    Document 3

So the inclusion of a weighting for term frequency within the database has altered the overall ranking in comparison to simple use of within document frequency.

These methods of document ranking have been tried and tested over many years and the third method, known as the inverse document frequency, is probably the most widely occurring ranking method.

Proximate pairs ranking

More recently research undertaken by Keen (1991) has investigated the use of word proximity as a means of document ranking. Ranking by proximity is a creative use of the fact that word proximity operators can be used in Boolean searching to require differing degrees of tightness of match. The argument is that term pairs adjacent to each other should be weighted more highly than term pairs with one intervening word, which are weighted more highly than term pairs with two intervening words, and so on. The approach is best understood by an example. Take a search with the search terms A and B and C. Then execute the following steps:

1. Take each of the pairs, that is
       AB
       BC
       AC
2. Determine the weight allocated to each pair for each document
3. Sum the weights of pairs for each document
4. Rank the documents according to sum of weights

Figure 6.17 contains a simple example in which there is one three-term query and two documents. The weighting assumes that it is only worth considering term pairs which are within ten words of each other. A simple scoring system is used so that an adjacent pair of terms is weighted as ten, a pair with one intervening word is weighted nine, two intervening words is weighted eight and so on. In the example, document 1 has a weighting of 27 and document 2 has a weighting of 17, and so document 1 would be ranked above document 2.

Best match retrieval in practice

While there has been much research on ranked output retrieval over a period of some 30 years, it is only since 1990 that it has had an impact on the practical world of information retrieval. Principally this has occurred through its widespread uptake by Internet search engines, but some CD-ROM products also offer ranked output and some major search services now are also making ranked output searching available as, for example, the Target facility on Dialog. Perhaps inevitably the search services are reluctant to reveal exactly how their particular algorithms operate. It is fairly common for ranked output search engines to make use of frequency of occurrence of terms in documents, frequency of occurrence of terms in database, exact position of terms in document and word proximity information. For example, it appears that Dialog's Target can be viewed as a refined form of coordination level searching. One attempt at explaining its operation has been offered by Keen (1994).

The use of word frequency as a means of ranking output is not without its critics. For example, it has been argued that the use of within-document frequency as a means of weighting enables a term which occurs frequently

---

Search terms: evaluation information retrieval

Document 1 Novel approaches to the evaluation of information retrieval systems

Document 2 Evaluation methodology for the testing of novel information retrieval algorithms

Proximate pairs

evaluation information
evaluation retrieval
information retrieval

Weightings

Document 1

evaluation information	9
evaluation retrieval	8
information retrieval	10
Document weighting	27

Document 2

evaluation information	4
evaluation retrieval	3
information retrieval	10
Document weighting	17

Figure 6.17   Hypothetical ranking by proximate pairs

in a document, but is not the most important within the search, to 'overwhelm' the impact of a term which is a vital component of the search but which does not occur with great frequency in a particular document. In addition, it is quite feasible that a term which occurs with great frequency in a database and so has a low weighting through the reciprocal of its database occurrence can be an important component of a search since it can place the other search terms into context. Thus the meaning of the terms 'water' and 'table' together are likely to be significantly different when combined with the term 'hydrology' than when combined with the term 'restaurant'. Thus it is encouraging that an increasing number of ranked output retrieval mechanisms such as Dialog's Target and the Excite search engine allow the searcher to tag search terms which must be present in any retrieved item.

It is less satisfactory, however, that search engine producers provide so little information about how their retrieval engines are ranking output. Indeed it must be open to question whether or not searchers are willing to place total faith in 'black box' search engines whose retrieval mechanism or impact on their search output they do not understand.

References

Brenner, E.H. (1996) *Beyond Boolean – New Approaches to Information Retrieval.* Philadelphia PA: National Federation of Abstracting and Indexing Services

Catching Sites (1997) *PC Magazine,* **6**(2), 109–153

Cleverdon, C.W. (1984) Optimizing convenient online access to bibliographic databases. *Information Services and Use,* **4**(1–2), 37–47

Ellis, D. (1996) *Progress and Problems in Information Retrieval.* London: Library Association

Galt, J. S. (1997) Does the future of the online industry lie in individually customised services? How hosts are adapting to the future. In D. I. Raitt, P. Blake and B. Jeapes (eds) *Online Information97. Proceedings of the 21st International Online Information Meeting.* Oxford: Learned Information, 13–18

Harter, S.P. (1986) *Online Information Retrieval: Concepts, Principles and Techniques.* London: Academic Press

Keen, E.M. (1991) The use of term position devices in ranked output experiments. *Journal of Documentation,* **47**(1), 1–22

Keen, E.M. (1994) How does Dialog's Target work? *Online and CD-ROM Review,* **18**(5), 285–8

Lawlor, B. (1997) The desktop information revolution: beyond 'the push'. In D.I. Raitt, P. Blake and B. Jeapes (eds) *Online Information 97. Proceedings of the 21st International Online Information Meeting* London 9-11 December 1997. Oxford: Learned Information, 19–23

Muhlhauser, G. (1985) Dawn of the next generation information retrieval. *Proceedings of the 9th International Online Information Meeting, London, December 1985.* Oxford: Learned Information, 365–371

National Information Standards Organization (1994) *Common Command Language for Online Interactive Retrieval* (ANSI-NISO Z39.58–1992). Bethesda, MD: NISO Press

Notess, G.R. (1997) Internet search techniques and strategies. *Online,* **21**(4), 63–6

Salton, G. and McGill, M.J. (1983) *Introduction to Modern Information Retrieval.* New York: McGraw-Hill

Webber, S. Baile, C., Cameron, A., and Eaton, J. (1994) *UKOLUG Quick Guide to Online Commands* 4th edn. London:UKOLUG

CHAPTER 7

Browsing

Browsing versus Searching

The previous chapter examined ways to retrieve information using what are called analytical searching strategies. Such strategies assume that the user is able to describe the information need in one or more terms that will match the terms used in the records themselves, whether these terms are found in the body of the text (natural-language terms) or have been assigned by indexers from a controlled vocabulary (assigned terms). This in turn is based on the assumption that users know what they are looking for: the task of the information retrieval system then is to match the information need with the information store and to display any resulting records (see Chapter 2).

A fundamental distinction can be drawn between this kind of analytical searching and an alternative way of finding information using a strategy called browsing. Borgman *et al.* (1995) define browsing as an interactive process of skimming over information and selecting choices. For Treloar (1993), browsing is the ability to navigate through an information space looking for items of interest. It relies upon recognition of patterns (sequences of words, pictures or sounds) rather than recall from memory of search terms to match against database contents, and requires less well-defined search objectives than does analytical searching. Browsing can prove particularly effective for information problems that are ill-defined or where an overview of a topic is the objective.

In practice, an information retrieval system may offer both approaches (see below), and individual users may avail themselves of these two different strategies. In everyday life, both browsing and searching are regularly employed. The shopper may search for a specific item, or simply browse the shelves on the chance that something useful will be found. The library user may search for a particular book in the catalogue, and then head straight for its shelf location; or the user may browse through one or more sections of the catalogue or the bookshelves themselves in the hope of spotting an interesting title. The same is true of retrieval systems. Although, as explained later, some information retrieval systems are designed primarily for analytical searching, and others primarily for browsing, normally they include elements of the alternative approach.

This chapter looks more closely at what is involved in browsing for information, and discusses the advantages as well as the limitations of such a strategy. Various browsing tools, of which hypertext is the most promising, are also considered.

Browsing Strategies

Although browsing is a common human activity undertaken in a wide variety of environments, including printed books and journals, computerized information systems did not initially lend themselves greatly to browsing. The typical Boolean-driven retrieval engines based on inverted file structures were intended to search a database and retrieve a set of records that matched the input search terms. It was assumed that users knew what they were looking for, and also knew how to convert their information need into an effective search strategy. The databases were not designed to facilitate browsing; the most that could be done was to browse through an online index (and occasionally an online thesaurus) or a set of retrieved records. Even these browsing techniques were discouraged by connect time costs that placed a premium on short searches. Furthermore, effective browsing is best undertaken by the actual client who wants the information rather than being delegated to an intermediary, but in practice most searches were carried out by information professionals on the users' behalf (the complexity of the early search systems as well as connect time charges based upon efficient searching discouraged end-user searching). Unlike searching, browsing cannot be delegated to a third party.

As Chang and Rice (1993) argue, library and information science has been biased towards specific, direct searching, based upon an assumption that users have static, well-defined information needs and know exactly what they want. In practice, users are often in what Belkin, Oddy and Brooks (1982) have called an anomalous state of knowledge (ASK) and do not have pre-defined search criteria (see Chapter 2). Assumptions that users know exactly what they are looking for in a database have more recently given place to a realization that they can often express their information need only in very general terms, and that the need can be met only by incorporating browsing as well as searching capabilities in the system.

Searching a database involves selecting specific search terms, devising a search strategy, implementing that strategy in order to retrieve any records that are indexed by those search terms, and examining those records to determine their relevance to the user's information need (see Chapter 6). It pre-supposes a specific target for the search; the search objective then is to find that target. The process may be iterative, involving modifications to the selected search terms or the strategy itself in order to obtain a different set of records, but at each iteration the user will be attempting to match a formulated information request with the contents of the database.

Browsing strategies, in contrast, are informal, interactive and opportunistic, depending upon the user recognizing relevant information when it is encountered. Browsing involves skimming information and making choices and is therefore highly dependent upon human perceptual abilities. As such, it is a natural and effective approach to many types of information-seeking problems. Marchionini (1987) suggests that people browse for three reasons: the search objective cannot be defined clearly; the cognitive burden is less than in an analytical search; or the information system itself encourages browsing (as in, for example, a hypertext system). Hildreth (1989) argues that 'the process of searching and discovering is more central to end-user searching objectives and satisfaction than the delivery of any pre-defined product.' He sees the search as 'likely to be largely a trial and error process, having no particular predetermined end or outcome'. As users browse they learn more about the topic and as a consequence may re-define the initial query in the light of ongoing results. Even when the user does know exactly what information is being sought, it may not be obvious how to articulate the need in terms used by the retrieval system. Borgman *et al.* (1995) believe that children have a natural tendency to explore, and this characteristic should be encouraged in information retrieval systems designed for children through the provision of browsing facilities.

Browsing is an attractive proposition because it requires a smaller cognitive load than does an analytical search strategy. There is no requirement to employ cognitive resources to recall from memory specific search terms that can represent the concepts related to the information problem. For tasks that are ill-defined or complex, browsing allows information seekers to devote their full cognitive resources to problem definition and system manipulation (Marchionini, 1995). Humans are better able to recognize something than to generate a description of it.

Types of Browsing

Several authors have refined the general browsing task into several distinct categories. One example is Marchionini (1995), who identifies three types of browsing, differentiated by the object of the search (the information needed) and the tactics employed:

- Direct or specific browsing that is both systematic and focused. A conference participant, for example, might browse the list of participants to establish how many are from a particular country (in contrast to a search in the alphabetized list of participants to find out whether a specific individual is present).

- Semi-directed and predictive browsing that has a less definite target and proceeds less systematically. An example would be the casual examination of records retrieved by an earlier search.
- Undirected or general browsing that has no real goal and very little focus (such as skimming through an encyclopaedia or 'zapping' through television channels).

Browsing Tools

Effective browsing requires specific tools that will facilitate the navigation of a database and provide sufficient feedback on results to permit successful browsing to continue.

As browsing is based upon an ability to scan information, any technique that fosters such scanning will enhance browsing. Scanning may be conducted in randomized collections, but it is much easier if like things have been grouped together. To take a library example, it would be possible to scan a library collection for books on a specific topic even if the books were arranged on the shelves according to the colour of their bindings. But it is that much easier (and faster) to scan the collection if it is already arranged in some kind of subject classification. It is therefore helpful to organize displayed information in conventional groupings whenever possible. For example, newspaper articles might be arranged chronologically, addresses by city and bibliographical records by subject.

Browsing assumes that the user can quickly pick out salient information from a display, and therefore any technique that emphasizes especially relevant data on the screen will be helpful. This topic is discussed more fully in Chapter 8, but a few words can be added here. Attention can be drawn on the screen to individual words or phrases by the use of highlighting, inverse video, colour or special fonts. In many information retrieval systems, for example, it is now common using one of these methods to pick out any terms in a record that were originally employed as search terms (in an initial analytical search). This helps the user to scan records (especially helpful with long full-text records) and quickly to locate the section or sections in the record that contain the search terms.

Full-screen images can be more quickly scanned if they are reduced to thumbnail sketches, either by reducing their size or by restricting the thumbnail to a detail from the full image. In this way, multiple images can be stored on one screen, facilitating rapid scanning and selection of relevant images by the user. A slightly different technique has been used in Figure 7.1. Here, the user can browse the 16 thumbnail sketches of book bindings in *The Islamic Book*, displaying them in the top right window, by moving the cursor through the image numbers (1–16) listed below (in this example, thumbnail 6 is displayed); any image can be selected by clicking on the number (image 1 is currently displayed in the large top left window).

Browsing is also facilitated by techniques that allow users to scroll through information quickly. Vertical (or, less commonly, horizontal) scrolling of windows enables information to be scanned quickly. This can be used with information displays that are too extensive to fit on one screen.

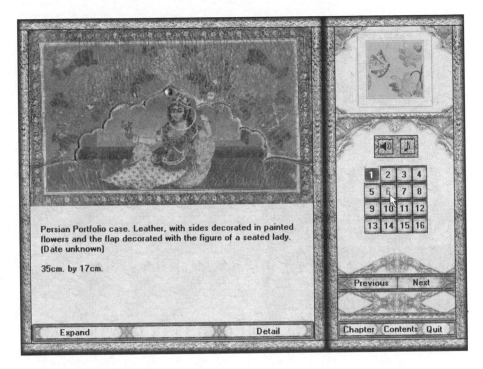

Persian Portfolio case. Leather, with sides decorated in painted flowers and the flap decorated with the figure of a seated lady. (Date unknown)

35cm. by 17cm.

Figure 7.1   Use of thumbnail images on *The Islamic Book* CD-ROM (McGill University)

Pull-down or pop-up menus also can be scrolled to display lists of search terms, articles, etc. Many CD-ROMs as well as the World Wide Web employ these techniques, and they are more fully discussed in Chapter 8.

Reference has just been made to lists of search terms or article titles. Such lists allow users to browse and select search entry points from the list rather than having to exert greater cognitive efforts in recalling such terms from memory. Figure 7.2, from the Microsoft Encarta 98 CD-ROM, shows a typical example of a scrolling list of encyclopaedia article titles from which the user selects (in this case, Greece has been chosen). Full-screen menus can also be scanned quickly to choose the relevant option. The ALEPH OPAC at the South African Library in Cape Town (Figure 7.3) offers an option on its main menu to browse the database (as an alternative to using one of the two analytical search strategies – Simple Find or Super Find). The browse function starts with a title (as in Figure 7.4), an author, a subject or a corporate entity (selected by scrolling the index to browse box) and can include all documents in the library, books only (as in Figure 7.4), periodicals or dissertations.

Browsing is now closely associated with the World Wide Web. Although the Web can be searched by keywords on several services such as AltaVista, Excite and Lycos (see Chapter 3), many services such as Yahoo!, the WWW Virtual Library and Magellan also offer hierarchical, structured directories

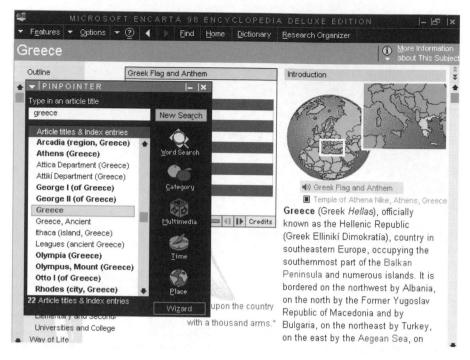

Figure 7.2   Scrolling menu from the *Microsoft Encarta 98 Encyclopedia* CD-ROM

(or menus) that can be browsed to locate sites dealing with particular topics. Figure 7.5 shows an example from Yahoo! Under each category (and sub-category) links are provided to appropriate Web pages (note that Yahoo! also provides a search box to go directly to a site rather than using the browse function). Unfortunately, creating such browsing tools, and especially keeping them up-to-date on the ever-changing Web, poses major problems.

Hypertext

The browsing tools already discussed facilitate rapid information scanning on the screen, and therefore undoubtedly help with browsing. The most dramatic browsing tool, however, is not so much concerned with the display of information on the screen, but with the way in which the information itself is organized so as to support navigation from one part of the database to another in what appears to be a seamless fashion. This tool is called hypertext, or hypermedia if it is used to organize still images, animation, video or sound as well as text. Hypertext (discussed in Chapter 5) is the navigational tool employed on the World Wide Web as well as on many CD-ROMs. Hildreth (1989) has argued for its use also on OPACs, citing examples such as linking books in the same series or from the same

Select one of the following options:

 View information on database contents.

To search the database, select:

 Browse an index, such as author, title, subject.

 Find documents by simple keyword search.

 Find documents by advanced keyword search.

To select a DATABASES:

 Change Databases

To view user information, choose:

 View account and activity log. Registered users only.

To register ILL request, choose:

 Register ILL request. Available for registered users only.

Please use **feedback** button to comment on system.

Figure 7.3 Browse option on main menu of ALEPH Ex-Libris OPAC at the South African Library

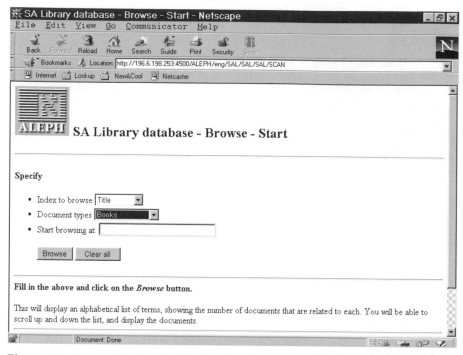

Figure 7.4   Browse Start on ALEPH Ex-Libris OPAC at the South African Library

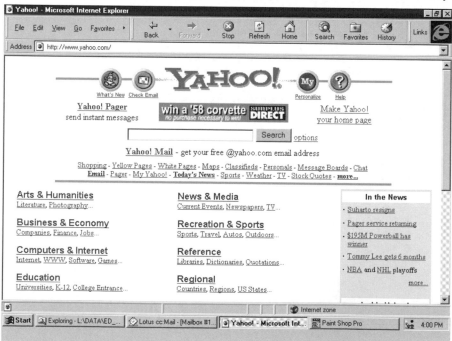

Figure 7.5   Full-screen menu from Yahoo! on the World Wide Web

Figure 7.6   Hierarchical hypertext links on the WWW – main sports index on WebCrawler

publisher, or even linking a book to other books that cite it (as in a citation index).

The inventor of the idea behind hypertext was Vannevar Bush, with his concept of the Memex machine (see Chapter 1). Credit for coining the term 'hypertext', however, is awarded to Ted Nelson, who in the 1960s used it to describe non-sequential writing. It was not until the introduction in 1987 of Apple Computer's Hypercard software that hypertext was launched as a major alternative approach to conventional information organization and retrieval.

Hypertext offered the prospect of creating semantic connections among logical units of information, a goal that information retrieval had found so elusive. Hypertext allows the presentation of information in a non-linear form. Information is no longer organized by the author in a predetermined sequence that the reader in turn must follow. In a hypertext system, information is presented in discrete chunks and the reader can jump directly from one chunk to another. Each information chunk is associated with a node, and the nodes are linked, thus allowing the user to move freely between them. Links usually appear as highlighted text or as icons at the edges of the screen. By clicking on the highlighted text or the icon at one location, the user immediately jumps to another part of the document, or alternatively to a completely new document, that has a semantic link with the original location. As Ellis (1991) comments, 'interaction with the database is constrained only by the network of links and paths which exist.' Users can browse the information store as they think fit, moving easily through large amounts of information according to their own needs.

Any one hypertext node can have links with many other nodes – not simply with its neighbours on either side as in a conventional document. Generally there are two ways of connecting nodes. Each node may be connected with nodes containing superordinate and subordinate information (unless the node is a starting or ending point of a conceptual information sequence). A node at one level can only access nodes directly above or below it in the hierarchy. This is called a hierarchical tree structure. For example, vertical hypertext links are followed from the WebCrawler Sports and Recreation index page (Figure 7.6) to WebCrawler's Baseball index page (Figure 7.7), then to WebCrawler's Major League Baseball page, (Figure 7.8) and WebCrawler's index page for the Montreal Expos baseball team (figure 7.9). From this page the dedicated fan who wants to maintain contact with the team can advance to the opening screen of the Official Site for the Expos (http://www.majorleaguebaseball.com/nl/mon/), shown in Figure 7.10.

Alternatively, each node can be connected to other nodes both hierarchically and horizontally, producing a much looser network structure.

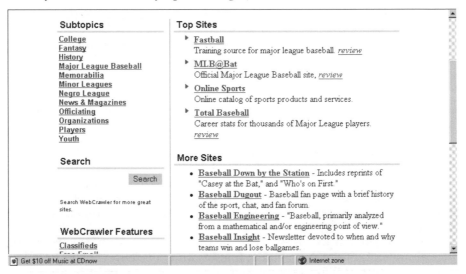

Figure 7.7   Hierarchical hypertext links on the WWW – baseball links on WebCrawler

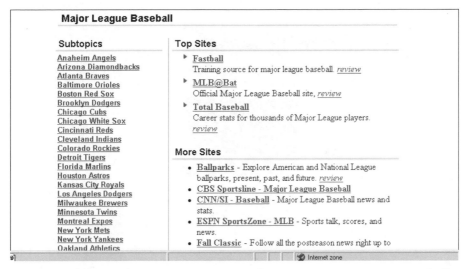

Figure 7.8 Hierarchical hypertext links on the WWW – Major League Baseball links on WebCrawler

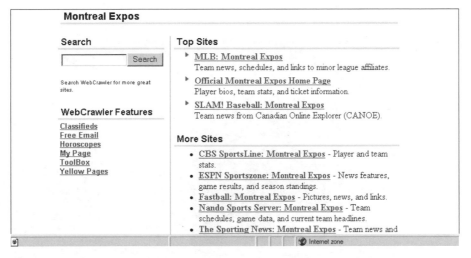

Figure 7.9 Hierarchical hypertext links on the WWW – Montreal Expos baseball team

Figure 7.11 shows the article on Microsoft Encarta 98 about penicillin. The encircled terms represent hypertext links that can be followed from the Penicillin article by the reader to locate other relevant articles on the encyclopaedia. In this example, a link is followed to the article on Sir Arthur Fleming, the discoverer of penicillin (Figure 7.12). The reverse link can then, if desired, be taken back from Fleming to the original penicillin article. Hypertext can also be employed to link a reference cited in an article to

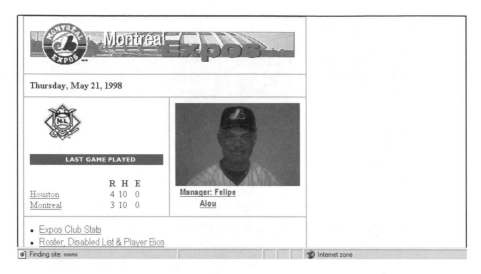

Figure 7.10   Hierarchical hypertext links on the WWW – Montreal Expos baseball team official Web site

Figure 7.11   Horizontal hypertext links on Microsoft Encarta 98 – Penicillin article

the full text of that reference if it is also available on the Web. For example, the January 1997 issue of the electronic journal *D-lib Magazine* includes an article by Shneiderman, Byrd and Croft (http://www.dlib.org/dlib/january97/retrieval/01shneiderman.html) that cites in its references an article by Van House, Butler, Ogle and Schiff. This latter article can be located by following the hypertext link to the February 1996 issue of *D-lib Magazine* (http://www.dlib.org/dlib/february96/02vanhouse.html).

Such linked nodes allow users to browse or navigate through the information space in a non-sequential manner – browsing here refers to the process of moving around a network by following links between information-containing nodes.

Much less research has been conducted on user search behaviour with hypertext-based systems than Boolean-based systems. Dimitroff and Wolfson (1995) recruited 70 students from a school of library and information science: half were familiar with the hypertext concept, but only three percent had actual experience of searching a hypertext-based system. After searching five queries using the hypertext system, 56 percent liked the hypertext system better than the Boolean system they had previously searched, 28 percent liked it less and 16 percent had no preference. The most frequent complaint was about the lack of Boolean search capabilities; hypertext browsing alone was not considered sufficient (but all the students

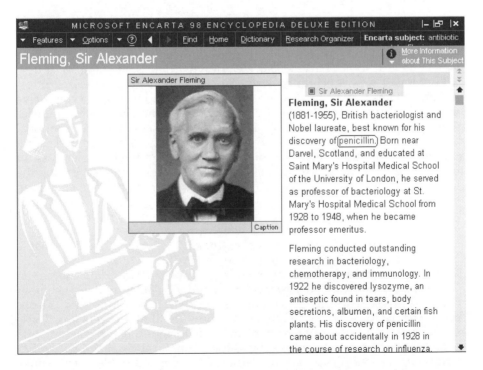

Figure 7.12 Horizontal hypertext links on Microsoft Encarta – Sir Alexander Fleming article

were already familiar with Boolean systems, which may have made them more conscious of the perceived shortcoming). Nevertheless, almost as many users cited browsability as a positive system feature. A majority was impressed with the overall simplicity of the system, finding it 'easy to use'. Liebscher and Marchionini (1991) believe that hypertext navigation is not intuitive but must be learned: novices tend to encounter more difficulties than experienced users because they have not yet mastered the analytical strategies necessary to exploit hypertext capabilities. Khan and Locatis (1998), however, found little difference between the strategies employed by novices and experts. Other studies have investigated the effects of higher or lower link densities. Some conclude that higher link densities increase efficiency as users now generally have to traverse fewer displays to access the sought information (Shneiderman and Kearsley, 1989). Others conclude that too many links may be confusing and introduce cognitive overload (Welsh, Murphy, Duffy and Goodrum, 1993). Khan and Locatis (1998) found that high school students, when required to make more choices among many links, also had more opportunities to make mistakes (looked at simply as a raw possibility). Choosing also added to the cognitive load because more information had to be processed. In this study low link densities produced more focused exploration.

Advantages of Browsing

Browsing offers a number of advantages to the information seeker in comparison with more conventional retrieval methods. First, it is an intuitive activity. Humans resort to browsing whenever they are seeking something but do not have a clear idea of what that 'something' is. If they did not resort very much to browsing in conventional computerized information systems it was only because these systems did not offer a conducive browsing environment. Second, as mentioned earlier, browsing imposes fewer cognitive demands upon information seekers than conventional retrieval techniques. The need to recall from memory terms that will represent the information need is replaced by the cognitively easier task of recognizing relevant information as and when it is encountered during the browsing session. Browsing can clarify an information problem, or help in the development of a plan or a more formal strategy. A major benefit that can accrue from browsing is the chance identification of information that was not actually being sought but which proves interesting to the user. Such serendipity can often prove extremely valuable. Finally, people browse to discover and learn, or just for plain fun.

Although textual information comprises much of the data stored on computerized information systems, it should not be forgotten that non-textual sources – still images, animation sequences, video, sound effects, music and the human voice – can also be found in digitized versions. These non-textual sources are much more difficult to index using conventional techniques than text sequences. They have no natural language text (other than perhaps a short caption) to form the basis for indexable entry points, and they are difficult and expensive to index manually (although a considerable research effort is now being expended to establish effective and economical ways to index images, in some cases using automatic indexing techniques based on 'recognizing' image content by shapes – see Chapter 4). For such non-textual information, browsing offers an opportunity for the user to explore these potentially rich sources in a way that is very difficult to equal using conventional retrieval techniques.

Browsing Limitations

Although browsing is both a natural and, in many cases, an effective technique for finding information, it does have a number of limitations.

First, browsing can be time consuming, especially if the information set is large. It is just to avoid the need for lengthy browsing that various kinds of indexing techniques are applied. If the information seeker knows exactly what is required from, say, a book, it is much faster to consult the book's index and identify the relevant page or pages than to browse through the entire volume. The analogy holds true for electronic sources. A well-defined task is better undertaken in a structured search.

Second, browsing accuracy tends to diminish if continued over a long time period. It is impossible to retain concentration indefinitely, and extensive browsing is likely to result in missed items. This problem is compounded by a distraction factor. The serendipity value of browsing has a down side: it is easy to become sidetracked into secondary tasks, thereby losing sight of the main task in hand.

Third, browsing can all too often result in disorientation. This is especially prevalent with hypertext systems. If hypertext offers users flexibility in following links from node to node, this very flexibility also poses a potential problem in keeping on track. Users can quickly become disoriented as they travel from node to node, losing sight of their original quest and unable to retrace their steps to *terra cognita*. The larger the information store and the greater the number of linked nodes, the more severe are likely to become such navigational problems.

Hypertext systems employ a number of techniques to cope with navigational problems. A 'map' of the information source may be provided to give an overview of the data structure (rather like a list of contents in a printed source). Search histories can provide a chronological list of the nodes visited in the current search session. On many World Wide Web browsers, for example, the 'go' button will reveal the trail followed in the current session; many CD-ROMs also include a similar feature. It is usually possible to backtrack through the traversed nodes, one at a time, until eventually the beginning of the search is reached (on the Web the 'back' button achieves this), or to jump directly back to any one of these intermediate nodes. It must be conceded, however, that even with such aids disorientation remains a problem in large hypertext systems. For that reason, O'Docherty *et al.* (1991) recommend that with large databases it is better to use hypertext only as a technique for browsing small sets of records that have already been retrieved by other means.

Another problem with hypertext is finding the way back to a valuable location that was found in a previous search session. On the Web in particular a circuitous path through many hypertext links may lead eventually to an interesting site. Unless the user notes the URL of the site, however, it may be difficult to re-discover in a subsequent session. The bookmarking facility provided by Web browsers is one way of coping with this problem: sites that are useful for the user can be added to a stored list (bookmarked) from where they can quickly be retrieved.

Fourth, browsing may result in information overload. If the information seeker does not apply a sufficiently fine filter when browsing a large information store, it is possible to find far more information than can subsequently be processed.

Fifth, in practice the flexibility of hypertext browsing is not totally unrestrained. The user can only follow the links that have been pre-determined by the product designer. For example, a user can only browse using hypertext links from one part of a document to another, or from one site to a another site, if the page constructor has established the necessary intra- or intersite links.

Finally, from the producer's rather than the user's point of view, a large manual effort is needed to create hypertext links. And one experiment found relatively little consistency between the assignment of links to the same data by different 'indexers' (Ellis, Furner-Hines and Willett, 1994).

The Best of Both Worlds

Browsing and conventional information retrieval should not be seen as rivals, but rather as complementary ways of finding information. Few information systems will fail to provide access to both these strategies, although the actual mix will differ greatly. Conventional retrieval systems utilizing largely analytical search strategies will nevertheless offer at least minimal browsing capabilities – for example, the ability to browse on-screen through a set of retrieved data, a chance to view indexes or to see a search history. Similarly, hypertext-driven browsing systems will normally provide some retrieval capabilities, if only because a starting point must be found in the database from which to commence a browse. The World Wide Web is perhaps the classic browsing tool, facilitated by browsers such as Netscape Navigator or Internet Explorer; yet the Web also offers opportunities to employ a growing range of search engines alongside hypertext links to search this enormous collection of information.

Both analytical and browsing strategies have their role to play in ensuring that information seekers can locate relevant information as effectively and effortlessly as possible.

References

Belkin, N., Oddy, R. and Brooks, H. (1982) Ask for information retrieval: Part 1. Background and theory. *Journal of Documentation*, **38** (2), 61–71

Borgman, C.L., Hirsh, S.G., Walter, V.A. and Gallagher, A.L. (1995) Children's searching behavior on browsing and keyword online catalogs: the Science Library Catalog Project. *Journal of the American Society for Information Science*, **46** (9), 663–84

Chang, S.J. and Rice, R.E. (1993) Browsing: a multidimensional framework. In M. Williams (ed.) *Annual Review of Information Science and Technology* **28**. Medford, NJ: Learned Information, 231–76

Dimitroff, A. and Wolfson, D. (1995) Searcher response in a hypertext-based bibliographic information retrieval system. *Journal of the American Society for Information Science*, **46** (1), 22–9

Ellis, D. (1991) Hypertext: origins and use. *International Journal of Information Management*, **11**(1), 5–13

Ellis, D., Furner-Hines, J. and Willett, P. (1994) On the creation of hypertext links in full-text documents: measurement of inter-linker consistency. *Journal of Documentation*, **50** (2), 67–98

Hildreth, C. R. (1989) Appropriate user interfaces for subject searching in bibliographic retrieval systems. *The Bookmark*, **47** (3), 186–93

Khan, K. and Locatis, C. (1998) Searching through cyberspace: the effects of link display and link density on information retrieval from hypertext on the World Wide Web. *Journal of the American Society for Information Science*, **49** (2), 176–82

Liebscher, P. and Marchionini, G. (1991) Performance in electronic encyclopedias: implications for adaptive systems. In J.M. Griffiths, (ed) *Proceedings of the 54th Annual Meeting of the American Society for Information Science* **28**. Medford, NJ: Learned Information, 39–48

Marchionini, G. (1987) An invitation to browse: designing full-text systems for novice users. *Canadian Journal of Information Science*, **12** (3/4), 69–79

Marchionini, G. (1995) *Information Seeking in Electronic Environments*. Cambridge: Cambridge University

O'Docherty, M.H., Daskalakis, C.N., Crowther, P.J., Ireton, M.A., Goble, C.A. and Xydeas, C.S. (1991) The design and implementation of a multimedia information system with automatic content retrieval. *Information Services and Use*, **11** (5/6), 345–85

Shneiderman, B. and Kearsley, G. (1989) *Hypertext Hands-On!* Reading, MA: Addison-Wesley

Treloar, A. (1993) Towards a user-centred categorisation of Internet access tools. Paper delivered at Networkshop 1993, Melbourne, Australia. Also available at http://www.deakin.edu.au/people/aet/nws93/nws93.html

Welsh, T., Murphy, K., Duffy, T. and Goodrum, D. (1993) Accessing elaborations on core information in a hypermedia environment. *Educational Technology Research & Development*, **41** (2), 19–34

CHAPTER 8

Interfaces

The Role of Interfaces

As described in Chapter 1, an information retrieval system comprises the following elements: an information store of some kind, organized in such a way that discrete data items within it can be retrieved; the hardware on which the information is stored; software which enables users to search or browse the information in order to identify and retrieve relevant portions; and an interface that enables the user to issue instructions to the search software and to display in some way the retrieved information. The interface governs what the user sees, touches and hears when working at the computer. All four elements are important, but some authors categorize the interface as being the most important factor in determining the success or failure of a system (see, for example, Baecker and Buxton, 1987). As Galitz (1997) says, a poor interface design will lead to user mistakes, aggravation, frustration and increased stress.

A great deal of research has been devoted to understanding how users interact with computers and how interfaces might best be designed to facilitate a productive dialogue between user and system. Beaulieu (1997) argues that 'we need to investigate further the nature of the cognitive load which different interface environments or features may impose' on users. Mandel (1997) states that 'the best interface is the one that lets users do what they want to do, when they want to do it, and how they want to do it.' Shneiderman (1992), more specifically, lists five measures that can be applied to any interface:

- How much time does it take the user to learn how to use the interface?
- How long does it take the user to issue an instruction via the interface and for that interface to display the retrieved information?
- How many errors does the user make in utilizing the interface?
- How well does the user retain a working knowledge of the interface over time?
- How satisfied is the user with the interface?

It should be noted that these measures will often force tradeoffs. For example, higher performance speed might be attained by an interface that employs short cuts, but these may take longer to learn and be more difficult to remember.

There can be no doubt that interfaces are far more sophisticated now than in the 1970s, and that when assessed by such measures as Shneiderman's would exhibit a marked improvement. Such improvements are partly a result of research that has shown how certain interface designs work more effectively than others. They are also a consequence of improvements in hardware (for example, the development of new input devices like the mouse and the touchscreen, larger and clearer monitors, and faster processors) and more sophisticated software environments (such as windows-based operating systems and enhanced graphic capabilities). Despite impressive improvements, however, much work remains to be accomplished. This can be seen most dramatically in the case of the World Wide Web, where designers are still learning by trial and error how to adapt existing interface principles into this new environment (Shneiderman, 1996).

Information professionals, and users of information systems more generally, should be concerned about interface design because it is a crucial determinant in a successful search. A familiarity with the basic principles is relevant to selecting new systems, and learning quickly how to use them. Furthermore, growing numbers of individuals now have the opportunity to design their own interfaces for use with microcomputer-based databases, locally produced CD-ROMs or Web sites. This chapter does not presume to offer a step-by-step guide to interface design; leading software companies like Microsoft, Apple and IBM have produced valuable design manuals, and these can be supplemented by excellent studies such as that by Shneiderman (1992). This chapter's more modest goal is to review the major components of an interface and comment upon design decisions that affect the information-seeking process.

Design Criteria

Users

Interfaces are found in numerous environments, and no interface will be equally suited, for example, to a video game, an automated teller machine (ATM), a computer-assisted design package, a wordprocessor and an information retrieval system. Even within the information retrieval domain, interfaces must be designed to cope with databases of varying sizes, retrieval software of varying complexity, and fast, local processing or remote, networked processing. Any successful interface also must take account of its users. These can form a relatively homogeneous group (such as lawyers or medical researchers) or, at the other extreme, a heterogeneous assembly such as will be found using a public library OPAC or, of course, the World Wide Web. Users vary by age (see Chapter 2): there is growing evidence to suggest that an interface designed with adults in mind may not function as well with children; and senior citizens, for example, may encounter problems in reading screen displays, hearing warning signals or operating a keyboard and mouse. Nor should cultural factors be ignored. These can influence many aspects of an interface, including text presentation (the user might read from right to left instead of left to right), capitalization and punctuation rules, character sets, interpretation of screen icons, design metaphors and colour coding, and reactions to the tone and style employed in error messages and help screens.

Perhaps the most crucial human variable, encompassing age and culture, is the level of knowledge that the user brings to the interface. This can usefully be divided into two categories: syntactic knowledge and semantic knowledge.

In order to drive a car it is necessary to know that separate pedals control the accelerator, the clutch and the brake, that the steering wheel turns the car left and right, that specific switches activate the lights, that certain levers work the windscreen wipers and the direction indicators, and so on. Furthermore, it is necessary to become familiar with the specific location of these devices in the particular vehicle to be driven, because they are not completely standardized. Similarly, users of computer systems must learn how to transmit an instruction (hit the return key, click on the mouse button, etc.), erase a character (delete key, backspace key, CTRL-H, etc.), open, move, re-size, scroll and close a window, pull down a menu, and so on. This can be termed syntactic knowledge. It will differ from system to system, and novices will have to learn the syntactic rules required to carry out a variety of basic operations that must be mastered before the computer can be 'driven'. This learning can be simplified by consistent application of the rules throughout the system, help screens, templates to overlay the keyboard, and clearly labelled on-screen menus, buttons and icons.

To return to the car metaphor, it is not sufficient to know that the middle pedal under the steering wheel is the clutch and the lever beside the driver changes from one gear to another when the clutch is depressed. It is necessary to understand the concept of a gear system, at least to the extent that the driver knows when to change up and down through the gears, and how to avoid stalling the engine. This can be described as semantic knowledge. Similarly, users must understand certain principles relating to computers: for example, that it is possible to display data on the screen, download them to a hard disc, or copy to another application; files must be given names, etc. Semantic knowledge does not stop here. The car driver must know the destination and how to reach it from the vehicle's current location. It is also useful to know about speed limits and other driving regulations if an unpleasant encounter with law enforcement officers is to be avoided. Finally, taking all these factors into account, which route should be chosen to reach the destination as quickly and safely as possible? Likewise, the computer user must have knowledge about the task in hand: the search's objective, how it is likely best to be met in this database, the fastest route to reach the required information and how the interface can best be employed to achieve the objective. This in turn involves a knowledge of the subject area as well as a familiarity with the retrieval software and, of course, the interface capabilities.

Users can be classified in terms of their syntactic and semantic knowledge as novice, intermittent or expert users. The interface may have to take account of all three user categories. This is best accomplished by offering either two or more separate interfaces (for example, Dialog offers on its CD-ROM products a choice between 'Easy Menu Search' and 'Dialog Command Search', and on its Web version, 'Guided Search' or 'Command Search') or by incorporating within one interface some basic options which can be chosen by novices, along with others that can be selected by the more experienced and enable more sophisticated strategies to be accomplished in a shorter time (see later).

Principles

Marchionini (1992) reminds us that most users want to achieve their search goals with a minimum of cognitive load and a maximum of enjoyment. They seek the path of least cognitive resistance and usually will trade time to minimize complexity. Furthermore, they will perform better on systems that give them pleasure or are interesting, and continue to use them in future. Microsoft's Windows Interface Guidelines (1997) remind us that 'a well-designed user interface is built on principles and a development process that centers on users and their tasks.' Shneiderman (1992) has suggested eight general design principles to provide the user with both success and satisfaction:

- Strive for consistency within all aspects of the interface. Shneiderman comments that although it is the easiest principle to apply, it is nevertheless the most frequently violated.
- Experienced users should be able to take shortcuts in order to avoid the more laborious routes established for novices.
- Throughout the search, the user should be supplied with informative feedback on the current state of the search. On completion of the search, it should be obvious to the user what happened and why. That is to say, users are not homogeneous.
- The user should be led by the interface through a sequence of actions, from the start of a search, through its implementation to its completion. It should also be clear to the user that this completion has been reached.
- Any errors committed by the user should be identified immediately by the interface and a simple, positive message delivered that will allow the error to be corrected (the ideal interface, of course, should not permit the user to make any errors, but these principles are meant to be realistic).

- It should be straightforward for the user to reverse any action taken; this both relieves anxiety and encourages experimentation.
- Users should feel that they, and not the computer, are in control and that the system is responding to their actions.
- Demands placed upon the user's short-term memory should be minimized; this is achieved by keeping displays simple, reducing the number of hierarchical levels in a menu system, providing a search history, etc.

An example of applying such principles to the evaluation of an actual interface (the DataStar web interface as it was at its initial launch in December 1996) is given by Barker (1997).

Galitz (1997) adds a number of more detailed criteria. The interface, in his opinion, should be:

- aesthetically pleasing;
- clear;
- compatible with the task;
- comprehensible;
- efficient;
- predictable;
- responsive;
- simple.

He concedes that some of these principles require a tradeoff: for example, efficient execution of instructions may clash with maintaining a simple interface.

Despite the progress made in interface design, the challenge to create effective interfaces for information retrieval systems continues; as the population at large becomes more accustomed to using computers (and therefore interfaces) for all kinds of purposes, both syntactic and semantic knowledge grow, simplifying the designer's task. At the same time, as computer usage spreads from a small number of aficionados to a wider public, a willingness (and even an eagerness) to overcome obstacles is replaced by an impatience with the obscure, the inconsistent and the unhelpful. In the early days of the car, the driver was also a mechanic, willing to resolve problems beneath the hood at the splutter of a piston; today's driver expects to reach the destination with as little inconvenience as possible and without oily hands. Computer users are undergoing a similar metamorphosis.

The Dialogue Transaction Mode

Any interface must provide a means by which the user can issue instructions to the retrieval system and receive its responses to those instructions, that is, conduct a kind of dialogue with the system. A typical search may include the following instructions being issued by the user: start the search; input one or more search terms; display retrieved information; review the search history, re-input new search terms; consult an online thesaurus; consult help screens; and terminate the search. In turn, the system may respond by displaying the number of records in the database that include the specified terms; displaying the records themselves; showing a history of the search steps to date; displaying a segment of a thesaurus on the screen, opening help windows; and confirming termination of the search.

Dialogue transaction modes differ greatly one from another. To begin, their structure is influenced by the underlying operating system being employed: an interface based upon a Windows operating system will look rather different from one based upon, say, DOS. A typical DOS interface has poor quality graphics, if any at all, and will be controlled by commands or menus rather than icons, buttons and windows. At the same time, it will be relatively uncluttered – straightforward to design and easy to manipulate for the experienced user. Graphical presentations of information use a person's information-processing capabilities more effectively: symbols can be recognized faster than text; the learning curve is shortened as graphics are easier to remember than text commands; graphical representations exploit the visual/spatial cues, which are more quickly understood than verbal representations; errors are likely to be fewer, the user has an increased sense of control; actions are easily reversible; immediate feedback is obtained; the interface is more attractive; and typing skills are less called for. At the same time, graphical interfaces also pose challenges to both designers and users: they are more complex to design; they are not always familiar to users; and they can be inefficient for frequent users. Frese, Schulte-Gocking and Altmann (1987) report that users of a word processing direct manipulation interface only outperformed users of a command-based interface on more complex tasks. As Shneiderman (1992) comments: 'Just because direct manipulation principles have been used in a system does not ensure its success.'

The interface can be constructed from a range of different tools: command languages, various kinds of menus, on-screen forms, buttons, icons, hypertext links and a variety of direct manipulation devices. In some interfaces only one tool is employed, but often a mixture is to be found in the one interface. It will prove useful to review these various tools individually despite the tendency for them to coexist within actual interfaces.

Command languages

The earliest interactive human–computer dialogue relied overwhelmingly upon command languages. This included online information systems, early OPACs and many early CD-ROMs. A command language, like any other language, comprises a vocabulary, together with rules – a syntax – for building this vocabulary into acceptable statements that can be interpreted by the computer's program. The searcher uses this language to issue instructions to the computer. Operating systems such as DOS use commands, and the command languages developed for information retrieval systems are similar in operation. For example, as described in Chapter 6, on the Dialog system the command SELECT searches the database for a particular term or combination of terms. The following command line is needed to find all records that contain both the terms 'Internet' and 'geography':

SELECT Internet and geography

The syntax rules of Dialog require that the terms be linked by an AND (to accomplish the Boolean matching) and that a space be left on each side of the AND.

Command languages offer several advantages, the main one being speed of interaction. Speed is especially important when search costs are related entirely or largely to the length of time the user is connected to the computer – the connect time. Command languages minimize the interaction between the user and the system and therefore economize on connect time. Each short command will execute one search/display function, and it may even be possible to stack several commands into one instruction, accelerating still further the search process:

SELECT truancy and poverty; TYPE1/6/1–3

Here the SELECT command and the terms 'truancy' and 'poverty' together with the Boolean operator AND are followed by a second command stacked in the same statement: TYPE followed by 1/6/1–3 instructs Dialog to display from this first set in format 6 (record accession number and title) the first three records retrieved.

Command languages are also flexible; a relatively small command set can implement very sophisticated retrieval capabilities including Boolean matching, truncation, proximity searching, field searching, and so on (see Chapter 6).

Third, a command elicits a direct response. When the searcher wants to find records about the Internet and geography, the response to this instruction is immediate and unambiguous: there are 1,578 records containing the term 'Internet', 6,411 records with the term 'geography' and 15 records that contain both these terms, constituting a first set (S1) in this Dialog search:

SELECT   Internet and geography
          1,578 Internet
          6,411 geography
S1   15 internet and geography

Fourth, command languages give users direct control over the interaction, providing them with a sense that they are in control of the dialogue.

At the same time, command languages present a number of drawbacks. First, any language must be learned, practised and regularly used, otherwise, fluency will not be maintained. This applies just as much to command languages as to any other kind of language. Of course, the vocabulary and syntax are very restricted, and learning the language of an information retrieval system is not like learning Arabic, Japanese or Russian. Nevertheless, it must initially be mastered and then used regularly if fluency and speed are to be maintained. Short commands whose meaning can be inferred from natural language (for example, EXIT or STOP to terminate a search session) are better than longer, cryptic or jargonized commands (for example, LOGOFF). Studies have shown, however, that naming commands is highly subjective and users can guess the names of commands chosen by designers only about 10 percent to 15 percent of the time (Mandel, 1997).

To this problem must be added a second: the multiplicity of command languages. Like their natural-language counterparts, command languages are numerous, often being unique to one specific information system. A search on several databases may involve the use of several command languages if these databases are hosted by different retrieval systems. Searchers may therefore be required to learn a number of different command languages. Figure 6.12 gives some idea of the problems users encounter if searching different command-driven retrieval systems. The same problem applies to Web search engines; for example, a wild card is signified on AltaVista and Yahoo! by the symbol '*' but on Lycos by '$'. Various attempts have been made to institute a common command language for traditional online search systems, notably some years ago by the Commission of the European Communities, but without success (see Chapter 6).

Third, systems utilizing command languages offer the searcher little guidance on search strategy construction – how to assemble commands into a meaningful discourse in order to retrieve the sought information. A search strategy must be formulated using the commands as building blocks. The user must therefore know at any particular point in the search which command to employ. The system itself does not normally prompt the user for the next likely command. In other words, command-driven retrieval systems do little to track the search and offer guidance on how to proceed. They pre-suppose that the user understands the system.

When most searching was carried out by librarians or other kinds of information experts, these shortcomings mattered less. Professional searchers could be expected to take the time to learn one or more command languages as a part of their job and to undertake searches for clients frequently enough to become adept in their use, and to retain fluency over time. If less-experienced and more infrequent end users were to become searchers then more friendly, helpful means of conducting the human–computer dialogue had to be found. Furthermore, as searching costs became less time dependent, the major time-saving premium offered by command languages became less significant. Users are not charged to search an OPAC; CD-ROMs are purchased or leased, and incremental, time-related charges are rarely if ever demanded; remote, online information services increasingly have directed all or some of the charges away from connect time and towards other costing criteria such as the number of records downloaded or unlimited use for fixed-fee leasing; and sites on the World Wide Web can be accessed with minimal or no connect time related costs (users without institutional access will have to pay a monthly charge for telecommunication links, and some sites do charge for the information they contain).

These developments have greatly reduced the importance of command languages as the preferred dialogue transaction mode. Nevertheless, many online services and some CD-ROMs continue to offer a command language as one choice from several possibilities. Even the search engines found on the World Wide Web include elements of the command approach. For example, Web users may have to learn the symbols and syntax required to truncate search terms or to confine the retrieved records to those containing the search terms within so many words of each other (adjacency searching). Figure 8.1 shows an excerpt from the Advanced Search Methods explanation on Excite, describing how to specify searches more precisely using symbols and Boolean operators: note the use of commands (the + and − symbols) and a syntax (to use the operators).

Searchers who have mastered and retained a command language may be reluctant to sacrifice the resulting efficiency by opting for an alternative dialogue transaction mode.

Menus

The first attempt to simplify the dialogue transaction involved replacing commands with menus. Menus are effective because they utilize the more powerful human capability of recognition rather than the weaker one of recall from memory – necessary with commands.

Each menu comprises a list of options from which the user chooses one. As a result of this choice, a change occurs in the state of the interface: either a new menu will be displayed, leading to another choice, or the sought information will be shown on the screen.

Menus are attractive for several reasons. They eliminate the user's need to learn and remember complex command sequences. Ideally, they are also self-explanatory, helping the user to make choices during a search session. The menus themselves provide a structure for the search by limiting the potential range of search options to just those listed in the particular menu or menus currently displayed (in contrast to commands where the user must decide which command to use with no such guidance). Users should have a clear idea of what will happen when they make a selection. In a menu system, it is also much easier to offer help than in a command-driven system. If help is requested, the current menu in use immediately locates for the help software the point in the search at which the user has encountered a difficulty; this enables what is called context-sensitive help to be provided by the software. This is help that is directly relevant to the user's problem rather than generalized, non-context-sensitive help that expects the user to find from many help screens that which might solve the problem at hand.

Surveys reveal that few command-language users employ more than a limited set of basic commands, even though their searches might be improved by exploiting more of the commands available. Menus may encourage users to explore more fully the search options available on the system, because they are listed on the screen. In fact, surveys show (for example, Connaway, Budd and Kochtanek, 1995) that in practice users of menu-driven systems tend to the same conservatism as command users, failing to exploit all the options available.

Overall, then, menus shorten the learning curve by obviating the need to master a command language and by providing a structure to the search and supplying the user with prompts at each step of the search. For this reason

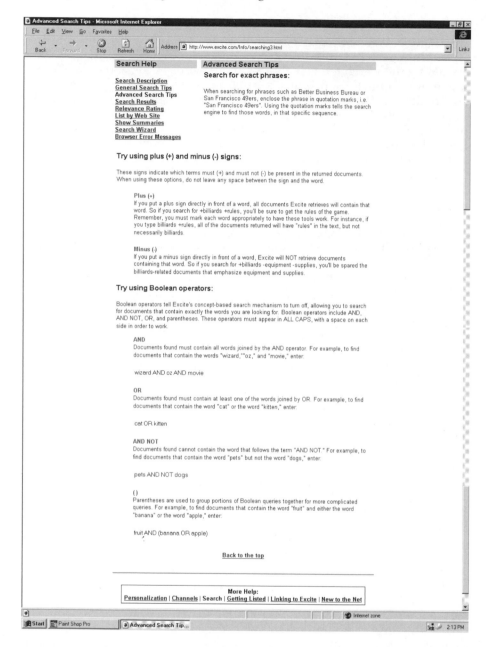

Figure 8.1   **Excerpt from Advanced Search Tips on Excite**

they are particularly advantageous if the user population comprises predominantly novices.

Menu-driven retrieval systems, however, pose several problems. Most obviously, menus can prove very slow to work through. Experienced users in particular can become irritated by the need laboriously to traverse menu after menu to reach their information goal. For this reason, some interfaces provide the option to jump intermediate menu sequences to reach a later stage in the search (called type ahead or menu jumping, using shortcut keys or hot keys). This does pre-suppose, of course, that the user knows the interface quite well and can select when and where to exercise this capability.

Searching tends to be an iterative process. An initial search is undertaken to see what can be found, with a view to strategy modification if necessary in the light of these early search results (see Chapter 6). For this kind of search, much greater flexibility is provided by commands than menus. A search that can be completed by using five or six commands might require cycling and re-cycling through many more menus to reach the same objective. Sullivan, Borgman and Wippern (1990) 'are inclined to conclude that the menu gets in the way of displaying and examining interim results . . . [and] that the time-consuming manoeuvring through menu choices discourages interactiveness'. Iterative searching through a system with many menu levels also can result in the kind of navigational problems typically encountered in hypertext systems (see later and Chapter 7). Users should be given a clear sense of their progress and position within the menus, and a means of going backwards (or forwards) to earlier choices if they so desire. The 'go', 'back', 'forward' and 'home' buttons to navigate the World Wide Web on Netscape are examples of such navigational aids. Even these measures, however, are not always proof against disorientation. Finally, it is vital that the menu structure really does provide appropriate options at each decision point if it is to guide users through their searches.

Menus have two dimensions: breadth and depth. Breadth measures the number of options listed in any single menu. Depth measures the number of menu levels through which the user must move to achieve the ultimate search objective. Ideally, both breadth and depth should be severely limited if users are to find the menu system helpful. Too much breadth results in screen crowding, as many options are crammed into a limited space. It also can make the selection of any one option more difficult for the user. Too great a depth of hierarchical menus increases navigational problems and error rates as well as searching time. Interface design guidelines typically recommend between four and eight items per menu (breadth) and no more than three or four menu levels (depth) (see, for example, Shneiderman, 1992). The complexities of many information retrieval systems makes the latter particularly difficult to achieve; many retrieval systems unfortunately must provide more than four levels if complicated searches, involving iterative searching, are to be accomplished. If more than eight items must be included in the menu, one solution is to display no more than this number at any one time, but to provide scrolling within the menu.

Designers can opt for several distinct menu models that each offer benefits and drawbacks to searchers: full-screen menus, pull-down menus, pop-up menus and command menus.

Full-screen menus

In a full-screen menu design, a menu is displayed on the first screen at the commencement of the search. This presents the user with a number of options. Depending on which option is selected, a new menu is displayed, and so on, until the information is located. The menus, then, are hierarchically structured and the user must travel through this so-called tree structure from the main trunk to the outer branches in order to accomplish the task. This might be considered as the purest menu form. It is familiar to any user of an ATM who has withdrawn or deposited cash. Its main advantage is that it guides the user through the search, because at each step the only options available are those listed on the current menu screen. Figure 8.2, from DialogWeb, shows the first level of the Guided Search menu that lets searchers select databases from among the several hundred available without the need for any command. Figure 8.3 shows another web-based, full-screen menu, this time listing special offers on Disney animated movies available on video. In four cases the user has the option of clicking on the image of the video cover instead of the titles listed alphabetically on the left of the screen.

Such strategy guidance is only achieved at a price. An information system using a complex retrieval engine and linked to a large database will often require the user to trek through many individual menu screens. Full-screen menus are particular suitable for occasional users, who need as much guidance as possible, or for relatively simple searches that do not involve many search steps.

Pull-down and pop-up menus

Pull-down and pop-up menus do not guide the user through the search, step by step. The user must decide which of several menus typically incorporated into any one screen display should be opened, and when. The user therefore must take more control of the search strategy than with full-screen menus. Typically, however, a menu will only be available to the user at a point in the search when it is appropriate, and to this extent the user is guided in menu selection. Pull-down menus tend to be employed for common and frequently used applications that can be activated in a wide variety of different windows. Pop-up menus are likely to be preferred for alternative applications within the context of a specific task.

The major benefit of pull-down or pop-up menus over full-screen menus is the much higher degree of user control afforded, and therefore enhanced flexibility in searching. Given that the user must exercise more decision making than with full-screen menus, it is probably more accurate to describe pull-down menus as offering menu-assisted rather than menu-driven searching. Pull-down menus are encountered in all kinds of software, and not simply in information systems. Figure 8.4 shows the *Microsoft Encarta 98 Encyclopedia* pop-up menu of article titles (Pinpointer) with a pull-down menu of options to copy, print, and so on superimposed upon Pinpointer.

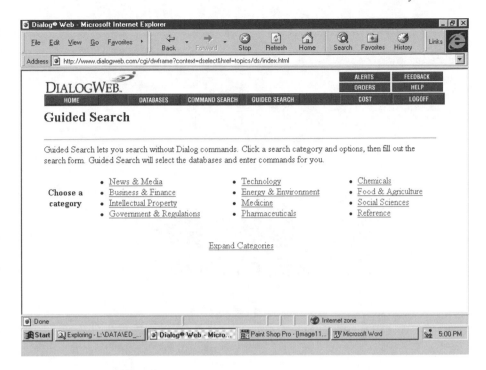

Figure 8.2   Full-screen menu on DialogWeb

Command menus

Command menus, or command bars as they are also called, combine
aspects of both the command and the menu dialogue transaction modes.
Commands must be chosen and implemented by the user, as with a
command language, but the commands are listed on the screen, introducing
elements of the menu approach. Two methods typically can be used to
display the commands: the command line (or bar) and function keys. In
the former, the individual commands, encapsulated if possible in a single
word, are displayed on the screen. A command is typically selected by
highlighting it using the arrow keys on the keyboard, or by typing the first
or several letters spelling the command. Alternatively, commands can be
represented by function keys, though the restricted number of function
keys on a keyboard (typically 12) means that commands must be limited
to this number or one function key must control more than one command,
either by using additional keys like Shift, Ctrl or Alt along with the function key, or by designating the same function key to undertake different
operations at different points in a search; the former is clumsy and the
latter potentially confusing. An example from the DOS menu interface to
the ERIC CD-ROM on the SilverPlatter Information Retrieval Service
(SPIRS) is shown in Figure 8.5: the commands are listed along the bottom
of the screen, and the FIND command has been highlighted to activate it.

Figure 8.3   Full-screen menu from Disney Videos on WWW

The command menu approach offers searching flexibility: the user can choose whichever command seems appropriate at a specific point in the search. The menu may be arranged either vertically or horizontally. The listing of the commands acts as an *aide memoire* for the searcher and obviates the need to remember specific commands (although their function must be understood by the searcher). Context sensitivity can be used by the interface designer to ensure that only commands of potential relevance to the search at that moment are available, thereby offering an element of guidance in strategy. Other than this, however, the searcher is not provided with help in strategy construction by the interface. The meaning of the individual commands must still be learned. It may also be difficult to encapsulate in these commands the many additional search features (such as truncation, word adjacency and field searching) available in the retrieval systems. Puttapithakporn (1990) reports on various problems encountered by novices using a command menu to search a CD-ROM bibliographic database (the ERIC educational database on SilverPlatter SPIRS version 1.4), an earlier version of the interface shown in Figure 8.5. These included failure to identify the next command needed in the search because it was not listed in the currently displayed command list, failure to understand abbreviations in the menus such as citn for citation, and misunderstandings about the functions of commands.

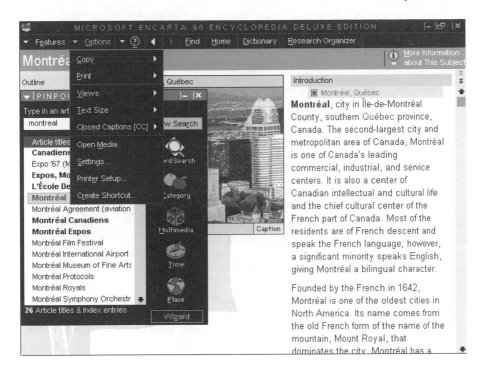

Figure 8.4   **Pull-down and pop-up menus,** *Microsoft Encarta 98 Encyclopedia* **on CD-ROM**

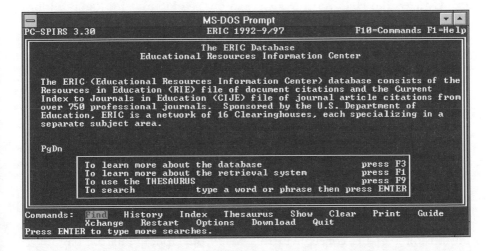

Figure 8.5   **Command menu from SilverPlatter's PC-SPIRS ERIC CD-ROM**

On-screen forms

On-screen forms are a popular way of providing guidance to users when data must be entered. Figure 8.4 shows a (partially concealed by the pull-down menu) example contained within the pop-up menu on the left of the screen: the user is invited to 'Type in an article title'. (This example from *Encarta* also demonstrates that a search for information need not always require a search term to be entered: the alphabetical list of article titles can be scrolled and selection made directly from the list). Figure 8.6 shows the web-based DRA OPAC at the State Library of Florida. Here the user has entered on to the form a title phrase, and two authors to be matched by a Boolean AND. Shneiderman, Byrd and Croft (1997) emphasize the importance of allowing plenty of space in text entry boxes, because longer search strings often give better search results and therefore users should be encouraged by the form design to use them. The boxes in the State Library of Florida OPAC are not especially big; the sought title 'Manual of Online Search Strategies' fits into the box only because it horizontally scrolls to accommodate titles of more than a few characters. (In the example in Figure 8.6 the title has scrolled off the left-hand side of the box, unhelpful if the user has made a typing error that is now concealed.) When complicated forms are provided (as with the HotBot Web search engine in Figure 8.7) it is important that all elements be clearly labelled.

Buttons, radio buttons and icons

A button is a small, normally square or rectangular area, often located on the vertical or horizontal edges of the screen, containing an instruction within it. Buttons along the top of *Compton's Interactive Encyclopedia* give access to the Find mode, go Back a screen, choose the Atlas or Timeline, Print, access the Help functions, and so on (see Figure 8.8). Radio buttons (or bullets) in the *Grolier Multimedia Encyclopedia* (Figure 8.9) allow a choice between browsing the full range of articles ('all' button) or a restricted range of articles selected by the user ('custom' button). Unlike a regular button, only one radio button can be selected (activated) at any one time (in this case 'All'). Note that the smallness of the radio buttons in Figure 8.9 requires their description to be included alongside rather than within them.

An icon, strictly speaking, is a graphical representation of an entity or an artifact; it presents on the screen a 'real' object rather than a text-labelled button. Users are supposed to remember the function of an icon more easily than that of a button. Some interface actions are easier to represent unambiguously than others using a graphical device (for example, a picture of a 35 mm camera can represent a still image, or a tape recorder can represent a sound sequence, without too much difficulty). More abstract concepts (such as repeat playing of a moving image sequence), however, are more difficult to portray because there is no familiar symbol that corresponds to the meaning of the concept. In this case a metaphor must be employed (such as two arrows formed into a circle to represent re-play). Problems of expressing meaning semiotically lead in many cases to an icon being accompanied by a textual description, thereby reducing the distinction between icons and buttons. In Figure 8.8, for example, the icon depicting

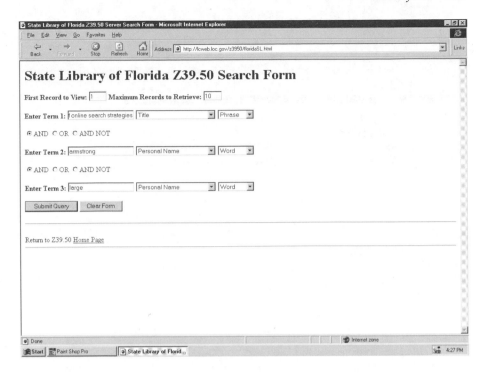

Figure 8.6 Form filling on the DRA Web OPAC at the State Library of Florida

a magnifying glass is accompanied by the description 'Find' (without the textual description it could alternatively have represented a zoom function), although the printer icon would be less ambiguous even without the accompanying 'Print' text caption.

In many cases the instructions encapsulated within buttons and icons are a subset of those also found in the interface's menus – the button is a faster way for the user, and especially the experienced user, to issue these instructions.

Ellis, Tran, Ryoo and Shneiderman (1995) provide an interesting discussion of the relative merits of buttons, icons and menus. It is crucially important, as with other aspects of interface design, that absolute consistency is followed in button and icon usage within any one interface. This might seem elementary advice, but it is not always followed. For example, on one CD-ROM product, best left unnamed, at least three different icons are used to represent the concept, 'go back one screen'. Although standards for icon representation have not been formally adopted, conventions are emerging. A video sequence, for example, is often represented by a movie camera, a page turn by an arrow, and so on. At the same time, developers of proprietary graphical interfaces may be tempted to differentiate their product from rivals by, among other things, designing esoteric

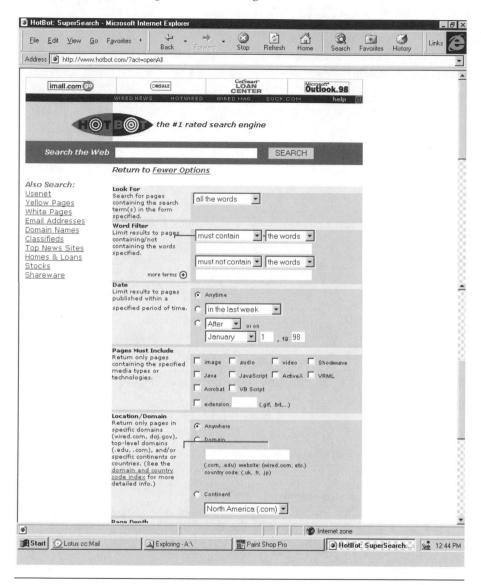

Figure 8.7   Form filling on HotBot

icons which are dissimilar from those of their rivals. To counter this tendency, at least in the case of bibliographic information systems, the International Federation of Library Associations and Institutions (IFLA) has commissioned the design of a standard set of icons which is intended to be language and culture independent (IFLA, 1996). Some examples of the proposed icon set are given in Figure 8.10.

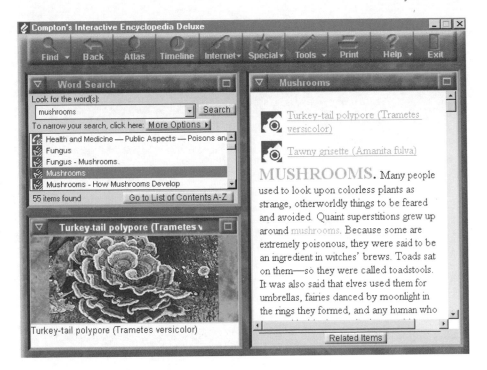

Figure 8.8 Buttons on *Compton's Interactive Encyclopedia* **CD-ROM, 1998** © **1998 The Learning Company, Inc.**

It is important when designing icons, as it is with other kinds of semiotic devices, to ensure as much as possible that the meaning of the icon is suggested by its structure. Too much detail should be avoided. Once learned, icons are likely to prove more memorable than commands.

Hypertext links

Hypertext links provide another way to navigate an information store, allowing the user to move from one location to another. They are more fully discussed in Chapter 7.

Graphical user interfaces

The graphical user interface (GUI), based on windows, icons and buttons, and using point and click devices like the mouse, allows users to manipulate directly on the screen objects that represent reality. A window is a rectangular area on the screen that displays a software application or a document file. Windows can be opened, closed, moved and re-sized with the click of a mouse. Several windows can be opened simultaneously, side by side or overlaid, and it may be possible to run several applications

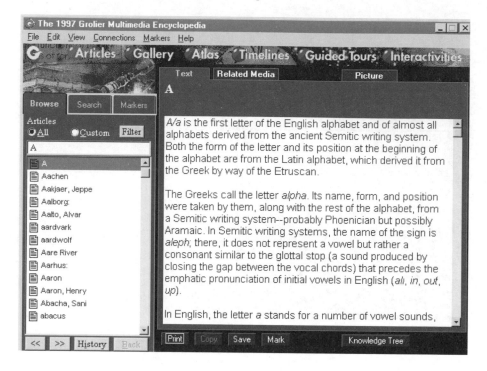

Figure 8.9   Radio buttons on the *Grolier Multimedia Encyclopedia*, CD-ROM 1997

simultaneously, each in its own window. Scroll bars enable a window to extend beyond the confinement of one screen. Typically the scrolling is vertical (up and down) but it may also be horizontal (right and left). A specific application of this technique is the time bar, used to identify and retrieve chronological information. Figure 8.11 shows an example from *Compton's Interactive Encyclopedia*; the scroll bar, at the top of the window, is used to scroll forwards (right) or backwards (left) through time.

Most current retrieval systems are based upon graphical user interfaces. These may be relatively simple, such as the covers of the most recent four issues of *Nature* on its Web site, where a click on the cover takes the user to the issue's contents (see Figure 8.12). AltaVista Maps uses a mixture of on-screen forms, and click and zoom to locate detailed maps of US cities. The user begins by filling in an on-screen form to locate the general geographical area; in this case San Francisco (Figure 8.13). The user in fact is interested in Berkeley – by clicking on this city the map re-centres (Figure 8.14). Finally the zoom bar on the right-hand side of the screen produces a street guide to one section of Berkeley (Figure 8.15). The *Castle Explorer* CD-ROM published by DK Multimedia provides another example (see Figure 8.16). Clicking on different sections of the castle takes the user to various locations. In Figure 8.16 the user has moved to the Middle Bailey,

Bibliographic Database Applications Standard Icon Set.

Below are the proposed standard set of icons for use in Bibliographic Database Applications. These Icons are in the Public Domain and may be freely used by all. More information on this project may be found in the Project report and Project Overview. If you wish to download the icons please follow this link.

Please Choose a Language :

English ▾   Go

Category : Actions

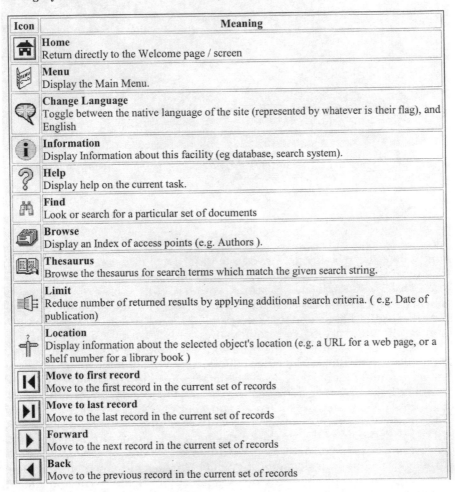

Icon	Meaning
	Home Return directly to the Welcome page / screen
	Menu Display the Main Menu.
	Change Language Toggle between the native language of the site (represented by whatever is their flag), and English
	Information Display Information about this facility (eg database, search system).
	Help Display help on the current task.
	Find Look or search for a particular set of documents
	Browse Display an Index of access points (e.g. Authors).
	Thesaurus Browse the thesaurus for search terms which match the given search string.
	Limit Reduce number of returned results by applying additional search criteria. (e.g. Date of publication)
	Location Display information about the selected object's location (e.g. a URL for a web page, or a shelf number for a library book)
	Move to first record Move to the first record in the current set of records
	Move to last record Move to the last record in the current set of records
	Forward Move to the next record in the current set of records
	Back Move to the previous record in the current set of records

Figure 8.10   Bibliographic Database Applications standard icon set (IFLA)

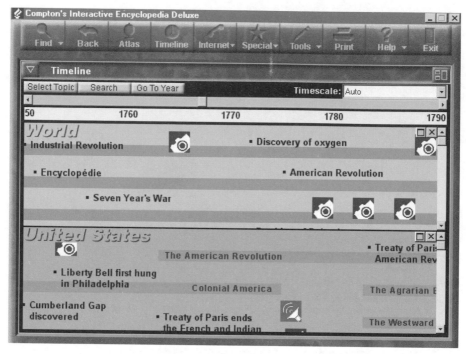

Figure 8.11   Time bar on *Compton's Interactive Encyclopedia* **CD-ROM, 1998** ©
1998 The Learning Company, Inc.

from where it is possible to move to another level of detail by clicking on,
say, the Gate Tower. Some OPACs use direct manipulation interfaces.
PACE, for example, is an experimental OPAC where users can browse a
bookshelf and 'pull' a book of the shelf to access its bibliographic description (Beheshti, Large and Bialek, 1996). The OPAC at the Informatics
Library of the Faculty of Mathematics and Natural Sciences at the
University of Oslo provides the user with a visual floor plan of the library
with zoom-in features. Shneiderman developed an interesting retrieval
system, HomeFinder, for real estate data (Shneiderman, 1994). Users see
points of light on a map representing homes for sale. As they shift sliders
to express their preferences for price, number of bedrooms, etc., the points
of light come and go presenting constantly changing visual representations
of how many homes are for sale and where they are located on the map.
Clicking on a point of light then produces a full description and picture
of the house. Golovchinsky and Chignell (1996) have designed an electronic
newspaper prototype that provides visualization of the 'local and global
structures' of the database being browsed. At the local level, each retrieved
article acquires a histogram of coloured bars, where the colour represents
the type of link used to find it (context setting, context specific or context

Figure 8.12 *Nature's* **graphical index page on the WWW**

independent) and the height represents the rank (the higher the bar, the more important the document). At the global level, each document is plotted as a point in a two-dimensional space; a point is highlighted if the document is selected, or the user may select an area in the space to view that neighbourhood of documents.

Such graphical interfaces are far from being full virtual reality systems (see later), but they do offer novel ways of putting the user in touch with the information.

Other graphical interfaces seek to complement a user's real-life experiences by providing a visual and tactile environment for the dialogue with the computer. Shneiderman (1992) lists the user benefits of such direct manipulation or object-oriented interfaces as mastery of the system, competence in performing tasks, ease in learning the system, enjoyment, and a desire to explore more powerful aspects of the system. He reports that studies have confirmed these advantages, at least for some users and some tasks. Head (1997) lists the following assets afforded by such interfaces:

● multiple methods for completing the same task, thereby allowing users to choose the easiest one for them;

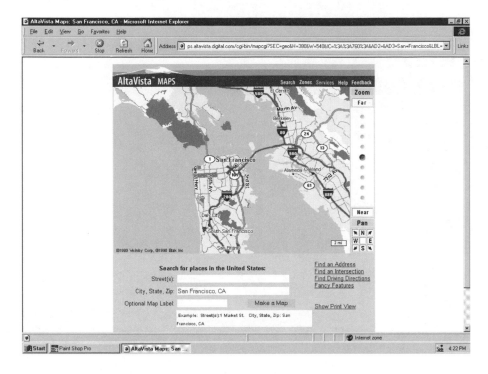

Figure 8.13   On-screen form on AltaVista Maps

- commands and menu options as needed, eliminating user memory overload;
- icons that rely on the user's recognition of real world objects;
- visual, auditory and tactile feedback about the system's operations;
- screen visuals, helping the user to focus attention on the current tasks.

On the other hand, the graphics can seem to be little more than gimmicks, and their novelty, while initially attractive to the novice, can become irksome for the more experienced. Shneiderman believes that the trick in creating a direct manipulation system is to come up with an appropriate representation or model of reality. With a card game such as Solitaire, for example, it is easy to design a screen-based visual reality where the cards are distributed on the screen as they would be on a table, and where the player can manipulate them on the screen exactly as would be done on the real table. Games of all kinds and levels of sophistication provide a fertile soil for the designer's imagination. Such visual representation is not necessarily as straightforward in the information retrieval domain. In PACE, for example, the book spines graphically represented on the screen have a thickness proportional to the number of pages as given in the appropriate MARC record (see Chapter 5 for more about MARC). The colours

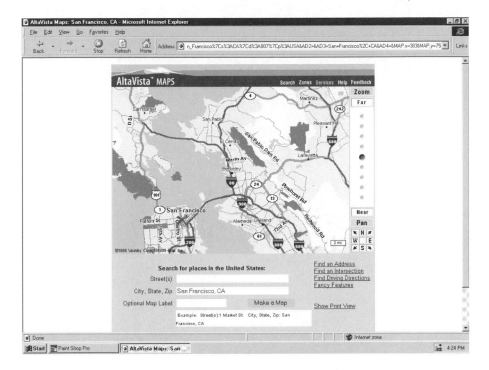

Figure 8.14   Point and click navigation on AltaVista Maps

used for the book spines on PACE are arbitrary, however, because the MARC record does not contain this information, even though some users may find colour a useful visual clue to a book's location on a real shelf.

Display Features

Screen layout

A well-designed screen should reflect the needs and capabilities of its users, be developed within the capabilities of the hardware on which it will operate and achieve the objectives of the application for which it has been produced: 'All elements of a screen must have meaning to users and serve a purpose in performing tasks' (Galitz, 1997).

Users easily can become disoriented in a complex interface involving many screens, or they may fail to explore useful features hidden within the recesses of a complex interface design. The answer to the problem of too many screens, however, is not to cram as much information as possible on a few screens. User performance tends to deteriorate with increasing display density. Cherry and Cox (1996) suggest a maximum of 600 characters per screen (30 percent density), with a display width of no more than 40 to

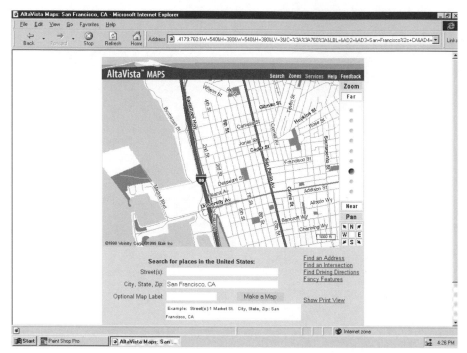

Figure 8.15   Zoom on AltaVista Maps

60 characters. Nor is scrolling necessarily a good way to reduce the number of screens as some users become uncomfortable or even disoriented when this technique is invoked. It is therefore important to omit unnecessary detail, use concise wording and employ where feasible tabular or form layouts. A standard way of expressing concepts concisely is to use special terminology (or jargon), but in such cases brevity may be purchased at the expense of clarity for those unfamiliar with this terminology. Abbreviations should be avoided where possible, as it is easy for the experienced user (or designer) to assume a familiarity which novices do not share.

Overlaying one screen on another can also become confusing for users. Frames clearly drawn around screens are essential if this problem is to be minimized. In the case of Web sites, unnecessary detail, especially pictorial, can overload not only the user but also the telecommunications: cleverly designed, complex graphics will dramatically slow response time. There is some evidence that menus displayed horizontally (as with many command menus) are more difficult to scan than vertical menu displays (Shneiderman, 1992).

Larger fonts are easier to read, especially for older users, but then less information can be accommodated on any one screen. Different fonts can be used to emphasize specific information components (for example, headings) but in this case should be used consistently for this purpose throughout the interface. Galitz (1997) recommends never using more than two font families (such as Times and Courier), two styles (for example,

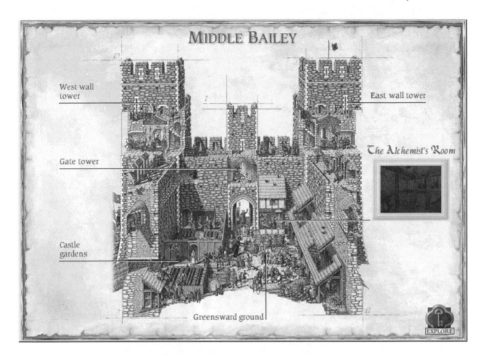

Figure 8.16   The Middle Bailey on DK Multimedia's *Castle Explorer* CD-ROM

regular and italic) two weights (for example, regular and bold) and three sizes. Italic fonts work much less effectively on the screen than in print: they are less crisp than standard fonts and therefore less legible. The information presented by *Compton's Interactive Encyclopedia* (Figure 8.17) uses various fonts, and although the screen includes three windows as well as numerous buttons and icons, it remains clear (although it cannot be seen in this monochrome figure, colour also is effectively used by this encyclopedia to aid screen clarity – see later).

Emphasis can be provided by inverse video, highlighting or blinking. These techniques can be effective if used consistently and sparingly, but overuse will simply reduce the clarity of the entire screen. Blinking or flashing messages in particular can prove irritating, at least to some users, and should only be used for urgent situations. It should also be borne in mind that directing attention to one part of the screen may distract attention from elsewhere, resulting in other important information on the screen being overlooked. Labels, instructions, warning messages and so on should be displayed in consistent screen locations, and consistent terminology employed throughout the interface.

Zooming techniques can be employed to magnify or reduce screen displays. They are relatively common with cartographic data where the user may wish to view a large area at a low magnification or zoom into a detailed, large-scale display of a map (see Figures 8.14 and 8.15).

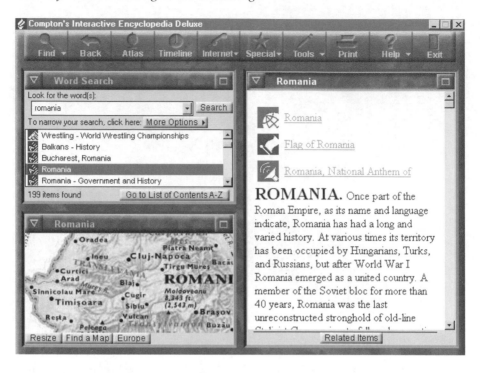

Figure 8.17   Screen layout on *Compton's Interactive Encyclopedia* CD-ROM, 1998 © 1998 The Learning Company, Inc.

Sequencing

Interfaces often present lists of items. These may be options within a menu or actual data elements such as bibliographical records. In the absence of other sequencing criteria, alphabetical or numerical sequencing should be used. But it is preferable to order the elements by a more meaningful criterion, such as conventionality, frequency of use or logical sequence of operations. There is general agreement that the menu sequence in which search options are offered will influence user selection: users are apt to choose an option higher rather than lower in a list. For this reason it can be argued that the essential search options should be located above their more esoteric cousins.

Colour

Many current information retrieval systems are designed to run on colour monitors and make extensive use of colour within the interface. If used properly, colour can play an important role in presenting information clearly on the screen. It can be used to express hierarchical levels within menus, to distinguish between different kinds of menus, to highlight search terms in data displays, and so on. At worst, however, it can distract, fatigue and impair the effectiveness of the interface. As Galitz (1997) puts it: 'The

simple addition of colour to a screen will not guarantee improved performance. What may have been a poorly designed product will simply become
a colourful poorly designed product.' The screen can become a psychedelic
colour assault, blinding the user to any significant elements in the display.
Screen backgrounds can prove more attention grabbing than the data themselves, a fault encountered, for example, with some Web sites.

Relatively little research has been undertaken on colour usage.
Shneiderman (1992) recommends that colours should be limited to four in
any one display, and to no more than seven in the interface as a whole.
Galitz (1997) agrees with four per screen (but normally prefers just two or
three) and recommends no more than four or five colours in total, which
should be widely spaced on the spectrum. All colours are not equal: the
eye is more sensitive to those in the middle of the visual spectrum such
as yellow or green which appear brighter than the colours at the ends of
the spectrum (blue and red). Red, yellow, green, blue and brown tend to
be good colours to use. For older viewers, brighter colours such as white
and yellow are better than blue or red. The ISO Colour Standard suggests
that for continuous reading tasks, de-saturated spectrally close colours
(such as yellow, cyan and green) should be used to minimize disruptive
eye problems. Some combinations, such as dark coloured text on a dark
coloured background, are difficult to read. Powell (1990) and Galitz (1997)
offer guidance on colour selection as well as many other facets of interface
design. As with other interface features, consistent use is vital.

Colour combinations that offer sharp contrasts and work well may prove
highly unsatisfactory when converted to their monochrome equivalents or
when used in ambient lighting conditions or by people with a colour-view-
ing defficiency. Therefore the display features should be designed to function effectively in a monochrome environment first, and only then in colour.

Certain colours have semantic values such as red to warn, yellow to
express caution or green to move on, and these should be capitalized upon
where possible. However, it should be borne in mind that such values may
be culturally dependent and therefore not universal in application (red, for
example, signifies danger in North America, death in Egypt, life in India
and happiness in China). Furthermore, users may have a very subjective
reaction to colours: what is attractive and coordinated to one user can
appear garish to another, and 8 percent of males (but only 0.4 percent of
females) in North America and Europe suffer to some extent from colour
blindness: for example, yellow may look like orange, and purple like dark
blue or red. For this reason, some CD-ROMs allow users to modify colour
use to suit their individual tastes, although this in turn can create problems in a multiuser environment such as a library where one user may
adjust the colour to suit his/her taste but not to the liking of the next user.

Multimedia

Display of multimedia information – incorporating combinations of text,
still images, animation, video sequences, music, sound effects and voices
– poses special interface problems. These include how best to combine
various media on the screen, the level of interactivity to be provided, and

ways of orienting the user to changes in multimedia displays. Multimedia features can be used in an interface to arouse and focus interest, but can also distract attention. What seems an attractive novelty on initial use can quickly become irritating. A fuller discussion can be found in Large (1996).

Output Options

The interface can present retrieved data in a variety of ways. First, they can be displayed on the screen either as text, still images, animation or video. Non-textual displays place greater demands upon the quality and dimensions of the monitor's screen and, in the case of remote systems, the speed and capacity of the communication channel. Images using the full screen (rather than quarter or half screens) and millions of colours (rather than, say, just 256 colours) will take longer to retrieve and display. Moving images likewise place greater demand upon the hardware and communication networks than still images. In some cases data may be presented as sound through speakers or headphones rather than displayed on the screen.

Usually the information retrieval system will also allow the retrieved data to be downloaded to a hard disc or diskette. Another common option is to print retrieved data at a local or remote printer. It may also be possible to transfer retrieved data electronically to email or other file addresses.

GUI environments allow text or images to be 'cut' from their original location and transferred (or pasted) to another. A CD-ROM, for example, may have a clipboard feature where items cut from the database can be pasted into a special storage area or transferred to an entirely new software application. Such portability is straightforward for ASCII text files but more difficult in the case of graphics and video images where format standardization has not been fully achieved (see Wusteman, 1996).

Input Devices

Keyboard

The keyboard is the traditional input device. It is a highly efficient way of delivering textual data to the computer. When searching for information it will normally be necessary to input one or more search terms, and this requires access to an alphabetical display. The standard way of accomplishing this is to use a keyboard.

The keyboard may be efficient, especially for those willing to spend a little time in acquiring touch typing skills. Nevertheless, it does have a number of drawbacks. Keyboards unfortunately are not completely standardized. The actual letter keys in the English-speaking world are normally arranged in a standard order (called QWERTY after the first six letters on the top line of keys). A keyboard designed for another language group may have a modified layout which plays havoc with the proficiency of a QWERTY-trained typist. The keyboard contains many other keys – numerical keys, function keys, direction keys, etc. – and their arrangement is less standardized than the letter keys. Furthermore, it cannot be assumed that all users are aware of these keys. A study of low literacy patrons at a public library OPAC found that many were unfamiliar with the keyboard layout (White, Deane and Livingston, 1996).

The main drawback of the keyboard, however, is its primary design as an input rather than a screen manipulation device. Function keys and directional arrow keys can if necessary be used to do things such as open a menu and scroll its options, but the keyboard was not designed for this purpose. The new graphical interfaces, requiring point and click actions, cannot efficiently be exploited using a keyboard.

Mouse

The mouse was designed specifically to meet the need for a point and click device. It enables the cursor to be moved around the screen and positioned accurately. An instruction can then be issued by clicking the mouse button in order to open a menu, activate an icon, scroll a screen or whatever.

The mouse is no more free from problems than the keyboard. It may be an excellent device to use with a graphical interface but it cannot efficiently enter textual information. It is true that the mouse can be used to click on an image of a keyboard displayed on the screen, but this is a far slower way of entering textual data than a real keyboard, even for the least accomplished typist. In information retrieval systems, with their requirement for entry of search terms, a mouse would therefore normally be used in conjunction with a keyboard.

A certain level of eye-hand coordination is required to operate a mouse properly. The mouse must be used to position the cursor accurately on a small area of the screen, and some users find this a challenge. In a cluttered screen it is remarkably easy to 'lose' the cursor from view; it is equally possible accidentally to take the cursor off the screen altogether. These problems are aggravated if the rotating ball within the mouse does not operate smoothly, establishing either too much or too little friction with the mat.

Touchscreen

An alternative to both the keyboard and the mouse is the touchscreen. Here users make physical contact with the screen, employing their own fingers to point at the screen much as the mouse points the cursor. Textual information is input by displaying a keyboard on the screen: the user can point a finger at the keys much more quickly than a mouse can point a cursor, and therefore this is not such an inefficient way of entering text. Touchscreen input devices have been used with some information systems, including CD-I applications and local information systems in public libraries. Considerable improvements have been made since the early models first appeared, and they can now give high precision. They certainly eliminate the need to control a keyboard or a mouse and therefore also the requirement for an add-on inputting device that might be stolen and needs a table on which to locate it at the workstation.

Nevertheless, touchscreen input devices are relatively uncommon for several reasons. Anyone who has stuck a finger on a glass surface knows that fingers have an unfortunate tendency to smear and leave a print, the intensity of which may be increased on warm days or if the finger has recently held a chocolate bar or a leaking pen. Touchscreens for public use will need constant cleaning. The human finger is rather large to envisage as a pointer to a regular monitor screen. It certainly does not have the precision of a mouse-driven cursor. Touchscreens must therefore be larger (and more expensive) than the standard monitor. At the same time, they are not as efficient as a keyboard at entering text. Screen touching can also quickly induce fatigue. Finally, touchscreens do not easily accommodate a verification stage. They do not have the equivalent of the 'return' key on the keyboard or the button on the mouse that must verify the initial cursor positioning: once the screen has been touched there is no further verification and the instruction will be implemented immediately.

Other possibilities

Marchionini (1992) argues for new input approaches to be tested and integrated into interfaces. He includes data gloves, speech recognizers, gesture recognizers and eye trackers. Currently, however, these have not figured to any extent in information retrieval systems.

Output Devices and Quality

The results from any search must be presented to the client, and therefore output devices are just as much a part of the interface as input devices. Ultimately, search results must be either displayed on a monitor (monochrome or colour), played through speakers or headphones, or printed (they may be first transferred in digital format to some other application program). It is not intended here to discuss such output devices in any detail.

The quality of the display produced by any interface will be affected by the size of the screen and the quality of the monitor and its video card (in the case of graphics). In the case of sound, the speaker and sound card quality are crucial, especially at the low end of the bandwidth. Impressive display characteristics of an interface will obviously be undermined by poor monitors and speakers.

Printers come in many shapes and sizes, and the quality of the print copy, especially in the case of graphics, will be determined by the particular printer being used. Effective colour use in the interface display will only reveal itself on a colour printer, and monochrome presentation (as in the case of a monochrome monitor) may mask important elements in the displays.

On-Screen Help

Help

Even the experienced user on occasion may encounter a problem during a search for which a solution is required. Trenner (1989) categorizes the questions that might be posed to the system by the user as:

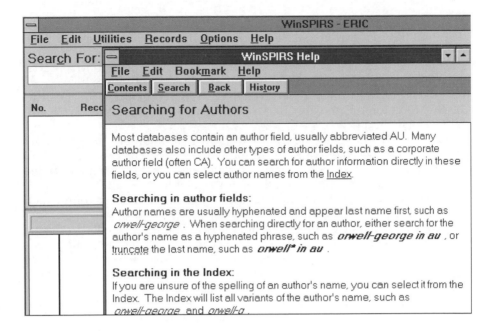

Figure 8.18   Help screen from SilverPlatter's WinSPIRS ERIC CD-ROM

- What have I done wrong?
- Am I doing the right thing?
- Where am I and what can I do next?
- How do I do something?
- How do I get some information?
- Why has the system failed?

Sytems that cannot respond to such questions are unlikely to be considered 'user friendly' and will deter subsequent use. Trenner (1989) suggests six guidelines for the design of a help facility:

- Online help should be available at all times.
- It should be easy both to enter and exit the help facility.
- The help facility should be well constructed.
- Help should be well presented on the screen.
- Help information should be well written.
- Help should include more than one user level to accommodate different users.

Many systems provide on-screen help in the form of complete user manuals or individual help screens (as well as printed documentation). Normally it is more helpful to provide context-sensitive help that is directed specifically to the user's current problem than leave the user to locate the relevant section of a manual. Indeed, a how-to manual is best provided in paper format so that it can be studied at leisure by the user prior to searching. Help facilities that expect users to work through numerous screens in order to solve one specific problem are unlikely to prove successful: there is considerable evidence to suggest that most users will abandon help after just a few screens. Figure 8.18 shows an example of a pull-down help screen from the Windows version of SilverPlatter's SPIRS (WinSPIRS) for the ERIC CD-ROM. As long as the user understands terms like 'field' and 'truncate', the message should be clear.

The only advantage for the user of an on-screen manual is that it cannot be lost or otherwise separated from the workstation. For the producer, of course, it may be cheaper and easier to update an electronic than a printed manual; indeed, where both versions are available it is not unknown for the electronic version to include revisions that have not yet found their way into the printed copy.

Help is particularly important for searches that are not producing satisfactory results. For example, when a search produces either hundreds of hits or zero hits, the user should be advised how to narrow or broaden the search. Retrieval systems that use term weighting should offer explanations in case the displayed results appear strange to the user. For example, THOMAS, a legislative retrieval system at the Library of Congress (http://thomas.loc.gov), was searched to find a bill on 'elderly black Americans' but retrieved a bill on 'black bears'. To prevent bafflement of users in such instances, THOMAS displays several general messages following every search, including the relevant one in this case: 'All of your search terms did not occur in any single bill' (Croft, Cook and Wilder, 1995).

The level of help and the language in which it is expressed must be suitable for the target audience, especially difficult if this is wide and diverse. It cannot be assumed that all users will understand terms that are commonplace for librarians, such as 'truncated', 'display', 'format', 'keyword', 'enter a line number' or even 'select' (White, Deane and Livingston, 1996). The instructions offered by the various Web search engines are often inadequate and confusing, assuming a knowledge of information retrieval techniques that many users are unlikely to possess.

Error messages

Error messages were notoriously bad on early mainframe-based online retrieval systems, all too often presenting the user with programming jargon that shed no light whatsoever either on the error or the means of correcting it. One manifestation of a general trend towards more user friendliness has been a great improvement in error messages, although exceptions can still be found. While researching this chapter, the following message was received from the Mosaic Web browser: Failure to find internal anchor '1996.'

Error messages should be clear, relevant, visible, consistently placed on the screen and above all helpful in warning the user that a problem has occurred and as much as possible suggesting a solution (unlike the earlier Mosaic message). Designers are recommended to opt for polite, constructive error messages. They should be non-threatening, avoid humour (which tends to be subjective and in any case wears thin after a while) and not be expressed anthropomorphically. Designers are urged to eschew terms like abort, boot, execute and kill, instead opting for the less emotive cancel, start, complete and end.

While not strictly an error diagnosis facility, a requirement that users must confirm decisions before they are implemented can prevent many errors in the first place. Puttapithakporn (1990) provides a good example of users who entered the 'Quit' or 'restart' commands when in fact they were trying to switch from one menu display to another. The consequence of entering these wrong commands was to erase the entire search history up to that point. A confirmation message asking whether they really wanted to execute such a drastic action would have given them pause for reflection.

Tutorials

On-screen tutorials are provided, for example, on some CD-ROM products and Web-based services. Unlike print-based tutorials, on-screen examples have the opportunity to be interactive. They must follow the standards for other kinds of computer-based training. These include a sharp focus, clear presentation of information, opportunities to practise examples, assessment of learning through quizzes or tests, and constructive feedback on any mistakes. Unfortunately, there is little evidence that such tutorials are followed by many users. To encourage use, they should be kept as short as possible (30 minutes maximum). It is preferable to provide several short tutorials rather than a single long one.

Interfaces Today and Tomorrow

Interfaces to information retrieval systems have undoubtedly improved as more experience has been gained in meeting user requirements. The original, online command-driven search systems reflected their programmer designers' backgrounds rather than their users' needs. They offered an enormous advance in retrieval capabilities compared with manual systems and therefore information professionals were prepared to cope with their many idiosyncracies. Information retrieval interfaces today must be suited not only to the occasional user but must also meet the high standards found in other software such as wordprocessors, spreadsheets, design programs and games.

A comparison of today's interfaces with those of just ten years ago would quickly reveal the progress that has been made. Yet it would be optimistic to think that high standards are met by all information systems. Take, for example, the principle that users should feel they are in control. There is growing evidence that user control improves search performance and increases satisfaction (Koenemann and Belkin, 1996). Nevertheless, not all systems even allow users to stop a search if they feel it is taking too long or is unsuccessful.

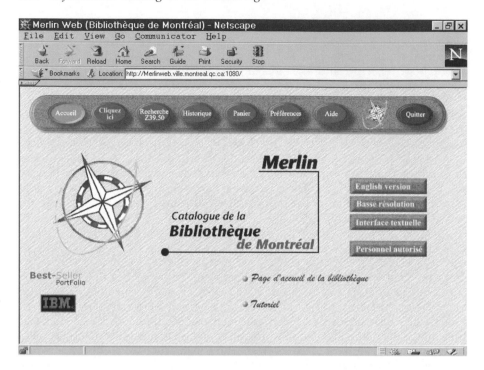

Figure 8.19   Opening screen of Merlin OPAC (Best-Seller) at the Bibliothèque de Montréal

Despite many common design features shared by different interfaces, their detailed operation still tends to vary from one to another. Networking of information resources permits users in one location to search databases on computers located elsewhere, but the benefits are compromised when it is necessary for the searcher to become familiar with an alien interface on the remote computer. For example, a search on another institution's OPAC via the Internet may still assume that the user can cope with that OPAC's interface. The extent to which this is feasible depends on the similarity of that interface with the user's own OPAC interface, the user's experience with various interfaces and the degree of help offered by the OPAC interface. It is not always easy to accomplish a search or even to find a way of ending the session. Fortunately, a new standard – Z39.50 – promises to overcome this problem.

Z39.50

The Z39.50 standard, developed by the American National Standards Institute, currently maintained by the Library of Congress, and approved as an international standard by the International Standards Organization, potentially represents a significant development for remote searching (Hakala, 1996). The searcher formulates the search using the local inter-

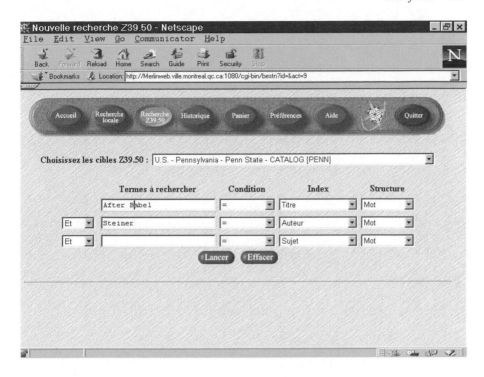

Figure 8.20 Z39.50 search interface at the Bibliothèque de Montréal

face. The client computer then converts this search into a Z39.50-compliant form and sends it to the host server on which the database is located. The server in turn converts the search into a form acceptable to the database and the search is carried out. The results are returned via the Z39.50 format to the client computer which finally converts into the local client computer's interface for display to the searcher. The intention is that the searcher need not be familiar with either the standard itself or the target system. An example from the Bibliothèque de Montréal illustrates this process. Figure 8.19 shows the opening screen of the public library's MERLIN OPAC, which includes a button from which a Z39.50 search can be selected (Recherche Z39.50). The Z39.50 interface itself is shown in Figure 8.20. The user completes a form with details of the sought document, in this case George Steiner's book, *After Babel*, and selects a library OPAC in which to search (in this case the Pennsylvania State University OPAC in the US) from a pull-down menu. The result of the search – the book is available at Penn State library – is displayed on the Montreal OPAC interface as shown in Figure 8.21. It is interesting to note in this example that the Z39.50 interface is working across two languages as well as two OPACs.

Z39.50-compliant server and client software programs are being implemented by OPAC vendors such as DRA, VTLS and Best-Seller. This standard currently does not offer, however, a complete solution to cross-

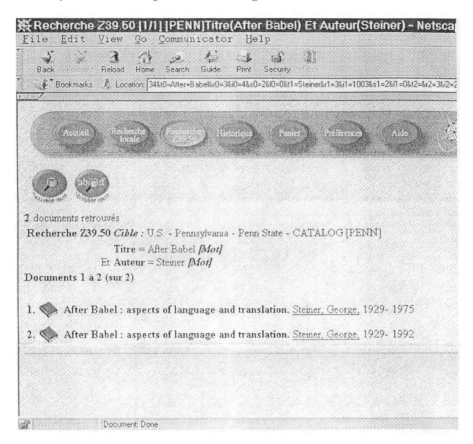

Figure 8.21   Z39.50 display interface at the Bibliothèque de Montréal

interface searching. Dorman (1997) tried out OCLC's WebZ server on a 'health care' simultaneous search against 12 university library OPACs. One search failed entirely, and the others returned hits ranging from the two lowest of nine and 250 to the two highest of 6,383 and a gargantuan 14,136. He surmizes that these results indicate little about the true holdings on this subject but were caused by differences in the ways fields were indexed, the thesaurus used and any automatic limits set on the number of records that were to be retrieved by the OPACs (see the comments on cross-file searching in Chapter 6). He concludes: 'Our standards need to go a lot deeper than the current Z39.50 products are capable of before we can do meaningful searches across multiple databases.' The virtual Canadian union catalogue (vCuc) pilot project suggests that library cataloguing practices need to be improved if searches through Z39.50 servers are to find relevant results and avoid false hits. In particular, unambiguous record identification data such as International Standard Serial Numbers (ISSNs) and International Standard Book Numbers (ISBNs) are essential. Lunau and Turner (1997)

Figure 8.22   Virtual tour of the National Library of Canada

conclude that 'Z39.50 is a solution for areas which require occasional access to several databases and where the databases are not searched frequently enough to develop the necessary expertise [in the use of the local system]. It is also applicable where the retrieval of a few [bibliographic] records is more important than the retrieval of all records for an item.' A side benefit of the Z39.50 standard, however, is that its very existence is encouraging different OPAC vendors to develop similar interfaces for their Web-based catalogues. Some further discussion on the use of Z39.50 can be found in Chapter 9.

A number of other interesting developments in interface design are taking place, and several briefly can be reviewed. Shneiderman, Byrd and Croft (1997) extol the virtues of 'dynamic queries' where the system would always be in a search mode. Search results are continuously displayed and updated as the search progresses, enabling users to broaden, narrow or re-focus their searches very rapidly and to see immediately the effects. Unfortunately, this approach requires a large screen to maintain the dynamic displays as well as high bandwidth if searching a remote database, and very rapid processing if the database is large.

Virtual reality

Another interesting area of research is virtual reality (VR), or virtual environment, as many of its proponents prefer to call it. VR simulates real environments in virtual worlds to represent them as realistically as possible. Stuart (1996) defines VR as a human–computer interface that provides interactive, immersive, multisensory 3-D synthetic environments. It uses position tracking and real-time update of visual, auditory and other (for example, tactile) displays in response to the user's motions to give the user a sense of being in the environment and being able to move through it. Although the history of VR can be traced back to the early flight simulators of the 1930s, and subsequently to the computer-generated graphics which appeared in the early 1970s, this field is still in its infancy. Much of the development work until very recently has been undertaken by the military and most of the research has used young, male fighter pilots, not necessarily ideal surrogates for users of information retrieval systems.

It is possible to envisage a virtual library reality, where users can approach the virtual catalogue, search it virtually, browse the virtual shelves, pull off virtual books, open and read them. The Leddy Library at the University of Windsor in Canada is experimenting with the Virtual Reality Modeling Language to generate 3-D bookshelves that can be browsed (not to be confused with the two-dimensional representations in the PACE graphical user interface mentioned earlier). In common with a number of other national libraries the National Library of Canada offers users a virtual tour of the building (Figure 8.22).

Jacobson (1993) suggests that people create cognitive schemes for themselves – inside virtual worlds – to provide order in their complex daily environments; technology can be used to construct outside virtual worlds that correspond as closely as possible to these inside worlds. It remains to be seen whether such realistic representations can provide helpful interfaces for information retrieval. VR in this field may have more to offer in creating metaphorical realities where information is displayed in more elaborate timelines, starfields and tree maps rather than reproducing a model of the library itself.

References

Baecker, R.M. and Buxton, W.A.S. (1987) (eds) *Readings in Human-Computer Interaction: a Multidisciplinary Approach*. Los Angeles: Morgan Kaufmann

Barker, A.L. (1997) DataStar Web: living up to the hype? An evaluation of the interface and search system. *Online Information 97. Proceedings of the 21st International Online Information Meeting, London, 9–11 December 1997.* Oxford: Learned Information, 213–222

Beaulieu, M. (1997) Experiments on interfaces to support query expansion. *Journal of Documentation*, **53** (1), 8–19

Beheshti, J., Large, V. and Bialek, M. (1996) PACE: a browsable graphical interface. *Information Technology and Libraries*, **15** (4), 231–40

Cherry, J.M. and Cox, J.P. (1996) World Wide Web displays of bibliographic records: an evaluation. *Proceedings of the 24th Annual Conference of the Canadian Association for Information Science.* Toronto: Canadian Association for Information Science. Also available at http://www.fis.utoronto.can/research/displays/caispck1.htm

Connaway, L.S., Budd, J.M. and Kochtanek, T.R. (1995) An investigation of the use of an online catalog: user characteristics and transaction log analysis. *Library Resources and Technical Services*, **39** (2), 142–52

Croft, W.B., Cook, R. and Wilder, D. (1995) Providing government information on the Internet: experiences with THOMAS. *Second Annual Conference on the Theory and Practice of Digital Libraries, 11–13 June 1995*, Austin, Texas. Available at http://csdl.tamu.edu/DL95/papers/croft/croft.html

Dorman, D. (1997) Technically speaking: new developments shake up Midwinter exhibits. *American Libraries*, **28** (4), 76–8

Ellis, J., Tran, C., Ryoo, J. and Shneiderman, B. (1995) *Buttons vs. Menus: an Exploratory Study of Pull-Down Menu Selection as Compared to Button Bars.* Available at CAR-TR-764. ftp://ftp.cs.umd.edu/pub/hcil/Reports-Abstracts-Bibliography/3452.txt

Frese, M., Schulte-Gocking, H. and Altmann, A. (1987) Lernprozesse in Abhängigkeit von der Trainingsmethode, von Personenmerkmalen und von der Benutzeroberfläche. In W. Schonpflu and M. Wittstock (eds) *Software-Ergonomie 87.* Berlin: Teubner

Galitz, W.O. (1997) *Essential Guide to User Interface Design: An Introduction to GUI design: Principles and Techniques.* New York: Wiley

Golovchinsky, G. and Chignell, M. (1996) *Merging Hypertext and Information Retrieval in the Interface.* Poster at SIGIR 1996. Available at http://anarch.ie.utoronto.ca/people/gene.html/publications/sigir96_poster/

Hakala, J. (1996) *Z39.50–1995 Information Retrieval Protocol: an Introduction to the Standard and its Usage.* Available at http://renki.helsinki.fi/z3950/z3950pr.html

Head, A.J. (1997) A question of interface design: how do online service GUIs measure up? *Online*, **21** (3), 20–29

IFLA. Information Technology Section (1996) *Feasibility of a Standard Icon Set for Bibliographic Information Systems.* Available at http://lorne.stir.ac.uk:80/icon-std/results

Jacobson, R. (1993) After the virtual reality gold rush: the virtual world's paradigm. *Computer and Graphics*, **17** (6), 695–8

Koenemann, J. and Belkin, N. (1996) A case for interaction: a study of interactive information retrieval behavior and effectiveness. *Proceedings of the Computer Human Interaction 96 Human Factors in Computing Systems.* New York: ACM Press, 205–212

Large, A. (1996) Computer animation in an instructional environment. *Library and Information Science Research,* **18** (1), 3–23

Lunau, C.D. and Turner, F. (1997) Vcuc Pilot project: status report and preliminary identification of issues. *Feliciter,* **43** (6), 40–45

Mandel, T. (1997) *The Elements of User Interface Design.* New York: Wiley

Marchionini, G. (1992) Interfaces for end-user information seeking. *Journal of the American Society for Information Science,* **43** (2), 156–63

Microsoft Corporation (1997) *The Windows Interface Guidelines for Software Design.* Available at http://www.microsoft.com/win32dev/uiguide/

Nicholas, D., Erbach, G. and Harris, K. (1987) End users: threat, challenge or myth? *Aslib Proceedings,* **39** (11/12), 337–44

Powell, J.E. (1990) *Designing User Interfaces.* San Marcos: Microtrend

Puttapithakporn, S.D. (1990) Interface design and user problems and errors: a case study of novice searchers. *RQ,* **30** (2), 195–204

Shneiderman, B. (1992) *Designing the User Interface: Strategies for Effective Human–Computer Interaction* 2nd edn. Reading: Addison-Wesley

Shneiderman, B. (1994) Connecting the DOE community: partnerships in information. *Information Technology '94, Oak Ridge, TN, 25–26 October, 1994.* Also available at ftp://ftp.cs.umd.edu/pub/hcil/Reports-Abstracts-Bibliography/94–12.txt

Shneiderman, B. (1996) *Designing Information-Abundant Websites.* Available at ftp://ftp.cs.umd.edu/pub/hcil/Reports-Abstracts-Bibliography/3634.txt

Shneiderman, B., Byrd, D. and Croft, W.B. (1997) Clarifying search: a user-interface framework for text searches. *D-Lib Magazine,* January. Available at http://www.dlib.org/dlib/january97/retrieval/01shneiderman.html

Stuart, R. (1996) *The Design of Virtual Environments.* New York: McGraw-Hill

Sullivan, M.V., Borgman, C.L. and Wippern, D. (1990) End-users, mediated searches and front-end assistance programs on Dialog: a comparison of learning, performance and satisfaction. *Journal of the American Society for Information Science,* **41** (1), 27–42

Trenner, L. (1989) A comparative survey of the friendliness of online 'help' in interactive information retrieval systems. *Information Processing and Management,* **25** (2), 119–36

White, M.A., Deane, L. and Livingston, B. (1996) Toronto Public Library's Online Public Access Catalogue Project. *Feliciter,* **42** (4), 30–31

Wusteman, J. (1996) Electronic journal formats. *Program,* **30** (4), 319–43

CHAPTER 9

Information Seeking –
Some Practical Issues

The Search Process

There are various ways in which electronic information resources can be made available to the searcher and these were described in Chapter 3. This chapter will provide an overview of the general search process before giving examples of a number of searches. Final sections will cover the impact of end-user information seeking on library and information staff and provide an overview of training issues for electronic information resource seeking.

Any search process, as described in Chapter 2, can be broken down into the following phases: establish the precise request, choose the appropriate information resource, prepare the search, and carry out the search. In some cases, where the search is done by an intermediary, a final stage will be the presentation of the results to the person requesting the search.

Obviously the time and effort spent on the various stages will differ greatly depending on the type of search being undertaken. A search to find what film is being shown at the local cinema tonight will be very different from a search on the appropriate drug to prescribe hay fever sufferers or a search on the latest news from the stock market in Malaysia.

Establish search request

For searches that are carried out by intermediaries, it is very important for the intermediary to establish exactly what information is required. This process, often known as the reference interview or the pre-search interview, involves the intermediary eliciting more information from the patron about what, why, when, where and how the search should proceed. The intermediary should ask for possible constraints, such as the publication date or language of retrieved items. The ability to build such constraints into the search request will depend on the search system being used and the way in which the data are structured. The patron can also be asked for any known relevant item that is likely to be included in the collection being searched. (Once that item has been found, it may suggest good search terms (assigned index terms or even words from the title, abstract and so on) to develop the search further.)

End-user searching became feasible during the 1980s and since then, especially with the advent of the Internet, there has been a huge increase in the number of users searching electronic resources for information, and mediated searches (i.e. searches carried out by an intermediary) tend to be decreasing in number. At the University of Birmingham, for instance, the number of mediated Medline searches fell from 526 during 1991/2 to 22 in 1995/6, with the comparable number for general searches dropping from 105 to 20 (Hewett, 1997). Similar results are reported from Denmark in an analysis of online searches carried out in public libraries for businesses (Clausen, 1997). However, as was noted in Chapters 2 and 7, end users do not always have a precise grasp of their information needs. So, even if doing the search for yourself you should spend a little preliminary time in working out as precisely as possible exactly what you are looking for.

Choose an appropriate information source

A major factor affecting the choice of information resource, obviously, is availability. The school pupil who has homework on, say, the art of Leonardo da Vinci, may have access only to the Encarta CD-ROM on the home computer and so that must suffice. A person working for a small firm which has Internet access from an office PC may not have access to online search services such as DialogWeb or OCLC FirstSearch. However, an art historian working in a museum or art gallery may have access to the Internet as well as to specialist bibliographic databases (for example, the ARTbibliographies Modern or the Bibliography of the History of Art on DialogWeb), the Art, Design, Architecture and Media (ADAM) subject gateway or to the OPAC of a relevant collection in another gallery such as the Louvre in France. In some cases a particular database may be identified as containing likely relevant material and that database may be available in various ways to the searcher – perhaps on several online search services, a Web site, one or more CD-ROMs or via a local OPAC. In such situations the user must decide which source is most appropriate. Factors affecting this decision include:

- Cost – if a CD-ROM database is already available then it is unlikely that there will be any added charge for carrying out a search. This may also be the case for a database available via an OPAC, a Web site or an online search service. In all these situations an annual subscription fee or licence will probably have been paid and there will be no further charge for each individual search. However, costs may be incurred for searching databases on some online search services which charge according to search time or number of retrieved items viewed. Searching many information resources (but not all) on the Internet is free. Medline, for example, is now freely available for searching on the WWW; one route is via the Healthgate service (http://www.healthgate.com). Figure 9.1 shows the available databases on Healthgate and a search form.

- Scope – type of material (bibliographic, full-text, multimedia, numeric), language coverage, geographic coverage.
- Currency – the frequency with which information is added to the information source and 'up-to-datedness' of the material in each 'update'.
- Date range of information covered by the database. The extent of retrospective coverage is likely to be more important in humanities or social science searches than in scientific, medical or technical searches. Sometimes only the more recent sections of databases are offered for searching.
- Record content – what fields can be searched? Is an abstract included? What is the overall quality of the record content? Is the full text available or can it easily be acquired?
- Indexing – how are the records indexed? Have terms been assigned from a controlled thesaurus? What is the overall quality of the indexing? Have indexing policies been adhered to?
- Search facilities – ease of use, interface issues. Is the search software user friendly and intuitive to use? More structured databases are likely to provide more sophisticated searching than basic keyword searching. However, if the searcher does not know how to make use of such facilities (e.g. searching by controlled subject terms or within specified number ranges) they will be of little use.
- Familiarity with the information resource. Searchers become more familiar with one resource than another and so are likely to make use of that resource first.
- Perceived reliability, reputation of producer and quality of material included.
- Output formats available.
- On-screen help facilities – is there context-sensitive help?
- Printed documentation.

In some situations when the user has access to a database on CD-ROM as well as on an online search service it may be more economical to use the CD-ROM to structure the search request and look for older material, and then use the online service to look for more up-to-date material. In other situations the user may have access to an online search service but not know the appropriate database for a particular search. For instance, if a search on 'noise of wind farms' was to be carried out on the Dialog Select search service (http://www.dialogselect.com) and the user did not know any relevant database, then the broad subject area 'Energy and the environment' could be selected from the opening screen (similar to that shown for a guided search on DialogWeb in Figure 8.2) which would result in the user being offered a range of energy-related databases including Energy Science and Technology, Pollution Abstracts and Ei COMPENDEX as

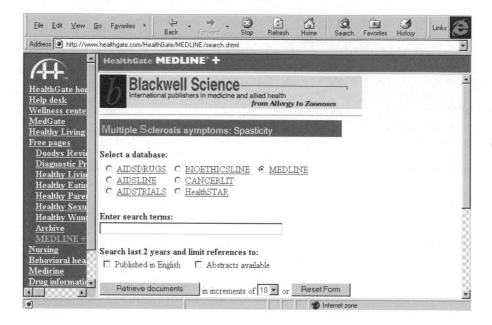

Figure 9.1   Search form for Healthgate

shown in Figure 9.2. This figure also displays some basic search hints for the user who might then enter the search statement:

(wind(w)farm?) and noise

For the user who decides to seek information on the Internet a further decision will need to be taken regarding which search engine to use. Some of the factors affecting this decision are covered by Nicholson (1997) who uses the following criteria to compare Lycos, AltaVista, Excite, Open Text, Yahoo! and Magellan:

- How are sites selected for inclusion? (is it automatic or carried out by people using some 'quality' criteria?)
- What types of Internet resources are analysed? (Web pages, USENET groups, ftp sites, etc.)
- What parts of the site are indexed and are these appropriate surrogates? (Open Text, for instance, indexes entire Web pages whereas Lycos indexes the title, headings and sub-headings and the 100 most 'weighty' words.)
- How is the keyword indexing accomplished?
- How can users search the indexed terms?
- What is included in a displayed citation?
- For what type of searching is the search engine best suited? (Is browsing by subject headings available?)
- For what type of searcher has the search engine been developed (casual or professional)?

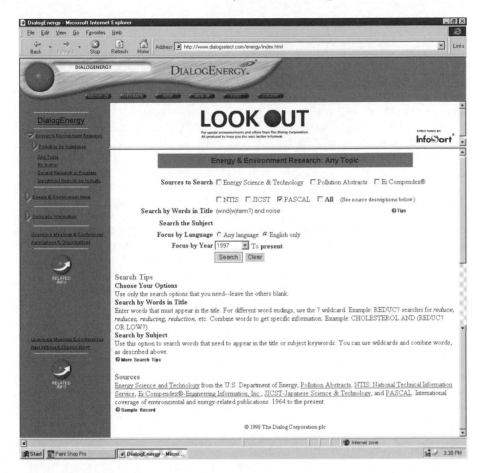

Figure 9.2   Search form for DialogSelect

Various Web sites attempt to maintain links to current comparisons of search engine performance and to provide information on searching the Internet.

If the user has access to systems that support Z39.50 (for further details see Chapter 8) it may not be necessary to choose a specific information source, as a search via one interface can be carried out on a number of separate search systems (which might well have different interfaces) and then the consolidated results can be presented to the user (Dempsey *et al.*, 1996). Thus, a single search could be used to search OPACs, CD-ROMs, locally produced databases, databases on remote computers, and so on. The advantages and limitations involved in setting up Z39.50 distributed search systems to enable resource sharing as compared to setting up union catalogues are described by Lynch (1997), who indicates that both approaches are relevant in the distributed network environment and that organizational, economic and political issues also need to be considered.

A study of the use of a common interface for searching multiple information resources using Gateway, an electronic library system at Cornell University's Albert R. Mann Library, is described by Payette and Rieger (1997). Gateway provides access to over 600 information resources including bibliographic databases (such as Agricola, BIOSIS, ERIC, Medline and PsycInfo), catalogue databases (including Cornell's OPAC and databases from OCLC and the Research Libraries Information Network (RLIN)), full-text documents, statistical datasets and spatial data. The study concluded that users would be interested in a common user interface for disparate bibliographic databases and that most were willing to sacrifice special features and advanced functionality. Some users, however, wanted to maintain a way of searching by concept codes and identifiers (e.g. for BIOSIS and ERIC), and using a specialized thesaurus, such as MESH for Medline, precluded use of Gateway. The study also found that users experienced very slow response times when searching the databases at different sites and were overwhelmed with the amount of information retrieved. The authors concluded that 'to satisfy user requirements for the presentation of results from a multi-database search, a system will have to support merged result sets, suppression of duplicates, and cross-database relevance ranking.' Another study, this time comparing versions of the same two databases (ABI/Inform and PAIS) on three platforms (Z39.50 via the library OPAC, OCLC FirstSearch and CD-ROMs from UMI and SilverPlatter) was carried out at Pennsylvania State University (Crawford, 1996). There was no overall 'best solution'. In some instances, for example, if access to a large number of databases was required, then OCLC FirstSearch was preferred for its single interface. In other cases, if consistency between the local catalogue interface and other databases is required then the Z39.50 approach is best. Finally, if there are a number of locally mounted CD-ROM databases then a common interface across all of them, such as that offered by SilverPlatter, may be best.

Deciding what, and how, information resources should be made available, say, in a school, a university, a public library, a hospital, legal practice or company, is often taken by the librarian or information professional, possibly following advice from users. Managing the range of information services, setting up and monitoring the use of appropriate passwords, dealing with the billing procedures, ensuring that appropriate hardware and software are available to access the services, dealing with the relevant licensing and copyright agreements and so on can be a challenge.

Prepare the search

Once the information source or sources have been chosen, the exact way in which the database should be searched must be decided. If the search is to be carried out on a single database, ideally the user will need to know how that database is structured and how it has been indexed to enable matches to be made effectively with search terms.

If the search is to be matched against several databases it is not possible to take account of individual database structures; this is the price to be paid for the increased speed of multifile searching. The search shown in

DIALOG Select

The measurement of noise from wind farms and background noise levels
Inter-Noise 96 : Noise control : the next 25 years, Liverpool, 30 July - 2 August 1996
HAYES M D ; HILL F Alison ed; LAWRENCE Roy ed
Hayes McKenzie Partnership, First Floor Office, 6 Penrallt Street Machynlleth, Wales, SY20 8AJ
United Kingdom
Conference : International congress on noise control engineering, 25, Liverpool GBR, 1996-07-30
Publication Date: 1996
Pages: 471-478
Publisher: Institute of Acoustics St Albans
Number of References: 7 ref.
Language: English

Descriptors:
Measuring methods
EFD wind generators
Sound pressure level
Acoustic radiation
Methode mesure
Aerogenerateur
Niveau pression acoustique
Royonnement acoustique
4328
4358

PASCAL
© 1997 INIST/CNRS. All rights reserved
DIALOG® File Number 144 Accession Number 12816255

Figure 9.3   Example of PASCAL record on Dialog

Figure 9.2 matches on all the databases indicated and a retrieved record from the PASCAL database is shown in Figure 9.3.

Having chosen the appropriate source, the user must prepare the search taking into account some of the features identified above (scope, date range, indexing policies, etc.). An initial task is often to break the search topic into its component parts, or concepts. Synonymous terms for a concept may need to be identified (e.g. woman, women, female, lady, ladies) and ways of combining different concepts should be worked out. If records have been indexed using a controlled thesaurus or a classification scheme then they can be consulted to find suitable search terms. Various techniques have been developed to help searchers who can now freely access the Medline database on the Web and who may not be familiar with the specialized vocabulary and structure of MESH, the medical subject headings used to index articles in Medline. The Healthgate service for instance, uses software which translates a user's search term (or terms) automatically into the appropriate MESH terms; thus lung cancer becomes the MESH phrase lung neoplasms, and a drug's trade name becomes the corresponding generic name. Often there are links to online documentation on the database structure and ways of searching a particular database.

Chapters in Armstrong and Large (1999) provide guidance on database selection and search strategy construction in a variety of subject areas such as agriculture, biosciences, business, law, engineering, natural sciences, earth sciences, social sciences, education and the humanities.

Carry out the search

The following steps typically are made in a search, although individual steps may not be appropriate in all situations.

Define the database (or part of the database) to be searched

Figure 9.1 shows the range of databases – AIDSDRUGS, AIDSLINE, AIDS-TRIALS, BIOETHICSLINE, CANCERLIT, HealthSTAR and Medline – that can be searched on Healthgate; the user can 'click' on one (or more) to limit the search to that (or those) database(s). In many OPACs the searcher has the option to search the whole catalogue, or perhaps just the catalogue of one particular part of the collection. For example, in Figure 9.4 the options available on the British Library's OPAC 97 are shown and the user could limit the search to collections of conference proceedings (from 1800), to journals (from 1700), printed music, and so on. The user has entered 'Alice in Wonderland' in the title phrase/keywords 'box' match to in the humanities and social sciences database.

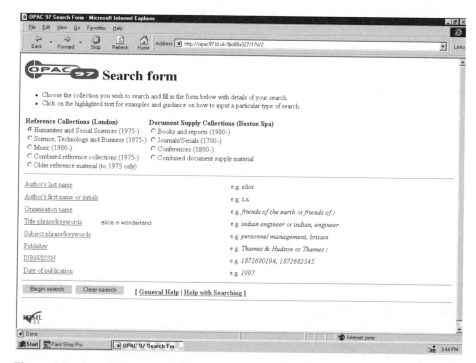

Figure 9.4   Search form for British Library OPAC97

Enter search terms

Search terms can be entered either singly, as a phrase or as a combination using Boolean (or other) operators as described in Chapter 6. The way in which phrases are dealt with varies from search system to search system and it is often not explicitly described at the point of search. It is most important for the searcher to realize how phrases will be analyzed by the search software. Looking at any appropriate help information, either online or in printed form, should clarify matters. As can be seen in many of the search form figures included in this book there are often buttons to call for search help, search hints, etc. Figure 9.5 shows a page of 'search tips' for the InfoSeek search engine on the Web. In common with many search engines, InfoSeek assumes that a 'simple' search is a relevance-ranked search and that an advanced or more complex search involves the use of Boolean operators.

Limit the search to specific fields of the record if necessary

If the database is structured into fields then these can be searched indi-vidually. In some cases the searcher must know the codes used for the particular fields e.g. tedd/au (for an author search on tedd), or Europe/ti

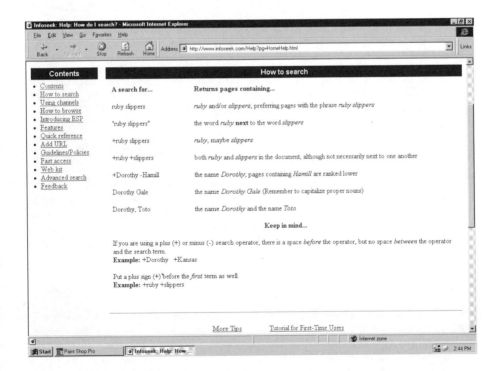

Figure 9.5   Part of page on search tips for InfoSeek

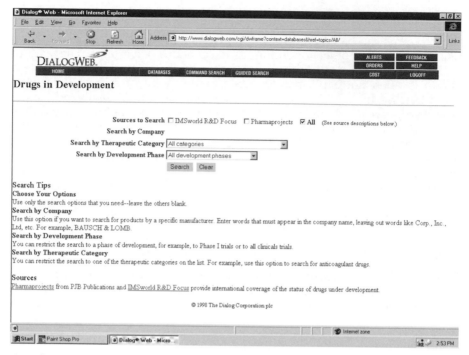

Figure 9.6   Search form for Drugs in Development on DialogWeb

(for a search with Europe in the title field). In other cases, where the searcher fills in forms to complete the search statement then the structure is implicit. The search fields for the British Library's OPAC 97 are shown in Figure 9.4.

Revise the search strategy if necessary

When a search has been carried out it is usual for the number of retrieved items to be displayed. This may vary from zero, through a manageable number of 10–40 items, to hundreds of thousands of items (which often result from a Web search). In the case of extremely low or extremely high hit rates it may be necessary to revize the search strategy by broadening or narrowing techniques (see Chapter 6).

Browse the information resource

Browsing is an alternative approach to searching as discussed in Chapter 7. Figure 9.6 shows the search form for seeking information on the Drugs in Development database on DialogWeb. Clicking on the 'Search by Therapeutic Category' field causes the full menu of options to be 'popped down' so that the user can choose appropriately from the list which contains subject heading such as: alimentary tract products; allergens and immuno-

Figure 9.7   Cyberstacks classification for medicine using Library of Congress Subject Headings

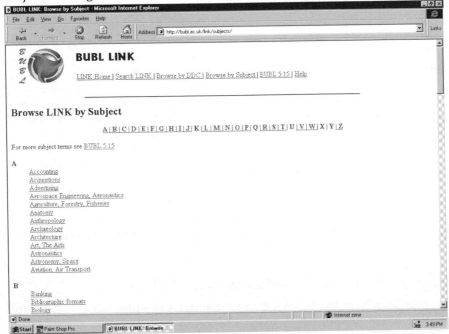

Figure 9.8   Alphabetic subject approach to electronic resources described on BUBL LINK

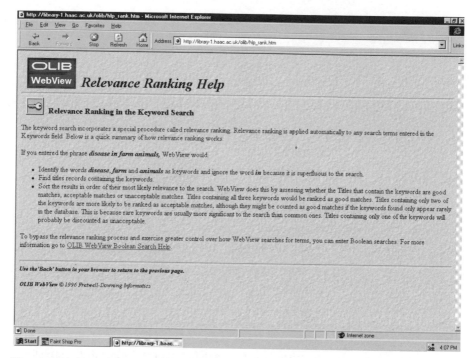

Figure 9.9 Example of relevance ranking help page from OLIB OPAC at Harper Adams Agricultural College

modulators; anti-infectives and so on. Many of the Internet search engines offer browse by subject facilities as well as the ability to search by keyword.

Various attempts have been made to 'classify' Internet resources and such classifications can assist browsing strategies. At Iowa State University, the CyberStacks(sm) system provides a centralized, integrated and unified collection of significant Web resources (of a research or scholarly nature) which have been classified using the Library of Congress Classification scheme (http://www.public.iastate.edu/~CYBERSTACKS/). Figure 9.7 shows the subject headings available under medicine. The Dewey Decimal Classification (DDC) scheme is used to classify Internet resources in the Libraries of Networked Knowledge (LINK) project in the UK. LINK is part of the BUBL information service which is based at Strathclyde University in Scotland and Figure 9.8 shows the first part of the browsing by subject approach.

View some retrieved items to check for relevance

The way in which the results of a search are presented can vary greatly and it is important for the searcher to be aware of the order in which the retrieved items are presented – sometimes the items are 'ranked' (as described further in Chapter 6) with the items identified by the search

Lycos

1)   Bonhams : Oriental and European Rugs and Carpets

> Oriental and European Rugs and Carpets Auction Items Auctions-On-Line
> "Lot 121 No images available A pair of Isfahan Rugs, each with an ivory ground sparsely
> decorated with vines around a medallion f
> htttp://www.bonhams.com/auct/a26653/Page31.html (2k)
>   [100% relevant]

AltaVista

1.   Isfahan Rugs : Oriental Rugs at Hard Cider Farm, Maine Antique Dealer Director

> Maine's largest selection of Persian and Tribal rugs at unbeatable prices. Thousands of
> beautiful rugs in stock. Visit our gallery or order by phone or

> http://www.metiques.com/oriental.rugs/isfahan.html – size 1K – 24-Feb-97 – English

Excite

76% Bonhams : Oriental and European Rugs and Carpets

URL: http://www.bonhams.com/auct/a26653/Page31.html

Summary: available A part silk Isfahan Rug, the ivory field of scrolling vines centred by a radiating
medallion framed by spandrels. 20K An Isfahan Rug, the cream field with birds of prey, trees and animals
enclosed by similar borders, 80 x 53in.

More Like This: Click here to perform a search for documents like this one.

Open Text

1.Re: Rugs from Iran (score: 1318, size: 6.8k)

> From: http://orientalrugs.com/public_board/messages/250.html

> [Follow Ups] [Post Followup] [WWWBoard Version 2.0 Test] [FAQ] Posted by Tom
Raffensperger on April 24, 1997 at 02:14:09: In Reply to: RE: Rugs from Iran posted by Anil Menon on
April 23, 1997 at 17:30:36::::::Hello, everyone! I recently moved here

> [Visit the page]

Yahoo

Isfahan Rugs : Oriental Rugs at Hard Cider Farm, Maine Antique Dealer Director – Maine's largest
selction of Persian and Tribal rugs at unbeatable prices. Thousands of beautiful rugs in stock. Visit our
gallery or order by phone or

--http://www.metiques.com/oriental.rugs/isfahan.html

Figure 9.10   Output from five Internet search engines

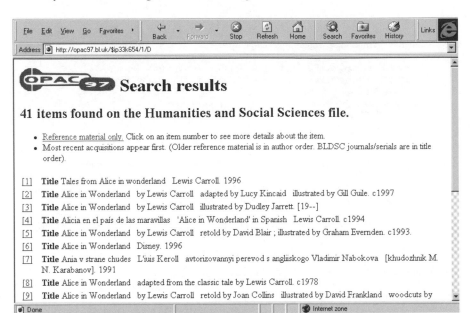

Figure 9.11   Display of items from OPAC97

engine as being most relevant appearing first. Figure 9.9, from the help pages on the OPAC at Harper Adams Agricultural College, explains how relevance ranking works with the OLIB software. Sometimes retrieved items are displayed in reverse chronological order (i.e. the most recent first), sometimes they are in alphabetic order and sometimes (but more rarely) they are not in any identifiable order.

A search using one of the Internet search engines will result in a list of retrieved items with clickable links to their home pages on the Web. The amount of information displayed varies between the search engines; Figure 9.10 shows the variation between the first item displayed for a search on Isfahan rugs carried out on Lycos, AltaVista, Excite, Open Text and Yahoo! in late 1997 using the default display options. Searching a bibliographic database will result in a list of references to items in published journals which may, or may not, be accessible in full-text format, searching, for example, a trade directory of suppliers of various products will result in a list of relevant contact details; and searching the shelves of the local 'virtual' supermarket should result in a box of groceries arriving on the doorstep.

It is important that the brief details initially displayed give enough information to enable the searcher to decide whether or not to request further details. Figure 9.11 gives brief information on the first nine matches to the search for editions of *Alice In Wonderland* covered by the BL OPAC – date of publication, author, adapter as well as illustrator. In many 'document'-related search systems, it is now possible to link from a retrieved reference about a document to the full text of that document.

Revise the search strategy if necessary

The records judged relevant by the searcher in a first search attempt can be checked to see if the index terms assigned to them might be used in a revised strategy to increase the yield of relevant items (increase recall). The amount of time and effort spent on this will inevitably be related to the 'importance' placed by the user on the search. Sometimes a few relevant items are sufficient. In other cases a much more detailed search is appropriate.

Retrieve the final set of items

The final set of items retrieved may be displayed on the screen, printed, emailed, downloaded to a local file or, if in the form of bibliographic references, added to the user's personal bibliographic database. There are a number of software packages (Endnote, ProCite, ReferenceManager) that researchers use to manage their own collections of bibliographic references.

End the search

This is obviously an important step, especially when using any service that may be charging by connect time. What is not so obvious is the decision as to when everything of relevance that might be found on the database actually has been retrieved. When should the searcher give up? Unfortunately, often there is no simple answer in the case of a subject search. (Known-item and factual searches are more likely to have an obvious termination point – see Chapter 3).

General Search Guidelines

Tenopir (1993) crystallizes her experiences of searching online databases over 20 years in the following 'loose guidelines' for online searchers:

- Pre-search planning is essential but over-planning is excessive.
- Know the purpose of, and motivation for, the search.
- Choose the best database or databases for each search.
- Use cost-effective search techniques.
- Use special care when searching for corporate or personal names.
- Know and understand the differences between databases.
- Plan your search strategy to match the type of database.
- Know and understand the differences between online systems and between the same database on different systems.
- Develop a style but know when to try something different.

These guidelines were formulated in the days when searching by end users was not as prevalent as it is now and although they contain relevant advice there are other helpful hints that can be given to today's searchers. Many of the search services provide such 'helpful hints' to searching information resources on their service and it is advantageous to inspect these. Some Internet search engines (e.g. Magellan's appropriately named Voyeur) display a random selection of search statements that are being processed. Some of the search statements viewed via Voyeur suggest further helpful hints:

- Make sure you understand the scope of the information resource being searched. Many Web-based search forms look fairly similar and the searcher needs to realize that a search statement that is to be matched against all sites on the Web should be quite different from a search statement for searching a local database of several hundred records, say, describing local clubs and societies.
- If using Boolean operators make sure these are used appropriately. On Magellan there were several examples of searches using the Boolean AND operator that looked appropriate (e.g. pacific AND northwest AND quilters, head AND hunter AND quebec). Caution is often advisable when using the NOT or AND NOT operator as it is easy to exclude relevant items.
- Make sure you understand how the search statement will be processed. Is it a relevance-ranked system? In what order are the Boolean operators processed? etc.
- Try searching for specific terms first, e.g. Reebok trainers instead of sports shoes.
- Beware of using single-term search statements when searching large databases. Examples on Magellan included: furniture, jokes, nature, rugby, all of which are likely to retrieve very large numbers of items.
- Try to ensure that you spell words correctly. Searches for the following were noted on Magellan: australian nurserys, naturopathic docter, 'hand mouth foot diseses'.
- Use a browsing approach, if available, to gain some familiarity with the information resource before searching it.
- Use an appropriate search strategy for the database. For instance, a search for 'sewage pollution in the Mediterranean sea' in the Pollution Abstracts database does not need to include the concept 'Pollution'.
- Be careful when using acronyms. For instance AA stands for Automobile Association (in the UK) as well as for Alcoholics Anonymous.
- Use the 'more like this' option, if available, to retrieve more references. Some search engines (e.g. Excite and Magellan make use of intelligent concept extraction to find relationships between words and ideas).
- Make sure you understand what happens in a search in a multilingual system. A search for the topic 'histoire ordinateurs' on the Web will only match with items written in French that contain those terms and will not match with 'history of computers'. However there are also some examples of multilingual databases where a search in one language will match with items that might have originally been written in another language. When searching the PASCAL BIOMED database on SilverPlatter, for instance, a search on keywords entered in Spanish will match with items described by those keywords in English or French as well as Spanish. There are indications (e.g. AltaVista's ability to trans-

late search phrases into other languages) that more multilingual searching will become available.

Staff from the Human Factors Unit at British Telecom laboratories in 1995 studied searches carried out by 'ordinary' users of search engines such as WebCrawler, Lycos and Yahoo! (Pollock and Hockley, 1997). The searchers were not trained in using the Internet and only were 'briefed as to its nature'. Some of the misconceptions found were related to the scope of the Internet, the fact that it was a global resource and that it was an 'unmanaged' resource. Many of the users had difficulty in formulating good searching keywords. One user seeking information on UK Local Education Authority student grants just entered 'grants' and failed to find anything of relevance. This research showed that users preferred being led through a process of browsing using a search engine such as Yahoo! rather than formulating a search request themselves.

More detailed hints and tips for searching the Internet also appear in many regular publications. In *Ariadne*, for instance, 'Search Engines Corner' in 1997 covered issues such as relevance ranking in search engines, and keyword spamming. The latter term describes less scrupulous developers of Web sites who deliberately add spurious or duplicated keywords to the metadata section of the HTML source of the document or within the Web document. Since many of the Internet search engines rank the items retrieved using the number of times the keyword appears in the text (and where it appears) this effectively ranks such items higher than their content justifies (in terms of the searcher's information need). Since many users only look at the first page or so of retrieved items from an Internet search it is therefore seen as advantageous for items to be ranked in that first set of ten items, and adding extra keywords is a way of achieving that.

Personal experiences of some 35 people searching for information on the Internet are included in Basch (1996). Further information on studies of information seekers are given in Chapter 2 and Chapter 10.

Search Examples

Query from a researcher in a university marine science laboratory: I would like to read some articles about El Niño, particularly with respect to its effect in Alaska.

A decision is made to use the Science Citation Index (SCI) database which is a multidisciplinary index to the international literature of science and technology. A particular feature of SCI (and its related databases, Social Science Citation Index and the Arts and Humanities Citation Index) is its inclusion of the references cited at the end of the articles themselves. This allows a search to begin with a known relevant item and from this item to find all the references to later published articles that have cited the known item. This provides an excellent way to track down recent references even if only older articles are known. The SCI database is available via many online search services and for this search a decision is made to use the BIDS service which was briefly described in Chapter 3. The searcher

BIDS ISI Easy Search

Easy Search	Advanced Search	Citation Search	Display Current Result Set	Display Marked List	Save/Retrieve Searches	Auto Journals	Help!	News & Info

Logout

Search for: `(el nino, ENSO)+alaska`

   in the ⦿ Title/keyword/abstract fields   or   ○ Title field only

Search for: ` `

   in the Author field

using the `Science Citation Index` ▾ database

   from `1994` ▾ to `1998` ▾ inclusive

Display the `Title, authors & journal` ▾ fields from articles found

[Run the search]   [Clear form]

You can phone the BIDS Help Desk on 01225-826074, or e-mail the Help Desk at bidshelp@bids.ac.uk. If you're using your own terminal (not a public one, in the library, for example) you can probably e-mail us by clicking here.

Figure 9.12   Search form for BIDS

belongs to an organization which has paid an annual subscription to use BIDS and so searching is 'free' to the searcher, although a relevant user name and password to access the service are needed.

In this case a known article is not available and so a subject search is carried out. In BIDS the Boolean operator AND is indicated with + or & symbols and an initial search statement el+nino resulted in 1121 items retrieved. The phrase 'el nino' however, reduced this to 811 items, and when this was ANDed with Alaska the result was 11 hits. Looking at the full records of some of these the phrase 'ENSO – El-Nino Southern Oscillation' was noticed and so that was included in the final search statement using the BIDS OR operator, as shown in Figure 9.12 – (el nino, ENSO) + alaska. The final set comprises 13 hits. The search statement is matched with the title/keyword/abstract fields for records in the database from 1994 onwards. The default display option (title only) of the first hits is shown in Figure 9.13. The format for the display of the records can be varied using the pull-down "Redisplay" menu. Most of the details included in the record for the third item retrieved are shown in Figure 9.14. This article is published in *Marine Pollution Bulletin,* a key journal in this area which the researcher can look at in the library. The items cited in this article are listed in the CR (Cited References) field. The citation search feature (chosen by clicking on the box at the top of the page) could be used to look for further possibly relevant references.

This search was carried out using the Easy Search option within BIDS. An advanced search option is available which provides limits to different languages (a large number are available) and type of material (article, editorial, news item and so on).

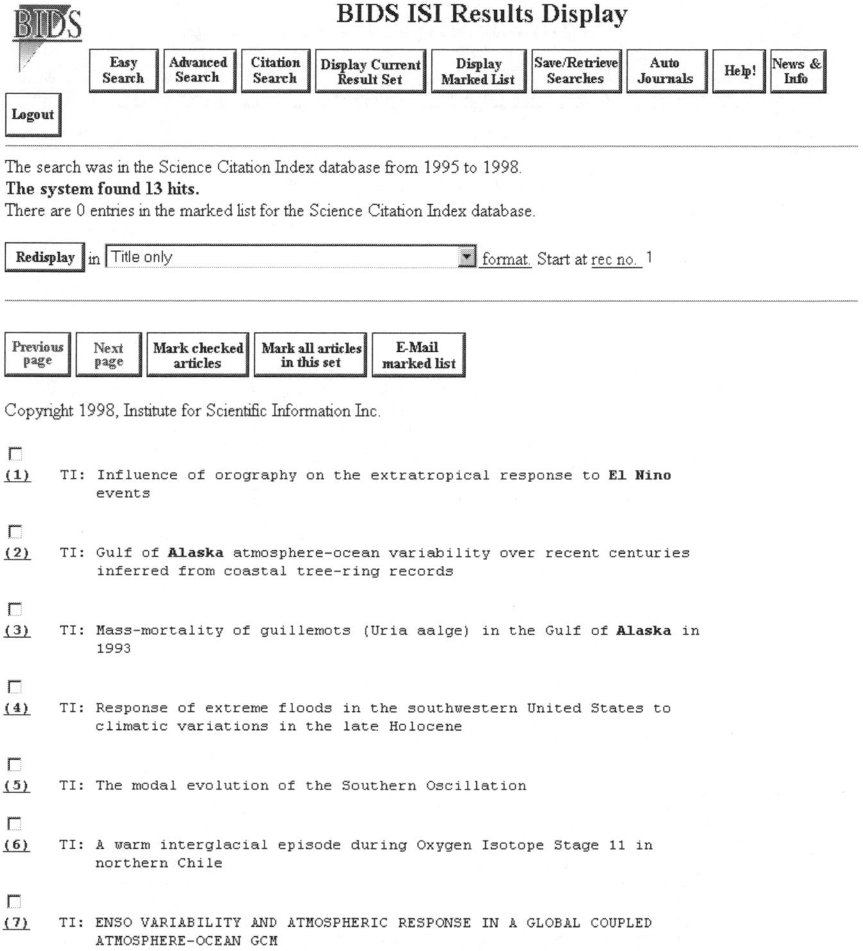

BIDS ISI Results Display

| BIDS | Easy Search | Advanced Search | Citation Search | Display Current Result Set | Display Marked List | Save/Retrieve Searches | Auto Journals | Help! | News & Info |

| Logout |

The search was in the Science Citation Index database from 1995 to 1998.
The system found 13 hits.
There are 0 entries in the marked list for the Science Citation Index database.

| Redisplay | in | Title only ▼ | format. Start at <u>rec no.</u> 1 |

| Previous page | Next page | Mark checked articles | Mark all articles in this set | E-Mail marked list |

Copyright 1998, Institute for Scientific Information Inc.

☐
(1)   TI: Influence of orography on the extratropical response to **El Nino** events

☐
(2)   TI: Gulf of **Alaska** atmosphere-ocean variability over recent centuries inferred from coastal tree-ring records

☐
(3)   TI: Mass-mortality of guillemots (Uria aalge) in the Gulf of **Alaska** in 1993

☐
(4)   TI: Response of extreme floods in the southwestern United States to climatic variations in the late Holocene

☐
(5)   TI: The modal evolution of the Southern Oscillation

☐
(6)   TI: A warm interglacial episode during Oxygen Isotope Stage 11 in northern Chile

☐
(7)   TI: ENSO VARIABILITY AND ATMOSPHERIC RESPONSE IN A GLOBAL COUPLED ATMOSPHERE-OCEAN GCM

Figure 9.13   Titles of some retrieved references on BIDS

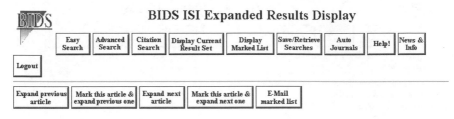

```
TI: Mass-mortality of guillemots (Uria aalge) in the Gulf of Alaska in
    1993
AU: Piatt_JF, VanPelt_TI
NA: ALASKA SCI CTR,NATL BIOL SERV,1011 E TUDOR RD,ANCHORAGE,AK,99503
JN: MARINE POLLUTION BULLETIN, 1997, Vol.34, No.8, pp.656-662
IS: 0025-326X
AB: During the first six months of 1993, about 3500 dead and moribund
    guillemots (Uria aalge) were observed throughout the northern Gulf of
    Alaska coast (ca 1800 km range). Mortality peaked during March.
    Highest numbers were observed in western Prince William Sound and
    along the south coast of the Kenai Peninsula. Large flocks of live
    guillemots gathered in nearshore waters, in contrast to most winters
    when guillemots reside offshore. Most guillemots recovered were
    extremely emaciated (ca 60% of normal weight) and sub-adult (80%).
    Based on carcass deposition and persistence experiments, we calculate
    that about 10 900 birds eventually came ashore on beaches that were
    surveyed. Even if most birds killed made it to shore, only a fraction
    of beaches in the Gulf of Alaska were surveyed and we estimate that a
    minimum total of 120 000 guillemots died. Results of other
    investigations on potential causes of mortality (biotoxins,
    pathogens, parasites, metals, etc.) were either negative or
    inconclusive, and necropsies lead us to believe that starvation was
    the proximate cause of death. Reduced food availability could have
    been related to anomalous sea conditions found during the prolonged
    1990-1995 El Nino-Southern Oscillation event. Published by Elsevier
    Science Ltd.
KP: EASTERN BRITAIN, FEBRUARY 1983, SEABIRDS, WRECK, DEPOSITION, PACIFIC,
    OCEAN, BIRDS, AUKS, SEA
CR: EC CONS INC ECI, 1991, UNPUB ASS DIR SEAB M
    AINLEY_DG, 1990, SEABIRDS FARALLON IS
    ARMSTRONG_IH, 1978 Vol.71 p.58, BR BIRDS
    BAILEY_EP, 1972 Vol.74 p.215, CONDOR
    BAILEY_KM, 1995 Vol.36 p.78, CAL COOP OCEAN FISH
    BLAKE_BF, 1984 Vol.76 p.89, J EXP MAR BIOL ECOL
    BODKIN_JL, 1991 Vol.69 p.1149, CAN J ZOOL
    BODLE_JE, 1969 Vol.55 p.329, CALIF FISH GAME
```

Figure 9.14   Part of display of a Science Citation Index record on BIDS

Query from an undergraduate distance learning student in a public library: I need to write an essay on the role of romance in Jane Austen's novels.

The public library has subscribed to a number of OCLC FirstSearch databases and so the student decides to use this online service for the search. The student may not be sure which database to use and by clicking on Arts and Humanities on the opening screen a list of possible databases is given, as shown in Figure 9.15, including the Modern Language Association (MLA) of America which is chosen for this search. The following screen is

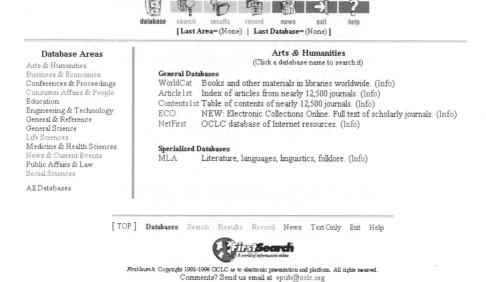

Figure 9.15   List of possible Arts and Humanities databases on OCLC FirstSearch

shown in Figure 9.16 and this provides a brief description of the MLA Bibliography database. The student must now enter the search term(s) and the help button can be used to explain how to link terms using Boolean and adjacency operators (as described in Chapter 6), limit searches and so on. The 'browse index' button could also be used to browse through the index terms in this database. The synonym for romance, 'love', is chosen and the student looks initially for austen and (love or romance); this results in 103 references. The student is offered a chance to limit the search and this is done by limiting the type of material to journal articles (other possibilities included theses and books), to the English language and to articles published between 1990–1997 (see top of Figure 9.17). Brief details of the resulting nine records are shown in Figure 9.17. An individual relevant item (or items) could then be acquired via OCLC's ArticleFirst service which, for a fee, will fax or post specific articles to users.

Query from an international politics student at the Australian National University: I would like a recent book covering political developments in Eastern Europe.

The Australian National University (ANU), as many academic libraries, provides access for its students and staff to a wide range of national and international databases (some via the Internet, some via an ERL server in the library) on workstations around the campus. At ANU this service is called Electronic Library Information Service at ANU (ELISA). The OPAC

database **search** results record news exit help

[**Database**= MLA Bibliography]

Welcome to *MLA Bibliography* ! By doing a search, you agree to the OCLC Terms and Conditions and the MLA Bibliography Terms and Conditions.

Word, Phrase (Help)   **Keyword Index** (Help)

Search for austen and (love or romance) in Subject ▼ Browse Index

Start Search   Advanced Search ▾

FirstSearch Database

Modern Language Association of America **MLA Bibliography**

Description	Literature, languages, linguistics, and folklore from over journals and series published worldwide.
Records	1200 K
Dates Covered	1963 ...
Updated	10 times per year.
Full Text	No
Periodicals Covered	4000
Producer	Modern Language Association of America
Date Added	1992-06-19
Optional Features	Document Delivery, Interlibrary Loan
Terms & Conditions	© 1998 The Modern Language Association of America

Return

[TOP] Databases **Search** Results Record News Text Only Exit Help

FirstSearch

Figure 9.16 Search form for MLA Bibliography database on OCLC FirstSearch

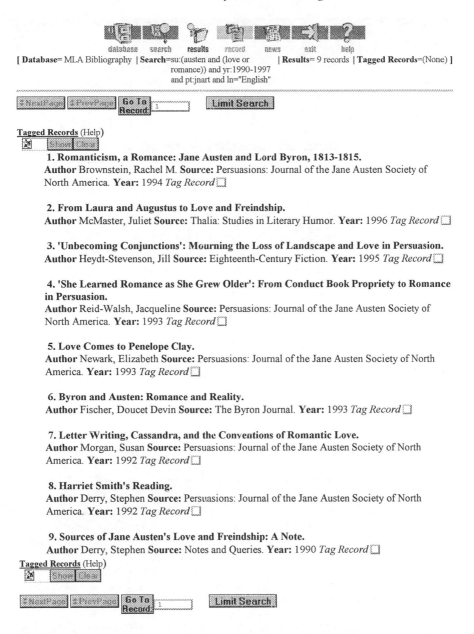

[**Database**= MLA Bibliography | **Search**=su:(austen and (love or romance)) and yr:1990-1997 and pt:jnart and ln="English" | **Results**= 9 records | **Tagged Records**=(None)]

Go To Record: 1   **Limit Search**

Tagged Records (Help)

1. Romanticism, a Romance: Jane Austen and Lord Byron, 1813-1815.
Author Brownstein, Rachel M. **Source:** Persuasions: Journal of the Jane Austen Society of North America. **Year:** 1994 *Tag Record*

2. From Laura and Augustus to Love and Freindship.
Author McMaster, Juliet **Source:** Thalia: Studies in Literary Humor. **Year:** 1996 *Tag Record*

3. 'Unbecoming Conjunctions': Mourning the Loss of Landscape and Love in Persuasion.
Author Heydt-Stevenson, Jill **Source:** Eighteenth-Century Fiction. **Year:** 1995 *Tag Record*

4. 'She Learned Romance as She Grew Older': From Conduct Book Propriety to Romance in Persuasion.
Author Reid-Walsh, Jacqueline **Source:** Persuasions: Journal of the Jane Austen Society of North America. **Year:** 1993 *Tag Record*

5. Love Comes to Penelope Clay.
Author Newark, Elizabeth **Source:** Persuasions: Journal of the Jane Austen Society of North America. **Year:** 1993 *Tag Record*

6. Byron and Austen: Romance and Reality.
Author Fischer, Doucet Devin **Source:** The Byron Journal. **Year:** 1993 *Tag Record*

7. Letter Writing, Cassandra, and the Conventions of Romantic Love.
Author Morgan, Susan **Source:** Persuasions: Journal of the Jane Austen Society of North America. **Year:** 1992 *Tag Record*

8. Harriet Smith's Reading.
Author Derry, Stephen **Source:** Persuasions: Journal of the Jane Austen Society of North America. **Year:** 1992 *Tag Record*

9. Sources of Jane Austen's Love and Freindship: A Note.
Author Derry, Stephen **Source:** Notes and Queries. **Year:** 1990 *Tag Record*

Tagged Records (Help)

Go To Record: 1   **Limit Search**

Figure 9.17   Some retrieved references from MLA Bibliography

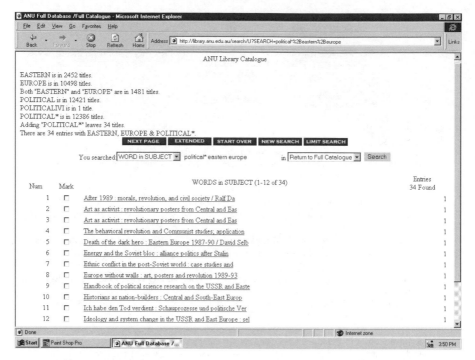

Figure 9.18   Search on the INNOPAC OPAC at the Australian National University

(which uses the INNOPAC software) is part of ELISA and offers searches by author, title, subject, words in subject, ISBN and so on. In this case the search statement 'political* eastern europe' was entered in the search box provided. On this OPAC the default is that terms are ANDed together, although they can be linked using OR or NOT if required. Figure 9.18 shows how the term stem 'political*' matches with variant words in the title and also shows the titles of the first 12 hits. The full details of one relevant looking text by Ralf Dahrendorf are shown in Figure 9.19 (and an indication that it is currently out on loan). This may well be sufficient; if not the searcher could click on the Library of Congress Subject Heading 'Europe, Eastern – Politics and government – 1989' and be linked to an index of other related material as shown in Figure 9.20.

Query from a school librarian: I have been asked to investigate the implementation of a workstation providing Internet access in the library.

Being a librarian, the user decides to use the bibliographic database Library and Information Science Abstracts (LISA) which covers the library and information science literature. The librarian does not have direct access to LISA but is able to use the library of a local university which has this database on CD-ROM. LISA has been produced in printed form by the UK

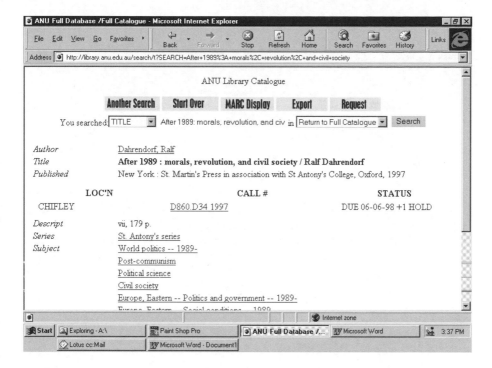

Figure 9.19   Display of one catalogue record at the Australian National University Library

Library Association since 1969 and was made available on the Dialog online service in the 1970s. In 1987 it was among the first bibliographic databases to be produced on CD-ROM by SilverPlatter. It is now published on CD-ROM by Bowker Saur as a product known as LISA Plus, and a review of the Windows interface is given by Kerr (1998). At the end of 1997 there were some 184,000 records in LISA.

Figure 9.21 shows the development of the search strategy using the 'Expert search' interface for LISA. The searchable fields of the record are shown in the box on the left hand side and the commands that have been entered to carry out a Boolean search:

Internet and school and (primary or secondary)

are shown in the box on the right hand side along with the number of records matching each set created by the search. By pressing 'view brief' the titles of 12 of the 17 records that match the search statement are shown in Figure 9.22, with some of the details of the first record displayed in the bottom box.

Query from a person in a public library: I have recently discovered that I am related to the architect Frank Lloyd Wright and I would like to know more about him, see some photographs of buildings designed by him and possibly visit some of those.

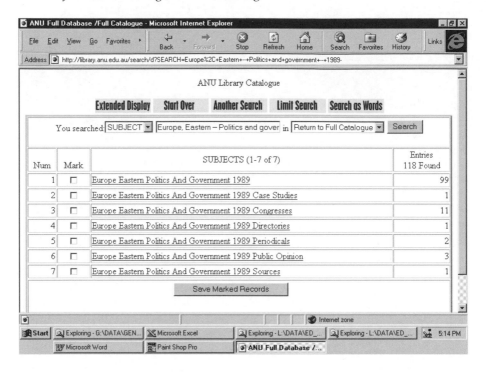

Figure 9.20   Example of ability to search by linking to LC subject headings

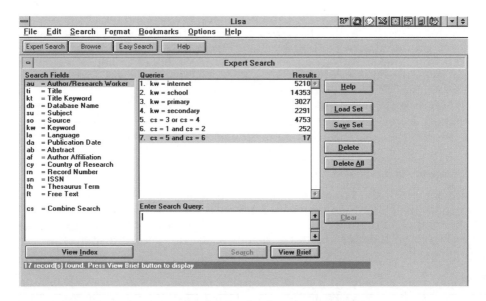

Figure 9.21   Inputting a search of LISA database on CD-ROM

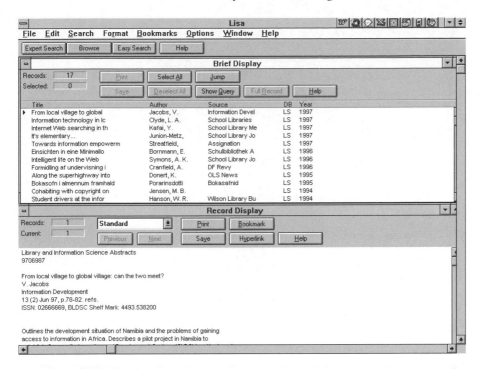

Figure 9.22   Results of a search on LISA

This search could be carried out on an OPAC that might contain a record for a book including pictures of buildings designed by the American architect, Frank Lloyd Wright. However, another approach is to do an Internet search. If the person is not sure about constructing a search statement then the Yahoo! search engine might be used. The opening screen for Yahoo! with the broad subject categories and more specific subject headings was shown in Figure 7.5. A click on architecture under arts and humanities results in a further menu of options as shown in Figure 9.23. The next step could either be to search by architects or by buildings and structures. A decision is made to search by architects and the next screen offers the options: commercial firms; group exhibits; individual resumes; masters and personal exhibits. Selecting masters results in a listing of various famous architects with Wright, Frank Lloyd as the last entry. Clicking on this results in the page shown in Figure 9.24 which has a selection of sites chosen (with some reviewed) by Yahoo! staff. The Frank Lloyd Wright in Wisconsin site is chosen and the first page is shown in Figure 9.25. By clicking on the site index it is possible to browse through the site and be shown many photographs of buildings designed by Wright as well as times when these buildings are open to the public.

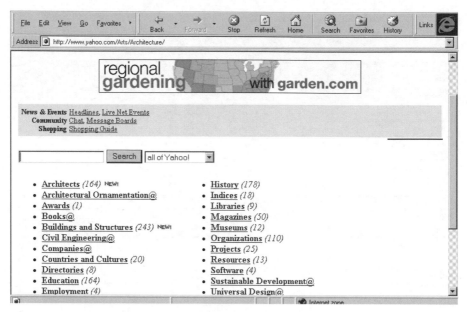

Figure 9.23   Architecture subject categories on Yahoo!

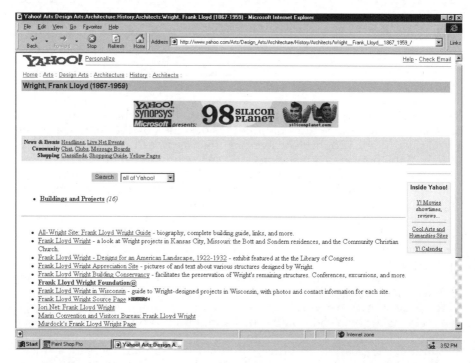

Figure 9.24   Selection of sites giving information on Frank Lloyd Wright on Yahoo!

FRANK LLOYD WRIGHT®

is widely regarded as this country's and this century's greatest architect.

His buildings are some of the world's most important architectural treasures.
Those in search of an intimate look at the life and work of Wright will find it in Wisconsin
- his birthplace and home for most of his life.

Frank Lloyd Wright® in Wisconsin is a presentation of the Frank Lloyd Wright® Wisconsin Heritage Tourism Program which provides these guides

WISCONSIN FLLW SITE INDEX LIST   EVENT

Included in the guides are photographs of these magnificent buildings,
maps which show how to find them,
and telephone numbers to call for descriptions of the tours.

The Frank Lloyd Wright® Wisconsin HeritageTourism Program is a membership organization.
Its mission is to promote, protect and preserve the heritage of Frank Lloyd Wright, his genius and architecture, located in his native state of Wisconsin.
For information write: PO Box 6339, Madison, Wisconsin 53716-0339 or call: 608-221-4111.
Author and copyright information
This presentation was updated 8/17/98

Figure 9.25   Frank Lloyd Wright in Wisconsin home page

Query from a tourist planning a visit to Eastern Europe: What times are the trains from Berlin to Warsaw?

This user has access to the Internet from home and has previously book-marked the Web site for the German rail service as http://bahn.hafas.de having noted the Web address given in a newspaper article. In the same way as individuals build up collections of printed reference materials (e.g. dictionaries, encyclopaedias, railway timetables, bus timetables and so on) Web users build up a collection of potentially useful Web sites and store these on the 'bookmark' facility of their Web browser.

Having accessed the specified Web site the user is presented with a search form as shown in Figure 9.26. The user initially enters Warsaw as the desti-nation station but is informed that 'Your input warsaw is ambiguous'. A list of all railway stations in Warsaw is then helpfully presented to the user who, more appropriately, chooses Warszawa Centralna. Details of some possible trains are shown in Figure 9.27 along with information about other functions such as ordering the tickets.

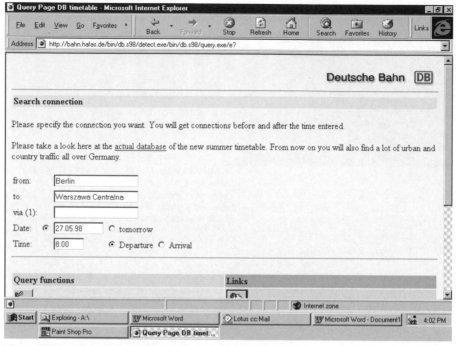

Figure 9.26   Search form for Deutsche Bahn timetable

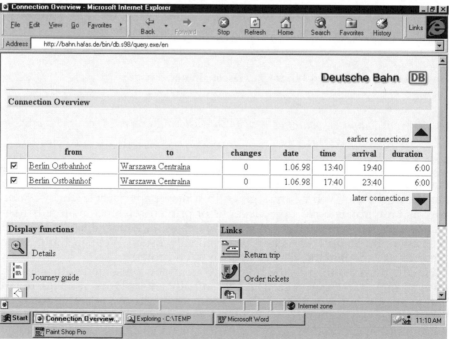

Figure 9.27   Display of possible train times from Berlin to Warsaw

Query from a consultant engineer: I am about to start on a contract that also involves the Swiss firm ABB. I would like to know more about this firm.

The engineer, who has Internet access from workstations at the office, could carry out a general search of the Web using one of the search engines. However, a search for ABB is likely to match with many different organizations. Instead the engineer decides to search the Edinburgh Engineering Virtual Library (EEVL) subject gateway and the opening page of the Web site is shown in Figure 9.28. The EEVL project started in 1995 with funding from the UK's eLib Programme and the aim of 'facilitating access to high quality networked information resources in engineering'. This is achieved by teams of experts identifying, describing and classifying potential resources which have to fulfill criteria of usefulness, relevance and subject content (Kerr and MacLeod, 1997). A database search from such a subject-based information gateway is therefore much more focused than a search via a general Web search engine. The search for ABB is inserted on the search form shown in Figure 9.29 and matches with just two items (Figure 9.30).

Impact on Library and Information (LIS) Staff of End-User Searching

The growth of end-user searching has an obvious impact on the role of the intermediary, as noted in Chapter 1. Blakeman (1996) comments that 'the role of the intermediary in locating and using information has generated debate ever since information was gathered to form the first libraries.' She provides a good historic overview of this debate since the late 1970s and outlines each new search development (CD-ROMs, Windows interfaces, the Internet) that have claimed to herald the demise of the intermediary. She concludes with her views on how professional LIS staff have a role to play in providing an evaluated list of recommended Internet resources that have an appropriate 'seal of approval' and in training and educating their users about searching.

Lancaster and Sandore (1997) outline some of the general effects of technology on LIS staff. Many of these are related to the provision of electronic information resources and include:

- Demands placed on the individual, e.g. the need for many LIS staff to become competent at answering users' queries related to accessing various electronic information sources as well as to more mundane tasks such as sorting out printer jams, misfunctioning software, etc.
- Different skills e.g. marketing, more IT competency generally, more database searching, project management.
- Training needs. It is important for the library manager to 'develop a culture in which the process of continuous learning and an acceptance of change by staff is the norm'. There is now a need for LIS staff to undertake both more training themselves and to be more involved with training and educating their users (Creth, 1995).

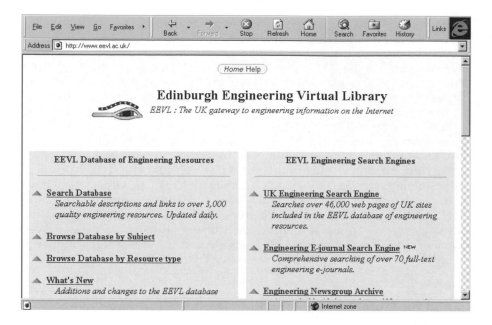

Figure 9.28   Part of Edinburgh Engineering Virtual Library (EEVL) home page

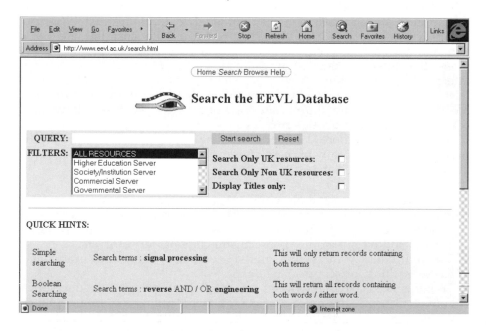

Figure 9.29   Part of search form for EEVL

(Home Search Browse Help)

 **Search results**

Your query **abb** has **2** results.

If you cannot find what you expected, some further advice including lists of other relevant indexing services is available.

1. Robot Simulations Ltd
[Full EEVL Record] *http://www.rosl.com/*

> Robot Simulations are the developers of the Workspace PC-based robot simulation and offline programming software and the Robotrak calibration device. The Robot Simulations server provides the latest information on these products as well as downloadable demonstration software. A substantial list and details (including downloadable VRML versions) of robot models for use with Workspace are provided, together with an **ABB** IR2000 robot moving in virtual reality. In addition, full-text case studies of product applications are given, including a waterjet cutting cell, an intelligent test rig for pre-paid gas metering schemes, arc welding workcells, and use on a BSc robotics and automation systems course. User Group messages and a dealer list may be accessed.

2. ABB Group [Non UK]
[Full EEVL Record] *http://www.abb.com/*

> **ABB** is a global engineering group serving customers in electric power generation, transmission and distribution, industrial and building systems, and rail transportation. The **ABB** server provides details of the company, its businesses and products, press releases and financial/investor information.

If you cannot find what you expected, some further advice including lists of other relevant indexing services is available.

(Home Search Browse Help)

Email: webmaster@eevl.icbl.hw.ac.uk
Copyright © 1996 EEVL.

Figure 9.30   Results of an EEVL search

Geleijnse (1997), of Tilburg University in the Netherlands, has also written about the impact of electronic information resources on libraries: 'Information technologies and the developments towards a digital library require not only changes in these traditional elements and changes in the organisation of the library but also changes for many individuals.' He suggests that libraries of the future should:

- Focus more on information management and on the selection of relevant information than on collection development as the shift from ownership to access is inevitable;
- Emphasize user support more.
- Emphasize user education and user training.
- Provide tailor-made services to end users, e.g. easy access to relevant sources.
- Support electronic publishing by researchers of the parent institution.

Lancaster and Sandore (1997) also note that 'computers and networking have made librarians and patrons more equal in gaining access to, storing, retrieving and representing information in novel and efficient ways, to the extent that fundamental changes in the relationship among libraries, users and information have occurred.' They argue that:

- Accessing electronic information sources has become more commonplace and can be achieved without users entering the library.
- Seekers of information can gain direct access to relevant information resources without the intermediation of library staff.
- Users are becoming information providers and publishers on the World Wide Web.
- Users have access to sophisticated 'tools' on the desktop that enable them to build their own personal electronic libraries.

There are many examples of LIS staff who provide links to suitable Internet resources for their users. Rusch-Feja (1997), for instance, describes the work at the library of the Max Planck-Institut für Bildungsforschung (Human Development and Education) in Berlin and notes that LIS professionals need to expand their abilities to 'provide adequate and appropriate information from various networked information sources suited to their user's information needs, thus taming and structuring the diverse, dispersed, and divergent sources to offer and maintain effective information retrieval services'. A set of relevant resources, with added information in German, has been developed at the Institute (http://www.mpib-berlin.mpg.de/DOK/ech.htm), one of the subject-oriented clearing houses being developed in Germany through the coordinating plans of the German Research Association.

It is important for LIS staff to understand the needs of end users and thus be able to support them. Kennedy, Cole and Carter (1997) suggest ways of introducing undergraduate students to the principles of searching by the developments of search strategies relevant to their information needs. Yuan (1997) reports on a longitudinal study which aimed to 'investigate user searching over an extended period of time for the purpose of understanding the behaviour of end users with different levels of experience'. The survey was undertaken at the University of Toronto in 1992–3 and involved law students searching the QUICKLAW online search service, which is command-based, and which provides access to many legal databases in Canada. Yuan's final comments in the paper are: 'As our understanding of end-user searching advances, we will be able to design a more user-oriented system to facilitate searching.'

Training Issues for Searching

Training for searching of electronic resources can be defined as the acquisition of the knowledge and skills necessary to realize the potential offered by such resources. As indicated in the previous section, with much searching being carried out by end users it is important that appropriate training facilities are available. Plutchak (1989) identified four states regarding end users and their searching capabilities:

- the satisfied ept user, i.e the person who knows how to search and can retrieve appropriate items;
- the dissatisfied ept user, i.e. the person who knows how to search but finds that the appropriate items are not being retrieved (and so will, hopefully, seek some help);
- the dissatisfied, inept user, i.e. the person who doe not know what to do and finds that appropriate items are not being retrieved – and will also ask for help;
- the satisfied inept user, i.e. the person who feels that the search has been successful but if any evaluation of the search were carried out (as described in Chapter 10) many improvements might be suggested.

Training can help the last category of user.

Topics that might be covered in education and/or training sessions for end users include:

- accessing electronic information resources on the World Wide Web;
- using the online public access catalogue;
- using specific CD-ROM databases;
- using specific remote online search services;
- accessing electronic journals and learning about document delivery services;
- gaining general information skills or information literacy.

Wade (1996), when describing experiences in running education and training programmes for students at Sheffield Hallam University in the UK, outlines her views on key features for success:

- The training is planned and integrated into the curriculum, and at an early stage.

- The training includes subject-based assignments (relevant to each student's area of study).
- There is an emphasis on hands-on, student-centred experience.
- Feedback and review are part of the process.
- The sessions are part of the student's formal timetable.

In many other situations education and training take place in the library/information centre as an 'extra' activity. O'Riordan (1996) reports on the development of a course on the use of the Internet as an information source and as a publishing medium at the University of Limerick in Ireland.

Some of the factors to take into account when designing training courses include:

- Define the level of training and the aims of the course.
- Structure sessions(s) to obtain an appropriate balance between lectures, practical exercises, self-help workbooks, discussions etc.
- Use appropriate teaching aids (overhead transparencies, live demonstrations, prepared exercises, Powerpoint demonstrations, videos, computer aided instruction (CAI), intranet, etc.).
- Take into consideration constraints of time, cost and location.
- Ensure that appropriate equipment is available – individual workstations, display facilities, suitable support software, etc.
- Develop appropriate course documentation – whether printed or online.
- Include a system for feedback on training from participants.

A number of aids are available on the Web to assist trainers in training people to use the Web and a brief description of some as well as a general overview is given by Balas (1997).

15 Minute series http://rs.internic.net/nic-support/15min

This series of presentations has been developed by InterNIC (a cooperative activity between the National Science Foundation, Network Solutions, Inc. and AT&T) and the Library and Information Technology Association of the American Library Association as a service to the US research and education community. The aim is to provide a resource that will assist users to incorporate the Internet into their daily routines.

TONIC http://www.netskills.ac.uk/TONIC

The Online Netskills Interactive Course (TONIC) is a modular course that introduces users to the Internet and to the major tools used to access information across computer networks. The course covers the technological background to the Internet, before describing specific tools used for accessing information. Short tests and quizzes at the end of each section help users to gauge how much they have learned. TONIC is one of the training packages developed by the NetSkills team at Newcastle University in the UK as part of the Electronic Libraries Programme.

TOURBUS http://www.TOURBUS.com

This package is based on the Roadmap workshop developed by Crispen at the University of Alabama. TOURBUS is a virtual tour of the best of the Internet, delivered by email to over 80,000 people in 120 countries.

BCK2SKOL http://Web.csd.sc.edu/bck2skol/bck2skol.html

Back to School comprises a series of 30 lessons covering searching the Internet (Chamberlain, 1997). It was first developed in 1995 and delivered by email to librarians in South Carolina. Since then it has been used in many countries and is being updated and maintained on a Web site.

Keeping abreast of developments in searching can be a challenge and making users aware of such developments through education and training programmes will be an important role for library and information staff in the future.

References

Armstrong, C.J. and Large, J.A. (1999) *Manual of Online Search Strategies*. 3rd edn. Aldershot: Gower

Balas, J. (1997) Training the Internet trainers. *Computers in Libraries*, **17** (3), 43–5

Basch, R. (1996) *Secrets of the Super Net Searchers: The Reflections, Revelations, and Hardwon Wisdom of 35 of the World's Top Internet Researchers*. Wilton, CT: Pemberton Press

Blakeman, K. (1996) The future role of intermediaries. In C.J. Armstrong and R.J. Hartley (eds) *Ukolug96@warwick.ac.uk. UKOLUG state-of-the-art conference, Warwick, 17–19 July 1996*, London: UKOLUG, 17–23

Chamberlain, E. (1997) Surfing the Internet with BCK2SKOL: an online tutorial. *Journal of Youth Services in Libraries*, **10**(2), 207–213

Clausen, H. (1997) Online, CD-ROM and the Web: is it the same difference. *Aslib Proceedings*, **49** (7), 177–83

Crawford, G.A. (1996) Varieties of access: a comparison of databases available via Z39.50, FirstSearch and CD-ROM. In M.E. Williams (ed.) *National Online Meeting Proceedings – 1996*. Medford, NJ: Information Today, 55–64

Creth, S.D.(1995) A changing profession: central roles for the academic librarian. *Advances in Librarianship*, **19**, 85 – 98

Dempsey, L, Russell R. and Kirriemuir, J. (1996) Towards distributed library systems: Z39.50 in a European context. *Program, 30* (1), 1 -22

Geleijnse, H. (1997) Human resource management and the digital library. *International Journal of Electronic Library Research*, **1**(1), 25–42

Hewett, S. (1997) The future for mediated online search services in an academic institution: a case study. *Online & CDROM Review*, **21**(5), 281–84

Kennedy, L., Cole, C. and Carter S. (1997) Connecting online search strategies and information needs: a user-centred focus-labeling approach. *RQ*, **36**(4) 562–8

Kerr, L. and MacLeod, R. (1997) EEVL: an Internet gateway for engineers. *Library Hi-Tech*, **15**(3–4), 110–118

Kerr, M. (1998) LISA Plus on CD-ROM, *Managing Information*, **5**(1/2), 53–55

Lancaster, F.W. and Sandore, B. (1997) *Technology and Management in Library and Information Services*. London: Library Association

Lynch, C.F. (1997) Building the infrastructure of resource sharing: union catalogs, distributed search, and cross-database linkage. *Library Trends, **45**(3), 448–61

Nicholson, S. (1997) Indexing and abstracting on the World Wide Web: an examination of six Web databases. *Information Technology and Libraries,* **16** (2), 73–81

Payette, S.D. and Rieger, O.Y. (1997) Z39.50: the user's perspective. *D-Lib Magazine,* April. Also available at: http://mirrored.ukoln.ac.uk/lis-journals/dlib/dlib/dlib/april97//cornell/04p

O'Riordan, G. (1996) An iterative development of a training programme in the use of the Internet as an information source and publishing mechanism. In D.I. Raitt, and B. Jeapes (eds), *20th International Online Information Meeting Proceedings, London 3–5 December, 1996.* Oxford: Learned Information, 77–83

Plutchak, T.S. (1989) On the satisfied and inept end user. *Medical Reference Services Quarterly,* **8**(1), 45–8

Pollock, A. and Hockley, A. (1997) What's wrong with Internet searching. *D-lib Magazine,* March. Available at http://mirrored.ukoln.ac.uk/lis journals/dlib /dlib/dlib/march97/bt/03pollock/html

Rusch-Feja, D. (1997) Subject-oriented collection of information resources from the Internet. *Libri,* **47**(1), 1–24

Tenopir, Carol (1993) Ten loose guidelines for online searchers. *Online,* **17**(2), 17–33

Wade, A. (1996) Training the end-user. Case Study 1: Academic libraries. In R. Biddiscombe, (ed.) *The end-user revolution. CD-ROM, Internet and the changing role of the information professional.* London: Library Association, 96–109

Yuan, W. (1997) End-user searching behavior in information retrieval: a longitudinal study. *Journal of the American Society for Information Science,* **48**(3), 218–34

CHAPTER 10

Search Evaluation

The Need for Evaluation

Information seeking is a practical activity with a very specific objective: to track down information that can be used to help clarify some uncertainty on the seeker's part. Attempts to evaluate this activity, however, have often been experimental in nature, removed from the realities of real searches by real clients to answer real information needs. More recently greater emphasis has been placed upon studies in a more naturalistic environment. Quantitative research techniques that attempt to express performance in mathematical terms have been supplemented by qualitative techniques that investigate how users themselves evaluate the search process.

Many of the best minds in information science have toiled with the problems of how best to evaluate information retrieval, but controversy continues over both the methodologies by which to achieve this goal and the results obtained in the many studies. Why should evaluation be so important?

Information retrieval evaluation is undertaken to answer one or more of three questions.

What is the best way to design a retrieval system?

- Should it be designed so that it can identify specific segments of information (or documents containing that information) within the database, or should it facilitate browsing through the database?
- What kind of retrieval or browsing techniques should be provided?
- Should it employ natural-language or controlled-language indexing?

- How should the interface be designed to simplify interaction between the searcher and the system?

What are the most suitable search strategies to employ?

Given a specific system, information store and information need:

- What kind of searching strategies should be used to identify all the information that is required while at the same time not finding any information that is not required?

What are the characteristics of the ideal searcher?

- Do information professionals conduct more effective searches than anyone else, including the clients who have the actual information need and are seeking the answers?
- Do experienced searchers really perform better than novice searchers?
- What particular combination of personal traits and skills makes a good information seeker?

These questions can only be answered by evaluating the information-seeking process. Such an evaluation in turn requires a methodology by which reliable and repeatable findings can be achieved, as well as a standard by which to determine whether a retrieval system, search or searcher is good, indifferent or bad.

Large-scale information retrieval systems are very expensive to develop. Searching costs, whether charged as fixed subscriptions or pay-as-you-go, are often considerable. Valuable time can be spent by both information professionals and end users in searching databases. And perhaps of most importance, a search can find, at its best, exactly what is being sought while eliminating all else, or, at its worst, can find lots of useless information while missing anything of interest. It is therefore important to know which kinds of systems, searches and searchers are most effective.

This chapter begins with an overview of the traditional measures applied in information retrieval evaluation. These measures have been subject to criticism, however, and the debate over quantitative evaluation techniques is also reviewed. Many studies have eschewed the quantitative approach to investigate how real users react when faced with a retrieval system: these more qualitative alternative means to evaluate information retrieval performance, therefore, are also considered.

Considerations of the search system, search process and searcher, while obviously important, are not the only criteria in determining the success or failure of a search for information. The database itself – its currency, coverage and reliability – is critical to the search outcome. A checklist for the evaluation of any database is therefore included. The chapter ends with a discussion of database content evaluation.

Recall and Precision Measures

The first tests of information retrieval systems took place separately in the UK and US in 1953, but large-scale evaluation studies began in earnest in the late 1950s at the Cranfield College of Aeronautics in England. The two Cranfield Projects tested the effects on information retrieval of various types of controlled vocabulary and natural-language indexing. In so doing, they established a standard for experimental design in information retrieval performance evaluation but also generated controversy over evaluation methodology that has continued to this day. Salton (1991) suggests that one reason for the criticism of the Cranfield methodology was that information specialists did not like the experimental findings – simple-concept indexing is more effective than more sophisticated indexing methods – and therefore sought to explain them away by faults in the test design.

The Cranfield Projects employed two measurements for an information retrieval system: recall and precision. The assumption behind the use of these measures is that the average user wants to retrieve large amounts of relevant materials (producing high recall) while simultaneously rejecting a large proportion of irrelevant materials (producing high precision). These measurements have remained central to subsequent evaluation experiments as well as to the controversy surrounding such quantitative evaluation techniques. It is therefore important that they be understood.

Recall

Recall is a measure of effectiveness in retrieving all the sought information in a database, that is, in search comprehensiveness. A search would achieve perfect recall if every single record that should be found in relation to a specific query is indeed traced. It is normally expressed in proportional terms:

$$\text{Recall ratio} = \frac{\text{number of relevant records retrieved from the database}}{\text{number of relevant records in the database}} \times 100$$

Supposing that the database includes 60 records that are relevant to the search. If all 60 records are retrieved then the recall ratio is 100 percent. On the other hand, if only 20 of these records are found then the recall ratio now will be $100 \times 20/60 = 33.3$ percent.

The thoughtful reader will deduce that the recall ratio in any search can theoretically be improved by finding more and more records; in fact, 100 percent recall can always be achieved by retrieving every single record in the database, including all the irrelevant alongside the relevant ones, although this defeats the purpose of a retrieval system. Clearly, a parallel measure is required to work alongside recall which will take account of the false hits produced. The measure of this filtering capability is *precision*.

Precision

Precision assesses the accuracy of a search, that is, the extent to which it finds only those records that should be found, leaving aside all records that are not wanted. A search would achieve perfect precision if every single record retrieved in relation to a specific query is indeed relevant to that query. Precision, like recall, is normally expressed in proportional terms:

$$\text{Precision ratio} = \frac{\text{number of relevant records retrieved from the database}}{\text{number of relevant records in the database}} \times 100$$

If in the search example only the 20 relevant records were found, then the precision ratio would be $100 \times 20/20 = 100$ percent. But if the search in fact found 30 records, of which only 20 are relevant to the information request, then the precision ratio is reduced to $100 \times 20/30 = 66.6$ percent.

The relationship between recall and precision

The relationship between recall and precision can be demonstrated using a two by two matrix (see Figure 10.1). A record can be retrieved and relevant (box a), retrieved but not relevant (box b), not retrieved and relevant (box c) or not retrieved and not relevant (box d). A perfect search would have records placed only in boxes a and d; boxes b and c would be empty. Any records in box b reduce precision; any records in box c reduce recall.

Using the imaginary figures provided in our two previous examples for recall and precision, it is possible now to attach figures to these boxes:

Box a contains the 20 records that were both found and relevant.

Box b contains the records that were retrieved (30) minus those that were relevant (20), that is 10 records.

Box c contains the relevant records (60) minus those that were retrieved (20), that is 40 records.

Box d contains all the remaining records in the database that were not retrieved and were irrelevant (and therefore correctly ignored in the retrieval process). If the total database contains 10,000 records then this figure would be 9,930 (the total minus the sum of the other three boxes). Normally the number of records retrieved by a search (a + b) will be very small in relation to the total database size (a + b + c + d).

	Retrieved	Not retrieved
Relevant	a	c
Not relevant	b	d

Figure 10.1   Recall/precision matrix

Recall and precision in use

The Cranfield tests found an inverse relationship between recall and precision. As attempts are made to increase one, the other tends to decline: higher recall can only be achieved at the expense of a reduction in precision. As a strategy is implemented to retrieve more and more relevant records, there is a tendency also to retrieve growing numbers of irrelevant records; recall is improved but precision worsened. As a strategy is implemented to eliminate irrelevant records there is a tendency also to eliminate relevant ones; precision is improved but recall worsened. There is a common sense logic to this inverse relationship which has been demonstrated in many, but not all, evaluation tests (Cleverdon, the chief investigator in the Cranfield tests, was unhappy about the widespread citation of this inverse relationship as a sort of general law applicable in all cases and all circumstances – he was careful to distinguish between the kinds of results that could be obtained in the laboratory when all the variables are controlled and those resulting from operational situations (Ellis, 1990). Such an inverse relationship between recall and precision will, nevertheless, often be noticed by searchers in their own results. As steps are taken to find more relevant records precision does have a tendency to fall, and as the search strategy is tightened to increase precision then the number of retrieved records will generally fall, the loss including some relevant as well as irrelevant ones.

This can be tried in any search on a CD-ROM, online database, OPAC or the World Wide Web. Techniques such as reducing the number of different concepts in a search that must be matched, adding more synonyms to represent the search concepts that are present, and truncating all terms will tend to improve recall but worsen precision. Adding more unique concepts, reducing the number of synonyms, using proximity operators and confining the search to specific fields in the record such as the title field and the index terms field will normally improve precision but worsen recall (for more on these and other searching techniques see Chapters 6 and 9).

Recall and precision have been used as measures in countless tests since Cranfield. For example, the evaluation by Lancaster of the MEDLARS database in the late 1960s found that on average recall was less than 60 percent and precision about 50 percent (Lancaster, 1968). A later evaluation of the Medline database gave very different results for recall (37 percent) but a similar precision ratio of 56 percent (McCain, White and Griffith, 1987). An evaluation of the STAIRS information retrieval system using a database of 40,000 full-text documents produced a recall of only 20 percent but a precision of 79 percent (Blair and Maron, 1990). Saracevic and Kantor (1988), in a study of online searches conducted on 21 Dialog databases, obtained overall scores of 22 percent for recall and 57 percent for precision, which they say correspond with the performance figures found in many other studies.

Saracevic and Kantor (1988) did not find an inverse relationship between recall and precision, however; they found a weak but positive relationship between the two – as one rose slowly, so did the other (they state that it was not one of their objectives to investigate why this occurred and refrain from speculating on this finding). Lancaster and Warner (1993) make the point that low precision scores may be less tolerable in a larger than in a smaller database. A user may be willing to look at 60 retrieved records to identify the 20 that are useful, but much less willing to examine 600 to find 200, although in both cases the precision ratio (33 percent) is the same. Clarke and Willett (1997) compare three Web search engines using recall and precision measures (estimates of recall were obtained by inspecting the retrieved items of many different searches on the same query and then pooling the sets of relevant retrieved items on the assumption that in this way all the relevant items had been recalled – see later). They did not find any significant differences in recall between AltaVista, Excite and Lycos, but AltaVista did significantly outperform Lycos in precision. All three engines achieved higher scores for recall than precision, and this was especially so for Lycos.

Criticisms of Recall and Precision Measures

Despite the widespread use of recall and precision as measures of retrieval effectiveness, criticism is frequently voiced, based upon a number of serious shortcomings.

Incomplete measures

In the first place, it is argued that even if these measures have validity, they offer an incomplete evaluation of information retrieval, at least from the average searcher's point of view. Searchers may well be concerned to maximize both recall and precision, but these are not the only criteria that can be applied in evaluating a successful search: factors such as the expense involved in completing the search, the amount of time taken, and the ease of conducting it via the system interface may all be important. Beyond the rarefied experimental environment, these are the realities for many information seekers. A retrieval system that gives impressive recall and precision ratios may win few friends if it proves very costly, takes a long time and requires the use of an unhelpful, frustrating interface. Lancaster and Warner (1993) report that studies have consistently shown that accessibility and ease of use are the prime factors influencing the choice of an information source.

Validity of recall as a measure

Second, as stated earlier in the chapter, recall depends on the assumption that a user wishes to find as many relevant records as possible. It can be argued, however, that in many cases users are not interested in exhaustive searches that find everything (Cooper, 1976). For such users, precision alone is the measure of retrieval effectiveness, and recall is irrelevant. One clear exception to this rule would be a search on a patent database where the objective is ensure that no patent exists on a particular invention and therefore the search must be exhaustive.

Problems in measuring recall

Third, recall in particular is extremely difficult to measure unless using a small, experimental database for test purposes. The precise percentages given for recall by many experimenters mask the estimations that in practice have generated these confidently expressed results. Remember that recall measures the percentage of relevant documents in the entire database that have been found by the search. In order to measure it, two figures are necessary. The first is produced by the search – the number of relevant documents actually found. But what of the second figure? This requires a count to be undertaken of all the relevant documents that have not been found by the search. How is this to be ascertained? In the case of the very small test databases sometimes used for evaluation experiments, it is feasible to examine all the documents and thus to determine which are and which are not relevant to any particular search query. Considerable doubt has been expressed, however, about the validity of extrapolating search results to much larger databases. This is one of the criticisms targeted at the Cranfield results: the database used in the Cranfield II tests contained only 1,400 records. The later Text REtrieval Conference (TREC) series of annual experiments, beginning in 1991 and coordinated by the National Institute of Standards and Technology in the US, seeks to answer this particular criticism by employing a much larger database: the TREC standard test collection contains several gigabytes of data – approximately 200 times larger than the Cranfield database (Robertson, Walker and Beaulieu, 1997). In practice, of course, most real databases are large, numbering tens of thousands if not millions of individual records. It is simply impossible to examine individually every record to calculate a recall ratio. Imagine the problems likely to be encountered in trying to measure recall on the WWW.

Several solutions to these problems of recall measurement have been adopted, but unfortunately none is beyond criticism in terms of reliability. One solution is to conduct many runs of a search query using different searchers and to aggregate all the discrete relevant records retrieved on the assumption that if the search is tried enough times eventually most, if not all, the relevant records will be found at least once (as used by Clarke and Willett and discussed earlier in the chapter). Any individual search results retrieved can then be compared against this aggregated set of relevant records in the database to calculate recall. A second solution is for one or more experts with both searching experience and subject knowledge to conduct the searches, and to assume that these experts will find all the relevant records in the database. Records found by other searchers, such as novices, can then be compared against these 'perfect' searches to measure recall. An alternative is to examine one by one the records in a small subset of the database to locate all relevant records and to assume that this sample is representative of the database as a whole. For example, all records on the database with a certain publication date could be examined. Finally, relevant records may be identified from another reliable source whose subject coverage overlaps that of the database, such as a subject bibliography, and which is so organized that all relevant items can readily be identified. It is easy to see that in all these cases recall figures are at best good estimates and at worst plain guesses. None of these solutions can guarantee an absolute measure of recall, as in each case it is possible still to miss potentially relevant items in the database. Furthermore, the constantly changing nature of the Web, where sites are added and dropped daily, precludes accurate comparison of search results that have been conducted in separate search sessions, even if these sessions are close together in time.

Blair (1996) discusses the importance of determining at what point an evaluator should give up the search for more relevant records in a large database. He believes that variation in both the persistence of the evaluators and where they looked in their search for non-retrieved relevant records are probably the most important factors explaining the different results of recall studies. He also comments that a careless or lazy evaluator who abandons this search for missed but relevant records too early can receive a bonus in concluding that the system has missed fewer records than is in fact the case, thereby producing higher recall ratios than the more diligent evaluator.

A final response to the difficulty of measuring recall is simply to use absolute retrieval as a substitute for proportional recall, while still using the term 'recall' for this measure. Ralph (1997), for example, tries to measure the recall performance of eight Web search engines. He does so by comparing the total number of documents retrieved by these engines over 25 test queries. This allows him to report that one search engine finds more than another in response to a given query. It is not, however, a measure of recall. Firstly, it does not attempt to establish how many relevant documents were not retrieved by the search engines (in reality an impossible task on a data set the size of the total World Wide Web holdings); and secondly, it does not distinguish between retrieved documents that were relevant to the queries and retrieved documents that were irrelevant. As Ralph concedes, such a measure of retrieval capability is not necessarily a measure of good performance, because the greater the number of documents retrieved, the longer the user must spend scanning manually through them on the screen, especially irritating when they prove irrelevant to the query.

Interactivity

Early information retrieval systems operated in batch mode: several search requests would be batched together and then matched in one pass against the database, the results being delivered to the requesters. Only in the 1970s did online interactive systems appear that would permit the searcher to view intermediate search results and, if necessary, revise the search strategy to increase the relevance of the hits. The Cranfield experiments pre-dated such interactive systems and later experiments, although using interactive systems, have normally been conducted with little or no actual interactivity between user and system, as if still in batch mode (Saracevic, 1995). Critics of evaluation experiments argue that such 'one-shot' searches are unrealistic, and ignore the role of the searcher who may be able to improve an initially unsuccessful search by revizing the strategy. As Robertson and

Beaulieu (1997) say: 'The rise of the interactive system has made evaluation methodologies that leave the user wholly outside the system less and less tenable.'

Furthermore, it cannot be assumed that each search is self-contained, having no links to previous or subsequent searches. In practice, as Spink (1996) has shown, users of information retrieval systems often conduct multiple searches over time on the same information problem, and these searches are connected. Which search should be evaluated, and to what extent will the results differ according to the search's actual position in a sequence of related searches? These are questions that no evaluator should ignore.

Definition of relevance

The most damning attacks on precision as well as recall measures are made, however, by those who query the reliability of the crucial concept underlying both – that of relevance. The *Concise Oxford Dictionary* defines relevance as 'bearing upon, pertinent to, the matter in hand'. It is employed as the acid test of whether any particular retrieved record is to be judged a hit (pertinent) or a miss (non-pertinent) in assessments both of recall and precision. The assumption is that such decisions can be made accurately and objectively; without such an assumption relevance becomes a matter of opinion and therefore so do the measures of recall and precision.

Relevance is a central concept in information science, serving as the fundamental criterion for evaluating the effectiveness of information retrieval and affecting the practical design and evaluation of information retrieval systems. Alas, relevance is also a confusing and much debated concept. Mizzaro (1997) lists 157 papers published between 1959 and 1996 that discuss it. Saracevic (1997) reminds us that by the end of the 1950s it had already become clear that relevance was neither a simple nor a consistent proposition, but that there are different kinds of relevance. Nevertheless, the concept survived intact and strong. The major problem, according to its critics, is its subjectivity. They argue that relevance is in the eye of the beholder – only the information seeker can determine whether any particular record is relevant or not to that specific information query. Experimentally, relevance judgements have typically been based upon a match between the subject content – the aboutness – of a retrieved record and the initial query that stimulated the search. In the Cranfield tests, for example, the subject content of the query and the subject content of the records were compared to decide whether a retrieved record was relevant or not.

It can be argued that decisions on aboutness, or topicality as it is also called, can be made objectively by subject experts, although the inconsistencies often revealed in somewhat analogous indexing tests where subject-competent and experienced indexers working with the same thesaurus chose different index terms to describe the same record cast some doubts on this assumption. According to Schamber (1994), the more judges know about a given subject area, the more their judgements tend to agree; the more judges know about the subject area, the fewer records in a retrieved set they deem relevant, and judges tend to agree more on judge-ments of non-relevance than on relevance. Many searches are now conducted by end users and not, as in earlier days, by information inter-mediaries. This means that in the case of many searches, the person judging the retrieved results as they are displayed is in fact the ultimate user of the information, who therefore can bring to play in this judgement what-ever subjective elements are involved (see later). On the other hand, Keen (1997), one of the original Cranfield researchers, has recently commented on the problems in evaluating relevance: 'Is it not a symptom of the post-modernist mind which eschews making judgements about anything, including relevance of documents to queries?'

Some writers argue that decisions about relevance, if taken by the infor-mation requestor rather than a researcher, are not necessarily confined to questions of subject topicality. Green (1995), for example, defines relevance as the property of a text being potentially helpful to a user in the resolu-tion of a need – user relevance. A real information seeker might judge a bibliographic record, for example, relevant on the basis of its author, the series in which it appears, its recency, local availability and so on, as well as on its subject content. On the other hand, would a retrieved document that the seeker has already read be considered relevant, even if directly related to the subject?

Lancaster and Warner (1993) prefer to distinguish between relevance and a related concept, *pertinence*. They define pertinence as the relationship between a document and a request, based upon the subjective decision of the person with the information need. They argue persuasively that pertinence decisions are essential to the evaluation of operating (rather than trial) information retrieval systems serving real users who have real information needs. Harter (1992) proposes the term 'psychological relevance' for records that suggest new cognitive connections, fruitful analogies, insightful metaphors or an increase/decrease in the strength of a belief. He argues that records about a topic may in fact prove less impor-tant to the user than relevant records which are not on the topic but that allow new intellectual connections to be made or cause other cognitive changes in the user. Furthermore, he believes that such a view of psycho-logical relevance is inconsistent with the notion and utility of fixed relevance judgements and with traditional retrieval testing as exemplified by the Cranfield tests and their successors. Nevertheless, most information retrieval experts do agree that subject aboutness is still the major criterion used in judging relevance. A search system can only be judged in terms of whether it is able to match the user's information need as expressed in the search strategy with the stored data. The additional facility to screen out from the retrieved records those that the user has already read may well be a highly valuable feature, but the failure of a system to undertake this extra step cannot reasonably be invoked to judge the performance of the system at *retrieving* relevant information.

Another problem with relevancy is that judgements about one record may be influenced by other records that have already been examined. After examining nine totally irrelevant documents, a tenth might be considered relevant, but had this tenth record been viewed after seeing nine spot-on records it might have been judged irrelevant. This emphasizes, of course the binary nature of relevancy judgements for recall and precision purposes: there is no place for fairly relevant, or marginally relevant, or even extremely relevant. A record is accepted as relevant or rejected as irrelevant.

Spink and Greisdorf (1997) argue that researchers should question the assumption that users always need even the most highly relevant items. At the outset of an information-seeking process a user's information problem is often ill-defined. The retrieved items considered highly relevant may well provide users with what they already know, as they are likely to equate strongly with the current state of the user's information problems: they may only reinforce the current state of the information problem. Items that are only 'partially relevant' may then play a greater role in shifting the user's thinking about the information problem, providing new information that leads the user in new directions towards the ultimate resolution of the information problem.

If these criticisms are accepted then there is no place left for relevance judgements by third parties such as researchers or expert panels of judges, both widely used in retrieval experiments. Only a genuine information query rather than a query 'invented' for an experiment can now be used, because relevance can only be judged in response to a genuine need for information, not an artificially generated need. And the search must be conducted and subsequently evaluated by the actual initiator of the query. Worse still, the decisions on relevance will now be intimately linked to the bundle of personal and cognitive characteristics shared by that one searcher, making generalizations about information retrieval performance difficult to draw. A different searcher, or even that same searcher on a different occasion, might have made completely different assessments.

The argument can be taken further. If relevance is really about the usefulness of information to a specific client, can it really be judged at the CD-ROM workstation or the OPAC? As Green (1995) concedes, users may normally be the best judges of relevance, but they are not always and, he says, perhaps seldom, perfect judges of what information might help resolve the need at hand – users may dismiss a record that could have helped resolve their need. Hancock-Beaulieu, Fieldhouse and Do (1995) point out that users often find it difficult while still at the OPAC to measure the relevance to themselves of documents they have just traced. Is it then necessary to follow the user further down the information-use chain, checking on the relevance of retrieved bibliographic records, for example, after the user has located the actual documents at the shelves or even after they have been examined in relation to the task in hand? A few OPAC user studies, for example, have followed the client to the library shelves to see if the bibliographic information retrieved and judged potentially relevant at the terminal actually results in the book being borrowed. Hancock-Beaulieu (1990) concludes that the main subject-searching activity is undertaken at the shelves rather than the OPAC: the latter merely points the user to the relevant areas of the collection. It is possible to take this objection even further: it could be argued that the real test of relevancy only comes when the borrowed book is used to write, for example, an

assignment, and is found useful or useless. This takes relevancy judgements a long way from the controlled experimental environment and in
most instances from any possibility of measurement.

Such doubts about the traditional view of relevancy as used in countless retrieval evaluation experiments clearly have implications for both the
results already gathered and the validity of further similar experiments.
Unfortunately, the critics of recall/precision measures are currently unable
to proffer any alternative quantitative evaluation technique. Yet everyone
agrees that the ability to evaluate information retrieval is crucial. All this
suggests that recall and precision ratios as reported in experimental studies
should be treated as relative rather than absolute indicators. The measures
of recall and precision based upon estimates of relevance remain valid evaluation parameters even if their precise measurement in experimental
studies is problematic. As Gordon (1990) comments, retrieval effectiveness
may be difficult to measure but it is nevertheless important that it be done.
In evaluating strategies and reacting to preliminary results during an interactive search, for example, the concepts of recall and precision are extremely
useful to help the searcher decide on strategy adjustments. A small number
of hits may suggest a need to broaden the search to improve recall, even
if this adversely affects precision. A search with higher recall but a large
percentage of irrelevant records is a prime target for strategy adjustments
to improve precision even if at the expense of lower recall (see earlier and
Chapter 6).

Making judgements during a search on the relevance of intermediate
results and then using these judgements to revize the search strategy is
termed relevance feedback. Some information retrieval systems do not
simply rely upon the searcher to initiate such feedback. The system
itself may automatically search, for example, to find more records that
share index terms with records already retrieved and judged relevant by
the user.

Navigational Retrieval Systems

A growing number of CD-ROMs as well as the World Wide Web now
include navigational retrieval systems based upon hypertext links.
Evaluation of retrieval systems based on navigational mechanisms such as
hypertext have tended to reject quantitative techniques in favour of less
formal evaluation. Ellis, Furner and Willett (1996) explain this in terms of
the backgrounds of researchers in hypertext who more typically are from
the field of human–computer interaction than information retrieval. This
in turn directs their attention to the user interface and ways of evaluating
its usability rather than its performance. They describe a method of
measuring the effectiveness of searches undertaken with a hypertext
retrieval system that used recall and precision, but nevertheless emphasize
that the traditional measures are not necessarily the most appropriate for
navigational systems. They found that higher levels of effectiveness were
achieved by searchers who were not given access to a keyword search
facility but only used navigational links, although the differences, especially

in precision scores, were small. Wolfram and Dimitroff (1997) evaluated searches by a mixture of novice and expert searchers on a bibliographical hypertext-based system. They measured the number of pages explored, whether relevant or not; search time; recall – the number of relevant records visited divided by the total number of relevant records; and browsing precision – the ratio of the number of relevant record pages visited divided by the total number of record pages visited. Using this data they were able to calculate a success measure:

$$\text{success} = \frac{\text{recall} \times \text{browsing precision}}{\text{search time}}$$

The success measure attempts to reward purposeful searching behaviour, resulting in higher values for high recall and precision searches with lower times.

User Studies

Fortunately, there is an alternative to the quantitative evaluation of information retrieval. Instead of seeking precise measurements of a retrieval system's performance it is possible to focus on the users of the system. How do they undertake searches, what kinds of help do they seek, how do they rate the system and their own searches, do they think a professional searcher could do a better job? Many studies have been conducted among both information professionals and end users to answer these and similar questions (and a few were mentioned in Chapter 2).

Data collection techniques

Data are collected in a variety of ways. Users may be interviewed after a search, or in some cases also before the search. An alternative is to ask users to complete a questionnaire, either on paper or online at the same terminal used to conduct the actual search. Observation of users has occasionally been employed. Think aloud techniques represent a compromise between interview and observation – the user is asked to describe the search as it progresses and this is captured on tape for subsequent analysis. Finally, transaction logs have proven popular, especially in OPAC studies, where users' keyboard or mouse actions as well as the system's responses can be captured as a log of each user's transaction.

Each technique has its advantages and disadvantages. For example, only transaction logs and questionnaires lend themselves to large samples of users (some OPAC studies have analysed thousands of transaction logs). Questionnaires must be carefully formulated to avoid misleading or ambiguous questions, and poor response rates can be a problem. Respondents may not remember accurately during a post-search interview what they did in the search. They may forget to keep talking in think aloud sessions, especially if they are familiar with the system and searching has become routine. It is difficult to observe users unobtrusively and still be able to follow screen activity, and in any case unobtrusive observation might be considered unethical; however, if the user is aware of being observed normal searching behaviour may not be followed. It may be difficult with transaction logs to establish where one search ended and a new one began (especially if there is no system requirement for a new user to logon from scratch) or to know the objective of the search, and the logs tell nothing about the user's personal characteristics – status, gender, age, searching experience, etc. The best approach, used now in many studies, is to employ several techniques simultaneously, such as transaction logs together with questionnaires.

User study findings

These studies will not provide recall and precision measures, but they can reveal a lot about how people actually use retrieval systems, where they encounter problems, and their levels of satisfaction. The results can surprise information retrieval researchers. Tenopir (1992), for example, found that users who conduct their own searches are often satisfied with large numbers of records and low precision when judged by the standards of experienced information professionals. Lancaster *et al.* (1994) studied end users of the ERIC database on CD-ROM. They comment: 'It is rather disturbing that so many library users seem completely uncritical in their evaluation of CD-ROM. Many express satisfaction even when they achieve very poor results.' Su (1992) looked at end-user reactions to searches conducted for them by information professionals. She found that there is not necessarily a high correlation between precision and users' judgements of success or users' satisfaction with the level of precision. Some users may assign high satisfaction ratings for searches with low precision scores because they expect a very low number of relevant records. Others may be satisfied with a small set of highly relevant records, rather than a large set including many more relevant records but also many other records that are only partially relevant. Su did not explicitly investigate recall because of the problems of measurement (see earlier). She found, however, that recall is important for users, indeed more so than precision when they assign success ratings. Satisfaction with completeness of search results was much more highly correlated with success than users' satisfaction with the precision of the search. This contradicts Cooper (1976), cited earlier, who reports that users are often not interested in exhaustive searches, but value precision more than recall. (It may well be that different categories of users strike different optimum balances between recall and precision; a university researcher, for example, might value high recall whereas a business person prefers high precision.) Tague-Sutcliffe and Toms (1995) analysed novice searchers' behaviour in full-text hypertext systems. They found that repeated internal browsing negatively affected recall and that on-screen help was inadequate. Borgman, Gallagher, Krieger and Bower (1990) concluded from their study of children's use of a hypertext-based OPAC that although the children could search the hypertext system without prior instruction, they were no more effective than when using a Boolean-based retrieval system.

Many studies have revealed a disappointing reluctance by users to avail themselves of the sophisticated retrieval mechanisms typically available. Most searches rely upon a few basic search features only. Users encounter many problems in choosing suitable search terms in which to represent their subject interest. Hunter (1991) found that some people at the OPAC entered very broad terms and then spent the entire search session paging through hundreds of titles without even looking at a fuller bibliographic display of any single title. Some entered long phrases or sentences but did not use Boolean operators to link terms. According to Hirsh and Borgman (1995), children encounter difficulties in formulating Boolean queries, understanding many terms used as subject headings, selecting appropriate subject terms, especially for complex topics, and generating alternative terms if the first attempt is unsuccessful. Borgman, Hirsh, Walter and Gallagher (1995) are blunt in stating that: 'With few exceptions the current generation of online catalogs are designed for adults and do not meet the special needs and capabilities of children.'

One suspects that older users do not fare much better. Yee (1991) has summarized the problems encountered by novice adult OPAC users. All too commonly they find it difficult to select appropriate search terms, do not know how to reduce a very large retrieved set to a more manageable size (increase precision), do not know how to expand the size of a very small retrieved set (increase recall), do not understand cataloguing rules, and make spelling and typographical errors. In addition, lack of under-standing of indexes, files and basic database structure leads to the use of definite and indefinite articles at the beginning of search phrases, stop words, entering an author's first name before the surname (instead of inverting them) and hyphenation problems.

Database Evaluation

The information retrieval system is a vital link in the chain from a user with an information need to the information that will satisfy that need. For this reason it is important to design systems that perform as effectively as possible, and to train users how to get the best from these systems. Nevertheless, it should never be forgotten that the most perfect retrieval system in existence will be of little help to the user if the informa-tion store – the database – with which it interacts has shortcomings in coverage, accuracy, currency and relevance. Users will often battle with a poor retrieval system so long as the quality of the retrieved information is excellent for their purposes, but they are (rightly) critical of retrieval systems that lead them to poor quality data. Large (1989) discusses evalu-ation criteria in relation to both online and CD-ROM sources, pointing out both the similarities with and the differences from the evaluation of print-based sources.

Unfortunately, database quality cannot be taken for granted. Information stored in electronic format is inherently neither more nor less reliable or accurate than other kinds of information. A few years ago, when much electronic information had been transcribed at the keyboard from hard copy originals, many typographical errors were detected in all kinds of databases. These errors not only affected data use but also data retrieval in the case of systems which allowed users to search on natural language terms in a record; only by similarly misspelling the term in the search would the record containing the misspelled word be found. More data are now generated at the outset electronically and scanning equipment is more reliable, but errors are still to be found in databases.

Technically, electronic data can be updated more easily and quickly than, say, printed information. Many databases are updated monthly, weekly, daily or even in realtime. Nevertheless, it should not be assumed that electronic information is always current. A number of encyclopaedias, for example, are available online that contain data long superseded even by print sources. Typically, online or Web-based sources are updated more frequently than CD-ROM or print equivalents (if these also exist), but occasionally technical problems have reversed this dictum.

The Internet in particular has highlighted the problems of data reliability. There is no umbrella organization to ensure data accuracy, currency or consistency. When anyone can create a Web site there is no longer an established publishing process to ensure some kind of quality control through market pressures or academic refereeing. The *New Yorker* magazine captured the anonymity of Web interaction well in its cartoon of a canine searcher at the terminal with the caption: 'On the Internet nobody knows you're a dog.' The cultural and linguistic dominance of the Anglo-Saxon world and the recurrent issues concerning pornography and hate literature further complicate discussions concerning Internet content. The ephemeral nature of much Web material also means that what can be found today may have vanished or been transformed by tomorrow.

Evaluation criteria

Evaluation criteria for databases have been proposed by a number of authors, and there is a large measure of agreement about these criteria. One influential evaluation checklist was formulated in 1990 by the Southern California Online User Group (Basch, 1990):

- Consistency – does the database maintain consistency in coverage, currency, etc.; if it is one of a family of databases, how consistent are these products in interface design, update policy, etc.?
- Coverage/scope – does the coverage/scope match the stated aims of the database; is coverage comprehensive or selective?
- Error rate/accuracy – how accurate is the information?
- Output – what kind of output formats are available?
- Customer support and training – is initial or on-going training provided; is a help desk available during suitable hours?
- Accessibility/ease of use – how user friendly is the interface; does it have different facilities for novice and experienced searchers; how good are the error messages; are they context sensitive?
- Timeliness – is the database updated as frequently as it claims, and as the data warrant?

- Documentation – is online and/or printed documentation clear, comprehensive, current and well organized?
- Value to cost ratio – finally, taking into account all these features, does the database give good value for money?

Anagnostelis and Cooke (1997) propose somewhat more detailed evaluation criteria to be applied to Web-based databases – in this case specifically for comparison of various Medline database services on the Web:

- authority of the service provider as well as the database;
- content – coverage and currency;
- retrieval mechanism – general search features, free-text searching, natural-language queries, thesaurus searching, command searching, display and output;
- ease of interface use;
- unique features;
- help and user support.

Similar evaluation criteria can be found in Tenopir and Hover (1993), who discuss specifically comparison of the same database available on different systems, and from the Organizing Medical Networked Information (OMNI) Consortium (1998), which is involved, among other tasks, with the evaluation of Medline Services on the Web.

Practical Results

As a result of the numerous studies undertaken, a body of research conclusions and recommendations has accumulated on information systems, users and search techniques. As is often the case, however, the research has been more successful in sweeping away simplistic assumptions and raising new questions about information seeking than in providing answers. One disappointing aspect has been the length of time it has taken the information industry to exploit researchers' findings to improve commercially available retrieval systems.

This reluctance can be explained by a number of factors. First, there are doubts about the extent to which generalizations can be drawn from the many completed studies. Can the results obtained from systems working in batch mode retrieval be applied to today's highly interactive commercial systems; can results obtained with controlled relevance judgements in experimental settings be applied to operational systems with real users and real information needs; and can results obtained from small test databases be applied uncritically to extremely large databases? Second, the research findings do not point uniformly in one direction. Debate continues over the relative virtues of natural-versus controlled-language indexing, browsing versus retrieval, Boolean versus ranking search engines, and so on. Third, the commercial world must take account of economics. As Ledwith (1992) points out, ultimately it is users' willingness to pay for new search capabilities that dictates system enhancements. They must perceive a benefit to using any enhanced retrieval system that is greater than the cost increase necessary to finance this enhancement. All too often researchers have failed to demonstrate conclusively that any performance improvement achieved in the laboratory will be transferable to the market-place, and that even if such a transfer can be accomplished the marginal searching improvement will justify the increased costs.

Nevertheless, it is possible to point to developments that are transforming research-based proposals into working systems. One example is the wide-spread use on Web search engines of relevance ranking – the system itself makes 'judgements' about the presumed relative importance to the user of the items retrieved in a search, and displays them in descending order based on this presumed relevance (see Chapter 6). Relevance ranking was expounded first by experimental system designers before it migrated to such public arenas. Interface design research has also positively influenced the look of current systems (see Chapter 8).

The economic, political and social importance of being able to locate that relevant segment of information when, where and by whom it is needed guarantees that the quest to enhance retrieval systems will continue, despite setbacks. As information stores become ever larger, the need for sophisti-cated retrieval systems becomes still more crucial. Current concern about retrieval problems on the Web is the latest manifestation of this pheno-menon. In order to develop better systems it is necessary to establish effective evaluation techniques, if only so that 'better' can be given concrete meaning. That the task is daunting, few would deny; but that it is neces-sary, most would concur.

References

Anagnostelis, B. and Cooke, A. (1997) Evaluation criteria for different versions of the same database – a comparison of Medline services available via the World Wide Web. *Online Information '97. Proceedings of the 21st International Online Information Meeting, London, 9–11 December 1997*. Oxford: Learned Information, 165–79

Basch, R. (1990) Measuring the quality of data: report of the Fourth Annual SCOUG Retreat. *Database Searcher*, **6** (8), 18–23

Bawden, D. (1990) *User-Oriented Evaluation of Information Systems and Services*. Aldershot: Gower

Blair, D.C. (1996) STAIRS redux: thoughts on the STAIRS evaluation, ten years after. *Journal of the American Society for Information Science*, **47** (1) 4–22

Blair, B.C. and Maron, M.E. (1990) Full text information retrieval: further analysis and clarification. *Information Processing and Management*, **26** (3), 437- 47

Borgman, C.L., Gallagher, A.L., Krieger, D. and Bower, D. (1990) Children's use of an interactive catalog of science materials. *Proceedings of the 53rd ASIS Annual Meeting*. **27** Medford, NJ: Learned Information, 55–68

Borgman, C.L., Hirsh, S.G., Walter, V.A. and Gallagher, A.L. (1995) Children's searching behavior in browsing and keyword searching online catalogs: the Science Library catalog Project. *Journal of the American Society for Information Science*, **46** (9), 663–84

Buckland, M. and Gey, F. (1994) The relationship between recall and precision. *Journal of the American Society for Information Science*, **45** (1), 12–19

Clarke, S.J. and Willett, P. (1997) Estimating the recall performance of Web search engines. *Aslib Proceedings*, **49** (7), 184–9

Cooper, W.S. (1976) The paradoxical role of unexamined documents in the evaluation of retrieval effectiveness. *Information Processing and Management*, **12** (6), 367–75

Ellis, D. (1990) *New Horizons in Information Retrieval*. London: Library Association

Ellis, D., Furner, J. and Willett, P. (1996) On the creation of hypertext links in full-text documents: measurement of retrieval effectiveness. *Journal of the American Society for Information Science*, **47** (4), 287–300

Gordon, M.D. (1990) Evaluating the effectiveness of information retrieval systems using simulated queries. *Journal of the American Society for Information Science*, **41** (5), 313–23

Green, R. (1995) Topical relevance relationships. Why topic matching fails. *Journal of the American Society for Information Science*, **46** (9), 646–53

Hancock-Beaulieu, M. (1990) Evaluating the impact of an online library catalogue on subject searching behaviour at the catalogue and at the shelves. *Journal of Documentation*, **46** (4), 318–38

Hancock-Beaulieu, M., Fieldhouse, M. and Do, T. (1995) An evaluation of interactive query expansion in an online library catalogue with a graphical user interface. *Journal of Documentation*, **51** (3), 225–43

Harter, S.P. (1992) Psychological relevance and information science. *Journal of the American Society for Information Science*, **43** (9), 602–15

Hunter, R.N. (1991) Successes and failures of patrons searching the online catalog at a large academic library: a transaction log analysis. *RQ*, **30**(3), 395–402

Hirsh, S.G. and Borgman, C.L. (1995) Comparing children's use of browsing and keyword searching on the Science Library Catalog. *Proceedings of the 58th Annual Meeting of the American Society for Information Science* **32**, Medford, NJ: Information Today, 19–26

Infoseek (1997) *Infoseek: Precision vs, Recall*. Available at http://www.infoseek.com/doc?pg=prec_rec.html

Keen, M. (1997) The OKAPI projects. *Journal of Documentation*, **53** (1), 84–7

Lancaster, F.W. (1968) *Evaluation of the MEDLARS Demand Search Service*. Bethesda, MD: National Library of Medicine

Lancaster, F.W. and Warner, A.J. (1993) *Information Retrieval Today*. Arlington, VA: Information Resources

Lancaster, F.W., Elzy, C., Zeter, M. J., Metzler, L. and Low, Y.M. (1994) Searching databases on CD-ROM: comparison of the results of end-user searching with results from two modes of searching by skilled intermediaries. *RQ*, **33** (3), 370–86

Large, J.A. (1989) Evaluating online and CD-ROM reference sources. *Journal of Librarianship*, **21** (2), 87–108

Ledwith, R. (1992) On the difficulties of applying the results of information retrieval research to aid in the searching of large scientific databases. *Information Processing and Management*, **28** (4), 451–55

McCain, K.W., White, H.D. and Griffith, B.C. (1987) Comparing retrieval performance in online databases. *Information Processing and Management*, **23** (6), 539–53

Mizzaro, S. (1997) Relevance: the whole history. *Journal of the American Society for Information Science*, **48** (9), 810–32

OMNI Consortium (1998) OMNI Guidelines for Resource Evaluation. http://www.omni.ac.uk/agec/evalguid.html

Ralph, R. (1997) WWW Search Engine Rankings, April 1997. http://www.netstrider.com/search/ranking.html

Robertson, S.E. and Beaulieu, M. (1997) Research and evaluation in information retrieval. *Journal of Documentation*, **53** (1), 51–7

Robertson, S.E., Walker, S. and Beaulieu, M. (1997) Laboratory experiments with OKAPI: participation in the TREC Programme. *Journal of Documentation*, **53** (1), 20–34

Salton, G. (1991) *The State of Retrieval System Evaluation*. Available at http://cs-tr.cs.cornell.edu/Dienst/UI/2.0/ShowPage/ncstrl.cornell/TR91–1206

Saracevic, T. (1997) The stratified model of information retrieval interaction: extension and applications. In C. Schwartz and M. Rorvig (eds) *Proceedings of the 60th Annual Meeting of the American Society for Information Science*, **34** vol. 34. Medford, NJ: Information Today, 313–27

Saracevic, T. and Kantor, P. (1988) A study of information seeking and retrieving. II. Users, questions and effectiveness. *Journal of the American Society for Information Science*, **39** (3), 177–96

Schamber, L. (1994) Relevance and information behavior. In M.E. Williams (ed.) *Annual Review of Information Science and Technology* **29**. Medford, NJ: Learned Information, 3–48

Spink, A. (1996) A multiple search session model of end-user behavior : an exploratory study. *Journal of the American Society for Information Science*, **47** (8), 603–609

Spink, A. and Greisdorf, H. (1997) Partial relevance judgements during interactive information retrieval: an exploratory study. In C. Schwartz and M. Rorvig (eds.) *Proceedings of the 60th Annual Meeting of the American Society for Information Science*, **34**. Medford, NJ: Information Today, 111–22

Su, L.T. (1992) Evaluation measures for interactive information retrieval. *Information Processing and Management*, **28** (4), 503–516

Tague-Sutcliffe, J. and Toms, E.G. (1995) Information system design via the quantitative analysis of user transaction logs. *Fifth Biennial Conference of the International Society for Scientometrics and Informetrics*. River Forest, Illinois

Tenopir, C. (1992) Is it any of our business? *Library Journal*, **117** (6), 96, 98

Tenopir, C. and Hover, K. (1993) When is the same database not the same? Database differences among systems. *Online*, **17** (4), 20–27

Wolfram, D. and Dimitroff, A. (1997) Preliminary findings on searcher performance and perceptions of performance in a hypertext bibliographic retrieval system. *Journal of the American Society for Information Science*, **48** (2), 1142–5

Yee, M.M. (1991) System design and cataloguing meet the user: user interfaces to online public access catalogs. *Journal of the American Society for Information Science*, **42** (2), 78–98

List of Acronyms

AACR2	Anglo-American Cataloguing Rules, 2nd edition
AARNET	Australian Academic Research Network
ADAM	Art, Design, Architecture and Media information gateway
ANU	Australian National University
AOL	America Online
AP	Academic Press
ARPA	Advanced Research Projects Agency
ARPANET	Advanced Research Projects Agency Network
ASCII	American Standard Code for Information Interchange
ASFA	Aquatic Sciences and Fisheries Abstract
ASK	Anomalous State of Knowledge
ATM	Automated Teller Machine
BIC	Booktrade Industry Communication
BIDS	Bath Information and Data Services
BLAISE	British Library Automated Information Service
BLDSC	British Library Document Supply Centre
BLR&DD	British Library Research and Development Department
BNB	British National Bibliography
BT	Broader Term
BUBL	Bulletin Board for Libraries
CAB	Commonwealth Agricultural Bureaux
CAS	Chemical Abstracts Service
CAS-IAS	Current Awareness Service-Instant Article Supply
CBIR	Content-Based Image Retrieval

CD-I	Compact Disc-Interactive
CD-ROM	Compact Disc-Read Only Memory
CEC	Commission of the European Communities
CIDL	Canadian Initiative on Digital Libraries
CIQM	Centre for Information Quality Management
COMPENDEX	Computerized Engineering Index
COPAC	Consortium of University Research Libraries OPAC
CURL	Consortium of University Research Libraries
DBMS	Database Management System
DDC	Dewey Decimal Classification
DIMDI	Deutsches Institut für Medizinische Dokumentation und Information
DJNR	Dow Jones News/Retrieval
DLI	Digital Libraries Initiative
DOS	Disc Operating System
DTD	Document Type Definition
DVD-ROM	Digital Video (or versatile) Disc-Read Only Memory
EARL	Electronic Access to Resources in Libraries
EC	European Community
EDINA	Edinburgh Data and Information Access
EEVL	Edinburgh Engineering Virtual Library
Ei	Engineering Information
eLib	Electronic Libraries Programme
ELISA	Electronic Library Information Service, Australian National University
email	electronic mail
EMBASE	Excerpta Medica database
ERIC	Educational Resource Information Center
ERL	Electronic Reference Library
ESA-IRS	European Space Agency-Information Retrieval Service
EU	European Union
FIZ	Fachinformations Zentrum Energie, Physik, Mathematik
FT	Financial Times
FTP	File Transfer Protocol
GUI	Graphical User Interface
HTML	HyperText Markup Language
IAFA	Internet Anonymous FTP Archive
ICT	Information and Communications Technologies
IETF	Internet Engineering Task Force
IFLA	International Federation of Library Associations and Institutions
INSPEC	Information Services in Physics, Electrotechnology, Computers and Control
ISBD	International Standard Bibliographic Description
ISBN	International Standard Book Number
ISI	Institute for Scientific Information
ISO	International Standards Organization
ISSN	International Standard Serial Number
JANET	Joint Academic Network

JIBS	JISC (assisted) Bibliographic data Services user group
JICST	Japan Information Centre of Science and Technology
JISC	Joint Information Systems Committee of the UK Higher Education Funding Councils
LA	Library Association (UK)
LCC	Library of Congress Classification
LCSH	Library of Congress Subject Headings
LINK	Libraries of Networked Knowledge
LION	Literature Online
LIS	Library and Information Science
LISA	Library and Information Science Abstracts
MAID	Market Analysis and Information Database
MARC	Machine Readable Cataloguing
MesH	Medical Subject Headings
MIDAS	McGill Interactive Data System
MIT	Massachusetts Institute of Technology
MLA	Modern Languages Association
MSC	Multimedia Super Corridor
NAFTA	North America Free Trade Association
NAICS	North America Industrial Classification Scheme
NASA	National Aeronautics and Space Administration
NC	Network Computer
NCSA	National Centre for Supercomputer Applications
NISO	National Information Standards Organization
NISS	National Information Services and Systems
NLM	National Library of Medicine
NT	Narrower Term
OCLC	Online Computer Library Center
OMNI	Organized Medical Networked Information subject gateway
OPAC	Online Public Access Catalogue
ORBIT	Online Retrieval of Bibliographic Information Time-shared
PC	Personal Computer
PDF	Portable Document Format
PIN	Personal Identification Number
PSLI	Pilot Site Licence Initiative
RDBMS	Relational Database Management System
RLIN	Research Libraries Information Network
ROADS	Resource Organization And Discovery in Subject-based services
RT	Related Term
RUDI	Resource for Urban Design Information subject gateway
SBIG	Subject-Based Information Gateway
SCI	Science Citation Index
SDC	System Development Corporation
SDI	Selective Dissemination of Information
SGML	Standardized General Markup Language
SIC	Standard Industrial Classification

SN	Scope Note
SOSIG	Social Science Information Gateway
SPIRS	SilverPlatter Information Retrieval System
STM	Scientific, Technical and Medical
STN	Scientific and Technical Information Network
TCP/IP	Transmission Control Protocol/Internet Protocol
TIARA	Timely Information for All, Relevant and Affordable
TREC	Text Retrieval Conference
TT	Top Term
UC	University of California
UDC	Universal Decimal Classification
UKOLN	UK Office for Library and Information Networking
UKOLUG	UK Online User Group
URL	Uniform Resource Locator
UWA	University of Wales Aberystwyth
VR	Virtual Reality
VTLS	Virginia Tech Library System
WAIS	Wide Area Information Server
WWW	World Wide Web

Index

Please note: The Internet and the World Wide Web are referred to so often in the book that these terms have not been indexed separately. See under individual topics, databases, systems, etc.

AACR2 113, 118–120
AARNET 65
ABI/Inform 47, 52, 110, 244
ADAM 99, 138, 240
Adjacency *see* Word proximity
Adobe Acrobat 7, 52
Agricola 244
AIDSDRUGS 246
AIDSLINE 246
AIDSTRIALS 246
ALEPH 183, 185–186
AltaVista 6, 10, 12, 13, 66, 68, 146–147, 149, 156, 183, 204, 216, 242, 251–252, 254–255, 282
AltaVista Maps 216, 220–222
America Online 49, 50, 58
American Chemical Society 43, 55
American Library Association 274
American National Standards Institute 232
Ameritech Library Services 42
Anaphora 97
Animation 10, 63, 192, 225
Antonyms 74, 78, 98, 99
Apple Computers 187
Aquatic Sciences and Fisheries Abstracts (ASFA) 110–111, 124–126, 153
Architecture 104
ARPANET 43, 65

Art 104
   See also individual databases
Art and Architecture Thesaurus 99, 104
ARTbibliographies Modern 240
ARTISAN 105
Arts and Humanities Citation Index 100, 255
ASK 31–32, 180
Australia 65
   See also individual libraries and universities
Australian National University 13, 259, 262–263

BCK2SKOL 275
Best-Seller 233
Best match 144
BIBLINK 140
Bibliographic databases 2, 8, 32, 36, 37, 42, 43, 44, 45, 46, 49, 50, 59–60, 78, 90, 97, 98, 138, 153, 210, 217, 244, 252, 253
   See also individual databases
Bibliography of the History of Art 240
Bibliothèque de Montréal 233
BIDS 9, 22, 24, 50–51, 100–102, 255–258
BIOETHICSLINE 246

Biology 47, 133
  See also individual databases
BIOMED 254
BIOSIS Previews 47, 49, 52, 113, 118, 244
Biz/ed 138
BLCMP 12, 132
BookData 46, 48
Boolean operators 6, 34, 38, 59, 66, 129, 136, 144, 148–150, 153, 158, 161–162, 165, 166–173, 180, 191–192, 203, 205, 212, 247, 254, 256, 259, 263, 290–291
Bowker-Saur 263
Briefsearch strategy 164
British Library 24, 246, 248, 252
British National Bibliography 46
British Telecom 255
Browsing 3, 5, 6, 59, 109, 132, 133, 143, 179–194, 218, 242, 248, 250, 254, 255, 259, 265, 277, 290
BRS Online 42
BUBL 22, 24, 249, 250
Building block strategy 164–165
Bush, Vannevar 43, 187
Business 2, 47, 52, 53, 56–57
  See also individual databases
Business Week 56
Buttons 34, 202, 212–213, 215–216, 223–224, 247

CAB 46, 166–168
Cambridge Scientific Abstracts 24
Canada 24, 50, 59, 65, 112–113, 234, 235–236
  See also individual libraries and universities
Canadian Initiative on Digital Libraries 24
CANCERLIT 246
CA*NET 65
Carnegie Mellon University 24, 67
Castle Explorer 216, 218, 223
CBIR 104–105
CD-I 227
CD-ROMs *see* individual titles
CD-Plus Technologies 42
CDS-ISIS 104
CERN 3

Chadwyck Healey 41, 46
Chemical Abstracts 43, 55, 78
Chemistry 43, 53, 54, 78, 113–115
  See also individual databases
ChemTox 113–115
Children 3, 31, 37–38, 181, 199, 290–291
China 7
CIQM 49
Citation indexing 100–102
Citation pearl growing strategy 165
Classification schemes 77, 88, 90, 95–96, 98, 104, 245, 250
Cleverdon, Cyril 281
Client-server 3
Clinton, Bill 3
Clumps 6
Colour 199, 218, 220–221, 223, 224–225, 228
Command languages 2, 6, 34, 49, 59, 61, 145–146, 161–162, 200, 202–205, 207, 231, 273, 293
Common command language 162, 204
Compaq 7
Compendex 43, 47, 54
Compton's Interactive Encyclopedia 63, 212, 215, 216, 218, 223–224
CompuServe 49
Computer science 133
Controlled vocabularies 34, 77–99, 100, 122, 160, 166–168, 179, 241, 245, 277, 278, 293
CONVERSE 43
Coordination level searching *see* Quorum function
COPAC 22, 99
Cornell University 244
Corporation for National Research Initiatives 13
Cranfield Projects 279, 281, 283, 284–286
Cross-file searching *see* Multifile searching
Current awareness services 58
Cybercafes 3, 4
Cyberjaya 3

Database (journal) 21
Database Searcher (journal) 21

DataStar 51
DEC *see* Digital Equipment Corporation
Denmark 240
Descriptors *see* Controlled vocabularies
Dialindex 159–160
Dialog 2, 6, 9, 14, 16, 24, 33, 42, 43, 44, 51, 52, 58, 95–96, 103, 110–118, 123, 145–147, 150, 151–152, 154–160, 176–177, 200, 202–203, 208–209, 240, 241–243, 245, 247, 248, 250, 263, 281
Dictionaries 2, 63
    See also individual titles
Digital Equipment Corporation (DEC) 64
Digital libraries 23
Digital Libraries Initiative 13, 23–24
DIMDI 54, 147, 162
Directory of Online Databases 45
Disney 208, 210
D-lib Magazine 13, 17–18, 24, 48, 191
Direct manipulation 34, 202, 219–220
Directories 44
    See also individual titles
Directory of Online Databases 45
Display (search results) 156–158, 253, 293
DK Multimedia 64, 216, 218, 223
Document delivery 9
DOS 202, 209, 211
Dow Jones 8, 55–56
Downloading 161, 199, 253
DRA 212–213, 223
Drugs in Development 248, 250
Dublin Core 13, 138–140
Dun & Bradstreet 56
DVD-ROM 2, 8, 9, 64–65

EARL (Electronic Access to Resources in Libraries) 4
ECHO 147, 162
Economist 56
EDINA 22
Education 14, 51, 66
EEVL 138, 269–271
Ei Village 54–55
Electrical engineering 42

Electronic journals 7, 13, 18, 42, 48, 51, 133–134, 273
    See also individual titles
Electronic Journals Online 9
Electronic Library (journal) 21
Electronic Reference Library 42
eLib Programme 24, 48, 138, 269, 274
Electronic shopping 49
Elsevier Science 47, 48, 54
Embase 47, 113, 118
Email 4, 5, 9, 49, 58, 65, 253, 275
Emedia Professional 21
Encyclopedia Britannica Online 8, 46
Encyclopedias 2, 37–38, 46, 63, 113, 183, 223–224, 292
    See also individual titles
End users 5, 6, 30, 31, 33, 34, 36, 38–39, 44, 56, 58, 59, 64, 158, 163, 180, 181, 204, 240, 253, 269, 272–273, 286, 289, 290
Endnote 253
Engineering 47, 54–55
    See also individual databases
Engineering Inc 54
English Poetry (database) 41
Enviroline 150
ERIC 14, 19–20, 46, 47, 52, 83, 85–89, 97, 155, 166, 209–211, 229–230, 244, 290
Error messages 199, 200, 230–231, 292
ESA-IRS 172
Evaluation 34, 36, 49, 163, 273, 277–294
Excite 8, 66–67, 68, 79–80, 177, 205–206, 242, 251–252, 254, 282

Fact searches 34, 38, 253
Field searching 153–154, 203, 210
File structures 123, 127–130, 151, 180, *Financial Times* Information 2, 8, 56–57
Finland 49
Finsbury Data Services 58
FIZ Karlsruhe 54, 55
Fonts 222–223
Forrester Research 4
Fees 204
Forms 212, 214
France 50, 53

Frost & Sullivan 57
FTP 65, 242

Gabriel 24
Gale Directory of Databases 45
Gates, Bill 3
Gateway (Cornell University) 244
Gateways 42, 60, 79, 99
Genie 49
Germany 50, 54
Gore, Al 3
GRIPS 54
Grolier's Multimedia Encyclopedia 63, 212, 216

Harper Adams Agricultural College 250, 252
Harvest 8, 136
Healthgate 241–242, 245–246
HealthSTAR 246
Help 123, 199, 205, 228–230, 241, 290, 292–293
History (online industry) 43–45
HomeFinder 218
Homonyms 76, 78, 81, 97
HotBot 212, 214
HTML 134–136, 255
Hybrid CD-ROMs 64
Hypermedia *see* Hypertext
Hypertext 3, 43, 65, 66, 132–133, 180, 181, 184, 187–193, 202, 207, 215, 288–289, 290

IAFA 138
IBM 7, 43, 198
ICONCLASS 104
Icons 7, 34, 188, 202, 212–215, 217, 220, 223–224
IFLA 214, 217
IHR-Info 138
Images 3, 104–106, 133, 134, 182, 192–193, 225
Index expansion 154–156
Index Medicus 44
Indexer consistency 99, 194
Indonesia 65
Information Access Company 59
Information intermediaries *see* Intermediaries

Information seekers *see* Seekers
Information Technology and Libraries (journal) 21
Information Today 21
Information World Review 21
Infoseek 6, 59, 100, 247
INNOPAC 262
INSPEC 41–42, 43, 47, 82, 88, 90–92, 95–96, 98
Institute for Scientific Information 47, 59, 100–102
Institution of Electrical Engineers 41–42
Interfaces 3, 6, 7, 34, 38, 44, 49, 59, 64, 88, 144, 182, 197–237, 241, 243, 244, 278, 282, 288, 292, 294
Intermediaries 5–6, 30, 31, 32–33, 34, 36, 38–39, 239–240, 269, 272, 286
Internet *see* note on page 301
Internet Explorer 7, 65, 194
Internet Movie Database 10, 12
Internet Scout Report 69
InterNIC 274
Interviews 289
Intranets 2, 8, 56, 58
Inverted file *see* File structures
Iowa State University 250
Ireland 274
Islamic Book 182–183
ISO 119, 232

JANET 65
Japan 3, 7, 50, 54, 65
JIBS 22
JICST 54–55
JISC 22, 24
Journal of Documentation 21
Journal of Information Science 21
Journal of the American Society for Information Science 21–22
Journals Online 9, 51

Keyboards 199, 226–228
Known-item searches 35, 61, 240, 253, 255
KOMPASS Canada 110, 112–113
Korea 7

LANs 8
Law 52, 57–58, 97
    See also individual databases
LEXIS-NEXIS 57–58, 149
Libertas 172
Library and Information Science
    Abstracts
    See LISA
Library Association (UK) 49, 262–263
Library of Congress 46, 230, 232, 249,
    250, 262
Limit 154, 158, 160, 167, 247–248, 259
LINK 250
LION 41
LISA 153–154, 169–170, 262–265
Literature Online 41
Los Angeles Times 113, 116–117
Lycos 6, 67, 69–70, 136, 204, 242,
    251–252, 255, 282

McGill University 7, 182–183
Magellan 66, 183, 242, 254
MAID 51, 52
Malaysia 3, 65
Managing Information 22
Manchester Metropolitan University
    12, 15–16
MARC 46, 59, 119–120, 220–221
Massachusetts Institute of Technology
    (MIT) 43
Medicine 44, 47, 54, 250
MEDLARS 281
Medline 6, 43, 47, 52, 54, 88, 113, 118,
    241, 240, 244, 245, 246, 281, 293
MELVYL 59–60, 145
Menus 34, 59, 61, 183–186, 199, 200,
    201, 202, 205–211, 220, 222
Metadata 136–140
Microsoft 7, 64, 198, 200
Microsoft Encarta Encyclopedia 7, 63,
    183–184, 189–191, 208, 211, 212, 240
Microsoft Music Central 133
MIDAS 7
Mintel 57, 88
MLA Bibliography 258–261
Mohamed, Mahathir Bin 3
Le Monde 56, 150
Mouse 227–228
Multifile searching 64, 160, 244

Multilingual searching 254–255
Multimedia 3, 4, 10, 48, 63, 64, 132,
    133, 225–226
Muscat 8
My First Amazing Dictionary 63

NAICS 78, 90
NASA 43
National Library of Australia 23, 24
National Library of Canada 235–236
National Library of Medicine 44, 53
    See also Medline
Natural language 6, 34, 97, 98, 99–100,
    160, 166–168, 179, 192, 277, 279,
    292–293
Nature 48, 216, 219
Nelson, Ted 187
Netscape Navigator 7, 65, 194, 207
Netskills Team 22, 274
Networks 2, 7, 8, 64–65, 232, 272
Newcastle University 274
New Review of Information Networking
    22
*New Review of Text and Document
    Management* 22
Newspapers 2, 46
    See also individual titles
NISO 162
NISS 60–61
Nordic Metadata Project 140
Nordunet 65
Northern Light 135, 158

Observation 289–290
OCLC FirstSearch 9, 14, 19–20, 42, 46,
    52–53, 60, 145–146, 244, 258–261
OCLC NetFirst 140
OKAPI 172
OLIB 132, 249, 252
OMNI 293
Online (journal) 21
Online journals *see* Electronic journals
Online and CD-ROM Review 21
Online Review 21
On-screen forms *see* Forms
OPAC 97 246, 248
OPACs *see* individual products
Open Journal Project 133–134
Open Text 8, 156, 242, 251–252

ORACLE 7, 132
Ovid Technologies 42

PACE 218, 220–221, 236
PAIS 244
Partial match 144
PASCAL 245, 254
Patents 51, 53, 144, 282
    See also individual databases
PC Computing 69
PDF 7, 52
Pennsylvania State University 233, 244
Pergamon ORBIT Infoline 53
Pertinence 286
Pharmaceuticals 52
    See also individual databases
Philippines 54
Phrase searching 59, 66, 152–153, 205,
    247, 256
Physics 42, 47
    See also INSPEC
PICK 22–23
Poetry 41
Pollution Abstracts 157–158
Precision 163, 165, 166, 278–289,
    290–291
Pre-search interview 33
Printers 228
ProCite 253
Prodigy 49
Profound LiveWire 52, 53
Program 22
Protocols 8, 9
Proximity *see* Word proximity
PSLI 48
PsychInfo 47, 83–84, 147–148, 244
Psychology 47
Pull technology 5
Push technology 5, 161

QPAT-US 53
Questel-ORBIT 53
Questionnaires 289–290
Questquorum 171–172
QUICKLAW 273
Quorum function 171–173, 176

Ranking 10, 136, 169–177, 247, 250,
    252, 254, 255, 293–294

Recall 163, 164, 165, 253, 278–289,
    290–291
Records 8, 9, 14, 34, 110–123, 129–132,
    138, 173, 241
Reed Elsevier 58
Reference interview 239–240
Reference Manager 253
Relational databases 131–132
Relevance 253, 279–289, 290
Relevance feedback 288
Relevance ranking *see* Ranking
Reuters 2, 5, 8, 56, 58–59
RLIN 244, 246
ROADS 138
RUDI 138

Schools 3, 4
Science Citation Index 47, 51, 100–102,
    113, 118, 255–258
Screen design 182, 199, 220, 221–225
SDC 43, 53
SDI 5, 161
SEARCH 97 8
Search formulation 6
Search process 31–34
Search strategies 6, 10–21, 163–165,
    180–181, 204, 207, 248, 253, 254,
    255–269, 278, 281
Search tactics 165–169, 248
Searchers *see* Seekers
Seekers (information) 5–6, 29–32,
    36–38, 41, 97, 143–144, 181,
    191–192, 197–200, 278, 287
Senior citizens 31, 199, 222
Sequencing 224
SGML 134
Sharp, I.P. 59
Sheffield Hallam University 273–274
SIC 78, 90
SilverLinker 42
SilverPlatter 42, 209–211, 229–230, 244,
    254, 263
Singapore 4, 24, 65
Social Science Citation Index 100,
    255
SOSIG 79, 138
Sound 3, 7, 10, 63, 133, 192, 225, 228
South African Library 183, 185–186
Southampton University 133

Southern California Online Users
　　Group 22, 49, 292–293
Spamming 255
STAIRS 281
Standard and Poor's Register 16
Stanford University 24, 66
State Library of Florida 212–213
STN 33, 42, 54–55, 148
Stopwords 121–122, 130
Strategies *see* Search strategies
Strathclyde University 250
Subject headings 38, 90, 93–95, 249,
　　250, 262, 265, 291
Subject searches 34–35, 38, 61, 143,
　　253
Successive fractions strategy 165
Sun Computers 7, 42
Sybase 132
Synonyms 33–34, 36, 74–76, 77–81,
　　95–96, 97, 99, 164, 168, 245, 281
SYSTRAN 66

Talis 12, 132
TCP/IP 8, 65
Telecommunication networks
　　See Networks
Telemedicine 4
Telnet 65
Term weighting *see* Weighting
Textline 58
Thailand 65
Thesauri 34, 77, 79–88, 90, 95–97,
　　98–99, 104, 122, 160, 180, 202, 241,
　　245, 293
Think aloud 289
THOMAS 230
TIARA 24
TONIC 273
Toronto Public Library 37
Touchscreen 227–228
TOURBUS 275
Trademarks 105
Training 39, 273–275, 292
Transaction logs 289–290
TREC 283
Truncation 34, 122, 146–148, 158,
　　162, 169, 203, 205, 210,
　　281
Tutorials 231

UK 1, 3, 4, 24, 46, 48, 50, 60, 65, 79,
　　138, 250, 274, 278
　　See also individual libraries and
　　universities
UKOLN 13
UKOLUG 22, 49, 161
UMI ProQuest 42
Unesco 8
University of Alabama 275
University of Bath 50
University of Birmingham 240
University of Boulder 136
University of California 1–2, 24, 59
University of Illinois 24
University of Limerick 274
University of Michigan 24
University of Oslo 218
University of Pittsburgh 42
University of Saskatchewan 60
University of Toronto 273
University of Wales Aberystwyth
　　10–11
University of Windsor 236
University Microfilms (UMI) 47, 49,
　　244
US 3, 4, 13, 23–24, 43, 44, 49, 53, 54,
　　65, 274, 278
　　See also individual libraries and
　　universities
US Office for Education 14
Usenet 65, 66, 145, 242
User studies 30–31, 36–38, 191–192,
　　197, 205, 227, 244, 255, 272–273,
　　285, 287, 289–291
Users *see* End users, Seekers, User
　　Studies

vCuc 234
Veterinary science 46
Verity 8
Video 10, 63, 192, 213, 225–226
VIRAGE 105
Virtual reality 219, 235–237
Voyeur 254
VTLS 42, 233

Wall Street Journal 56
Washington Post 56
Web *see* note on page 301

WebCATS 60, 62–63
WebCrawler 66, 187–189, 255
Web crawlers 136
Weighting 173–175, 177, 230
WHOIS++ 138
Wilson, H.W. 59
WILSONLINE 149
Windows 6, 7, 34, 198, 202, 215–216
Word proximity 130, 150–152, 158,
    167, 169, 175–177, 203

Workstations 7, 8, 9, 31, 44, 63, 64, 227
WorldCat 52, 119
World Databases 45
WWW Virtual Library 183

Yahoo! 59, 68, 78–79, 183–184, 186,
    204, 242, 251–252, 255, 265–266

Z39.50 9, 232–236, 243, 244
Zoom 216, 223